S0-BYY-581

Gia

Height 5′8 Dress Size 6-8-10 Bust 34 Waist 24 Hips 35½
Shoes 8½ Hair Brown Eyes Brown
Hauteur 1.73 Confection 36-40 Poitrine 86 Taille 61 Hanches 90
Chaussures 39½ Cheveux Bruns Yeux Bruns
SAG

This book belongs to me
Gia Carangi

WOMAN INTO MAN, PARIS 1979

HELMUT
NEWTON
P R I V A T E
PROPERTY

Gia

Height 5′8 Dress Size 6-8-10 Bust 34 Waist 24 Hips 35½
Shoes 8½ Hair Brown Eyes Brown
Hauteur 1.73 Confection 36-40 Poitrine 86 Taille 61 Hanches 90
Chaussures 39½ Cheveux Bruns Yeux Bruns
SAG

*This Book belongs to me
Gia Carangi*

WOMAN INTO MAN, PARIS 1979

HAMILTONS
13 CARLOS PLACE LONDON

**HELMUT
NEWTON**
PRIVATE
PROPERTY

CHRISTIAN CHENEAU GALERIE
5 R.B. DE L'ARSENAL PARIS

COSMOPOLITAN

July 1979 • $1.50

Be a Scarsdale
Loser—32 Tips
to Eat Skinny
From the Famous
Diet Book

Depressed?
What Zaps You,
Why, and How
to Get Yourself Up

Finding Out
His Turn-Ons—
and Making Sure
He Knows Yours

How Diane
von Fürstenberg
(Mogul, Mother,
Woman in Another
Workaholic's
Life) Keeps Her
Many Worlds
From Colliding

Putting on
Your Best Face:
The New
Plastic Surgery for
Girls of All Ages

Girls Who Make
Outrageous
Demands—and
Think Their
Sexuality Is Fair
Exchange

Bucky Dent,
the Yankees'
Most Valuable
(and Sexy) Player

8 Terribly Rewarding
Things to Do
on a Rainy Saturday
Afternoon

Victoria Holt's
New Novel,
My Enemy the
Queen, a Stunner—
and 2 Surprise
Short Stories

VOGUE

ITALIA

VIAGGIO
IN
KENIA
CON
LA NUOVA
MODA KAKI

*TENUTE IN
PELLE,
BLOUSONS,
GOLF GRANDI*
pezzi forti della
prossima stagion

Di Gianfranco Ferré
il blouson di pelle
con fazzoletto di lino

In command of the elements with an umbrella from the Christian Dior collection.

CHRIS VON WANGENHEIM

Reigning is Your Dior.

VOGUE

AUG.
$2.00

right!

What you
want first for fall
150 terrific new looks

Saint Laurent's
dream house

Erica Jong's
surprise new novel

The
working
...you

Romeo
a fash

Fur appeal

THING OF BEAUTY

THE TRAGEDY OF
SUPERMODEL GIA

STEPHEN FRIED

POCKET BOOKS

New York   London   Toronto   Sydney

For information regarding special discounts for bulk purchases,
please contact Simon & Schuster Special Sales at
1-800-456-6798 or business@simonandschuster.com

POCKET BOOKS, a division of Simon & Schuster, Inc.
1230 Avenue of the Americas, New York, NY 10020

ISBN: 0-671-70105-3

First Pocket Books Paperback printing June 1994

20   19   18   17   16   15   14   13   12   11

POCKET and colophon are registered trademarks of
Simon & Schuster, Inc.

Cover photo by Lance Staedler

Printed in the U.S.A.

Photo inserts conceived, researched, and edited by Vincent Virga; designed by Stanley S. Drate/Folio Graphics, Inc.

8-page insert credit: Gia's modeling portfolios courtesy of Elite and the collection of Kathleen Sperr, courtesy of *Philadelphia Magazine*—page two, poster from Helmut Newton show *Private Property;* page three, American *Cosmopolitan* tearsheet of Francesco Scavullo cover from Gia's portfolio; page four, Italian *Vogue* tearsheet of Renato Grignachi cover from Gia's portfolio; page five, tearsheet of Dior ad by Chris von Wangenheim, courtesy of Gene Federico; page six, tearsheet of Armani ad by Aldo Fallai from Gia's portfolio; page seven, American *Vogue* tearsheet of Richard Avedon cover from Gia's portfolio; page eight, American *Vogue* tearsheet of Denis Piel photo from Gia's portfolio

16-page insert credits (*asterisks indicate pseudonyms): 1. Jim Graham; 2. from the collection of Rochelle Rosen*; 3. Jim Graham; 4. from the collection of Alice Kensil; 5. from Lincoln High Yearbook, from the collection of Elaine Moon*; 6. Urban Archives, Temple University; 7. from the collection of Nancy Adams; 8. from the collection of Karen Karuza; 9-10. Joe Petrellis; 11. Maurice Tannenbaum; 12. *Philadelphia Magazine;* 13. collection of Kathleen Sperr, courtesy of *Philadelphia Magazine;* 14. Joan Ruggles; 15. from the collection of Nancy Adams; 16. collection of Kathleen Sperr, courtesy of *Philadelphia Magazine;* 17-18. Lance Staedler; 19. Italian *Bazaar* tearsheet from Gia's portfolio; 20. from the collection of Lizzette Kattan; 21. Lizzette Kattan; 22. Ralph Gibson; 23-25. Lizzette Kattan; 26. *New York Magazine;* 28. Arthur Gordon, from *Disco Beauty,* published by Simon & Schuster; 29. American *Vogue* tearsheet; 30. Chris von Wangenheim, from *Fashion: Theory,* published by Lustrum Press; 31. Lizzette Kattan; 32. Joan Ruggles; 33. collection of Kathleen Sperr, courtesy of *Philadelphia Magazine;* 34. *Philadelphia Magazine;* 35. David King; 36. *WWD;* 37. David King; 38-40. *WWD;* 41. collection of Kathleen Sperr, courtesy of *Philadelphia Magazine;* 42. American *Vogue* tearsheet from Gia's portfolio; 43. collection of Kathleen Sperr, courtesy of *Philadelphia Magazine;* 46. from the collection of Rochelle Rosen*; 47. from the collection of Monique Pillard/Elite; 48. American *Cosmopolitan;* 49. Francesco Scavullo, from *Scavullo: Women,* published by Simon & Schuster; 50. collection of Kathleen Sperr, courtesy of *Philadelphia Magazine;* 52-53. from the collection of Dawn Phillips; 54. from the collection of Rochelle Rosen*; 55. from the collection of Dawn Phillips; 56. painting by Joe Eula, from the collection of Lizzette Kattan; 57. Alice Kensil; 58. American *Harper's Bazaar* tearsheet

To my wife, Diane Ayres

Contents

Contents

A thing of beauty is a joy forever:
Its loveliness increases; it will never
Pass into nothingness; but still will keep
A bower quiet for us, and a sleep
Full of sweet dreams, and health, and quiet breathing.

John Keats,
from *Endymion*

Prologue

The newsmagazine anchorman thanks a correspondent for his report on "this fascinating subject of near-death experience," turns to face another camera, and reads the teaser for the upcoming segment of the January 6, 1983, edition of ABC's *20/20*.

"Next," he says, "inside the world of the fashion model . . . a world that is not always as it appears. Right after this."

After the commercial, the anchorman introduces reporter Tom Hoving, who presents a report meant to detail "the dark and anxious side" of the modeling business but manages somehow to make the whole enterprise seem extremely glamorous anyway. There's top model Christie Brinkley being coaxed by a photographer. "Make me chase you," he's saying. "Tease, tease. Look at me like you're naked. That's it. *Fabulous.*" After the shooting, Brinkley—the industry's quintessential blond-haired, blue-eyed California girl—says that she'll never have to worry about money again.

"Models can earn two million dollars a year," Hoving explains in his booming TV-overvoice. "Once you make it, you become a member of an exclusive international club, where the sun always shines, the parties are glowing. A land where there's no ugliness, no sickness, no poverty. A land where dreams come true and everyone is certified beautiful. The club has special fringe benefits. Top model Apollonia knows them all."

"Rolls-Royce, flowers, dresses, limousines, tickets," lists

the Dutch-born Apollonia von Ravenstein, a long-reigni
queen of the more specialized, dark-haired, European-exo
look. "I mean, anything you want, anything a woman wou
want, really, just ask."

Flamboyant hairdresser-turned-fashion-photographer A
Gallant appears, wearing a leather Jeff cap, Mr. Spock si
burns and nearly as much makeup as any of the girls. (
modeling, women are always called "girls.") He is asked
reflect on why the fashion model has such appeal. "They'
become a glorified version of what ladies imagine themselv
to look like in their fantasy," Gallant explains. "And th
set a kind of standard. Without models, women in gene
would have no guideline with which to identify. So they'
become icons, the modern icons."

Hoving then takes the viewer through the cattle-call au
tions and explains that there are 7,000 girls in New Yc
who "call themselves models"; 1,500 actually work, and
these, 500 are the "so-called 'glamour guns' " who get m
of the good jobs. Because his report is focused on N
York, he doesn't even mention the international farm syste
for modeling: the untold thousands of girls enrolled in
gional schools, or signed up at local agencies in Ameri
and Europe.

Several models attest to how difficult and degrading t
grind of traveling and groveling for work can become. Shagg
haired John Casablancas—the president of Elite, the upst
agency that has recently toppled the decades-old studio sy
tem in modeling and, almost overnight, tripled the price
professional prettiness—explains that when and if succe
finally comes, models "have a moment where they appre
ate it very, very much, but it's very, very short ... they g
too much too quickly."

Then the camera cuts to Francesco Scavullo's studio
East Sixty-third Street. In the reception area, decades
Cosmopolitan, Vogue and *Harper's Bazaar* covers shot
the precious, prolific photographer hang high on the whi
walls. The girl whose face and "bosom"—as Scavullo wou
say—appear on some of his more recent covers is in t
small dressing room being prepared for a demonstrati
photo session being staged for the TV cameras. Seated
front of a large makeup mirror, the girl doesn't squirm a

her face is painstakingly primed, painted and powdered
r nearly two hours. She has learned to hold still while
er naturally beautiful face and hair are made unnaturally
eautiful so that the camera—which sees things somewhat
fferently than the human eye—will capture her as preter-
aturally beautiful.

She is Gia. At seventeen, she was a pretty girl from the
ortheast section of Philadelphia who worked the counter
her father's luncheonette, Hoagie City, and never missed
David Bowie concert. At eighteen, she was one of the
ost promising new faces and figures in modeling, discov-
ed by the agency run by sixties cover girl Wilhelmina Coo-
er and launched in American *Vogue* by the most influential
shion photographer of the day, Arthur Elgort. Now, at
wenty-two, Gia is a member of the elite group of so-called
op models. At any given moment, there are only a dozen
r two such girls, who end up splitting most of the very best
litorial, advertising and catalog jobs.

Even among the professionally beautiful, Gia is consid-
red special. She is more like the quintessential painter's
odel—an inspiration, a "thing of beauty"—than a working
rl, a professional mannequin. A disproportionate number
f the beauty and fashion shots she appears in transcend the
ccepted level of artful commerce and approach the realm
f actual photographic art.

But Gia is legendary in her industry for other reasons,
nly a few of which can even be mentioned on network
elevision. Her celebrated androgyny is no provocative put-
n: the female makeup artist who is brushing Gia's lips shiny
ed is the recurring object of her affections. Her rebellious
ttitude toward the business—no model has ever come so
ar while appearing to care so little—has alternately out-
aged and delighted the biggest names in fashion. And her
rug problems have been so acute that if she didn't have
hat incredible *look,* she might never work at all: lesser girls
ave been blackballed for doing once what Gia has managed
 get away with many times.

Behind the scenes, where the world of a fashion model is
ally not always as it appears, Gia has given new meaning
 the industry catchphrase "girl of the moment." It usually
st refers to a model's popularity among photographers, art

directors and ad agencies reaching such a critical mass th
her face is suddenly everywhere. But Gia is such a girl
her moment that she is about to become either the face
the eighties, or a poster child for the social ills of t
seventies.

While Gia is being photographed by Scavullo in the bac
ground—"Great, like that, turn your head over a bit .
fabulous, fabulous, laugh, *laugh;* beautiful, marvelous .
smile, if you can smile"—reporter Hoving talks about t
supermodel. "A virtual symbol of the bright side and t
dark side of modeling," he calls her.

"I started working with very good people ... I mean
the time, very fast," Gia says, in a metered tone created
professional voice instructors who are trying to neutrali
her unsophisticated Philadelphia accent so she might get in
acting. "I didn't build into a model. I just sort of becar
one."

"Then the troubles began for Gia," Hoving intones, I
post-recorded commentary interspersed with edited inte
view snippets. "The real world became clouded by illusions

"When you're young," Gia tries to explain, "you do
always ... y'know ... it's hard to make [out] the differen
between what is real and what is not real."

"Particularly when adulated ..."

"Innocent," she corrects, "and there's a lot of vultur
around you."

"She became erratic," Hoving booms on, "failed to she
up for jobs." Then he turns to Gia. "At one point, you g
kind of into the drug scene, didn't you?"

"Ummm," she pauses for a long time, as the reporter a
cameraman anxiously wait to see if the loaded question w
yield a usable sound bite about a still-taboo subject. Gia h
been in front of the camera enough times to know how
dodge the question or spoil the take but, finally, she decid
to do neither. "Yes, you could say that I did. It kind
creeps up on you and catches you in a world that's, y'kno
none that anyone will ever know except someone that h
been there."

"You're free of it, aren't you, now?" he asks, even thou;
many on the *20/20* crew believe her to be high on somethi;
as she speaks.

"Oh yes, I am, definitely," she says. "I wouldn't be here right now talking to you if I wasn't, I don't think."

"Are you happy with your success?"

Gia thinks for a second, running her tongue across her painted lips. "Ummm, yes," she says. "I am, I am."

"You . . . hesitated."

"Well, I just wanted to *think* about it," she quips back, laughing, trying to defuse whatever poignancy her pause has taken on, now that it has been captured on film and can be offered for individual interpretation to each of the program's fourteen million viewers.

"No, I am happy with it," she says.

"Didja ever do it for money?" asked the tall, haggard young woman, not even bothering to brush away the long hair that covered her red eyes and broken-out cheeks.

"Do what?" asked the nurse, a big-boned woman who sat crosslegged and shoeless at the opposite end of the bed—a posture she found put the more depressed patients at ease.

"Y'know, sex. Ever do it for money?"

"No, of course not. Why?"

"I have," said the woman, lighting a Marlboro. "I've turned a lotta tricks. For drugs, y'know. You gotta do what you gotta do."

The nurse guessed that the patient was just trying to shake her up, throw her off guard. But she didn't doubt the truth of the statement. The young woman's body had been violated in half a dozen different ways. She had been addicted to heroin for a long time and had attempted suicide with a massive overdose only weeks before. The bruises on her upper body suggested that she had been badly beaten up. She had recently been raped. And she was suffering the effects of exposure from sleeping outside in the rain several nights before.

The young woman had no visible means of support. She had registered as a welfare patient in the emergency room of this small, suburban hospital outside of Philadelphia. There was a mother who came to visit sometimes, but otherwise the girl seemed very much alone. Only twenty-six, she was one of the youngest street people the hospital had ever admitted. Turning tricks was probably the only way she could survive.

The nurse was encouraged that the young woman wanted to talk about anything. "Carangi, G." had been severely depressed and mostly uncommunicative during her stay. She had first been admitted to the medical wing for treatment of pneumonia and low white-blood-cell count. When blood tests revealed that she was HIV-positive, she was placed in an isolation ward and treated gingerly, if at all, by hospital personnel largely uninformed about the disease. Even though it was already the summer of 1986 and health care workers were supposed to know better, unfamiliarity was still breeding contempt. Some nurses and orderlies were donning rubber gloves or "space suits" before entering her room, and they were wiping down her phone every time she used it, which only exacerbated her depression and suicidal feelings.

When the patient's medical condition stabilized, she was put on lithium and shifted to the mental health wing. There, it was hoped she could get a handle on her depression and figure out where she would go after discharge. "The stepfather"—mental health professionals had a way of referring to the people in a patient's life in the distant third person, as if each was an interchangeable actor taking a role in a little play—had refused to let her come back home. And the mother, who some hospital personnel had already grown to dislike because she was "difficult," insisted that she had no choice but to acquiesce to his wishes.

It was a pretty bleak case history that filled the files of Med. Rec. #04-34-10, not many positives to reinforce. So, if turning tricks for drugs was a topic that this extraordinary patient wanted to talk about, it was better than not talking at all. Or crying, which was how she had been spending many of her days.

So she and the nurse talked about turning tricks. They talked about junkie life: the shooting galleries, the filth, the sprawled-out bodies. They talked about different types of heroin and how many bags the young woman usually shot.

"You married? D'ya have any kids?" the patient later asked, trying to turn the conversation away from herself.

The nurse explained that she had a beautiful little daughter—so beautiful, in fact, that one day they were walking through one of the casinos in Atlantic City and a photographer asked if he could take the little girl's picture. The shot appeared on the cover of a casino magazine. After that, the nurse explained, she began driving her six-year-old to New York on weekends to auditions for modeling jobs. It had been very exciting for both of them, but the daughter got few jobs and the travel expenses had piled up. After a year, they had stopped going to auditions altogether. But her daughter was begging her to resume the trips.

"Don't do it," the patient said. "Even if she wants it, don't let her do it. I used to be a model. You don't want your kid to be a model."

1
Family Matters

The 1970s came early for Gia Marie Carangi. Many people would later recall 1973, the year the Vietnam War ended and the Supreme Court made abortion legal, as the official start of what they remembered as "the seventies": that slice of time when the social changes people talked about in the sixties actually started happening, when sexual liberation and drug experimentation left the rarefied laboratory of the college campus and, in the hands of regular parents and regular kids, mutated into something else entirely. Some would recall 1974 as the benchmark, the year one group of investigative journalists dethroned a U.S. president and another group created *People* magazine. Others would say the decade didn't officially start until 1975, the year TV spawned *Saturday Night Live*, New York City teetered on the brink of bankruptcy, mass marketing was reinvented by "designers" and America started to realize that freedom really *was* just another word for nothing left to lose.

But for Gia, the seventies began earlier, in February of 1971, when she had just turned eleven and trends like free love and women's liberation showed up on her doorstep at 4027 Fitler Street: one of the nicest single-family homes in one of the nicest pockets of Northeast Philadelphia. The seventies began the night that the regular evening argument between her parents—Joseph and Kathleen Carangi, a chronically overworked restaurateur and his forever dissatisfied second wife—ended with Gia's mother leaving the house for good, without really even saying good-bye.

The departure was the talk of the neighborhood. Even in the rising tide of separations and divorces, a mother leaving her husband *and her children* was unusual. And the two clans brought together by this marriage had become somewhat *known* because so many of them lived in the Northeast and had, at one time or another, worked in one of the family's restaurants. Joe Carangi had built a little culinary empire for himself. A second-generation Italian Catholic, whose father had run a jewelry business under the de-ethnicized name Crane, Joe had returned from World War II and started out in the food business delivering Bond bread. With his fraternal twin brother Dan in tow, Joe had then parlayed a series of local luncheonettes into, first, a respectable restaurant and a poolroom and, later, a lucrative chain of sandwich shops, each named Hoagie City, after the Philadelphia version of the submarine. A small jocular man with thinning dark hair, he took his family on nice vacations and gave his wife and children nice things, but mostly what he did was work. He was out early in the morning to catch the breakfast trade and home late in the evening after all the transitory employees the restaurant business attracted had finished their tasks.

Joe Carangi's first marriage had ended in divorce, he always said, because he was "too young." And he had no intention of making the same mistake twice and having his attentions diverted from financially supporting his family. Instead, he made a *different* mistake. He married a twenty-one-year-old neighborhood girl—eleven years his junior—who wanted not only his success and stability but his constant understanding and attention, neither of which he was able to give. She also wanted his help in raising the children and keeping the house straight, neither of which he felt was part of his job description.

Kathleen Adams Carangi was the second of five daughters born to an Irish Navy machinist and his Welsh, farm-bred, fundamentalist housewife. The Adams family had relocated to the Northeast from a farm in Maryland when Kathleen was six, after their only son died in infancy. At a young age, Kathleen had rejected her mother's strict beliefs. What

Kathleen came to believe in was glamour. She believed in beauty, too, but beauty was something she hadn't really been born with: she was a chubby, big-boned teenager with thick glasses. Glamour, however, was something she knew she could work at, develop and, with enough money, simply buy. Beauty was truth but glamour was a way to do something *about* the truth. It was a way for a woman to cast an alluring spell using powders and creams and incantations from fashion magazine headlines. Glamorous things made a woman feel the way a woman was supposed to feel; they were the wages of the job of being female. And as Kathleen Adams was proud to say, "I always thoroughly enjoyed being a woman."

Until she married in 1956, glamorous things had been Kathleen's livelihood as well. In high school, she studied retailing and joined the teen modeling club at the local Strawbridge and Clothier department store: she had been on TV a few times modeling for the Board of Education. After graduation, she worked at the most exclusive women's shop in the Northeast, Saks Frankford, with a name borrowed from the famous New York retailer and a location under the Frankford El. With her lightened hair elaborately coiffed and her face boldly made up behind her oversize spectacles, Kathleen sold clothing to those women who could afford higher fashion items and didn't have to buy knockoffs or sew from a pattern book. She also helped to prepare fashion shows. She loved everything about the women's retail business, but found working with the models especially fascinating.

But after she was married—to a man her parents initially objected to because he looked old enough to be her father and was not only divorced, but had a child from his first marriage who visited on occasion—Kathleen was content to be a mother and a wife. It was "an important job," she said, "what you were created for . . . if you failed at that, you failed at being a woman." She had three babies in three years, two sons and then a daughter, Gia, whose unusual name Joe Carangi said he remembered hearing while stationed in Italy during the war.

While Kathleen had struggled with her babies and Joe with his business, they had been able to maintain the outward appearance of happiness and growing prosperity. There was no time to even register dissatisfaction among the numerous distractions and family responsibilities. Kathleen's parents and several of her sisters, as well as Joe's mother and one of his two brothers, lived nearby. At different times, almost every uncle, aunt, nephew, niece and cousin had worked for Joe, who was always a soft touch for a job or a loan he knew would never be paid back. His kindness was most often extended to his twin brother Dan, who had periodic problems with gambling debts.

As the kids grew older and the Carangis moved up in the world, Kathleen became, with each new fur and Cadillac, increasingly dissatisfied with her life while Joe became increasingly impatient with her complaints. They brought out the worst in each other. He was a man who wanted life to be simpler than it was and she was a woman who wanted life to be more complicated than it needed to be. He also liked to tease, especially "the girls," and she was incapable of rolling with what she saw as malicious punches. While he had always managed to ignore her shrill lecturing and dramatic exits before—even joking with the kids, "Oh, look, we got mommy mad"—she began getting his attention. And when his very long fuse burned down, his frustration could turn to violence. He threw things, he broke things. It was his house, he said, and he could destroy it if he wanted—while Kathleen figured out how many fifty-cent hoagies and forty-five-cent steak sandwiches he would have to sell to redecorate the wall he had just smashed.

Sometimes he hit his wife and she hit back. Sometimes he would storm out of the house for an hour or two. Sometimes she would run out, with Gia in tow, and ride the El train until she calmed down; on occasion she even left, with or without the kids, for a day or two. While the children were never hit, they were often caught in the crossfire. An argument might typically begin with Kathleen telling the kids to set the table, and Joe ordering them not to because that was "Mommy's job."

"He didn't think the kids should have to do anything," Kathleen recalled. "He thought they should be allowed to enjoy themselves. He'd take the kids to work and pay them before they started working."

While there were a great many problems between the Carangis—it had always been a marriage made in purgatory—Kathleen came to see her husband's jealousy and his violence as the main issues. He once, she recalled, "smacked me in the face during sex and accused me of thinking of someone else." But after a while, it wasn't entirely clear that he didn't have some reason to be jealous. "He accused me, but he didn't know for a fact," Kathleen recalled. "He tried to prove it, but he couldn't prove it. He had been insanely jealous, always. I couldn't smile at a customer—if I did he said I was making out. A customer comes in and I'm not supposed to smile?"

"Joe didn't know about it for a long time," recalled Dan Carangi, Joe's brother, "but I saw her with other men. She just wasn't happy in marriage, she wanted men falling all over her. I just wanted to see my brother happy, so I never said anything. One time I was back in the kitchen of the restaurant and Kathleen said 'You know, I could *make* you if I wanted.' This was the way she thought, that every man in the world was in love with her."

Kathleen's youngest sister believed the problem was more subtle than Kathleen wanting other men. "I think she wanted Joe to give her all kinds of attention and think that she was like a sex goddess and make that fantasy come true," she said, "but she wasn't willing to respond to him and make that happen."

Joe and Kathleen's sons would later try to make sense of the problems their own ways. "My dad wasn't around a lot," said Michael Carangi, Gia's middle brother, "and Kathleen couldn't deal with that. She wanted to go out. You know, women like to go out and enjoy the money."

"Most of the fights were after we went to bed," recalled Joe Carangi, Jr.—known as "Joey" to the family. "Kathleen would always have some crying story about it afterwards, y'know. 'Oh, oh, what am I going to do,' and this kind of stuff, crying. In the meantime, we were pretty much taking care of ourselves. I mean, Kathleen never prepared us meals or anything. We ate whatever was around in the place. Once in a while she cooked something, not too often. The way I remember it, she was mostly either in bed or out of the house."

Kathleen saw it all in far simpler terms. Her husband was a sexist, violent man who had learned too well from his own father—who was referred to as "The Mister" by Joe's mother. To Kathleen, Joe was a good provider—he certainly supported his family materially—but an intolerable companion. And she was still young. She felt more attractive than ever. She had lost all the weight that came with her three pregnancies and then some. There had to be more to life as a woman than this.

Joe Carangi became more aggressive and jealous, Kathleen more combative and troubled. She was never an early riser, but she stopped getting up in the morning altogether. She had a doctor check her into a hospital psychiatric ward and later made a suicide attempt. "I tried to kill myself because Joe tried to examine me to see if I had sex with someone else," Kathleen recalled. "He sat and watched me take all the pills. He thought I was being dramatic. Then when I started falling asleep, he finally called the police and took me to the hospital.

"All the years that he abused me, I had gone to the cops, but I knew it was a man's world. I would call the cops and he would be in a rage, and when they'd come he would be as nice as pie."

The situation finally reached the point that Kathleen believed if she didn't leave "he was going to kill me or I was going to kill him. . . . There have been times when I thought, for the sake of the children, maybe I should've tried to work it out more. But leaving them with him was the only way I could get out. He *never* would have let me take them. And I really never thought it would hurt them as badly as it did.

"I didn't realize the full impact of what I did until much later. I came to understand that kids only want one thing. As long as Mommy and Daddy wake up in the house with them, whatever they're conditioned to is just normal. If you cry all the time, your kids get used to it. They think everybody's mommy cries, everybody's father punches holes in the wall."

And so on that night in February of 1971, a new decade began for Gia Marie Carangi. The next day her father would be devastated, his rage yielding to heartbreak as he began to realize that his second marriage was over; Gia and her

13

brothers would be slightly relieved because, with one parent gone, at least the yelling would stop.

The aunts, uncles, grandparents and cousins descended on 4027 Fitler Street to help Joe Carangi take care of his kids and his home, an enterprise for which he was ill-prepared, except he knew how to cook. But even with all of this activity—and the knowledge that somewhere, at the other end of a telephone line, their mother was out there—it was impossible to blot out the feeling that someone had died.

When the decade was well upon them, social commentators would declare the seventies "the me decade" and attempt to dissect the phenomenon of a decaying social order that transformed self-revelation into self-deification and the search for personal freedom into the demand for personal license. For Gia Marie Carangi, the seventies would be the "me decade" for a far less esoteric reason: because there was no more "us."

Until the divorce, Gia had always been, in every way, her mother's child. She was supposed to be the little girl to whom Kathleen could pass on the mantle, or yoke, of womanhood. But Gia never seemed to be interested in joining the "girls' side" of the Carangi family. "Joe would spoil her," Kathleen recalled. "We would go to Atlantic City every weekend in the summer and she would just put her arms up—she wanted to be in the rolling chair [on the Boardwalk] or be carried—and he would give in to her. Well, she was absolutely beautiful, you couldn't refuse her.

"But, in other ways, the boys could do anything they wanted and Gia had to toe the line."

Gia would remember what her father denied her more than what he gave. "My Dad was always working," she would later write of her childhood, "and when he was around he paid more attention to my brothers. I would try to get his attention and he would reject me by putting me down, making fun of me, teasing me. He would do this in front of my brothers. I felt like they were better than me and the only difference was they were boys. I feel my father never gave me what I needed growing up which was love, understanding, time . . . he never gave me the time of day. When I was little my parents had this big closet. I used to go in there to play dress-up. Instead of choosing my Mom's clothes to look at I would look at my Dad's. I would go into my brother Joey's closet and try his clothes on. I think I thought if I was a boy my father would love me."

Gia was a bright, quiet child with thick, long brown hair and bangs. Her hair was the focus of much motherly fussing: Kathleen liked to braid it and tie it with ribbons, which Gia always immediately yanked out. The hair was never cut, except to trim the bangs, until she was eight years old; her mother had the shorn locks washed, rebraided and put into a box that the young girl sometimes took to school for show and tell. Gia loved stuffed toys—her favorite was Smokey the Bear—and she slept in a frilly white four-poster bed full of them. She also loved animals. The family had a white cat named Creampuff and they went through a series of dogs, all of which managed to get run over. After a school bus killed their black poodle, Sam, all the neighborhood kids would chant "dog killer, dog killer" whenever the poor driver pulled up to the bus stop. Unlike some small children, Gia had no fear of animals. Just down the block from their house was a family with a huge black dog that terrorized neighborhood children. Gia would astonish her mother by walking right up to the dog and bonking it on the head, which immediately stopped the barking.

Gia's early childhood mannerisms were considered so adorable that she was encouraged to speak in baby talk long after it was appropriate. She also wet the bed long past infancy, a problem that, like much of what went on in the Carangi household, was exaggerated rather than constructively addressed. "That was always a big thing," recalled Nancy Adams, Kathleen's sister. "You knew that it was always disrupting and my sister just bitched about everything and Gia's brothers used to make fun of her for [the bed wetting]. So even though all the kids were together—my oldest sister had eight children of her own, so there were a lot of us—Gia kind of kept to herself. You know shy people . . . as they get older, you're not as conscious that they're shy. They're *quiet,* they're *intellectual,* they're *withdrawn.* I think they thought she was either shy or miserable. They weren't sure which. But she was always pretty bratty."

Much to Kathleen's irritation, Gia was as strong-minded

as she was, and insisted on learning everything her own way. "Always the hardest way possible," recalled Kathleen. "We went through a period when she was two that she couldn' have birthday candles because she was playing with matches. And she would eat things. I found them on the way out. . . . couldn't believe it. She ate a big chunk of snake plant. She swallowed a great big wooden button." When shopping with her mother, Gia would sometimes disappear, purposely getting lost so she could fiddle with the EMERGENCY STOP button on the escalator or hear her name announced over the department store public address system. That unusual name also became an obsession when Gia learned penmanship. She would practice writing her name on nearly any blank piece of paper or open space. While looking under her daughter's bed for something, Kathleen discovered "Gia Marie Carangi" written all over the slats.

Gia rejected out of hand much of what her mother tried to explain to her about the way a young girl should think. "She had a boyfriend in grade school," Kathleen recalled, "and she was describing him as a little smaller than she was. And I said to her, 'Why don't you want a *bigger* guy, girls are supposed to have a big guy to protect them.' She said, 'I'll protect *him.*' That was another side of her: she thought she could always protect you."

They often disagreed and were clearly locked in a battle for attention, but Gia and Kathleen were nonetheless extremely close, in a way that mothers and daughters often are almost despite their actions or intentions. As a small child Gia had often wandered across the hall in the middle of the night to come sleep next to her mother. And there were times when the young girl wanted to do nothing more than be in the house with Kathleen. Her mommy was, she often said, her best friend.

There is perhaps no more significant time in a girl's life than the age of eleven, when she is poised on the gangplank of adolescence and her body is about to confirm what her mother has always insisted—that girls are different from boys. It is a time that researchers in female development have come to single out as the pivotal "moment of resistance" against societal forces to which most girls eventually succumb.

16

And there probably had never been a more confusing time for a girl to turn eleven than in 1971, the year *Ms.*magazine first appeared on the newsstand and *All in the Family*'s Edith and Gloria Bunker first began debating feminist issues on television. Politics, The Pill and Pantyhose were conspiring to free women socially, sexually and comfortably. But, it was one thing to be an adult woman in 1971 and sense that a female's place in society might be changing. It was quite another to reach the age when girls are taught to covet their first training bras just as public burning of brassieres became a symbolic sexual protest. When women's liberation began, Gia was still a Brownie.

Even for girls in the most supportive households, it was a time of dramatically mixed signals. It wasn't easy to become a woman when everyone seemed surer of what a woman *wasn't* going to be anymore than what she *was*. In what was left of the Carangi household, a woman's place was more precarious than ever. Gia was both the youngest child and now the only female in a house of very disoriented, and even vengeful, men.

It was a physically bruising time for the entire extended family, as everyone waited out what they initially believed to be a temporary separation. Joe and his brother Dan were convinced that Kathleen had abandoned her family for another man. "I saw her about a week after she left," Dan recalled, "and I told her it was one thing to leave the boys but she had no right leaving Gia. She said, 'You don't understand, I have my own life to take care of.' She was running with a bartender, a guy who knew my brother."

Kathleen remembered that time quite differently. "I didn't leave him for someone else or anything like that," she said. "Dan doesn't know what he's talking about. I don't even remember him being around at the time: he was probably out gambling somewhere. He didn't want Joe to marry me in the first place.

"Sure, I knew this bartender, but I also knew he was a gigolo and I had no intention of marrying him. He was a *bartender*, I knew he couldn't keep me in the style to which I was accustomed. I convinced my husband I had to get out for my own sanity; he even helped me get my own apartment initially. When I left him he wasn't aware that I intended to divorce him off the bat. If he had known, wouldn't have lived to get out the door. When it started sinking in that this was for keeps, he started giving me trouble. When I filed for a separation agreement, he threw a ram. I wanted the kids, but I knew he wouldn't let me have them. He wouldn't even let me see them. He would call me and threaten me about the lawyers. He came to my apartment once and broke the window to get in to see if I was with someone else."

The temporary separation began to look more permanent when, a month after she moved out, Kathleen met Henry Sperr at a local bar. Henry had actually been a high school classmate of Kathleen's, although they hadn't known each other then. He was now a CPA who had just left the grind of Price Waterhouse to make a career as an independent financial adviser. Beneath his drab accountant's garb, Henry was nearly as lean and mean as he had been during his high school football days. An auto accident during tax season had left him with a permanent tracheotomy that occasionally made breathing difficult and day-to-day living uncomfortable, but Henry was still a steady, commanding presence with a ruggedly spent look and a distaste for overly emotional outbursts. He was also a relatively social man, with a growing list of client-friends.

Henry had separated from his wife the year before, and he was already immersed in the growing culture of divorcées, recently single parents, remarried couples and holdout bachelors that was offering a new kind of adult teenagehood—the malt *beverage* shop—for Ozzie and Harriet refugees. In the record books, 1972 would go down as the peak year in U.S. history for remarriage of divorced men and women. Society might not have been quite prepared to embrace this new class of emotionally disenfranchised men and women in their thirties and forties, but the business community was more than willing to create institutions to serve their needs. There were boutiques for those reentering the social scene; bars and clubs where the newly single, and those "cheaters" who weren't yet ready to make (or unmake) the commitment, might show off their colorful plumage.

It was a lifestyle that Kathleen Carangi immediately took

18

o, and Henry Sperr was her escort. "Henry swept me off
my feet," she recalled. "I couldn't believe that a man could
make you feel like that—especially after what I'd been
through. I started living with him almost immediately after
I met him."

While all this went on, the Carangi children were the sub-
ject of the most concern but the least actual attention.
"When Mom first left, we didn't see her for a while," said
Michael Carangi. "She would call to tell us she loved us.
Later she started to come around."

Kathleen recalled the situation differently. "I know Michael *thinks* there was a time period when I wasn't around,"
she said, "but it isn't true. Also, he was a boy, Gia was a
girl. There were lots of times when I would go over there
and Michael would have ten million pals around. I realized
that was important to him, so I didn't bother him . . . and,
really, I don't remember *any* of them begging for me to
come back. For a while Joe wouldn't let them come to visit
me. Then he started letting me have Gia over for dinner."

In the midst of all this, Joe Carangi felt he had no choice
but to maintain his hectic work schedule. The Hoagie City
chain was doing well—he would build up business at one
shop, sell it off, and open another—but it required his constant attention. He was gone most days before the children
rose for school and he often came home late. When he realized that his wife wasn't coming back, he too began to socialize—he got himself fitted with a hairpiece, bought some new
clothes and started staying out even later at night. Although
he could afford it, Joe didn't want to hire anyone to help him
take care of the children. So, Joey, Michael and Gia were
often left to their own devices. "It was real peanut-butter-
for-breakfast time, at least from the way Gia described it,"
recalled one friend. "Nobody was paying attention to
those kids."

"We could've used some discipline," said Michael. "Every
child needs it. We were allowed to do what we wanted. I
could stay out as long as I wanted and nobody would know.
I don't think my parents ever talked to us about sex. In the
back of your mind, you want discipline, you want to be told
stuff by your parents—just to know that they care and that

they know what you might be going through. Gia was t**
youngest, the breakup affected her the worst. And I fe**
girls need more attention than boys anyhow."

Since Joe's own mother had died in the mid-sixties, son**
of the tasks of surrogate motherhood for the Carangi ch**
dren fell on Kathleen's mother and four sisters. Because**
the wide range in their ages, experiences and religious b**
liefs, the Adamses were a catalog of the incongruities **
womanhood—especially since each was so firm in her disp**
rate perspective. "I never met a family with such stro**
personalities, especially so many strong women," recall**
one family friend.

Kathleen had been the first in the family to challenge h**
mother's strictness. "My mother said she was so *defia**
when she was a child—none of her other girls were li**
that," recalled her sister Nancy. "I remember my moth**
talking about disciplining her children and with Kathlee**
she could beat her to death and she wouldn't move, s**
wouldn't bat an eye. She wouldn't act like it bothered h**
at all. Kathleen and my oldest sister sort of grew up t**
gether, and everything the oldest sister did was wonderf**
and everything Kathleen did was all wrong."

Kathleen's contentiousness laid the groundwork for h**
younger sisters, Barbara and Nancy. Barbara was a child**
the early sixties and grew up imbued with some of th**
decade's spirituality and irresponsibility. She married, had**
son, divorced and all but left the child to be raised by h**
mother, but she was still adored by her siblings in a w**
that Kathleen never would be. Nancy, considered the mo**
physically attractive of the bunch and a wild child of t**
late sixties, never made any pretense to adulthood at a**
She was the baby even to her siblings—her oldest sister w**
over twenty years her senior, her mother was old enough **
be her grandmother—and she would forever remain a litt**
young for her age.

Barbara was the sister with whom Kathleen had alwa**
been the closest: she had often been the Carangis' bab**
sitter before the separation. With Kathleen out of the hous**
Barbara, and occasionally Nancy, tried to fill in as somethi**
more than baby-sitters and less than a mother—especial**
for Gia, who appeared to be taking the breakup the harde**

"She was spending a lot of time hanging out with her older brothers and just being lonely," recalled Nancy, who might have been Gia's aunt but, with only six years separating them, was young enough to be considered in many ways her peer. "She couldn't understand why her mother had left, why her parents weren't together. I don't think she ever understood it. And she was totally unsupervised. I would go over to see if she had been at school, if she was planning to go the next day, if her father had been at home.

"And, at the same time, Kathleen was mad at us. I remember my sister Barbara coming home one day crying after baby-sitting for Gia. She said she was sitting on the sofa with Gia and Kathleen came in the house and grabbed Gia, stuck a finger in Barbara's face and said, 'You stay away from my daughter, she's mine!' She did the same thing to me once: she pulled me out of a car when I was with one of my boyfriends. She treated Gia like her possession. But, it was like a kid with a discarded toy: this is mine and even if I leave it under a sofa it's still mine and I don't want anyone else to use it."

Kathleen believed that Nancy was more of a corrupting influence than a positive one. "When I left that house, Nancy would bring her boyfriends there and sleep with them in Gia's bed," she said. "She would stir up trouble between Gia and I. She could've helped Gia and all she did was make things worse. I have a lot of problems with Nancy. I think she was always jealous of me and of what Gia and I had."

But the Carangi home itself might have been the most corrupting influence of all. The impressive stone house, wrapped in ivy and set back on one of the largest and lushest residential plots in the area, had once been a fitting symbol of how far Joe Carangi had come. He was a man who still basically made a living selling sandwiches in a smeared white apron and a T-shirt. Yet he lived in what anyone would describe as "a beautiful home," where his children had large bedrooms of their own, his prized pool table had a separate room with plenty of space for tricky shots, and, for a time, his wife had plenty of space to decorate and redecorate as she wished. Now it was, in every way, a broken home. And because Joe was rarely there, it was also becoming the big hangout spot for his sons' school friends.

In almost every residential community, there was a handful of houses where all the kids hung out after school, in the evening, on weekends. Some were supervised playhouses where parents purposely created youth-friendly environments—even if it meant feeding everyone else's kids—so they could keep an eye on their own children. The others were houses left unattended for such long stretches that anything went. These were the homes where adolescent rebellion was being pushed beyond even the thresholds dared in the sixties—when at least there had been some modicum of reverence left for the physical power of drugs, some residual respect for the emotional potency of sex. These were the homes where seventies kids would remember first trying marijuana, first vomiting from cheap jug wine, first acting upon sexual feelings. These were the homes where the minimum age for certain rites of passage had gone from twenty-one to eighteen to fifteen to thirteen in a matter of years, where high school kids were suddenly having college and postgraduate fun. These were the homes that were the epicenters of the quakes that were beginning to crumble the dream of the Great Northeast.

The Northeast section of Philadelphia—or the "Great Northeast" as it came to be called in the fifties, when its first major department store, a Gimbels, emblazoned those words in twenty-foot-high stainless steel letters on its facade—was the ultimate creation of the city's burgeoning middle class. It was far more than just another faceless suburban development, another destination for white flight. Located just north of the center of Philadelphia, the Northeast was serviced by Philadelphia's public transit system, educated by the city's school system and policed by city cops, many of whom lived there to satisfy residency requirements for municipal employees. The area offered the inexpensive single-family homes and drivable streets of the bedroom communities, the ample parking and access to modern shopping. But, confined by the city limits, it eventually became relatively crowded for a suburb—mostly a sprawl of tract homes and twin houses with tiny yards. And it came to develop its own industries, its own class system and its own ethos. It even had its own accent, a loud, nasal singsong that was instantly recognizable. *Gia* was one of those words most altered by the Northeast dialect. It came out something like "Jay-ya."

Unlike a prefab, residential Levittown, the Northeast was really a whole world unto itself—or really two worlds, one predominantly Jewish, the other predominantly Catholic, roughly divided spiritually and physically by the sprawling sixteen-lane Roosevelt Boulevard. But in the Northeast, these particular Jews and Catholics somehow found they had more in common than not—adherence to middle class values, fear of blacks, dedication to an ethnic dream of prosperity. And they created something so attitudinally different from mainstream Philadelphia and its more traditional suburbs—it was a suburban city, a superburb—that local politicians were continually proposing that the Northeast should secede from the city, and maybe the state as well.

But, like all suburbs, the idealized Northeast had really only lasted through the first generation of its postwar inhabitants. Those first striving settlers were the ones who had seen the Northeast as the best of both worlds. Their vast numbers—and the predictable difference between parents who worked hard to earn what they had and children who just *had*—slowly turned the Northeast into what some perceived as the *worst* of both worlds. It had neither architectural nor natural beauty. Its citizens had neither the true street smarts of the city nor the true safety of the pristine suburbs; they seemed informed neither by time-honored wisdom nor by up-to-the-minute thinking. To cynical outsiders—who assumed the "mall culture" was a small but controllable cancer on the America body politic—the Northeast came to embody how quickly the newly manufactured middle-class dream could turn nightmarish.

An incident at Abraham Lincoln High School—Kathleen's alma mater, where both Joey and Michael Carangi were students—typified the vast differences between the generation that had built the Northeast and the one about to inherit it. The drugs of choice in the early seventies were still marijuana and LSD, but suddenly Lincoln High was being flooded with phenobarbital pills. It wasn't just an unusually large supply of sedatives working its way through normal drug distribution channels. There were suddenly just phenobarbs *everywhere*. Kids had pocketfuls of them; they were toting around bottles that contained not ten or twenty pills but a thousand. Students were throwing them across the 107 Lunchroom like confetti, swallowing them like candy.

There were scares, overdoses, investigations. Eventually, there was police action; over a dozen Lincoln students were arrested, many at a teen dance at the Jardel community center at Cottman and Penway. The story made the evening news and was covered by all the newspapers—especially when the source of the phenobarbital pills was discovered. They hadn't been clandestinely manufactured in some shack in rural Bucks County. Nobody had robbed a drugstore or broken into nearby Byberry State Hospital and stolen all the inmates' sedatives. The pills had been discovered by students in medical kits in a forgotten Civil Defense bomb shelter, located in the *basement of Lincoln High itself.*

It was anyone's guess what authorities in the 1950s had imagined that high school students might do with thirty-four thousand downers if the bomb got dropped.

2
The Low Spark of High-Heeled Boys

Karen Karuza was a sight to behold, especially in the setting of a drab high school classroom. If the fourteen-year-old had antennae protruding from her high forehead, instead of just the space where her eyebrows had been, she couldn't have stood out more among the flannel-shirted boys and peasant-bloused girls. In her glittering stretch pants and platform shoes, her brightly dyed hair nearly glowing and her multicolored fingernails sweeping rainbows when she talked, Karen decked the halls of Lincoln. The fact that she was one of the brightest students in the ninth grade only added to the mystery of her physical mutation from yet another Polish–Catholic Northeast girl into one of *them*. Lincoln had large ramps between floors instead of stairs, and each major clique in the school claimed a ramp as its exclusive territory. But there was no incline for the kids who looked "outrageous" like Karen Karuza. They found each other in different ways.

One day Karen was walking out of a classroom when she encountered a vision as startling as herself. It was a girl her age but taller, wearing a quilted red satin jumpsuit and shiny red boots with black platforms. She wore her thick hair cropped short and shaggy in the back. It looked like a coonskin cap had been glued to her scalp.

The girl made eye contact and awkwardly approached her.

25

At first, Karen flinched: not long before, she had been sucker-punched and knocked off her platform shoes by a female classmate who considered the way she dressed a personal affront. But this girl simply shoved an envelope into Karen's hand and galloped away. Inside the envelope was a picture postcard of David Bowie. Scrawled on the reverse side was "because you remind me of Angie"—which any fan would recognize as a reference to Bowie's wife.

The next day the tall girl was waiting outside Karen's classroom again. And she continued to come back every day after that. Before long the two were friends, and their relationship—and outfits—were topics of constant comment and speculation among the students at Lincoln. They were the women who fell to earth.

Karen Karuza's pal was the new and reproved Gia: now identifiable only by certain physical features—the broad lips and tiny nose, the thick hair and perpetually bitten fingernails—as the spoiled little girl whose life had been leveled by the separation, and eventual bitter divorce, of her parents. Some of the changes in her had been the standard ones brought on by adolescence: the spurt in lanky height and the very beginnings of a curvy figure.

But other changes were attributable to the sheer volume of weirdness she had endured and, in a way, perpetuated. A year after she moved out, Gia's mother married Henry Sperr, in a private ceremony that the children were told about only *after* it happened. Gia didn't know her new stepfather, but she disliked him on general principle. She was envious of the way Henry monopolized her mother's attention. And after hearing her father's jealous rage, she decided that Henry was the sole reason for the dissolution of her parents' relationship. No matter how often Kathleen tried to explain the irreconcilable problems she had with Joe, Gia continued to see Henry Sperr as the main obstacle to her parents' reunion.

In fact, just the opposite was true: Gia was the only thing that remained between Kathleen and Joe. The boys had sided completely with their father and showed no interest in being part of their mother's new life. But Gia continued to exploit whatever connections remained between her parents by yanking at their heart-and-purse strings, an emotional exercise made both simpler and more complicated when she chose that newest form of home life: Divorce–Dual Residency. Gia maintained a bedroom in her father's home. But she officially moved in with her mother, or her "mommy," as she always referred to her, and her stepfather, who she referred to as Henry if she referred to him at all.

The three of them shared a small, two-bedroom duplex just a few blocks from the Carangi home. And suddenly child support, scarcely mentioned at the time of the divorce, became an issue. Kathleen and Henry did not have the kind of money Joe Carangi did. Henry had just begun free-lancing as an accountant and financial adviser, and building a client base took time. It seemed only fair that Joe pay them something—especially since the original divorce settlement had not favored Kathleen.

"I ended up walking away from everything," she recalled. "I gave away quite a bit. I didn't fight him for anything I might have been entitled to, and those businesses were very healthy. But Pennsylvania didn't have no-fault divorce then. A woman leaving had no rights at all. When I originally moved out, he co-signed a lease for an apartment because he thought it was temporary. When it started sinking in that this was for keeps, he started giving me trouble. I wanted out so bad, I told my lawyer I just didn't care."

An amount of child support was agreed upon, along with a payment schedule, but Joe rarely kept to either. It wasn't that he didn't care. In a way, it seemed he even liked it when Kathleen stormed into the restaurant screaming about money if he was a day late. It was like a little soap opera all the Carangi men could watch.

"I remember one day Kathleen came in yelling about something," said Dan Carangi, "and Gia and I were sitting there. I said to Kathleen, 'Hey, how's that guy of yours with the hole in his neck?' Gia just laughed and laughed."

The war between the families had not abated with the remarriage. "My one sister, my older sister, I *know* would invite Joe to dinner and she *never* invited me to dinner," said Kathleen. "I got the message that they all thought Joe was having such a bad time—because he played on it. And a great deal of the time, I didn't want to listen to them, so I didn't stay in touch.

"Joe put me down all the time—in front of the kids, too—which was totally wrong. He would curse me out. I finally put Henry on the phone and then he stopped that. Henry can be *very* intimidating."

Henry Sperr was trying to be a good sport about it, but having a teenager around the house was not exactly what he had bargained for. He was accustomed to leading an active social life, and assumed Kathleen would join him. Soon after they got married, Kathleen announced that she wanted to have another child, which he definitely didn't favor. Having Gia move in was a little more palatable, but it still meant changes he hadn't planned on.

The biggest problem was rules: Gia wasn't accustomed to having any. And it was an uphill battle to get a fourteen-year-old to abide by more restrictive regulations than she had when she was twelve. Besides, now that Gia had two homes, there was really no bottom line to the demands made by her mother and stepfather. "As long as you live under my roof," wasn't much of a threat when another roof was readily available. Especially when Henry found himself caught between two parents who weren't very good at sticking to their own edicts. If it had been up to Henry alone, the heads of the household would have prevailed. But Gia wasn't really Henry's to discipline. He did so occasionally out of sheer frustration: "One time we were all together—the father, too—and Gia started on her mother," he recalled. "I finally just grabbed Gia, picked her up and threw her in the car myself." But generally, it wasn't appropriate for the stepfather to play the heavy—even if the real father was unwilling and the real mother unable to be a strong parent.

And Kathleen *was* unable. Perhaps it was her sense of guilt over leaving Gia when she was eleven. Or perhaps Gia was just stronger and more resourceful than Kathleen. For whatever reason, Kathleen couldn't stay mad at her daughter long enough to really discipline her. When she announced a punishment, it was rarely carried out. And sometimes Kathleen's social life kept her out so late that she and Henry weren't home to receive a phone call that Gia was going to be late. It was almost as if Kathleen wanted motherhood to be a nine-to-five job with frequent vacations, and she simply refused to work overtime.

In the midst of all this, Gia found David Bowie. By 1973, being a "Bowie kid" was an act of individual rebellion complete with its own thriving subcultural support group. The club of trailblazers had already been formed, the glittery dress code had been established and the "outrageousness is next to godliness" ethos was set in stone. Bowie's 1972 concept album, *The Rise and Fall of Ziggy Stardust and the Spiders from Mars* (and the ensuing U.S. tour and *Rolling Stone* cover story) had made him an international phenomenon. But he had been recording in England since 1966, and he had been wearing dresses on album covers and publicly declaring his bi-or-homo-sexuality (depending on how the presence of his wife Angie was interpreted) since 1971. *Ziggy* was simply the most successful packaging of twenty-six-year-old Bowie's basic themes: alienation, androgyny, otherworldliness, production values. And his highly theatrical act was the perfect innovation in a rock concert business where demand for showmanship was outpacing supply.

There were Bowie kids all over America and England. In every municipality and suburb, a certain number of people heard Bowie—or his character, Ziggy—speaking to whatever it was that made them feel different: their sexuality, their intellectual aspirations, their disaffection, their rebelliousness. It was mass marketing to those who wanted to be separate from the masses. And since Philadelphia had been among the first American cities to embrace the bisexual Barnum of rock, his cult of personality had grown particularly strong in the Delaware Valley. His fall 1972 shows were such a huge success that when he returned in February of 1973, local promoters were able to sell out seven nights at the Tower Theater, where audiences showed up in outfits that rivaled those worn by Bowie and his band, turning the whole scene into a rock 'n' roll performance art piece with a 3,072-member cast. When Bowie then announced his retirement from performance in July of that year, his marketed mystique was solidified.

"He was a genuine guru, a rock star who seemed to hold some secrets in a way that nobody really expected of, say, the Beatles," recalled Matt Damsker, Philadelphia's reigning rock critic at the time. "Everyone was so caught up in the shared moment, and Bowie represented somebody so mysterious and so calculatedly brilliant. There was a power to his very best music that suggested a lot of withheld information: it seemed that if you got close to him, he might dispense it to you. He seemed to have a political and metaphysical program in mind. These weren't stupid kids. They weren't into Bowie just because they were bored with everything else. They were caught up in something that was pretty broad in its implications."

Bowie himself would recall of the time, "I never ever thought my songs would help anybody think or know anything. Yet it did seem that at that time there were an awful lot of people who were feeling a similar way. They were starting to feel alienated from society, especially the breakdown of the family as we'd known it in the forties, fifties and especially the sixties, when it really started crumbling. Then, in the seventies, people in my age group felt disinclined to be a part of society. It was really hard to convince oneself that you *were* a part of society. [The feeling was] here we are, without our families, totally out of our heads, and we don't know where on earth we are. That was the feeling of the early seventies—nobody knew *where* they were."

For Gia, Bowie and adolescence would be interchangeable. Her first haircut since the age of eight—and the first time she ever chose her own hairstyle—was the bushy Bowie cut. It was executed by Nadine at Bonwit Tellers, almost perfectly replicating Bowie's look on the *Pin-Ups* cover photograph. "She went from this beautiful long hair to this *Bowie* hairdo," Kathleen recalled. "I couldn't stand it. I avoided seeing her for two weeks."

Gia's first experimentations with makeup were definitely not done to make her look more womanly. She and her Aunt Nancy spent an afternoon singing along to Bowie records and perfecting a red lightning bolt from Gia's hairline to her cheek, like the one on the cover of the just-released *Aladdin Sane*. Among the first clothes Gia bought for herself *by herself* were red platform boots, a white shirt decorated with black hands that appeared to be wrapped around her upper body, and a feather boa. The red satin jumpsuit had been handmade by her mother as a gesture to befriend this gawky space creature that had once been her adoring daughter.

Even Gia's handwriting was affected. She began dotting her *i*'s with circles and signing her notes and letters "Love on Ya!" It was the same way Bowie had scrawled his handwritten liner notes on *Pin-Ups*.

To her parents, Gia seemed to have been transformed overnight after attending a Bowie show. "She got involved with rock concerts, *okay?*" her stepfather, Henry Sperr, recalled. "And a bunch of people who went to rock concerts. They weren't from around here. She got a Bowie haircut and that changed her personality completely. She seemed like a sweet, young little kid before, and then afterward ... well, you know it probably had something to do with the drugs. She would be disrespectful, she would be constantly fighting, just over nothing. And she'd be very rebellious. You'd say, 'Be home at ten o'clock,' and she'd come home the next day."

But that was the way it was for many of the kids caught up in the glitter crowd, some of whom had yet to actually *see* this creature David Bowie perform. They viewed Bowie—not just his records and his image, but the whole scene he was musically documenting—as the doorkeeper to a new world that really was brave.

Joe McDevit was converted at The Tunnel at Cottmann and Bustleton, where teen dances were held on Saturday nights. It was there that the blond, broad-shouldered forklift operator—a seventeen-year-old Catholic school dropout—was first inspired by a friend with a Bowie-do and a rhinestone shirt.

"Next thing I knew, I shaved my eyebrows off, hit the sewing machine to make glitter clothes and found out about this man in Hialeah, Florida, who made custom platform shoes," McDevit recalled. "I sent him a tracing of my foot and ordered a pair with eleven-inch heels and eight-inch platforms, navy blue with silver lightning bolts down the side. They came in the mail, a hundred five dollars—I had to work two weeks to pay for them. In a matter of weeks, I went from a normal kid who played baseball at the local field to parading around in full drag. Suddenly, I was bisexual. I had a steady girlfriend, and my boyfriends were all neighborhood kids who played on the baseball team."

McDevit's first Bowie concert was also his debut to the Delaware Valley's David throng as a fanatic to be reckoned with. "We camped out for a week for tickets," McDevit recalled. "And I had a friend of mine whip up a silver lamé space suit, with a blue lamé jock strap attached to the jacket. I remember waiting for Bowie to come on stage for *my* entrance. I felt so special. He was on stage singing and I walked down the aisle. They put the spotlight on me and I started throwing kisses." On that night, Joe McDevit became "Joey Bowie."

For others, the evolution was less theatrical. "The way I remember it," recalled one friend of Gia's, "I was a little kid watching *The Brady Bunch* one day and the next day I was in a bar with a Quaalude, even though I was only fourteen. It was just a very crazy time to be in high school. I remember staying out all night on a weeknight and then hailing a cab to take me straight to school from the clubs."

The Bowie crowd at Lincoln, though small, quickly developed its own hierarchy and heroes. Although it was mostly girls—a male took a much higher risk coming to school wearing makeup—the leader of the pack was Ronnie Johnson,* a sixteen-year-old dead ringer for Bowie. Ronnie wasn't so much the ultimate Bowie fanatic. Ronnie Johnson *was* David Bowie—or as close as you could get and still have a locker at Lincoln. He designed and sewed his own Bowie-inspired clothes: did his own embroidery, affixed his own sequins. He combed the high fashion magazines for the latest trends in hair, makeup and clothing. He understood that Bowie's outfits, extraterrestrial to girls who shopped in

---

*This designates the first appearance of a name that has been changed to protect the privacy of a character or source. Each pseudonym refers to a specific person and no other personal details have been altered: there are no composite characters in the book.

malls, were merely the most futuristic designs of top European and Oriental dressmakers.

Ronnie and Gia immediately hit it off. When they saw each other, Gia made it a point to bite Ronnie, as a sign of playfully outrageous affection. Besides Bowie, they shared the bond of emotional, broken homes. "His father left the family when he was like three," recalled one of Johnson's high school friends. "And his mother was this *wild* woman, a waitress at the diner."

And Ronnie and Gia had something else in common. The Bowie kids did a lot of sexual posturing. Bowie was bisexual so, at least in theory, they were, too: they cross-dressed, they cross-flirted. In practice, however, few of them did in private what they claimed to do in public. And some of them didn't do anything at all. All of which made life that much more confusing for people like Gia and Ronnie, who, deep inside, suspected that they really were gay, and wanted to do something about it.

The reinvented Gia who Karen Karuza met was still basically a quiet girl who did not yet possess great beauty. Still, there was something about her that drew attention and made people stare: even the severe Bowie haircut couldn't dilute her visual appeal. Young men and women alike were stunned by the way she looked, her wicked grin, her perfectly squared shoulders, the utter fearlessness in her gait, the sad burn behind her wide eyes. She smoked Marlboros with cool distance and danced with abandon. At thirteen, she had already found in herself a seductive posture that made people want to break rules for her.

Nobody knew her from conversation. A dispassionate "Yeah, yeah, yeah," a laugh and a shrug were her responses to most situations. She was personably vague one-on-one, and even her closest relationships were shallow. She rarely shared personal details with anyone. "She never talked about her family life or anything," recalled one friend. "You know how teenage girls whine and cry about their moms? She would *never* do it."

At fourteen, she was already becoming a sort of icon to those who saw her walking in the school hallways or working behind the counter in her father's shop. She was a first crush for many teenagers at Lincoln—male *and* female—and her shirt with the fabric hands wrapped around it would, years later, remain an indelible image of growing up in the early seventies. But she did what she could to defuse that sort of attention.

"I was sitting in a class once," recalled one close friend, "and I heard a voice yell, 'Yo, Ellen.' I looked out the window, toward the window of the *boys' bathroom* across the courtyard, and there was Gia's ass sticking out. She was a wild child."

"It was great at Lincoln," Gia would later recount. "I guess they remember me because I used to chuck moons out the window all the time. It was real fun. Nobody knew my face, but they sure remember my ass."

But along with the outrageous antics were telling gestures of friendship and affection: the Bowie card, homemade cookies thrust into the hands of someone she barely knew, flowers and handwritten poems delivered to startled girls she hoped to woo. In most cases Gia was both wealthier and a few years younger than those she spent time with, so she often seemed to be trying especially hard to fit in. Her handwriting and spelling resembled that of a grade-schooler, even though she wrote incessantly, practicing her name or copying down lyrics to her favorite songs. She liked to give people silly nicknames and dropped dopey terms like "okie-dokie" into conversation. Her enthusiasms for anything from the sound of traffic to the pure junk-food joy of an oily steak sandwich suggested to her friends that Gia possessed some heightened sensitivity.

Karen and Gia were in completely different programs at Lincoln. The only course they had in common was art, which was primarily an exercise in trying to make each class assignment fit a drawing of Bowie or an analysis of his lyrics. While Karen was college bound, Gia was struggling to pass the basic courses. She was the kind of student the school systems were seeing more of: kids who, a generation before, would probably have dropped out and gotten jobs because classrooms had nothing to offer them. Now, they just showed up for school: to fulfill parental dreams of having children who graduated the way they never had, or simply

o be baby-sat by the system. They were the ones who accu-
ately answered "present" when roll was called.

At Lincoln, a half-dozen or so girls would sit on the grassy
awn outside the 107 Lunchroom and smoke what teachers
night have even believed were hand-rolled cigarettes. A girl
icknamed Cricket sometimes brought a guitar and played;
nother girl had a bulky tape deck and recorded their con-
ersations. One of the group's leaders was Ellen Moon,*
vho shared her school locker with Gia because it was closer
o the lunchroom: their Bowie-bedecked compartment was
mmortalized in the high school yearbook. There was usually
nly a joint or two to pass around, and marijuana in 1973
vas rarely as potent as the industrial-strength pot the late
eventies would produce. But the lunchtime ritual—followed
y the Marlboros that everyone smoked—would produce a
leasant, giggly buzz that took the edge off the rest of the
lay. For those who bothered to wait for lunchtime to get
igh, grades in courses with afternoon classes were often
narkedly lower than those scheduled in the morning.

Gia was often counted upon to provide the marijuana,
ecause her brother Michael happened to be one of the
chool's better pot connections. In the subtle sociological
lelineations of the schoolyard, this made both of them
lightly different from their peers. The distribution system
or pot was very simple and, generally, very friendly. At the
op were layers of "real dealers"—who actually knew people
:ven *they* thought of as criminals. The pot dealers sold to
everal layers of middlekids who paid for what they used
hemselves—and made a little profit, as well—by selling to
heir peers.

Since pot was such a social drug, many people got high
ut never really bought. When it appeared at social events,
:veryone was happy to smoke someone else's, but many
veren't prepared to spend their own money—or felt uneasy
bout being so deliberate about getting high. Even though
l lot of people used pot, there was still a difference between
hose who just smoked and those who bought. The buyers
vere taking a bigger risk if they ever were caught: they were
lso placing themselves in a position of both power and
rustration. "We were amazed at Gia's ability to get pot,
:ven during the worst dry spells," recalled one member of

the 107 Lunch bunch. "But, actually, sometimes she became paranoid and thought people were using her. She said we only wanted her around for pot."

On Saturdays, Karen and Gia would go downtown, walking over to Frankford Avenue in the morning to catch the elevated train. The Frankford El was the most convenient way to Center City from the Northeast. Its route was also a trip up and down the socioeconomic scale. Each stop closer to the city was in a poorer neighborhood, and from the point where a rider was afforded the most spectacular view—with the expansive Ben Franklin Bridge on one side and the skyline on the other—the train dove underground into the middle of one of the city's most bombed-out sections. It then headed up Market Street East, a once-posh commercial district that was now all discount record stores, head shops and porno theaters, still awaiting a promised "urban mall" development that was supposed to save the area. The girls got off at Thirteenth Street, the stop that shared an underground walkway with the John Wanamaker's store, the traditional refuge of the refined Philadelphia lady.

As soon as they stepped off the train, the girls rushed to light up their Marlboros. But before their shopping began, Karen and Gia had to stop at the recently opened Center City branch of Hoagie City at Twelfth and Chestnut. There they received soda, sandwiches and other sustenance.

"Dad, I need twenty-five dollars," Gia would begin.

"What do you want this for?" her father would ask, wiping the oil and tomato seeds off his hands with his apron before hugging his daughter.

"C'mon, Dad, really, I need twenty-five dollars."

"Didn't I just give you money?" he asked, in the soft voice he had passed on to all his children. "Didn't you bring any money with you?"

"Yeah, yeah, yeah, c'mon, how about twenty-five dollars? I gotta get stuff."

No matter how tough he got with her—it varied with how busy he was—the end of the time-honored family ritual was always the same. He always gave Gia money, just like he always put his hand up to check when Gia would joke,

"Dad, the toupee's crooked," when he was on his way out the door for a date. But before they left, the girls had to eat. "Okay, let me make you a hoagie," he would begin. And on the subject of feeding, he was always firm. If it was nice out, they went up to the apartment Gia's father was redoing upstairs and ate at the open window, watching people go by and occasionally dropping a pickle round on a passerby's head.

With money in hand, the two girls would set out to do Center City. Downtown Philadelphia was not very large—only twenty blocks by twenty-five blocks. But the area was in the midst of a rebirth, and any one of the city's better shopping streets could end up taking a whole afternoon.

The city was blossoming, in spite of the neomilitary reign of police-chief-turned-mayor Frank Rizzo. Like the rest of the country, Philadelphia was feeling the economic impact of the baby boom. Woodstock graduates were reclaiming the urban areas their parents had fled for suburbia and starting businesses that provided the products and services *they* wanted. And a few purely local phenomena were helping transform the dowdy town with its legendary inferiority complex about nearby New York into a place that might actually attract its *own* tourists.

Federal funds were pouring into the city: not just the dwindling urban renewal money sent to save all municipalities, but additional dollars earmarked to spruce up Philadelphia for the upcoming bicentennial celebration. Graduates of the pioneering Restaurant School were turning the previously tasteless town into a culinary capital. The local music scene, moribund since Dick Clark had moved *American Bandstand* west in the sixties after a payola scandal, was soaring again. Even the city's newest sports franchise, the Philadelphia Flyers hockey team, was showing great promise. The city was beginning to look exciting, sound exciting, even taste exciting.

Their platform shoes clomping on the historic red brick sidewalks and cobblestone streets, Gia and Karen would set off to shop. First they walked down Chestnut, in and out of the new boutiques like The Hen's Den and The Horse You Rode In On, as well as Dan's Shoes, which sold the most outrageous footwear in Philadelphia. After a while they got to know some of the store owners—or at least be recognized by them—just as they did in the record and poster shops. Both the newer, independent record stores—which made as much money selling bongs and rolling papers as music—and the more established Sam Goodys had to be shopped. It was hours of letting your fingers do the walking through the bins of alphabetically sorted rock albums: searching for obscure import versions of Bowie's earlier releases and for records by the other stars of what was now a genre known as glitter-rock.

A well-informed Bowie kid needed a lot of information, and it wasn't available in mainstream newspapers, magazines or TV news reports. To these media, rock music was still basically for children. So the musical minutiae had to be gleaned from the pages of "alternative" publications. There were rock tabloids like *Rolling Stone, Crawdaddy* and the local *Drummer,* and magazines like *Creem* and *Circus,* which at least *attempted* to employ standard journalistic techniques in covering pop culture. And there were glossy magazines like *Hit Parade,* which, like most fanzines, were mostly pictures to be cut out and affixed to bedroom walls and notebooks. While schoolbooks held little interest for her, Gia pored over these publications for details.

Appreciating Bowie meant more than memorizing lyrics, liner notes and David-news flashes. You had to understand the world he had packaged for mass consumption to speak the language. You had to know about Lou Reed and the Velvet Underground, the first rock band ever to sing about homosexuals and heroin, and you had to know about pop artist Andy Warhol, who made the Velvets the toast of a downtown Manhattan club you had to know about called Max's Kansas City. You had to know about the rivalry between Bowie and Marc Bolan of T. Rex, and how Bowie had rescued Mott the Hoople from obscurity by giving them his song "All the Young Dudes." And you had to know about the Rolling Stones—not because of their venerated position in the history of rock but because Bowie had recorded their "Let's Spend the Night Together." And the Stones's recent number one single "Angie" was supposedly a love song from Mick Jagger to Bowie's wife—or to Bowie himself.

* * *

To get to the rest of the stores they liked, Gia and Karen would walk up across Broad Street through the more expensive part of town. This was where Nan Duskin and Bonwit Teller sold the clothes their mothers hoped they would one day wear. Between the stores were the fancy restaurants and hotels, and the salons of the top hairstyle superstars—like Julius Scissor, Vincent Pileggi, Mister Paul and Barry Leonard, the Crimper—where the "looks" from the pages of the fashion magazines were dispensed to those who knew to ask.

The very center of Center City was where the wives of old and new money alike went to indulge themselves, asking for as much daring in their do's as they could socially afford. It was not New York—nothing in Philadelphia ever was, a fact that Philadelphians rarely allowed themselves to forget. But a sufficiently high level of regional fabulousness was available to those who wanted to separate themselves from the fuddy-duddies: those who the trendy cutters sneeringly referred to as "the wash-and-set ladies." The top shops in Philadelphia didn't set any trends—that was done in New York, Paris and London—but they were the fashion franchisees licensed to dispense them.

Just beyond the toniest shopping and salons was Sansom Street, the city's original bohemian enclave. The street's rebirth had begun in the mid-sixties, supposedly as a Philadelphia version of London's Carnaby Street, and it maintained a foppish air even after some of the mod, fashiony shops were replaced with hippie and glitter-rock stores. But Sansom Street was more than just stores. It was a *scene,* the site of the city's first stationary freak show of painted hippies, outlaw bikers and drag queens. Those extremes made the street a place where Philadelphia's traditionally powerless—the young, the black, the female, the homosexual—could feel powerful, or at least relatively safe in numbers.

In recent years, Sansom Street had also begun to attract tourists: little kids from the suburbs and the Northeast who came in on Saturdays to gawk at the interracial couples publicly kissing, the men holding hands with other men, the latest tattoos. Entrepreneurs seized the moment by carving a mini-mall, Sansom Village, out of spaces on the standard, store-lined shopping block. It was suddenly possible to comparison shop for items that were once impossible to find anywhere. There was Stosh's Hide, the leather store; Mr. Tickle's, the poster shop; boutiques like Picadilly's, Dreams, Distant Drummer and the Pants Pub; as well as the Alice's Restaurant ice cream parlor, which had to change its name to Alice's Restaurant of Pennsylvania because someone else had already franchised the title of the Arlo Guthrie song.

The commercialization had taken its toll. The hippies and art students who settled the area were certain that if thirteen-year-olds knew about Sansom Street, it had clearly passed the point of hip exclusivity. The developers of Sansom Village were actually trying to clone another site in the Northeast. But the street had been reborn with the recent opening of a restaurant and nightclub called Artemis. The cuisine at Artemis was the sort of college gourmet fare of elaborate burgers, French onion soup and spinach salad that was beginning to find a niche between fast food and fine dining. The decor was simple wood walls and butcher-block tables. But it was what the owner referred to as the "bouillabaisse of people" that made the place unusual. Artemis was one of the first establishments that attracted crowds that were white and black, Catholic, Protestant and Jewish, straight and gay, young and not-so-young, sports fans and art aficionados. It was where local heroes met for drinks: it was the one place that out-of-towners—businessmen from Texas or fledgling rock stars from London—simply *had to go* while in Philadelphia. It had a supper crowd, which even Gia and Karen could join, and a glitzy late night party scene. Artemis was where girls like Gia and Karen dreamed about dancing the night away.

In the evening, Gia and Karen would ride the El train—or, if it seemed too late, the bus—back to the Northeast. Gia didn't really have a curfew that anyone was going to enforce, but Karen had to be home.

Karen's rebelliousness did not include ignoring her parents' wishes. Her mother and father—a bookkeeper and an auto mechanic—cringed at her outfits, and twinged with each plucked eyebrow hair. But they sort of understood what was going on. Mrs. Karuza would sometimes recall her girlhood fascination with Frank Sinatra, and suggest that perhaps Karen was going through a similar, if more colorful, phase. And besides, her grades were good.

Gia—who Karen's father called "Danny," because her haircut reminded him of Daniel Boone's cap—was a different story. She was an incredibly loyal friend to Karen and had a very endearing, little girl side. But something about her was unsettling. She was, if nothing else, a constant reminder of how normal their daughter with the clothes from Mars really was.

The mommy–daughter relationship between Gia and Kathleen was far from perfect, but at least they finally *had* a relationship. And even though Gia flaunted her disinterest in Henry and Kathleen's house rules, "the girls" were, in some ways, "the girls" again. They would go shopping together occasionally or go out for lunch. "We would talk, and Gia wanted to know everything about my marriage to her father," Kathleen recalled. "And I told her everything. She knew in explicit detail all the things about Joe I didn't like. She knew about his sense of humor. She knew the ins and outs of our sexual relationship. I thought he had a lot of fetishes. He couldn't be in a loving situation, he always needed me dressed up. If I was Mrs. Mommy in my nightgown, he had no interest. If we went to dinner he expected, you know, a *payback*." Kathleen also explained the gruesome details of her last year of marriage: her suicide attempt, where she really had been when she disappeared for several weeks.

In return for her mother's openness, Gia divulged one of *her* most closely held secrets: she had been sexually abused when she was six years old. Gia said that a teenage boy down the street from their old house—a member of a large family the Carangi boys often played with—had been her abuser. The abuse had occurred only once, but she was traumatized by the incident. She worried silently, as abused children often do, whether the violation made her a "bad girl." And she lived in fear that someone might violate her again—a fear that could manifest itself in many different ways.

Gia told Kathleen about how uncomfortable she had sometimes felt after the divorce living with her father and

41

brothers. Sometimes late at night, when Joe Carangi returned from work and everyone was asleep, he would wander around his home and look in on his kids. "Gia told me he would come into her room in the middle of the night and sit on her bed," Kathleen recalled. "Nothing ever happened, but she was uncomfortable. She'd wake up and he would be beside her, staring at her."

But all these heart-to-heart talks did not really clear the air, or convince Gia that her parents were better off apart. Nor did they lay the groundwork for coping with the adolescent traumas to come.

Drugs and alcohol were two of Kathleen's biggest concerns. She had recently driven by Lincoln when Gia hadn't come home from school and found the fourteen-year-old passed out on the front lawn from a lunchtime vodka chugalug contest. "She picked her up every day after that," recalled Karen Karuza. "Drove up in her big white Cadillac, with her fur coat and big blond hair. She gave us all rides home."

Henry was also getting tired of the spent joints he kept finding in the front yard, which led him and Gia to have frequent arguments about drugs. "I'm totally against drugs, one hundred percent," Henry explained, "but then Gia would come back at me because I drank. She'd say drinking was the same thing. I'd say, but when a person drinks they don't do it to get drunk. When a person does drugs, they do it to get high, to escape. When a person drinks, they do it just to drink, not to get drunk. It's not the intent when they start out. Maybe they *get* drunk, or maybe they get a little high. But how many times do they get high when they drink compared to the times that they don't? But with drugs, you do it to get high. Not too many people I know drink to get a high."

Abused substances had always been a big issue between Gia and Henry. "From the beginning, she confronted him about drinking," Kathleen recalled. "It was a big joke. The first time she met him, he had stopped on the way home and had a couple of drinks. She started imitating him—just the way he held his keys in his hand, and the way he walked after he had a few drinks. Henry's not an alcoholic or anything, but he drinks a little too much socially. I say he has a problem; he says he doesn't.

"But Gia was just disrespectful to him about it. Once, Gia and Michael grew marijuana plants on the TV. Henry was into plants at the time, and the big joke was that he was really admiring this marijuana plant, not knowing what it was. I finally made them get rid of it because it showed such a lack of respect for him.

"I also had a big problem with her taking drugs, but you couldn't stop her. She would go into my bathroom in the back of the apartment, open the window and smoke pot. Then she'd spray perfume all over."

Gia tried to point out that her mother, like most mothers in America, wasn't exactly drug-free. "Gia told me about her mom taking diet pills to lose weight," recalled one high school friend, "and she would get mad at me when *I* did diet pills. I was always obsessed with my weight and always did diet pills to get weight off me. She'd say, 'I love you just the way you are.' But, I think it bothered her mostly because of her mom. From what she told me, her mom took a lot of diet pills. To us, she was like a speed freak, really."

"I was *strictly legit*," Kathleen said. "Over the years I've been on diet pills. But, I've always taken legitimate drugs and never taken the amount that was prescribed. I don't want to become drug dependent, and I always felt like the doctor was giving me more than I possibly needed. I also took some kind of tranquilizer for a short period of time because I noticed that traffic was really bothering me. One doctor prescribed Quaaludes, and I would be so nervous taking them. I would announce I was taking a Quaalude and the kids would roll on the floor laughing, 'Oh, Mom's taking a *Quaalude!*' "

But it wasn't long before Kathleen Sperr was wishing that drugs and alcohol were her biggest child-rearing concern. While cleaning Gia's bedroom one day, Kathleen began going through her daughter's dresser drawers. It was something she did periodically, seeking incriminating evidence of pot and pills. If she got caught snooping, she usually explained that she was "looking for a phone number." This time she found something so shocking to her that she didn't even bother to apologize for the search. It was an emotional letter Gia had written to a girl. It didn't take much reading between the lines to realize that Gia was upset because the girl had spurned her romantic advances.

Kathleen, stunned, called her family doctor, who suggested Gia see some sort of counselor. It was, of course, impossible that Gia could be gay, as far as Kathleen was concerned. This was obviously a phase, clearly all tied in with Bowie and these kids she was hanging around with. Kathleen was certain that a therapist could help Gia get over it.

Still, Kathleen was deeply troubled by the prospect of her daughter being attracted to women. "It's very difficult for me to relate to all that because I don't have feelings or inclinations that way," she said. "I can really say that I can accept a person no matter what their sexual preferences are, but I simply can't identify with that. For another woman to turn on to me—that's very scary. Actually, when I was married to Joe, this one situation came up. I bowled in a league with these four sisters, and then this other sister of theirs started showing up. I took an interest in her because the other sisters seemed to really have it together in a way this girl didn't. She obviously needed a friend and pursued a friendship with me. She told me that she was attracted to me and she kissed me.

"I made it clear that I wasn't interested in anything like that. But, I was so shaken by it, knowing that I had made her feel that way. I discussed it with the psychiatrist the first time I was in the hospital. He said I was attractive and it was normal that a woman would be attracted to me and I shouldn't feel one way or the other about it. Actually, this all happened during the week I went into the hospital because of the trauma with Joe. But, it just happened to happen at the same time. I went into the hospital because of *Joe.*"

Gia's friends never doubted that she had some personal problems. But they thought her sexual preference was one of the only things she *wasn't* confused about. In a group where the sexual posing was becoming absurd—especially as people began actually having sex, which really complicated the issue—Gia had always been considered a beacon of clarity. She had briefly dated a few effeminate, pretty boys, but she had soon realized that her real physical attraction was to women.

The feeling wasn't as unusual as her response to it. At that age, it was uncommon even for those men and women who would one day live exclusively homosexual lives to act on their feelings. Even the Bowie boys who dressed like drag queens weren't necessarily involved with men. But Gia was ready to act. She wanted a first love, and she wanted it to be a girl.

Most of Gia's friends were doing their best to sneak into the city's gay and mixed nightspots. But most of them went because gay bars always seemed to have the best music and, since they were often private, they stayed open later and checked ID's less stringently. Gia was certainly at the gay bars to maximize her access to dance, drink and drugs. In fact, she often economized by taking a Quaalude on her way to the club (two dollars for a high that lasted all night) or by carrying a large aspirin bottle hand-filled with vodka or tequila or whatever anyone's parents had around. But she was also at the clubs to meet women who wouldn't be surprised when she flirted with them. And she always seemed wholly unconcerned about what others might think about her intentions.

"Gia was the purest lesbian I ever met," recalled Ronnie Johnson. "It was the clearest thing about her. She was sending girls flowers when she was thirteen, and they would fall for her whether they were gay or not."

"She was the most perfect woman, and the most perfect lesbian ever," recalled Keith Gentile, a gay club habitué from South Philadelphia who met Gia and Ronnie at the first Center City gay club they all frequented, Steps. "She wasn't masculine and she wasn't feminine. Guys liked her because she wasn't that prissy kind of woman, women liked her because she didn't have the worst qualities of women or men. And she had that I-don't-give-a-shit attitude and it wasn't fake."

That sophisticated androgyny led her to a new style of dressing. She had recently jettisoned her glitter clothes for a wardrobe of army fatigues and men's pleated slacks, worn with a tee shirt or men's oxford cloth shirt and army or cowboy boots. And she never wore makeup, unlike all of the women, and many of the men, she knew. It was a fashion statement that nobody in Philadelphia—man, woman, straight or gay—had even *thought* of making.

Although she didn't really want to, Gia went to see the therapist recommended to her mother. The male psychologist turned out to be more sympathetic than Gia could have ever dreamed. She did not tell him much about her life, and delighted in making up stories for him that she would later recount to her friends: at fourteen, Gia was already legendary for spinning seamless yarns that added years to her age and mature substance to her wild life. But the therapist was not totally unsupportive about her feelings toward women. Two years earlier, the organized mental health community had officially changed its mind about homosexuality, which previously had always been described in the literature as a "disease." In 1971, both the American Psychiatric Association and the American Psychological Association announced that homosexual orientation was not, by definition, a mental illness. They identified something called "ego-dystonic homosexuality"—which described those patients who were deeply troubled about being gay. But homosexuality itself was no longer to be routinely discouraged or looked at as a condition requiring a cure. The counselor basically told Gia it was okay to be gay. So at the end of one of their sessions, Gia decided that the real problem was that she couldn't confront her mother about her feelings.

By this time, Gia had any number of older male friends with cars who would take her places. It was one of the fringe benefits of being a pretty girl, a prerogative she was not about to give up just because she preferred women. She had arranged for one such young man—a classmate with a well-established crush on her—to pick her up after the session. Karen and another guy were with him in the car. Gia asked if they would all come back to her mother's apartment. She was, once and for all, going to tell her mother she was gay, and she needed moral support. She cajoled them all into agreeing to do it, although none of them really believed she would go through with the plan.

The four walked into the apartment, sat down on the powder-blue velveteen sofa and love seat in the living room and began to chat. Kathleen came in and joined the conversation. Suddenly, in the middle of a completely unrelated topic, Gia turned to Kathleen. "Mommy," she said, "I have something I want to tell you."

Karen and the two teenage boys immediately turned their eyes floorward, stiffening, staring at their shoes and mentally chanting "Ohmigod, ohmigod."

"I like women," Gia said. "I'm gay."

Kathleen stared at Gia and started to cry, her runny mascara streaking her powdered cheeks. Then Gia started to cry and soon they were all crying. After a few weepy minutes, Karen managed a feeble, "Well, I think we better go now," and they sneaked out the door. Once out of earshot of Kathleen's living room, they hollered in disbelief over what they had just seen. Even in outrageous times, *that* was truly outrageous.

Kathleen and Henry had bought a cabin in the Poconos to get away and entertain friends—"a party house," they called it. They learned the hard way what could happen if they went to the cabin for the weekend and left Gia by herself. One Saturday evening they called home at midnight to make sure Gia was in, and got no answer. Kathleen convinced Henry that they had to drive home immediately, and when they pulled up to their duplex two hours later, Gia was nowhere to be found. But some guy whom Gia had come home with from Oz—a Center City gay club with a Judy Garland theme—had just finished emptying their home of its valuables. The guy, a friendly Oz Quaalude connection in his mid-twenties, had apparently fallen victim to his own fare. Before getting away from the house with Kathleen's jewelry and some rare coins, he had passed out on the front lawn—where he still was when the Sperrs, and then the police, arrived. When Gia returned home about five A.M. and saw her stepfather's car, she took off.

Kathleen and Henry assumed that Gia ran away because she was afraid of getting into trouble. But Gia later confided to a friend that she had been very messed up on Quaaludes and the guy had "taken advantage of her."

After that incident, Gia started coming along more often to the cabin. She could bring a friend, but she had to come.

Downtown Stroudsburg on a Saturday afternoon did not exactly hold the mystique of Sansom Village, but Gia would often invite Karen along and they would make the best of it: frightening the townspeople with their hair, smoking a couple of joints to make the day a little more amusing, eating whatever was edible in the pizza joints and diners and seeing whatever was at the one movie theater. When they returned to the cabin, they were often confronted with a scene that they might have considered wild and wonderful if it wasn't populated by ... *parents*. Everyone was drunk or getting there, grown men were groping grown women. The sexual revolution had reached the suburbs—wide sideburns, see-through blouses, leisure suits and medallions. And *they* complained that the Bowie kids looked weird.

At one such weekend party, Gia was introduced to a client of Henry's, a bachelor lawyer named Meyer Siegel. He said that Gia looked like she might be able to model. That was high praise, because Meyer had a reputation for always dating pretty models and stewardesses. He suggested that Kathleen have some pictures taken of Gia and recommended Joe Petrellis, a well-known commercial photographer in Center City. Petrellis shared Siegel's interest in "magnificent women." They had been bachelor buddies for years until Meyer sent the photographer a girl named Patty Herron, whom he not only photographed but eventually married—ending his single life at the age of forty-six.

Petrellis was a heavyset, handsome man with a studio decorated with antiques he had personally and painstakingly refinished. Fashion photography was what he loved doing best, but the demand for it had dwindled. The local department stores started doing their own work in-house. The city had just a handful of major clothing manufacturers and only one magazine, *Philadelphia*, that published the low-paid editorial fashion pictures that helped photographers get more lucrative display advertising and catalog work. And there were always newer, younger, cheaper photographers vying for those jobs. Petrellis didn't want to move to New York, where most of the better national jobs were: he had worked to become an above-average fish in America's fourth- or fifth-largest pond, and he wasn't interested in starting from scratch. So he began taking pictures of accident scenes for local law firms that billed the costs of the massive enlargements to their clients. And he was doing model portfolios for cash.

Petrellis rarely did free test shootings with prospective models anymore. That was how very young or very successful photographers, each with a continual need for fresh faces, found new girls and experimented with new techniques. The photographers were paid in loyalty and other more personal tokens of a model's gratitude, an occasional model agency finders' fee, and, once in a while, a terrific picture; the girls got shots for their portfolios that made them look sort of like models. But Petrellis could no longer afford to do free tests, for both professional and personal reasons—his time was too valuable and the temptations too great. Now he charged $850 for a session and eight finished photographs. Beauty was suggested, but not required. Once in a while he came across a girl worth recommending to an agency. But, as he would bitterly point out, as soon as anyone he "discovered" found any measure of success, she promptly forgot that she was from Philadelphia and had ever known a Joe Petrellis. Meyer Siegel arranged for Gia to be photographed as a favor to him. "I think Meyer sent me a few hundred dollars as a present," Petrellis recalled. "He didn't have to."

The night before the session, Gia and some friends spent the evening at Oz and came home on the El a little after three A.M. "I remember she called her mom when we got off the train and said she was sleeping at my house," recalled one friend. "She said she had to go get pictures taken at nine-thirty the next morning. I said, 'Why don't you just go later,' and she said her mom had paid for the pictures. What I found unusual about it was that she had left this little bottle of pink L'Oréal Color-Wash at my house. She *never* wore makeup like that, not the Gia I knew."

The sessions, one indoors and one outside, produced dozens of uninspired and uninspiring photos of a gangly fourteen-year-old with a forced smile and a hairstyle that, no matter how skillfully manipulated, would never pass for ladylike. Gia looked presentable if uncomfortable in women's clothes, and her awkwardly posed bikini shots revealed spindly arms, small breasts, chubby thighs and a broad bottom: a typical model's figure only from the waist up. Nothing about the pictures was reminiscent of the shots in the *Vogue*s and *Harper's Bazaar*s that filled her mother's coffee tables, except they were of a girl and they were in the kind of sharp focus that only professional cameras and lighting could consistently produce.

But the process of being photographed interested Gia. Mostly, she liked cameras, and was fascinated by the technical aspects of what was going on. She also didn't mind the attention being focused on her. She liked that Petrellis told her she was pretty good at modeling. Even under the raccoon-like makeup job, there was a little something in her eyes that was catching the camera's attention.

And in nearly every shot, her eyes were wide open. She already knew not to flinch when exposed to the harsh light.

3
Suffragette City

When the announcement came over WMMR-FM, word spread through the Bowie community like a batch of bad hair dye. The T. Rex show scheduled for the Tower Theater was canceled. Ticket holders could get a refund at the box office or, for an extra dollar, could trade in the tickets for the same seats to see David Bowie, who was coming out of retirement to support a new record.

Diamond Dogs was to be the turning point in Bowie's career. Renaming 1974 "The Year of the Diamond Dogs" was part of the campaign by Bowie's management to explain his formative year away from performing and to sell his new image. Bowie wasn't going to be Ziggy Stardust anymore. He was going to throw a wrench into the time-honored machinery of pop stardom by splitting with his past image and repositioning himself as a musical chameleon, a pretentious changeling with no real identity beyond the parts he played and the costumes he wore. The futuristic hell portrayed in the lyrics and on the album cover suggested a reason for throwing Ziggy to the dogs: the decadent life of rock stardom had destroyed his sensibilities. Luckily, the album *Diamond Dogs* had a few catchy tunes among the dystopian posturing: "Rebel, Rebel" was Bowie's most radio-ready hit yet.

Bowie was now big enough to play to sold-out stadiums: under normal circumstances, he would have been expected to play the cavernous Spectrum. But as a gesture to his Philadelphia fans, he had instead decided to play the smaller Tower Theater for as many nights as he could sell out.

The Bowie fans camped out for several days for tickets. In the year since Bowie's last appearance, there had been many converts: the outdoor slumber party became a sort of family reunion for people who never knew they were related. It was also, for the uninitiated, a major rite of passage. The older fans tried to scare off the kids with a special harassment technique. "They called it 'reading you for filth,'" recalled one ticket camper. "We'd protect the younger kids in line. They would torment them, dare them to do drugs, tease them with lots of sexual innuendo." Another ticket-line veteran remembered a Bowie-nut removing her in-use tampon and throwing it at one of the kids. "I think they had seen too many John Waters movies," he laughed.

The night of the second show, Karen put on the outfit she had been planning for months: the tightest jeans she could find, a glitter tube top and silver, glittery, four-inch-high platform shoes. She knew she was bucking the Bowie dress code, which had been established when David stunned the first-night audience with an entirely new look. Instead of glitter clothes, he appeared in baggy pleated trousers, suspenders, a white cotton shirt and black ballet shoes. His hair was slicked straight back. Karen heard that during opening night intermission—a theater convention rarely used at rock concerts—the scene in the bathrooms was frantic. Some glitter boys and girls hurriedly altered their outfits, wetting down their spiked hair, rubbing off their makeup lightning bolts and rolling down their pants legs.

Gia, of course, had been on top of the new Bowie look for months, since *Diamond Dogs* was originally released. She went to the show in what had become her new uniform: a white T-shirt, patch-pocket fatigues, heavy boots and a red beret from the I. Goldberg Army–Navy store. And no makeup.

Passing through the crush of weird-looking people outside the Tower, who had managed to turn the blue-collar Upper Darby neighborhood into a Bosch painting, Gia and Karen went in to take their seats. But the ushers said there was a problem. Extra sound equipment had been brought in at the last minute and a mixing board now sat where they were supposed to: fans would later find out that the shows were being taped for a double live album. As a way of apologizing for the inconvenience, management had arranged for the displaced fans to sit in the orchestra pit. Down front. If they had ever needed a sign that their love of Bowie was divinely ordained, this was it.

As the lights went down, all eyes were directed to the stage, where Bowie appeared with two male dancers on leashes, dancing on all fours. He sang "1984" while spotlights revealed the show's elaborate set, a Broadway-on-acid display that redefined the parameters of rock spectacle. In the front rows, the Bowie kids began the frenzied process of getting David's attention: waving signs, flashing breasts, tossing flowers and notes onstage, or just staring intently at his face, hoping to catch his eye when he scanned the throng. Ownership of those passing glances was hotly contested — glitter girls would argue between songs, "He looked at me," "No, he looked at me" — and if David actually read your sign out loud or acknowledged your offering, status was immediately conferred.

As the second half of the show came to a close, Bowie shocked the crowd by doing an encore, something he generally avoided: the hardcore Bowie fans took it as a personal gift, something they had willed by their own enthusiasm. About halfway through the song, Gia grabbed Karen's hand and dragged her out the side exit of the theater and around back. As Bowie shuffled out the stage door and slid into his waiting limo, Gia vaulted over the yellow police barricade and leaped onto the hood of the car, face against the windshield. Bowie slunk down into the back seat as Karen waved to him from the sidelines. And when it became clear that the driver wasn't going to stop, Gia rolled off the hood, victoriously brushing off her hands. "Geez, we just wanted to say hi," she said.

It was the beginning of a week of Bowie madness, with Gia meeting and making a reputation for herself among the older Bowie kids like Marla Fuzz, Fat Pat, Purple and, of course, Joey Bowie. The hardcore fans found out what rooms the Bowie entourage had commandeered in the Bellevue Stratford

Hotel, and they staked out his floor. They called the Bellevue front desk repeatedly trying to get connected to his suite. They set up positions in the hotel's grand lobby, and chatted up roadies, sound technicians, or anyone who looked vaguely rock 'n' roll, in the hopes of being invited up. One group even followed Bowie's dry cleaning up in the elevator.

Gia was one of the few Bowie kids whose mother sometimes tagged along. She even attended one of the later Tower shows. "I tried to understand why Gia liked Bowie so much," Kathleen recalled. "So I ended up going to some concerts with her and learned to appreciate Bowie as an artist, a real talent. Gia was tickled to death. I went to the Tower Theater and you could get high just from being in there. I couldn't *believe* an establishment could have a smell that strong and get away with it. I tried to sit down and talk to some of her Bowie friends, who absolutely drove Henry crazy. I always got along great with her friends. They thought I was really neat because I really tried to understand them."

"The mother would come to concerts," recalled Ronnie Johnson. "It was so ridiculous. Gia would be high and the mother would be there thinking she was protecting her daughter."

"I didn't find it strange for her mother to do that," said Karen Karuza. "I had another friend whose mother came to all the concerts. In fact, I remember Gia telling me about one time her mother came back to Bowie's hotel with her after the concert. She was saying, 'Here's my mom with her blond hair and her white Caddie and her big fur coat and she's talking to Jimmy James, Bowie's bodyguard.'"

One afternoon, Gia actually managed to wedge herself into Bowie's elevator before the door closed. Realizing he'd been caught, he leaned against the wood-paneled elevator wall and closed his eyes. Gia just stood there and stared at him, too stunned to act. She finally managed to say hello, introduce herself and even shake his hand before he got off. She was left dumbfounded. A few days later, she wrote about it in a letter to Ellen Moon—who spent summers with her parents in the Poconos.

"Howdy Ellen . . . I got to shake hands with Bowie Friday night because me and my mummy followed his limo. His arms really feel nice. He's one nice piece of ass . . . I've done a couple 7–14's [Quaaludes]. I'll try to get you two.

They make me too horny and tired. There's a lot of reds going around here ... My mother got her hair cut into a Bowie. Ha! Ha! I think she's a bit nuts. When you do come back to old Philadelphia if you want to you can take some coke! Take care ... see you later alligator ... Bowie is the most beautiful person! Don't cry like me, Love, Gia."

In the top margin of the letter, Gia explained, "Don't write me cause I might be living somewhere else."

But the seminal event in Bowie fandom was still to come, a moment in pop music history that would make Gia and her friends the envy of rock fans the world over. Several weeks after the Tower concerts, in mid-August, Bowie returned to Philadelphia to make a record with hit-making sensations Kenny Gamble and Leon Huff, whose Philadelphia International label was suddenly the second coming of Motown. Mixing smooth rhythms and lush orchestrations at the local Sigma Sound Studio, the company had been cranking out hit after hit, each one breaking first on black radio and then crossing over to white audiences. Bowie's celebrity at this point was still far grander than his album sales: he hoped Gamble and Huff could help him make a record that would appeal to young Americans.

His extended visit made the Bowie kids feel they had been somehow chosen for a divine mission. A core group camped out in front of the studio each evening while Bowie worked through the night, and waited in front of his hotel all day while he slept. During the two weeks Bowie was in town, Gia and the other apostles didn't even go to the Jersey Shore, where Philadelphians usually migrated each summer. Several of the older fans were fired from their jobs because of the time spent waiting. They grew so chummy with Bowie's entourage that one night they convinced his limo driver to let them pick David's hairs off the car's back seat and empty the cigarette butts from his ashtrays.

Their perseverance did not go unrewarded. As the week wore on, Bowie began stopping to chat with the fans outside the hotel and the studio. "I introduced Gia to David at Sigma," recalled Toni O'Connor,* who as an eighteen-year-old from Chestnut Hill had only started coming to Bowie concerts the month before, but was making up for lost groupie time. "I had met him at a big party at his hotel after the show a few weeks before. He fell in love with me instantly."

Then, at five in the morning after the final session, Bowie took the unprecedented step of inviting the ten fans who remained into the studio. They were played rough mixes of the record, they danced with Bowie and personally offered him their ecstatic comments about *Young Americans*. They even had their exploits detailed in the newspaper. Bowie had made sure that a reporter was in attendance before "spontaneously" inviting the kids in.

The story made the front page of the *Evening Bulletin*, accompanied by a picture of Toni O'Connor that caused her to skyrocket to subcultural fame. Then the writer capitalized on his rock world scoop by selling a version of his story to *Rolling Stone*. Within a few weeks, every rock fan in the English-speaking *world* knew that the sycophancy envelope had been pushed by triumphant Philly fanatics. But, for once, Gia was left to join those noninsiders kicking themselves with jealousy: she had grown impatient during the last hours of the Bowie vigil, and left before the grand finale.

One night during the fall of 1974, Karen Karuza got a phone call at home from Gia. "She was hysterical crying," Karen recalled. "She didn't really say much of anything except she was alone and wanted to get out and *'he'* was bothering her. She wanted my parents to come pick her up. We went and got her, and brought her back to the house. She was so upset—nobody pushed her for any details.

"A while later, her mother showed up at our front door. Her car was double-parked outside our house. My mother went out to talk to her: she told her Gia was very upset and she thought it would be best if she stayed with us for the night."

The exact details of what happened that night would remain a secret, although its various interpretations would forever color many of the family's relationships. "Whatever happened between Gia and Henry was forgiven and was settled between the two of them," Kathleen would say. "She was capable of doing *anything* to get her own way, and she wanted her father and me back together again. I know that if Henry had not been drinking, that's one way that it would never have happened. I also know he was so glad that she was being nice to him that it warped him a little bit: she was usually belligerent to him at that time. But I blamed both of them."

"Gia's sexuality was the strongest thing in her life," recalled her aunt, Nancy Adams. "It was the one thing she could control. I think she enticed Henry into coming on to her and knew exactly when to yell 'uncle.' He tried to kiss her or something in the kitchen and she really thought that because this happened, her mother would get rid of him. But Kathleen didn't leave Henry. I don't know what I would have done in her situation. Whose fault was it? Well, it's both their faults, but because she's the child and he's the adult, he's responsible."

Not long after that evening, Henry and Kathleen began coming to counseling with Gia. The sessions were becoming more intense. "The therapist thought he had gotten her to the breaking point and she was gonna spill her guts," Kathleen recalled, "and she ran out of his office, came home and told me she was moving back in with her father. He told me to let her go because she was suicidal."

Moving back in with Joe wasn't quite as simple as it would have been the year before. Joe Carangi had remarried and bought a home in Richboro, a suburban community due north of the Northeast in bucolic Bucks County. Since it was so far from Center City, where he worked, he still kept an apartment over the hoagie shop in town. Moving in with her father meant leaving Lincoln for the more rural Council Rock school system, where someone like Gia was less likely to be considered "unique" than just plain weird. And the new Carangi home was an even less hospitable environment for a young woman than before. The third Mrs. Carangi came into the marriage with four sons of her own. It was going to be six boys and Gia.

"When we lived up in Richboro, the new wife and Gia just couldn't get along," recalled her brother Michael. "The move goofed me up because I was used to having the house to myself. I wasn't sixteen yet, but in the city I didn't need wheels. Out there, we were really out of town.

"The new wife was a real witch. My father said, 'Yeah,

each one got worse.' She gave him hell, maybe a jealousy problem, or maybe she just wanted to be accepted too much. She created total chaos with Gia one night—I just remember she took some clothes Gia had and tore up some stuff. After that, it was never right. Then I remember she got some sort of face-lift, and that was pretty traumatic. And she always had pills ... I always knew what stuff they had—my mom, too—because I used to take them from them."

Timmy Mills was a neighborhood kid made bad, and one of the more extreme examples of the fringe characters who populated Gia's life. Originally an older friend of Michael Carangi's, Timmy had grown up right around the corner on Primrose Lane, and had been what his father described as a "model son" until the age of fourteen. That year his parents divorced, he changed schools and he discovered drugs.

"Timmy always had a little bit of everything," recalled Michael. "He carried it around in this burlap bag hanging from his tenspeed. I was kind of his go-between, although I usually didn't make any money on it. He was always great at a party: always had plenty of smoke, four different kinds, and he would just put it out, angel dust, PCP."

Timmy's mother left the Northeast for an apartment in Center City on Spruce Street, the notorious gay cruising district. It was there that he met an entire new group of people, including a rich old hippie named Fanshawe Lindsley, who went by the nickname "Togo" and was once a prominent member of Main Line society. Togo had been reduced to running a butler and maid service for people throwing parties, enabling him to meet an inordinate number of handsome young men like Timmy Mills. At fifteen, Timmy dropped out of school and began to stay out all night, sleep all day, and sell drugs to maintain his lifestyle. He remained friends with Michael Carangi. And as Gia grew older, he developed a crush on her.

Gia's girlfriends found Timmy's persistence pretty amusing. "I remember one night we all had tickets to see Roxy Music," said Karen Karuza. "He was older than us and had a car so he was going to drive. It was a whole group of us girls and we met at my house. He came with Gia. They had been out to dinner, and it was around Valentine's Day so he had bought her a corsage with rosebuds, which was a sweet thing to do. When she got to my house she tore the corsage apart and gave everybody one of the roses: right in front of him, like it was nothing. She said she didn't want anyone to feel left out."

The next week, Timmy and Gia made plans for a small party at a mutual friend's house in Bucks County. A number of people were driving up from Center City. One was Stevie Beverly,* a Sansom Village fixture who, in his oversize red glasses and high-waisted baggy pants, had made a reputation for doing makeovers and selling clothes—and occasionally sleeping with his new customers. Stevie had also taken a liking to Gia. Among the other guests were Ronnie Johnson and his new girlfriend, Roseanne Rubino.

Roseanne and Gia had become friendly while waiting in line at the Spectrum for several days to buy tickets to the next Bowie concert. "I'll never forget, Gia showed up at the Spectrum with these orange marshmallow pumpkins for Halloween," Roseanne recalled. "And she took a real liking to me: she would just hang around me. She was really friendly, lovable—this sweet girl with orange marshmallow pumpkins."

At around eleven o'clock on that Friday evening in late February of 1975, Gia and Timmy arrived at the party. Timmy pulled out a combo platter of powders and fine smokeables. "He laid out lines of something that we just assumed was coke because nobody ever said it wasn't," recalled Roseanne. "Naturally the first people in line were me, Ronnie and Stevie. We each did two of these big lines and that was the last thing I remember. From what I hear we just keeled over on the floor. Somebody must have called an ambulance, because I woke up the next day in a hospital with my arms and legs strapped to a bed."

The lines were PCP, and the afflicted five were in the hospital for weeks. Timmy and Gia had avoided the paramedics and police by hiding in the bathroom, eventually sneaking out the window. The police towed Timmy's car away and eventually issued a warrant for his arrest on various drug and morals charges.

Those charges became a moot point several weeks later, when Timmy Mills was arrested for causing or aiding the suicide of Togo Lindsley. The charge was later raised to murder when the bizarre circumstances of the death were revealed. Mills told police that he and Togo had made a suicide pact: they were to drive to a deserted stretch of highway where the twenty-year-old would shoot the sixty-five-year-old with a shotgun and then take his own life. If he fulfilled the bargain, Mills' parents would receive a stipend from the Lindsley will.

Timmy claimed that at the moment of truth, he balked: Togo allegedly grabbed the gun, put it between his legs and pulled the trigger with his toe. Police experts insisted that Togo's wound could not have been self-inflicted, but Mills was finally allowed to plead guilty to voluntary manslaughter, and was sentenced to less than two years in prison.

The sensational case was the subject of several front page newspaper stories. But one of the unreported highlights of the proceedings—or so the story circulated through the Center City club world—was that Gia dramatically kissed the defendant one day as he was being led into the courtroom. During the kiss, it was said, she passed Timmy a Quaalude she had popped into her mouth.

To some of Gia's friends, the Timmy Mills saga was a billboard-sized omen. "I stayed away from Gia for a while after that whole thing," recalled Ronnie Johnson. "It was starting to get a little scary."

But nothing seemed to scare Gia. She was fearless the way only pretty girls can be when they realize they can get away with anything, even if they get caught. And she was dauntless the way only Quaaluded teens can be: so oblivious that they can trip down a flight of concrete steps—like the ones leading to the good seats at the Spectrum—only to get up and walk away like nothing ever happened. It wasn't that Gia walked through minefields and miraculously missed every mine. The occasional explosion just didn't seem to phase her.

One of Gia's favorite ways of daring life was to shoplift. Although she had never actually been arrested, Gia was well-known to the security departments at most of Center City's better department stores and boutiques. Friends had noticed that her wardrobe seemed to be expanding. She began to mix inexpensive vintage clothes and army surplus with pricey pieces by Ralph Lauren and other top designers: never dresses or skirts, but blouses, sweaters, trousers and blazers. Few of these designer pieces had been paid for.

"She always ripped off good stuff," recalled Nancy Adams. "Gucci, Halston ... it wasn't like she was going to the five and dime and ripping off lip gloss. She got briefcases, bathing suits, whatever she needed she got. She knew what she liked, she had expensive tastes and she couldn't afford to buy these things herself. She was spoiled, but how many $500 sweaters does your father buy for you when you're a teenager?"

Gia was amazed, she told friends, at how easy it was to take stuff from stores. It was incredible what you could get away with if you didn't look the type. "Gia and I actually once went into Nan Duskin," recalled Roseanne Rubino, "and we had army pants on, those balloon-leg army pants. We went into the dressing room, took a zillion things in, and we were very gracious. We ended up tying silk blouses around our legs under the army pants and walking out. I still wear some of those blouses today."

"We all wore this cologne called The Baron, and patchouli oil, we got it at Wanamaker's," recalled Joe McDevit. "She'd get that during her daily shopping trips."

Sometimes, Gia would go into Bonwit's or Nan Duskin or Wanamaker's and fill up an empty shopping bag, just to prove she could do it. Other times, she had specific goals in mind: birthday gifts, courtship presents.

Gia had fallen for a girl she met in the clubs called Nina*, a working-class Roxborough native with Main Line airs and long blond hair. Nina saw a silk Halston dress in the window at Bonwit's that she *loved*. She just had to have it. Gia snuck into the window, undressed the mannequin, and smuggled out the dress. When Nina broke up with her, Gia cut up the dress with a pair of scissors.

Gia and some of her friends would also steal credit cards. Joanne Grossman, an established hairstylist in her mid-twenties when she met fifteen-year-old Gia in an all-women's club, was among those who had their credit cards stolen. Several days after the theft, Gia quietly came and told her where the cards were.

"I thought she did a lot of this stuff to get her mother's attention," recalled Grossman. "Gia had the kind of personality that yielded to a baby-sitter sometimes. She needed guidance—whether a mother, a lover, a sister, a nanny. She needed not to be left alone. And the one person she really wanted was her mother. Kathleen obviously wanted her own life and wanted her daughter to be strong enough to do it on her own, without her doing anything."

By this time, it was clear that Gia's living situation with her father wasn't going to work out so well: her new stepmother was now pregnant, and Gia missed Lincoln and her friends in the Northeast. So she moved back in with her mother and stepfather. Kathleen was determined that things would not get out of control again, and tried to be much stricter than before. She dragged Gia to the family doctor and insisted he test her blood for the presence of cocaine. When she tested positive but denied having taken anything, Kathleen dragged her back again. The doctor refused to do the test. "What are you going to do?" Kathleen recalled the doctor telling her. "She went out, she partied, she did a little drugs. What are you going to do?"

None of Gia's friends recalled her doing any more drugs than anybody else was doing at the time. "People did a lot of Quaaludes back then," recalled Michael Carangi, who was in a position to know. "Gia didn't drink a lot, she smoked pot, did ludes, did some acid. It wasn't a big thing to her."

"Gia loved Quaaludes," recalled Toni O'Connor, who, by that time, was maintaining her new lifestyle by selling the big, pale-yellow sedatives. "Sometimes I thought Gia only loved me because I always had Quaaludes. I was, in my day, the Quaalude queen of Philadelphia—although I was so paranoid about getting busted that I told everyone I was a prostitute. I made a lot of money selling Quaaludes. I'd just go to the doctors and get them anytime. I had three different doctors I would go to. I would tell them I couldn't sleep at night. Each doctor was good for thirty Quaaludes every two weeks. One doctor would mail prescriptions from California, can you believe it?"

Others in Gia's crowd had also discovered the Quaalude

doctors. "I started going to a lot of the Quaalude doctors with a couple other friends," recalled Roseanne Rubino. "We'd make the circuit. There was one doctor, this seedy little fag, always fucked up on something. He had this awful cinder block office in West Philly. You'd go and wait for hours with slimy people. He had this big sign: THE DOCTOR DOES NOT DISPENSE THE DRUGS. You'd sit down with him. He'd say, 'What seems to be the problem?' You'd say, 'I can't sleep, I'm trying to lose weight.' He'd say, 'Okay, I'm going to prescribe methaqualone and Valium,' and black beauties, whatever they were called. He'd give us these incredible prescriptions for great drugs.

"I started doing the Quaalude doctors after Ronnie Johnson and I broke up. That's also when Gia and I had our little affair. She told me she was in love with me the first time we slept together. I thought that was kind of weird. I guess that, somehow, love wasn't supposed to be part of it."

"I know there were a lot of drugs," recalled Joanne Grossman, "but in Gia's case, at that point, I think her sexual habits were a lot more extreme than her drugs."

"She was as promiscuous as everyone else in our group," recalled a high school friend. "Pull out the phone book and I'll tell you who I dated. I think there's a memorial to me on the front lawn at Lincoln."

"All our sex lives then were so bizarre," recalled Joe McDevit. "I remember this huge orgy in a synagogue. We were all at Digits one night doing acid, and one of the guys announced that he had keys to a synagogue nearby—his father worked there or something. We went there, upstairs to this big conference room, put cushions on the floor and had this big party. At one point we dared my girlfriend to put on a show for us. She had never slept with a girl and she picked another girl who hadn't either and they took off all their clothes and made love. Then I had to pick a boy who had never had sex with another boy, and we had fun, petting and fellatio and such. It was bizarre."

As an alternative to the kinds of people Gia was encountering in the clubs and at concerts, photographer Joe Petrellis—who had become socially friendly with Kathleen and Henry—suggested that she meet his friend Jane Kirby Harris. A tall, handsome woman in her late thirties, Harris was a former New York runway model and a fixture in Philadelphia. She was fashion director for the Philadelphia area Bonwit Teller stores and coordinated all their fashion shows. She maintained her reputation and continually expanded her public by teaching beauty and modeling courses.

In the store, she ran a beauty workshop for the daughters of Bonwit's patrons, taught with manuals made available to retailers by *Seventeen* magazine and personalized by each instructor. Harris called her version "Project You." The *Seventeen* course was devised to give young girls the basics of posture, exercise, diet, hair care, skin care, makeup, grooming, fashion and manners. By providing the service, the store hoped girls would come to Bonwit's for the many products they had just learned to need—including makeup applied every day "at least twice, even three times if you can."

One of the longest chapters in the manual—and the only one that did not contain practical information pertinent to all young girls—was the one about fashion modeling. It began with a lengthy excerpt from a *Seventeen* article by Eileen Ford, of the Ford Model Agency, about "what it takes to join the ranks of today's top models." Besides the basics of the model's life, the excerpt pointed out that, at most, one in one thousand of the girls who applied to Ford became successful models. The manual then asked girls if they felt they met all the requirements to be a professional model. "NO! Perhaps you should do non-professional modeling through your local store's teen board. However, if the answer is YES, and you do want to go full-steam ahead to a modeling career . . ."

Harris regarded the in-store course as a mere trifle compared to the intensive modeling sessions she gave several nights a week in the grand ballroom at the Bellevue Stratford hotel. There, the girls with even the slightest bit of promise would be painstakingly trained in actual modeling techniques. Harris paid special attention to walking: it had been considered her great talent as a runway girl, and was a skill she felt that even many top models had failed to master. She couldn't stand it when Bonwit's would bring a top girl down from New York for a big show and the girl couldn't even *walk* properly; it was better to use a local girl who had been properly trained.

Harris' course was meant to turn out models—or at least good "nonprofessional models." And she did differentiate between girls who "had something" and those who had nothing but enough money to pay the fee. That distinction separated her from the local franchise of the national John Robert Powers schools, which had been spun off from New York's first-ever model agency. Begun in the thirties and, for years, so synonymous with the profession that it spawned the 1942 film comedy *The Powers Girl* with George Murphy and Dennis Day, the Powers agency itself had been toppled by Eileen Ford in the fifties. But its schools lived on, surviving by adopting a new creed: If you didn't have the looks to be a model, you could at least learn to be a "model girl."

A "model girl" knew the basics of Good Grooming: her face shape, her body type, the hues that best suited her, professional makeup techniques and how to achieve that "well-put-together look." She understood the building blocks of Visual Poise: proper placement of hands and feet, how to enter and exit a room (both the informal three-touch method and the formal four-touch method, each including a hesitation for effect). And she minded her many Manners, like the rules of Cigarette Etiquette: "Avoid looking masculine, never dangle the cigarette in your mouth, never flick ashes man-style, always use a feminine cigarette case and lighter." Powers was sort of a charm school for girls who would have to get real jobs eventually.

Gia's Aunt Nancy also signed up for Jane Harris's course. Gia still looked up to her aunt in some ways, but many of her new friends were Nancy's age or older, so the two had effectively become peers. There was also such a strong family resemblance between them that they looked like sisters— although Nancy was pretty in a more conventional, less ethnic way, and she wore all the feminine clothing and makeup that Gia rejected.

Nancy led Jane Harris to believe that she was signing up for the course as a favor to Gia, whom she sort of watched over. She explained to Harris that Gia was the way she was—distant, generally uncommunicative—because she came from a broken home and had some drug problems.

While there was some truth to this, Nancy was hardly taking the course just to look out for her niece. She hoped that there might be a place for her in modeling. Nancy had never vigorously pursued it. She was working as a bank teller, filling in at Hoagie City. And she was, at twenty-one, already a little old to *begin* modeling. But people had always told Nancy that she was the prettiest of the Adams sisters. And she looked like a model. It was something to dream about. It was certainly something she dreamed about more than Gia ever did.

Jane Harris found Gia difficult to talk with, but she was taken by her looks and her ability to coordinate clothes. "There was an innate sense you felt," she recalled, "this girl was so put together, without being contrived. I don't know if the clothes were expensive, but she *looked fashion*. And she did well in the course. She learned to walk *beautifully*.

"I wanted her to go to Eileen Ford after she was done with me. But she disappeared off the face of the earth. I remember her class well because we held graduation at the Bellevue and that was the summer of Legionnaires' disease."

Besides the runway classes, Gia also answered an ad in the paper for amateur models at Gimbels department store. "We had always used regular models, and then somebody decided we should try ten-dollar-an-hour models and just have a cattle call," recalled well-known Philadelphia photographer Michael Ahearn, who was then director of fashion photography for the store. "Most of the people were just awful, and then in comes this little girl and she was *wonderful*. She was always late, always had some excuse. The fashion director used to get pissed and wanted to shoot without her. And she sometimes came in bruised up. She said that her stepfather did it because she was running around late. We had to patch up the bruises. But I used her as much as I could, even when she wasn't really right for the shots. I remember stuffing up her chest and behind the straps in the back so we could use her for these ads for old ladies' bras.

"She had a way of looking at you at certain times. It was this look, the face of a little girl. She learned how to drop it for the camera, but sometimes I would still see it."

Joe Petrellis also did another series of tests with her: this time, in more sophisticated poses and clothes, including a purple see-through blouse with nothing underneath. "She projected like a cheetah," he recalled. "She was *born* to be in front of the camera. The way she would move ... she knew her face, she knew her body. She was born with that. She was born to model. And it was no big deal to her. She was only doing modeling because she needed something to do."

Petrellis also suggested that Gia go see Paul Midiri, who ran the top modeling agency in Philadelphia. She went with her mother, who did most of the talking, and Midiri put her in his teen division. But nothing happened. "She didn't get one booking with us," said Midiri. "The trend toward using younger models and making them look older hadn't yet caught on in Philadelphia. She had a mildly ethnic and exotic look, which Philadelphia just wasn't that familiar with. She was also a little rough around the edges. In New York, you can get away with that because there are makeup artists at the shootings. In Philadelphia, you're expected to be more of a complete package."

As she did more modeling, Gia started paying more attention to the names in the credits in the fashion magazines her mother got. In her journals, along with the rock lyrics, she would errantly jot down the name of a photographer or a designer or a model she had noticed: itineraries of imaginary modeling trips and technical information she gleaned from photographers soon followed.

"We would sit in Gia's bedroom," recalled Nancy Adams, "and try on clothes, putting ultrasuede outfits together to be fashionable. Patti Hansen was on the cover of *Vogue* for, like, five months in a row. Gia said all she wanted to do was one cover of *Vogue:* that was it, just one cover."

After their classes with Jane Harris, Gia and Nancy sometimes walked *like ladies* to the clubs, many of which were only a few blocks from the Bellevue. They often went to a women-only bar, because that's where Gia said she felt the most relaxed.

"I loved to go out with Gia and Nancy," remembered Joanne Grossman. "You could sit at the bar and have every single decent-looking person in the room come over. Gia never moved, and Nancy just kept everyone at bay. I used to just love to sit on a bar stool and watch this: it was a night in itself. And you never had to pay for a drink.

"Gia just had this charisma. She wasn't extremely smart and she didn't have extremely interesting things to talk about, which bothered her. She thought of herself as sexually boring, too. She used to say, 'People look at me and they think I'm this beautiful thing and I must be extremely hot. And what they don't realize is that I'm extremely boring . . .'

"Nancy played around. I was involved with her on and off for many years and I finally had to accept it: she was straight. She just loved people in different ways. I wouldn't even say she was clearly *bi*sexual. Just because you have one or two people who come into your life and you're sexual with them doesn't mean that you're gay."

The biggest, newest club in town was the DCA—or, as Gia and her friends referred to it, the "DCGay." It was a cavernous building hidden from plain sight on a small, pedestrian-only street. The main floor was devoted to the kind of flamboyant, multimedia disco scene that a new generation of gay men were coming to favor. But DCA was large enough to have a separate floor just for women.

"Oh, it was a scene up there on the second floor," recalled Toni O'Connor. "We all lived in our own little world, nobody else could get in, we could do whatever we wanted. One night I can remember at the club, Gia had this water pistol and we were in the ladies' bathroom taking pictures of each other and shooting the gun. She was just posing with the gun. We had such a good time. Sometimes we would all dress in three-piece suits. We were like the gay Mafia."

"I remember one night at the DCA," said Roseanne Rubino, "Ronnie showed up with his new boyfriend. We were all very fucked up: I was hanging with a new bunch of weirds then. Gia was there. Gia was *always* there. When we walked into the place, we would immediately go get a drink: Southern Comfort Manhattans were the big thing. Somebody had Quaaludes, we were all dancing. I had this, like, white thing on—white shirt and pants. All I know is that I woke up on the men's room floor and it was about four A.M. and the place was closing. Ronnie and his boyfriend took me home.

"Gia always amazed me during that DCA time, because we would go out and get trashed and all sleep over at somebody's house, and we'd wake up the next afternoon and we all looked a mess. Except Gia, who looked gorgeous. She didn't have to do a thing. She looked great. She could eat whatever she wanted to, never had to diet. It was like, 'Oh man, *fuck you,* you always look perfect.' "

It was at DCA that Gia met twenty-one-year-old Sharon Beverly*. A small, energetic woman with blond hair, almond eyes and a friendly smirk, Sharon worked at a department store makeup counter. She had always been overshadowed in town by her older brother Stevie, who was well-known (if not always well thought of) in the clubs, and had dated Gia himself. When friends debated if Gia was "really gay," the purported fact that she had slept with Stevie was often invoked. But it was Gia and Sharon who dated on-and-off for a year and then finally became involved.

"The first time I was with her was at her mother's apartment," recalled Sharon, with a giggle. "I was dressing to leave the next morning and she was sitting on the floor in this terry cloth robe she wore, saying, 'Don't leave, stay with me.' I realized immediately how needy she was, and how far I had already fallen for her.

"Gia and I kind of revolutionized the gay world in Philadelphia. Before we went out together it was always butch-fem couples where there was one 'masculine' and one 'feminine' girl. We were seen as two fems. I mean, really, Gia was butch, she dressed like a boy. But she wasn't the kind of butch that Philadelphia girls were—muscular, big. To them, Gia was a fem, because of her aesthetics. We were, I think, pretty much a shock to them.

"And they were pretty boring to us. That's why we always went downstairs and danced with the boys. The boys were more fun, they were out there dancing and knew how to have a good time. And the girls were sitting upstairs crying in their drinks."

At first, Kathleen seemed to like Gia's new friend Sharon—until she figured out that they were involved. Then she called Sharon's mother. "She told my mom that she thought I was too old to be hanging around with her daughter," Sharon said. "She didn't say we were sleeping together, but my parents already knew I was gay. They had received a letter from some other girl's parents."

Sharon had no doubts about her own sexual preferences at that time—she had been seeing only women for over five years—but she felt that Gia was still vacillating. "Gia *always* had a question about her sexual preference," Sharon said. "There was always a question in her mind, and she always *wished* she loved men—it would have made life so much less complicated. But she just always really loved women. And she was a lot of fun, very mischievous and she had a lot of energy. She really loved to wrestle. We would have wrestling matches: she was pretty strong, but I'm strong, too. Wrestling made her happy. It brought her out of her depressions."

It was immediately clear to Sharon that Gia had no emotional middle. "She was an extremist, and she found emotions traumatically hard to deal with," Sharon said. "There was a very sad side of her. It wasn't a sadness that was really blatant—she was always in a good mood, always laughing, joking—but it was there. She always questioned why she would get upset. She felt that she had a very rough life and felt that it took a lot of energy to deal with the world as it was. She could never pinpoint where the unhappiness came from, just something inside of her that she could never satisfy. I don't think she was talking about her parents. I don't even think she meant anything that *tangible* was rough. She just meant living and thinking and breathing and having to mentally deal with waking up and living was a hard thing for her."

By the end of her junior year in high school—which came officially at the end of summer school, 1976—Gia had moved back and forth between her parents' homes several more times, living wherever she was in the least amount of trouble. In her journals, she would sometimes make lists of the pros and cons of living with one parent or the other: "Living with Mom & Henry—own room, far away, pool, dinner, behave."

She was now also completely mobile because her father had bought her a new car. "When she turned sixteen, he bought her a car, a '76 Capri, just like that," said Henry

Sperr. "I didn't think any kid should be given a car. I thought she should have to work for it."

While Kathleen wasn't thrilled about Gia's newfound freedom, she was quietly proud of how aggressively her daughter drove. A car enthusiast herself, Kathleen believed that strong women should know how to handle cars. "Gia could drive a car better than any guy," she recalled. "She was an absolute daredevil behind the wheel."

Sharon Beverly once got a glimpse of Gia's road acumen. "One day I was really mad at her because I found her at my house down in the basement fooling around with my brother," she recalled. "She snuck upstairs, past my parents, to come apologize, but I wouldn't talk to her: I just got dressed, walked out, and drove away. So I'm going down East River Drive and suddenly she pulls up beside me in the other lane. She's screaming, 'I love you, I love you!' I pulled away and no matter how fast I drove, every time I stopped she pulled up right next to me."

Once Gia had a car, there seemed to be no chance of reining her in. Kathleen and Joe were so resigned to their inability to exert parental authority that they agreed to a plan that was clearly post–last resort, but somehow seemed rational given all the irrational things that had happened. After she finished her junior year in summer school, Gia proposed that she start her senior year fresh, in a new school and new surroundings. She asked if she could move permanently into Center City—where she spent much of her time anyway—and attend South Philadelphia High School. She could live in the apartment above Hoagie City, where her father rarely stayed anymore and which her brother Michael, just out of high school himself, had commandeered. It was a two-bedroom place with windows overlooking Chestnut Street, which was completely deserted except for buses after business hours. The living room was dominated by a slate pool table, on which Gia was becoming quite accomplished. "Gia could play pool like a man," recalled her uncle Dan Carangi. "She had a slide stroke just like a guy."

Gia was given permission to move into Center City. She knew hardly anyone at her new school, and barely kept her head above water academically. Her life was so unlike that of a normal teenager that it sometimes seemed pointless to even pretend to play the game.

One of the people who helped her struggle toward graduating was John Long, a twenty-seven-year-old jack-of-some-trades. A struggling painter, martial artist, concert promoter and slightly self-amazed Renaissance guy, Long had taken Gia under his wing several years before and got in the habit of helping her with her homework when she bothered to do it.

"When I first met her, she told me she was a sophomore at the University of Pennsylvania," he recalled. "Later I found out that just about everything else she had said was a lie, too. She had fabricated an entire life. I never figured out why. I got to know her mother and stepfather a little bit. Hank seemed like a bright guy, but he stayed out of it. After all, he just wanted to marry Kathleen and instead he got all the problems of her juvenile delinquent daughter in the bargain. Kathleen was just trying to make her marriage work and Gia wasn't any help. I mean, Kathleen was more tolerant than *any* parent should be in trying to hold on to her kid's love. And Gia learned very early what she could get away with. When you have people around who you can tell 'Jump backwards through a hoop of fire,' and they do it, pretty soon you find yourself becoming a really overbearing bastard. And then you have to make a conscious decision to be *less* abusive."

One of the many things John Long knew a little bit about was fashion photography. When he had first seen Gia in Hoagie City, he asked if she had done any modeling and offered some advice. But while she didn't seem interested in his counsel on fashion, Gia was happy to have him as a big brother for other reasons. He had great connections with all the promoters in town so he could get good concert tickets. And he was a convenient heterosexual front. She could make it appear to her family—and anyone else—that John Long might be her boyfriend. But quite the contrary was true. Mostly, she was using him to meet other women, or to run interference with her cast-off one-night stands.

"I remember one time I got a phone call from this girl," said Long. "She's crying and she's saying, 'I know you're having an affair with Gia, but what you don't know is that she's only fifteen years old and she's gonna blackmail you.' To break up with the girl, Gia had told her she was romantically involved with me."

After moving into Center City, Gia's social and sex lives became even more complicated—especially after she and Sharon uncoupled. They had always had the kind of relationship that went from crisis to crisis, breakup to makeup, over the silliest things imaginable. But when they finally split for good, it was over a much more serious issue. Sharon had decided to "go straight." She came to believe that her involvement with women—Gia and those before—had been mostly a reaction against men.

"I think that I had a lot of anger inside for men because, besides being raped, I was also sexually abused by someone when I was very young, and that went on for about a year," Sharon recalled. "I think that's one big reason that it happened that I turned to women, 'cause I felt much safer with them. I guess, looking back, that it was somehow a phase. I don't know, I can't explain it, but I guess it was a phase because it's over and it's been over for a long time."

Gia was crushed by Sharon's decision. It was a terrible personal loss, the kind that Gia was never very good at handling. She wrote in her journal, "When she kisses me I feel all four winds blow at my face/But now Sharon tell me what do you do with a woman who has no love for you/my love for her shall never die for she opens my eyes/she is my lost captive and no longer lies along my legs."

After the breakup, Gia used her unwanted freedom to get involved with all kinds of women. "Gia liked to play games with women, she liked the challenge," recalled David Cohen, another DCA regular. "She could be a great seductress, sending flowers and really wooing girls. Or sometimes she would just get horny, bring some chick home and throw her out the next morning."

In Center City, it was not uncommon for late weekend nights to end the next morning at any one of the dozen or so twenty-four-hour diners. The most legendary of them, the Melrose Diner, was too deep in South Philadelphia to walk to from the clubs. So people usually ended up in the Greek-owned places that seemed to pop up wherever life was being lived twenty-four hours a day—near a hospital, a hotel, a bunch of clubs or a gay cruising area.

"There was a diner right around the corner from her dad's apartment," recalled Nancy Adams, "where Gia used to take all her dates for breakfast the next morning, if there was a next morning. Either way, I would meet her there for lunch, or at the hoagie shop, and she would, like, critique her dates. If I had seen who she was with, she'd ask what I thought of her. Or she'd say, 'Well, I think she's really dumb, but she's really cute.' The funny thing was, I think she took her relationships very seriously and she took sex very seriously. It was just . . . people were in a frenzy to have sex then. That was the whole outcome of a night. Going out, doing drugs, getting really wacko and picking someone up."

"Gia just fell in love easily and when she had a crush, it was a very passionate crush," recalled Sharon Beverly. "And she didn't take sleeping with women lightly. She took sleeping with *men* lightly, but not sleeping with women. I mean, it wasn't as if she'd sleep with someone one night and then go on to the next. I mean, I know she *did* that. But it was basically looking for more of a relationship.

"But, you know, that was a bad time to fall in love with the people you slept with. People weren't really looking for love. Although, no, wait. I take that back. In the back of their minds they were looking for it, but in all the wrong places and in all the wrong ways. You know, looking for it by sleeping with three people each week thinking one of them might be the one. You know what I mean? Even through their promiscuity there was, like, a *goal* to it."

4

Mr. Maurice
Reinvents Himself

It was time for Mr. Maurice to reinvent himself again.

The first time had come when he was fifteen and still Maurice Tannenbaum, a neighborhood kid who had given haircuts door-to-door for a quarter and then learned how to style in a little basement salon below the busy intersection of Bustleton and Tyson in the Northeast. He found he had an instinct for hair and, just as important, an understanding of the power of saying "fabulous" convincingly—an ability to make women feel good, or at least better, about themselves on a weekly basis. At sixteen, he was reported for working without a license by the owner of a competing shop, who wanted to steal him away and used his position on the state licensing board to do just that. Eventually Maurice outgrew that second shop, and then another, and ended up on the Main Line, working at a well-known shop and then opening one of his own with a partner. When that partnership failed, he opted for some stability—he had a wife and a child—and in 1969 took a job as director of the salon at the newly opened Saks Fifth Avenue store in Bala Cynwyd, just outside the city limits.

It was at Saks that he had come to be known as Mr. Maurice—at first jokingly but then, as his fame grew, a little more seriously. He had gone from well-known hairdresser to the most celebrated and expensive stylist in town by perfecting the new "layering" technique made popular by Jane Fonda's radical chic coif. "He studied that hairdo with the intellectual detachment of a scientist," one of his devotees told *Philadelphia* magazine in a 1972 article about the new hairstylist superstars. "In the end, he was the only one in Philadelphia who really understood it."

With his stardom came several life changes. He got involved with a woman who worked in his salon and he divorced his wife. Then, in a sort of bisexual version of the just-released film *Shampoo,* he got involved with a man who worked in his salon and divorced his sexual preference. By 1977, he was ready to divorce Philadelphia, too.

Maurice wanted to move to New York, where he often went on weekends and where some of his clients had already migrated. But he hoped to relocate as somebody more interesting than just a *hairdresser.* Being a top stylist in New York wouldn't be that much better than being *the* master cutter in Philadelphia. Certainly, it would *be* New York. The rich people there would be richer, the celebrities more celebrated, the fast lane faster and the gay life gayer. Salons depended on a handful of clients who would go to any expense to make sure they looked their best: only in New York did any expense really mean *any* expense. Since the magazines and manufacturers were based in Manhattan, there would be fashion photography and fashion show hair work, which often involved exotic trips and led to exotic friendships.

But Maurice had met enough of the "name" stylists in his travels—like Harry King in New York, Jean Louis David in Paris and Michael Rasser in London—to understand how the high-fashion business really worked. Cutting models' hair didn't pay very much in itself: the day rate was often less than what he grossed daily in his Philadelphia salon. The work wasn't always very creative: you were generally hired by the photographer, who often told you what to do just like the ladies in the salon. Basically, you cut models' hair cheap for the magazine credits—and cut some celebrities' hair free for the word-of-mouth—in order to get your name around, fill your salon with less glamorous but full-paying heads and perhaps snag a promotion deal with the manufacturer of some hair-care line. Most of the big money was generated through the salon where you worked. And since Maurice, like many top stylists, was far better at the cut-and-shtick than at running a business, he would undoubtedly end up as a star in someone else's shop, losing up to fifty percent of the income he generated to the owner.

And it still wasn't art or anything. It was just haircuts.

"Women were demanding, they were tiresome," Maurice recalled. "I had reached the pinnacle of what I could be in Philadelphia. I was thirty-two years old. I wanted adventure. I wanted to travel. And then I found photography. It seemed uncompromising."

He had hired enough photographers to shoot his hairstyles that he understood what was involved. He didn't think photography looked *easy*, but it looked like something he could learn. And, more important, it seemed like photographers had so much more control over their lives than hairstylists did. Photographers were respected, indulged, even worshiped. They didn't suck up to people for a living, people sucked up to them. Photographers were the centers of their own little universes: models, hair and makeup people, and stylists orbited around them, always at the mercy of their selective gravitational pull.

Maurice knew that untried photographers, no matter how great their connections were in the business, didn't just walk in and get paid to take pictures. He would have to create a "body of work"—a bunch of pictures—that showed his ability to bring something singular to photographs that still looked like they could sell something. He would then have to put this body of work into a portfolio, which he would properly refer to as a "book." Fledgling still-life photographers and photojournalists could develop a body of work largely on their own. Would-be fashion photographers, like aspiring playwrights, needed a cast to play the other roles in these nonprofit theatrical ventures. In fashion photography, there was a name for these continual dress rehearsals for pictorial plays unlikely to ever be premiered. They were called "tests."

The test was, and always would be, the essential process in the fashion photography business. It was the intermediate

step between dreamy amateurhood and possible profession-
alism for photographers, models, hairdressers, makeup artists and the new breed of visual professionals known as
"artistic directors" or simply as "stylists," who claimed responsibility for "bringing the whole thing together." The test
was passed if any one image among the dozens or hundreds
or even thousands produced caught the eye of someone who
mattered—an agent, an art director, the friend of an editor's
brother-in-law—and convinced that person that *somebody*
involved in the shot knew what they were doing. The finished pictures could result in almost any cast member being
singled out—one good picture might show up in a half-dozen
books. But, the test was the photographer's show to direct
and produce and, in most cases, fund: with film and pro-
cessing charges, working "for free" generally cost the photographer more than everyone else combined.

To nonbelievers, and those whose livelihood depended on
Mr. Maurice remaining a haircutter, his "testing" was nothing more than a waste of valuable coif time and a hobby
with very expensive equipment. It was a joke, a drain of his
creative energy. Only Maurice understood why he had to
keep doing it.

The actual picture-taking was only one part of testing.
After Maurice paid a lab to develop the film, he had to edit
the shots. This was the other essential process in fashion
photography: lining up images and winnowing away at them.
Usually, Maurice worked with thirty-five-millimeter slides,
which came back from the lab in a hard plastic box, or with
2¼-inch-square transparencies, which came back in oversize
strips. The transparent images were laid on a light table and
surveyed through a magnifying eyepiece called a loop. With
a grease pencil, he marked the images worth looking at
again and then separated them from the others.

Editing was an inexact science, especially since it was easy
to see something different in a picture every time you looked
at it. It was also a very personal science: ultimately, the
only thing Maurice was gauging was which image was more
interesting to *him* at that particular moment. And learning
the process of taking your aesthetic pulse, making a decision
and living with it—and, in fact, *celebrating* it by making a

beautiful print of the image, showing it around as your Work—was perhaps more important than the choice itself.

Once the best shots were chosen, Maurice had to decide how to print them. Should parts of the image be cropped away? Should colors be corrected? Should certain areas of the picture be printed darker or lighter than the rest? Or should the image be printed "full frame," exactly as the camera and photographer originally saw it, untouched by thoughts that came after the preserved moment?

Maurice had begun doing test shots in the back of his salon on free evenings and on locations near his farm in Bucks County on weekends. He chose models from among his younger clients and friends, and sometimes he would approach girls on the street or in clubs and ask if they would consider working with him. In a city like Philadelphia, with three major art colleges, any number of beauty-related trade schools and a handful of modeling agencies, there were always many people involved in what could loosely be defined as testing. But being asked to test by Mr. Maurice, a well-known personality in a town with few resident celebrities, was a real honor—second only to being asked to work with one of the city's few full-time fashion photographers.

One night at the DCA, Maurice spotted Gia on the main dance floor. He took her aside and asked if she would test with him. She came in on a Thursday evening, he made her up and did some shots, and she returned several days later to view the finished results. They found they got along so well that it became a weekly date.

"It happened that every Thursday night I'd shoot her," Maurice recalled. "And while we did it we talked. It's a very personal thing to work like that—especially when you're doing the hair and makeup, too, you're right up close. She was really shy and quiet, and she was totally untrusting. She was obviously used to being abused because she was so beautiful. People wanted to be around her because she was so beautiful. They didn't care who Gia was; her mind and her person weren't important to them. It was only important that she was beautiful and she was this thing they could carry around with them. She had become very hardened to that. She realized it young, and tried to protect herself.

"This girl had done *everything* by the time she was sixteen.

79

She had tried almost every drug, had all kinds of sex, and she was going with a very fast crowd. She liked being the center of attention. If I shot her with other people and they got the attention, she'd get pissed. Yet she seemed, deep down, to be a regular sixteen-year-old kid, wholesome, loving, involved with her family. She loved kids—because they were pure and going to love her for the right reasons.

"And it was pure things that made her laugh, simple things. Once she came up to our house in New Hope for the weekend and I gave her a haircut outside. It was really windy and as we were cutting her hair it was drying. She would bring that up every once in a while, the memory of having her hair cut and letting it dry in the wind. That was fun for her."

By the fall of 1977, Gia was thinking about joining the thousands of girls who annually took a shot at modeling. Her face and body had matured in such a way that a successful career was now more than just a fantasy of hers or her mother's or her Aunt Nancy's. And it wasn't as if modeling would interfere with her going to college or pursuing some other dream. She was really just killing time, working part-time at Hoagie City—like her brothers—and following in the wobbly career paths of her older friends.

The hardcore Bowie fans never took jobs they couldn't afford to quit in order to perform some outrageous act of worship. (Toni O'Connor and Joey Bowie, for example, left town unannounced to follow David to LA and then drove to Arizona to crash the set of *The Man Who Fell to Earth,* in which Bowie was making his major film debut. They were supposed to be extras in the film, but were prematurely banished from the location after Angie Bowie drunkenly seduced Toni to get her husband upset.) The club kids worked as assistants in salons or as salespeople in fashionable stores by day and then slept from dinner until midnight so they could dance the night away at the night spot of the moment. A number of the Lincoln girls had already realized that the party was over. Two of the 107 Lunchroom crowd were already getting outpatient help for drug problems. Another disappeared after discovering she was pregnant too late to get an abortion: she quietly carried the baby to term and put it up for adoption.

Gia had no idea what she wanted to be. And unlike the young women who saw a modeling career as something they would do *anything* to have, Gia considered professional posing the path of absolute *least* resistance. Everyone she knew was encouraging her to do it, everyone seemed to agree that she was destined for it. And it was the only career path that even vaguely interested her that she also knew her mother would approve of.

Gia had never been ordered to model, but she knew that the pictures with Joe Petrellis and the department store ads were among the very few things she did that really pleased Kathleen. The modeling allowed Gia's mother to vicariously live the life she had wanted for herself as a teenage glamour girl. It also produced photographic evidence of the womanly, feminine daughter that Kathleen believed was trapped in Gia's man–woman body. While Kathleen had encouraged Gia's modeling, she had never been truly overbearing about it. And there was, at the moment, an international standard for such overbearance: Teri Shields, mother of child model Brooke Shields.

Teri's name had been mentioned passingly in gossip columns for years, but she had finally captured the media's attention and revulsion during the pre-publicity for Louis Malle's *Pretty Baby,* in which her twelve-year-old Brooke played a child prostitute. In a September 26, 1977, *New York* magazine cover story on Brooke, Teri was portrayed as a bitter divorcée who drank too much and had all but sold into slavery the beautiful child of her five-month marriage to a Revlon executive. The lives of the mother and daughter seemed hopelessly, even dangerously intertwined. If the basic facts of Brooke's career didn't raise eyebrows—her mother had been dragging her into photographers' studios since infancy, and had never discouraged nude shots—Teri's widely circulated quotes in the magazine story were sure to send the world's tongues clicking. She went on about how Brooke's "titties" had sprouted and she got her first period between the time she was cast and the actual filming—discussing her daughter like she was a particularly prime piece of livestock.

Although she certainly had dreams of her daughter becoming a model, Kathleen was no Teri Shields. But not long after Gia finished her senior year of high school—again, in summer session—her mother became more aggressive in her encouragement. In October, Kathleen and Henry arranged with Joe Petrellis for Gia to meet a modeling agent during the intermission of a Donna Summer concert. The agent was impressed, and said he might send Gia over to Europe the following summer—along with Petrellis' wife, model Patty Herron—to test and try out for some of the photography and runway jobs generated by the collections in Paris, Rome and Milan. Petrellis also offered to use his connections with Eileen Ford to get Gia an interview with the Ford agency.

Gia decided on her own that losing a little weight wouldn't be a bad idea, since she had a tendency to be a little chunky below the waist. "I remember her eating cereal with water on it to try and get skinnier," recalled one friend. "And she would take an hour to eat it so she wouldn't be hungry later."

Ultimately, it was Maurice Tannenbaum's photos that made the difference. As his body of work grew and he began taking his photography more seriously, Maurice decided to hire a makeup artist instead of doing it himself. Making that further commitment to the testing process was another way to separate Mr. Maurice from Maurice Tannenbaum, fashion photographer. Like so many people at every level of the beauty business, the makeup artist he hired was a former model. She had remained friendly with her old agent, Wilhelmina Behmenburg Cooper—known to the fashion public simply as Wilhelmina since the sixties, when she was one of the world's top fashion models.

Willie, as she was called by close associates, was always looking for new models, and Wilhelmina Models Inc. also had an entire testing division where promising photographers could shoot new girls in the company's studios. The makeup artist offered to show Maurice's book—which, by this time, was almost all shots of Gia—to Willie. The model agent was impressed enough to summon both Gia and Maurice to New York, at their own expense, to be seen.

Kathleen, Gia, Maurice and the makeup artist drove to New York together in January for the meeting at the agency's offices on Thirty-seventh Street just off Fifth Avenue. At Gia's request, Kathleen waited in a coffee shop across the street while the hopeful trio rode the small elevator to the twelfth-floor office. The small front lobby was, as usual, overflowing with young (and pretending-to-be-young) women, all waiting to be looked over by a member of the Wilhelmina staff and, god-willing, by Wilhelmina herself. Some of the girls ended up sitting on the floor, trying to minimize the mussing of the outfits they had been planning for weeks, months or even years in anticipation of the ultimate blind date, the five-minute beauty pageant.

The screenings were done by a core group of three or four people who were nearly exact physical opposites of the statuesque, Dutch-born, antelopian model whose magazine covers adorned the lobby walls. Like many of their contemporaries at other agencies, the division heads and top bookers at Wilhelmina tended to be small, plain, comforting women and men, as often as not battling with weight problems. They had made professions of being the homely, sensible friends of pretty girls. They dressed in loose, casual clothes and had calming voices, which could make even the most brutally blunt comments seem somehow constructive.

At the front desk, a receptionist repeated the litany of screening questions to each expectant caller: "How tall are you?" "How much do you weigh?" "How old are you?" "How long is your hair?" Any incorrect answer would be used as a way to emphatically dissuade the caller from spending her life savings to come to New York just to give the same incorrect answer in person.

Many of the young girls came anyway. The model fantasy was too deeply ingrained. It began in the mid-1800s when a Parisian shopgirl at the fashionable Gagelin et Opigez named Marie Vernet married a salesman at the store, Charles Worth, an Englishman with designs on designing. After winning an international award for his crinoline hoopskirts, Worth began his own business and Marie became his model—the first human "mannequin." (Marie also turned out to be the birth mother of the *couture:* she convinced the wife of the Austrian ambassador to try her husband's crinolines, which led to his becoming the first *grand couturier* to European royalty.)

But the Victorian fantasy of a shopgirl being able to wear the clothes she once sold had given way to something more powerful in twentieth-century America. With the rise of fashion photography, models grew from glorified salespeople into women whose lives might actually resemble the fantasy images they were employed to create. The top models became professional muses, quasi-celebrities, visual role models, human billboards. And then they even started getting paid.

When American women started thinking about careerism, it was hard to overlook the fact that, as a recently published history of the "model girl" had flatly stated in its first sentence, "Today modeling is the most highly paid profession a young girl can enter." Cinderella had met Miss America and the Working Woman. When the Kenner Toy Company did market research in its endless quest to dethrone Mattel's Barbie Doll, it found that America's little girls had a new primary fantasy. They wanted to be models. A new model doll named "D'Arcy" was being developed.

With Brooke Shields breaking all the age barriers, the pool of young girls trying to fulfill the model dream had doubled almost overnight. The offices of the few nationally recognized gatekeepers to the world of modeling were jammed like never before. Those who actually made it to the lobby sat and listened to the receptionist trying to dissuade others. The discouraging words gave the girls-in-waiting pause, and almost simultaneously fortified their resolve that the industry standards would be waived for them.

Many of those who came in were being weighed, measured, briefly interrogated and then completely discouraged from modeling—although the bad news often came in the form of encouragement to try some other fashion-related field. They walked back through the lobby after their bubble-bursting interviews with stunned looks on their faces, barely holding back the tears from what was often the first rejection of their lives. Another tier of girls was encouraged, however slightly, but not accepted. They were given a firm "perhaps" with several concrete suggestions. Screeners knew that a certain number of the girls would actually do what they were told they needed to do—lose weight, radically change their looks, expend endless amounts of time, money and emotional virginity trying to get better pictures, and "come back to see us" in a prescribed number of weeks or months. And they would do it without any real commitment, financial or otherwise, from the agency. These were the girls who walked out stupefied, but full of firm resolve. They had a mission and a timetable and hope. Many would also soon have an appointment for a second opinion at another of the big agencies.

Gia, Maurice and the makeup artist did not wait in the lobby for long: it helped to come in with a friend for the boss. As was true in so many professions, the standard procedures existed to politely process those who *wouldn't* make it, rather than to identify those who would. When the three Philadelphians were announced, protocol was jettisoned. Maurice's photographs of Gia had preceded them, and the fact that she was nearly an inch shorter than the Wilhelmina *absolute minimum* of five feet, eight inches had already been discounted. Instead of a pre-interview, Gia was immediately whisked in to meet Wilhelmina. Seated behind a white desk, elegantly smoking a cigarette, the thirty-seven-year-old time-less beauty rose regally to her full five-foot-eleven-inch stature.

"Wilhelmina went absolutely crazy," recalled Maurice. "She was trying to contain herself. She was saying, 'Come stand here, my darling,' and she was really in awe." And Wilhelmina's awe *mattered*. New York was the richest mod-eling market in the world, and there were only five agencies in Manhattan that really made a difference—Ford, Wilhel-mina, Stewart, Zoli and the recently opened Elite. By almost any standard, Wilhelmina was clearly the agent of the mo-ment. In a tiny business where everyone was a close friend or a close enemy, Wilhelmina was one of the handful of people whose enthusiasm could be *very* contagious.

Willie began to speak excitedly about Gia's future model-ing career as if a deal had already been struck and signed in triplicate. The office was so frothy with expectation that Willie sent Gia home to talk to her parents about the spe-cifics of the contract without actually giving her the docu-ment. "We were on our way out when Willie came running down the hall after us with the papers," Maurice recalled.

Willie also had some nice things to say about Maurice's

pictures. But her encouragement was clearly more a way to thank him for finding Gia than any comment on his photographic vision. "When they came down and got me, Gia said they had offered her a contract," Kathleen recalled. "She also said they spent a lot more time talking to her than to Maurice." It wasn't long before *that* observation was cattily making its way around the Philadelphia club circuit.

When they got the contract home, Gia and Kathleen went over it with Henry; it was one of the first times that Gia had ever honestly needed something from her stepfather. Like most modeling contracts, it included no financial guarantees whatsoever. There were no signing bonuses, stipends or salaries: there was no health insurance or retirement plan. Models were complete freelancers—the agency simply collected for them and from them. And models got paid only after they generated income for the agency and worked off the upfront costs of being added to the roster: the Wilhelmina-embossed portfolio and datebook, various printing charges, the messenger fees that accumulated rapidly as constantly updated portfolios were circulated. Those charges could be offset only by a fraction of what each modeling assignment generated.

The standard arrangement was that the agency got a commission on each modeling fee. The commission began at twenty percent and was sometimes negotiated downward if the model's fame rose dramatically—which happened to maybe one in every hundred models with agency contracts. The agency also received a twenty percent fee from the client for making the booking. So, if a model's fee was $1,500 a day—the absolute top rate at the moment, which perhaps five or ten models in the whole industry could demand—the client paid $1,800 and the model received $1,200. But only the model's commission, in that case $300, was used to offset her charges.

The agencies felt the high fees and the commission structure were entirely justified—not only by the cachet associated with their names but by the monumental cash flow problems associated with the business. In essence, a modeling agency was little more than a bill collection service and a telephone sales office with a healthy direct mail promotion budget to get pictures of the models to prospective clients. Most of the glamour accrued from the businesses the company served. Most of the energy emanated from the girls themselves. And most of the money came *through* the agency, not from it.

Almost all the jobs were arranged over the telephone, many at the last minute. A bank of "bookers" sat at phones all day soliciting appointments for beginners and juggling requests for the established names. There was rarely a signed contract before a job was executed, or even a formal billing. Nearly everything was done by verbal handshake— although it was a not-well-kept industry secret that phones in the booking rooms were rigged so the booker could clandestinely record the client repeating and agreeing to the terms.

Models were given vouchers on the set by the client after finishing a job, which they redeemed weekly or biweekly for an agency check. Then the agency had to try to collect the money from the client. To help cover its risk, the agency temporarily deducted an extra fee from the model's money. But, ultimately, if the payment was late or never came at all, it was the agency's problem. The industry ran on a great deal of faith—faith that the model would show up and look like she did in the photos the client had seen, faith that the client could and would pay its bills. When faith was violated, the agency was often at the greatest financial risk. So they didn't throw too much money away on beginners, even promising ones.

Sending Gia to New York was going to require an upfront expense of thousands of dollars. Fortunately, she had recently wrecked her new car, and the insurance company had just paid her father about two thousand dollars to settle the claim. Joe let her have the money even though he had his doubts about Gia moving to New York to become a model. Henry chipped in some as well.

"I never got the right vibes from [my father]," Gia would later tell an interviewer. Part of his concern was that the agency wanted his daughter to drop her family name professionally. Many of the top models went by one name—either their own, or one provided to them by their agent—and Willie had insisted that Gia alone was perfect. It was exotic,

European and short. It was an uncommon name for a model, sure to create curiosity. And it came early in the alphabet. Models often took new names beginning with *A* through *G* so their pictures would appear closer to the front of the alphabetically ordered agency rosters sent to clients.

Gia decided it would be better to move to New York with someone she knew than to live alone. A number of her friends were also thinking about relocating, so she started asking around. Sharon Beverly had recently taken a job at the cosmetics counter at the same Saks Fifth Avenue where Maurice had his shop, so they would sometimes see each other when Gia came to test. For the past several months, they had been doing their best to turn a broken love affair into a friendship. Gia asked Sharon if she wanted to move to New York with her.

Neither of them knew very much about Manhattan: Gia's interview with Willie had actually been her first time there *ever*. It was such a huge place, New York. Philadelphia had once seemed that big to Gia, but over the years it had grown smaller and smaller. She developed favorite places to eat and shop and dance. She became known in certain establishments. She realized that most of her friends hung out in a handful of places that could be easily combed; nearly everywhere she went, she knew or recognized someone. After a while, she *owned* Philadelphia. But New York seemed scary to Gia—so unfathomable, so difficult to find your way around, especially during its snowiest, coldest winter in forty years.

To begin to get their bearings, Gia and Sharon went up several weekends to scout out the apartment situation. To do this, they had to figure out, basically, how Manhattan was laid out. The sections of town had to be memorized like some school assignment. East Side meant it was east of Fifth Avenue, West was west; uptown was anything above Fifty-ninth (the bottom of Central Park), midtown went down to about Twenty-third and downtown was everything south, getting increasingly *downtown* until you hit Wall Street. Among the areas where they had a *chance* of finding restaurants they could afford, Greenwich Village was downtown on the West Side, Chinatown and Little Italy were way downtown on the East Side. SoHo, the mysterious, dark district of artists' lofts and new wave rockers, was somewhere in between, like its budget annex, the East Village.

But no matter how hard they tried to remember sections of town, it was easier to just locate the few essential places in their lives and work backward. Bloomingdale's was at Fifty-ninth and Third Avenue. Studio 54 was on Fifty-fourth near Sixth Avenue. The center of the Village was around West Fourth Street and Sixth Avenue. The Wilhelmina agency was at Thirty-seventh and Fifth. Until she and Sharon could find an apartment, Gia would stay at the Barbizon Hotel at Sixty-third and Lexington. And until she figured out the subway, she would just take cabs.

On Wednesday, February 22, 1978, Gia began her first "go-sees." These were appointments set up by agency bookers during which the model was sent to one address after another to be eyeballed by a testing photographer or, sometimes, an established photographer's assistant. They looked at you, looked at your book, and either bluntly said they weren't interested, suggested they would be in touch and gave a time frame, or sometimes even started snapping pictures.

Go-sees were scheduled one an hour, on the hour, sometimes six a day: models called in the night before to get their next day's schedule. On her first day, Gia's first appointment, ten A.M., asked if she could come back in four weeks. Her second appointment, eleven A.M., said he'd call her in two weeks. Her third appointment, noon, had arranged with Wilhelmina bookers to do some test shots of her. He shot for four hours and told her to call back in five days to see the slides.

When she went home for the weekend—to give Sharon a progress report and see her friends at the DCA—Gia had already seen ten different photographers, tested with two of them, and had three others ask her to send more photos. Each photographer had his or her (but usually his) own studio space. Each photographer had his own personal and professional agenda, his own claim to relative fame and his own maze of connections and clients.

Each photographer also had his own range of reputations. At any given moment, there was somebody powerful who considered him a nobody, another who believed in him as an up-and-comer, still another who revered him as a star and yet another who disdained him as a has-been. But all these photographers had one thing in common. Each had the ability to almost single-handedly launch Gia's career, either by taking a picture that looked outstanding in her book, or by offering her a job for an assignment he had already been given.

And she was seeing the entire spectrum of photographers. At the high end was Alex Chatelain. The thirty-eight-year-old former assistant to Richard Avedon, Hiro and Guy Bourdin—all fashion photography legends—had just come from Paris to test the U.S. market. He worked for British, French and American *Vogue*. At the low end was Maurice Tannenbaum, whose only real claim to fame was that he had discovered *Gia*. To thank Maurice, Wilhelmina had arranged for him to shoot the girls in the testing division and he was allowed to use the agency's studios when he was in New York.

In March of 1978, Gia and Sharon Beverly finally moved into their New York apartment—350 East Sixty-second Street, Apt. 3G—and embarked upon their brilliant careers and their just-friendship. The few times they had come to New York together to look for apartments, Sharon had gotten a little too drunk, Gia had been a little too persuasive and things had gotten a little intimate. But that was over, Sharon insisted. She was seeing only men now. She had said the same thing over a year before, but now she meant it. Her new life in New York didn't include any room for sexual ambiguity: it would be hard enough just finding a good job.

Sharon ended up at the cosmetics counter at Fiorucci's on Fifty-ninth Street. In the year since its opening, Fiorucci— which imported kitschy, pop-art clothes, accessories and glittery trash, like the $110 gold cowboy boots that were *the* chic footwear statement of 1977—had established itself as one of the handful of New York's truly trend-setting, or at least trend-selling, stores. The supermarket of high-class camp had a vast selection of things that it seemed like you could *never* find at the mall (although, in reality, there were already seven tiny Fiorucci boutiques sprinkled across the country). Sharing Fiorucci's moment was the recently opened vintage clothing warehouse Unique Boutique in the East Village, where Gia shopped for the men's clothes that dominated her wardrobe. Fiorucci didn't pay much—still just a percentage on what you could successfully smear on a client's face and get her to pay for. But it had great cachet. It was the right place at the right time.

Gia just kept going on appointments. There were lots of go-sees, which her agency requested, but people were also beginning to ask to see her specifically. Some of these were "callbacks": people she had seen who wanted another look. Others were "requests," generated simply by her circulating portfolio and the buzz that could be manufactured in a world as small as fashion photography when one of the handful of major agencies had a new girl it was excited about. These intermediate appointments were not jobs, or "castings" for jobs, or even tests. But they were a step above go-sees. They meant that someone in the massive beauty-industrial complex knew Gia existed.

Thousands of companies made up the American beauty-industrial complex: some were established giants with huge product lines, others little more than sketchy business plans in search of investors. For Gia, they all had only one thing in common: on any given day, any one of them could give her a job.

At the top of the food chain were the manufacturers: the diverse and diversified makers of clothing, and the chosen few creators of cosmetics and other beauty and health products, each followed by an entourage of subsidiaries and licensees. Then came the sellers of products: the department stores, the specialty clothing stores, the drugstores, the catalog companies, the beauty salons and sometimes even the manufacturer's company-owned or franchised boutiques. To increase sales there were advertising agencies large and small, national and regional marketing boards (for the finished products or the raw materials used to make them), and in-house advertising departments. They created everything from print and TV ads to countertop "point of purchase" displays.

All these companies and products met on the pages of the publications. The monthly magazines and weekly newspaper magazines printed all these advertisements, along with stories and "editorial" photographs of the products in use. The women's magazines did the most editorial photography in fashion and beauty every month, but others had begun to follow suit, hoping that coverage would lead to fashion advertising.

Every civilized country had its own indigenous beauty–industrial complex tied to its own standards of beauty, but there was a good bit of international overlap. Many American and European manufacturers either exported or created foreign divisions and licensees. The same was true for magazines: *Vogue, Harper's Bazaar* and *Cosmopolitan* all had separate foreign, and even foreign-language, editions.

But at the highest levels of fashion, national borders were superfluous. Some European and a few American designers were simply above all that, creating fabric fantasies that were shared the world over. Some models were the same way, their looks and careers transcending national boundaries.

Despite its vast power, the beauty–industrial complex was really just a huge nursery of fashionable babies that had to be fed and changed astonishingly often. At bare minimum, the manufacturers needed to reinvent part of their product lines once or twice a year. Many major advertising campaigns and catalogs changed quarterly. Most of the magazines came out monthly. And some larger department stores needed new newspaper ads every week or even *every day*. Invariably, these changes required new photographs, sketches and fashion shows, all of which required models.

Some companies trusted photographers or ad agency art directors to choose their models. Others had executives who wouldn't dream of missing the entire thrilling process of picking "their girl"—a combination of judging a beauty pageant and choosing merchandise at a brothel. They scanned agency headsheets of professionally beautiful young women. They discussed the girls' attributes and narrowed down the field. They often asked the agency for more pictures—perhaps bathing suit or lingerie shots—and sometimes even had a few of the girls come in person before picking a model. If the girl wasn't free or wouldn't work for the budgeted price, she was replaced by someone else who was singularly perfect for the job.

Every fashion or beauty picture that was printed anywhere—as well as every picture that was rejected and reshot along the way—was cast by the same systematically arbitrary procedure. It was a process no simpler or more complicated than deciding what scarf or necktie to wear to work. The fact that hundreds of careers hung in the balance didn't—or couldn't—make the decisions any less capricious. And it was the ability to make such utterly arbitrary choices seem objective and *correct* that separated the men from the boys, the women from the girls, and those in between from everyone else in between.

Sharon was slowly learning the process of her business, figuring out where a beginning makeup artist might fit in among the manufacturers, the major salons that hired staff makeup people and the hundreds of editorial and advertising photographers who hired freelancers. She could see there was a lot of politics involved—more, it seemed, than in photography or modeling, where at least you had to have *some unique quality* to get ahead. The top makeup artists seemed to her almost completely interchangeable, their careers built on nothing more than contacts and friendships. Still, Sharon liked doing makeup, and she felt like she was basically on the right career ladder—although on a much lower rung than she had hoped for.

But after only a few weeks in New York, it became clear to Sharon that Gia wasn't really suited for what she was trying to do. "She would go out on her go-sees and just hated it," Sharon recalled. "She hated it from the beginning. She felt like a piece of meat. I know it's an old cliché in the business, but that's what she said. You take your portfolio around to thousands of photographers around the city, and they're very cold-hearted when they look through the book. They flip through it while you're standing there.

"I'm a makeup artist and I've had people look through my book like that. It's very disillusioning. But it's bad enough to have someone look at your art—what you *do*—that way. It's another thing to have someone look at your person that way.

"She felt uncomfortable about doing it, but she knew she

was good at it. She also knew it was no big deal to *be* good at it ... it wasn't anything meaningful. But I would catch her every now and then, kind of looking in the mirror and giving a look that I knew was for the camera. She didn't do this regularly or anything. I just caught her a couple of times doing it and we would both laugh about it. She would think it was a big joke.

"She was still so much like a little girl. She would come home from her day and throw her book to the side and put cartoons on. And there would be men all over the city daydreaming about her—men who had seen her or her book—and there she was watching cartoons."

For the first few months Gia was as focused on making it as a model as she ever had been on anything in her life. She was playing the game, or at least her version of the game. She went where her booker sent her, showed up on time to appointments and attended agency classes. To a large degree, she did what she was told. But her behavior was not so much a sign of growing up as it was a testimony to her deep feelings for her boss and mentor. Gia was not accustomed to being so impressed by anyone, so influenced, so awed. But she had never met anyone like Willie before.

Wilhelmina Behmenburg Cooper was born and raised in Holland, and moved to Chicago with her family at the age of fifteen. It was there that she began to model, eventually finding favor with the one world-class fashion photographer who remained in Chicago long after his reputation rose to the top in New York: Victor Skrebneski. Wilhelmina became a Ford model in the early sixties—when the only way to be a professional model was to be represented by Eileen Ford—and had an amazing professional career.

Willie's name hadn't been as well-known as Jean Shrimpton's or Twiggy's. Both of them had become larger than life—and briefly bigger than modeling—because of their association with the sixties British Invasion in fashion and music. Shrimpton especially benefited from her professional and personal relationship with David Bailey, the British *Vogue* photographer. Bailey was the designated shutterbug of the Invasion and the likely inspiration for the 1966 Antonioni film *Blow Up,* the erotic thriller that cemented the world's image of the high-living fashion photographer, riding around in a Rolls-Royce and seducing models on the seamless paper used to make backgrounds disappear.

But Wilhelmina had actually done more magazine covers than Jean Shrimpton and Twiggy *combined*. And instead of disdaining her chosen profession and leaving as soon as her ability to make big money was secure, Wilhelmina stayed in modeling. While she was still at the peak of her earning power, she left Eileen Ford in 1967 to open her own agency with her new husband Bruce Cooper, a tall, Chet-Bakerly handsome, divorced TV producer she had met during her first appearance on *The Tonight Show*.

Wilhelmina Models Inc. wasn't designed to reinvent the wheel as much as make it a little smaller and rounder. Eileen Ford had invented the wheel. It was she—with her husband, Jerry—who had made modeling as professional and respectable as it was going to get, inventing a set of rules for billing and fair work that were, in their own way, as revolutionary as the first child labor laws. The Fords also created the prototype of the mom and pop with a percentage of earnings, taking new models into their own home to protect them from the big bad wolves of the fashion world. But Eileen Ford could be a harsh, conservative, overprotective and downright vindictive parent: *Life* magazine had called her "The Godmother." And she ran what had become a very big business, over $10 million in annual billings, with an eye toward her bread-and-butter accounts: the middle-of-the-road magazine, catalog and advertising clients, who were looking for blond-haired, blue-eyed, flat-chested, all-American-looking girls. Wilhelmina had wanted a boutique agency that would cater to models like herself—more exotic, more ethnic, more high-fashion, sexier.

Financially, things hadn't worked out according to plan. The agency struggled for years, paying bills with Willie's modeling fees. Nearly a third of its billings were for TV commercials—which didn't really interest Eileen Ford, unless they were for cosmetics or other fashion-related products—rather than fashion photography and print advertising. And just as Willie began successfully to create and then corner the market for girls with high-class looks and big attitudes, American fashion magazines began responding to feminism and the rise in working women by becoming less fantasy-oriented and more practical. The agency was eventually forced to hire two Ford executives to broaden its roster to include some models with that increasingly popular "girl next door" look.

But Wilhelmina Models still had a reputation for sexier girls than Ford. It had begun with a roster of the more exotic Ford girls who followed Willie—like flamboyant Elsa Peretti, who had moved on to jewelry design, and Naomi Sims, one of the first top black models—and built a glitzy image with several high-profile launches. When Margaux Hemingway decided she wanted to parlay her beauty and name recognition into a modeling career, she debuted, and immediately won the contract for the Babe perfume ads, as a Wilhelmina Model. When photographer/socialite Peter Beard met Iman in Kenya and convinced her to come to America to model, she was signed with Wilhelmina, who helped concoct the preposterous—but salable—story that the upper-middle-class college student was actually an exotic African princess who had been discovered by Beard in the bush.

Wilhelmina had successfully linked her name to the model fantasy that was once exclusively Eileen Ford's. Some young girls even knew enough to dream about Willie's special "Hollywood Board," where the agency's top girls were handled by their own special bookers. The Hollywood Board was, at the moment, handling calls for Patti Hansen, the industry's top blond cover girl, dark-haired Pam Dawber and Juli Foster, and black models Toukie Smith (a Philadelphian whose brother Willi would become a major designer) and Rasheeda Moore (who, many years later, would be the bait in the drug bust of Washington mayor Marion Barry).

Willie and Bruce Cooper had two children—besides Bruce's from a previous marriage—and a personal relationship that many knew was on shaky ground. But their business was finally becoming established. It was finally not only hot, but solvent. That success was transforming the supermodel into a superwoman, possessed of a mature personal strength not always common in her industry.

She was offering a new kind of role model. The Ford model was, no matter how much the agency kept up with the times, still somehow a creature of the fifties and early sixties. She was going to make some money and have some fun before marrying a really rich guy. She was, basically, a prude, or was expected to pretend to be. The Wilhelmina model was, like the agency itself, a creation of the late sixties and early seventies. The agency still sold sexual stereotypes and represented everything the growing women's movement abhorred. But Wilhelmina attracted the kind of girls who drew that backhanded compliment of being described as "strong-willed." They were, in the jargon of the business, "more modern."

Gia felt very strongly about Wilhelmina, describing her as more than a role model. "I finally found a mother," her uncle recalled her telling him during a visit home. She would also tell gay friends that she and Willie had been lovers. But several people who worked closely with Wilhelmina said they doubted she and Gia were involved in that way. "Gia got the customary amount of attention from Wilhelmina," said one executive at the agency. "But my impression is that there were other models with whom Willie had a much closer relationship."

"I could give you a list *this long* of people I've heard Gia was involved with," said top hairstylist Harry King. "Some of them are laughable, *laughable*. Married women, famous women. I mean, it might be true, but it's laughable."

"I don't believe they were involved, and I'd be surprised if they were even that close," said Kay Mitchell, who was head of Wilhelmina's women's division. "I do remember Willie helping Gia a lot with her makeup and that kind of thing. I don't know if Willie was ever involved with a female, although she had a very European attitude about sexuality in general. I remember once being horrified when one of the kids called from location and another female model had come on to her. She was very upset and didn't know how to handle it. I went in to Wilhelmina and I was ready to kill the photographer because, well, I'm from Ohio, you know. Anyway, Willie just laughed at me. She wasn't, like, mean or anything, she said 'Kay, it'll all work out. It will be okay.' And it did all work out in the end. The model got more blasé about things and learned how to handle it, and I got my eyes opened to the fact that my values were not necessarily the only values.

"I don't think we saw Gia's sexuality the same way Gia did. Everybody just thought she was like a puppy. I got that response from a lot of people, because no one was *offended* by Gia. It wasn't like, 'Damn, get the hell away from me!' It was more like, 'Gia, give me a break.' You know? She was like a puppy, like somebody who needed love."

5
Go-See

Manhattan in the late seventies was chaotic and decadent for those who could afford it and a voyeur's paradise for those who could not. It was almost as if New York had responded to the famous 1975 *Daily News* headline—"Ford to City: Drop Dead"—by giving up on the failing institutions of the daylight hours and going unquietly into that dark night. With the traditional infrastructure of the city crumbling, it was no surprise the public was looking for new heroes to replace the power politicians and captains of industry.

They settled on the Beautiful People, those international jet-setters from whom fashion and style were to trickle down to the masses. They were originally christened, during Jackie Kennedy's shopping spree in the White House, by young John Fairchild, then a reporter for and heir to his family's Seventh Avenue trade publication *Women's Wear Daily*. The rise of the Beautiful People—or BPs, as they were shorthanded in *WWD*—seemed perfectly timed with the cult of personality journalism that was sweeping America.

The first shot in the "soft news" revolution was fired in 1974, when *Time* magazine took its "People" page—where it had always banished reports on movie and TV stars, rock groups, socialites and athletes—and turned it into the instantly successful *People* magazine. As *The Washington Post* capitalized on its newfound national profile after Watergate, its highbrow soft news section "Style" taught newspapers how to incorporate *People*'s lessons. While *Ms.* magazine was the first mainstream feminist publication, *People* and "Style" were probably more accurate measures of media response to the women's movement. Or perhaps they were a subconscious response to other social changes—creating a centralized system of international gossip and people-talk to replace the crumbling network of neighborhood and family chatter.

The Beautiful People filled a great many needs in the soft news revolution. And, as print and broadcast media followed the lead of *People* and "Style," demand for celebrities increased exponentially. Eventually the traditional BPs—redefined as anyone who could actually *afford* the clothes and the lifestyle, regardless of social standing—were joined on the bandstand by their beauti*fying* people.

It was a whole new world for the *fashionistas:* the army of models, photographers, designers, hair and makeup people, stylists and editors who toiled daily in the beauty trenches. The "famous non-famous people" were joining the ranks of the truly famous. And the first place where the BPs and the *fashionistas* could be seen together in public was on the global dance floor at Studio 54.

"That whole curtain just dropped," recalled fashion illustrator Joe Eula, who had been a famous non-famous person for decades—doing elegant illustrations for all the top designers and publications—but became a celebrity in the mid-seventies because he was responsible for all of Halston's preliminary sketches and fashion illustrations. "They invited us all to dinner, lunch and to sleep with them. The Studio took care of that. Suddenly they didn't mind rubbing asses with anybody, or even the front of them according to what gender they were."

Eula was particularly tied to the Studio scene because his apartment just happened to be right down Fifty-fourth Street from the club. "We got drugged here first, and then went up there," he explained. "We were living in some kind of incredible ... well, we were living in our own publicity world. Party and work became synonymous. It was twenty-four hours a day, no goddamn limit, never any nine-to-five. And having all these rich, international people around just lent credence to the party. They had money. They certainly dressed the style. And all those girls needed an arm to lean on.

"It was a heyday for those social people. And the reporters were very bright. Suddenly, every night, they had something to write about. There were South Americans, there were French, the English, who had such bad pimples, and those converted liras certainly went around big. It was just another goddamn League of Nations.

"Everybody was there until late and then people split off. There was the after-hour go *drug* group, the after-hour go *gamble* group, the after-hour go down and *faggot* group, the after-hour *leather* group ... always pretty much the same people.

"But it was *ours*. It was a world that had nothing to do with Europe. This whole crazy thing came out of New York. Everybody had to stay up all night. You took what you could. I personally took as many drugs and fucked as many people as possible. They did it half-assed in Europe. They never knew how to mix fags with straights in those discotheques. They were beginning to, but they didn't know how to put it together like me and Halston and the people who made it at that time."

"Studio was a phenomenon; every night was like a Fellini party. Everyone was there and you could do whatever you wanted there," recalled Peter Beard, cameraman, playboy, photo-opportunist and legendary Studio regular, whose home in Montauk, Long Island, was a regular retreat for the Warhol crowd and whose home in Kenya (near *Out of Africa* author Karen Blixen's place) was where the jet set went to get down, get dirty and touch nature. Beard's fortieth birthday party at Studio was highlighted by a huge white elephant cake lowered from the ceiling, in honor of his famous pictures of dying wildlife. "That was the last hurrah for New York. Karen Blixen said it beautifully: 'When the wildlife is gone, the only comparable thrill may be found in the middle of the biggest cities.' "

In May of 1977, Steve Rubell and Ian Schrager had done something quite ingenuous. They took the huge, ethnic discos in the outer boroughs—like the one Rubell ran in Queens, which was similar to 2001 Odyssey, immortalized in *Saturday Night Fever*—and crossbred them with the gay dance clubs. They established unheard of exclusivity by creating the most restrictive door policy a public place could get away with, and making sure that enough went on inside that people would wait. The club's watershed event was Halston's birthday party for Bianca Jagger, where she was led around on a white horse by a naked black giant rolled in gold glitter.

Once the stars started coming, Studio maintained a constant flow of celebrities (and people who looked as if they deserved celebration) by elaborate party-planning. They actively merchandised the club as a place to hold private parties and public relations events. And anyone whose presence would rate a mention in a newspaper gossip column or *People* magazine might be asked if Studio could throw them a party.

By the time Gia and Sharon got to town, Studio 54 was, to those who paid strict attention to such matters, already peaking or even slightly beyond its peak. It had already been open for a year. The best parts of its clever concept were already being copied, or rebelled against, by other clubs. Even the recently established VIP catacombs—created when Bianca, Halston and Liza Minnelli needed a dressing room to prepare for the club's first anniversary party—were proof that mere mortals and people from New Jersey were overrunning the main entrance and the dance floor.

But the *fashionistas* had too much spiritually invested in Studio 54 to let it pass so easily: it had become the Grand Ole Opry of Style. And, besides, appearances to the contrary, the fashion business was not really in the habit of changing bandwagons when the cutting-edgers started looking for the next big thing. They were usually still responding to the *last* big thing. In the beauty–industrial complex, it took at least three months to turn *any* idea—for an editorial photograph, a piece of clothing, a nail polish—into reality. Many of the top people at the magazines, clothing manufacturers and ad agencies stopped going out dancing when they got those powerful jobs. They heard about new things before Middle America did, but often in the same way parents heard about new things: from their kids, or *somebody's* kids.

There were a handful of New York publications that kept up with the scene at its own pace—*The Village Voice,* Andy Warhol's *Interview* and the new nightlife rag, *Night.* But most of the fashion business was decidedly uptown and slow to respond to trends unless they could be assured that the hipness would outlast their lead times. To Seventh Avenue, where the manufacturers had their offices and showrooms, a trend wasn't over until there was no more money to be wrung from it. There were no fortunes to be made by selling to the fringes. It was the people who followed the trendies, and those who followed the followers, who really spoke at the cash register.

So it was no surprise that fashion people were still hanging out at Studio 54. Gia's personal taste in music tended more toward rock n' roll than Studio's trademark disco music. But she started going to Studio regularly, anyway: you couldn't really expect to be a fashion model without being seen there.

"I moved to New York around the same time Gia did," recalled John Long, "and I went to Studio with her a couple times. We liked to dance together and she used me to meet girls. It's not easy for a girl to score other girls. She could get any man she wanted, but she said she envied me because I had a better shot of scoring with Juli Foster than she did. Juli Foster was a big Wilhelmina model at that time, and Gia had a crush on her. Gia would say, 'Ask that girl to dance.' Then she'd join with us and pull the girl off into a corner and buy her a beer."

On one of her first nights at Studio 54, Gia was approached by Ara Gallant. Once among the top hairstylists in the industry, the flamboyant Gallant was now establishing himself as a photographer. His more experimental work appeared often in *Interview,* and although his conventional fashion pictures had yet to make a huge impact, he was shooting for a start-up women's magazine called *Ambiance.* Gallant was popular with the models; he always wore a cap, for which the girls would bring him pins. He asked Gia if she would come by his studio.

Two days later, Gallant photographed her for *Ambiance.* It was her first job in New York. She arrived at nine A.M., had her hair and makeup done by a professional for the first time, and modeled until five P.M. For this she earned $23, which wasn't going to do much to offset the $50 advances she had begun taking from the agency each Friday. Like all modeling jobs, it would be two months before she found out—when the magazine's third issue was published—if the pictures were used at all and how she looked.

A week after the shooting with Ara Gallant, Gia went on a go-see to Lance Staedler's studio. The young, excruciatingly quiet, Montana-born photographer had moved his freelance business from Chicago to New York in 1976, and was still trying to build up a clientele for his artful, seductive, black and white fashion shots. He had done an assignment for *GQ* and some advertising and catalog work, but most of the pictures he took that he really liked weren't considered appropriate for fashion. They had an intimacy that big commercial magazines only wanted in celebrity portraits, not shots of professionally anonymous models.

"Gia came by the studio, and her hair was a mess, and all in her face," Staedler recalled. "I asked her if she wanted to do some tests. I remember the first time I shot with her, I was doing her hair. She was looking in the makeup mirror and I was looking at her and I didn't quite know what I was going to do. She looked at me and said, 'Well, don't look at *me,* I'm just some dumb girl from Philadelphia.' She just seemed so real, not like the other models."

During one session, Staedler heavily made up Gia's eyes and lips, and had her remove her top and just wear his own leather bomber jacket. In each shot, she threw her hair back at a different angle and left the jacket open a little more or less. In between poses, she ate raisins from a box—he clicked off a few shots of her doing that as well. He used a mounted, rectangular camera that took 2¼-inch-square photographs: film cartridges were attached and detached from the camera body so it could be reloaded without moving it. Staedler took thirty-six shots in the first pose, and then had Gia change positions. He told her to lay down and prop herself up on one arm. As in the other shots, her breasts would be partially or even completely exposed, depending upon how far she opened the jacket. But in this pose, her bared breasts wouldn't be as prominent and obvious: the nudity would be more subtle and sensual. Staedler took a few shots in that position, and the session was over.

After the film was processed, Staedler sat down with the images to figure out what he had. Of the standing poses, seven frames interested him enough to try cropping them with a grease pencil and a ruler on the contact sheets. But the shots he found himself drawn to were the reclining ones. And after painstakingly editing down the images, one finally emerged.

It was a stunning photograph. The oversize prints he made of the shot drew the viewer into the folds of the jacket, the shiny sweep of hair, and a pair of sadly seductive eyes. It was the kind of shot that would stop even the most jaded photographer as he hurriedly paged through yet another model portfolio, or the most harried magazine reader leafing through five hundred pages of pretty girls. It was easily the strongest picture anyone had ever taken of Gia. When Staedler showed it to her, she immediately asked to see the contact sheets. "I had gotten into the habit of not showing contact sheets," Staedler recalled. "The contact sheet is just so free, you see everything. I want people just to see what I was working towards, not everything it took to get what I wanted. She got really upset that I wouldn't show them to her."

But even in her upset, Gia was smart enough to know what to do with the shot he *did* show her. She walked it over to Mann and Green Color lab on East Forty-third and had copies made for her portfolios—the more calls that came in requesting a model's book, the more duplicate books she needed. And she had a hundred Xeroxes made for whoever she thought should have one.

It was the kind of picture that could make a model's career. "I remember when Gia's book came into the studio," said Sean Byrnes, longtime assistant of photographer Francesco Scavullo. "I stole that black and white picture and sent the book back. I never did that *ever* before. I finally met Gia when she came around the studio to get the photo back."

It was also the kind of picture that, ironically enough, would do absolutely nothing for Staedler's career. "At the time, nobody had any use for a picture like that," he recalled. "I also did another one of her, just at her apartment one night after we had gone out, just a snapshot with a little camera. She was just wearing a pair of gym shorts, no top, and holding this little Charlie Chaplin doll she had in her room. No makeup, totally natural. That was something that, in 1978, nobody had any use for. 'It's nice,' an art director would say, 'but what's it for? It just looks like a snapshot.' Today, you'd try really hard to make a picture look that natural. You'd be on a shoot with hair and makeup artists, everybody working at being that natural. I printed it up for myself, but I never showed it to anyone."

The copies of Staedler's picture came back from the lab just in time for a week with several important appointments. Gia went to the offices of *Cosmopolitan* on Fifty-seventh Street—in the Hearst Building, along with *Harper's Bazaar*—and dropped off her book. And two days later she went to the offices of *Vogue* at 350 Madison Avenue, just above Forty-fourth. *Vogue* was on the thirteenth floor of the Condé Nast Publications building, which also housed the editorial, art, production and sales offices for four other American magazines—*Mademoiselle, Glamour, House & Garden* and *Bride's*—and the U.S. offices of the British, French and Italian editions of *Vogue.*

On American *Vogue's* floor, where a tastefully decorated lobby led to a maze of extremely plain and relatively small offices and cubicles, Gia met with Sara Foley, who had the impressive-sounding title of assistant to the model editor and an equally impressive résumé. The position was Foley's fifth within Condé Nast—she had already worked at every Condé Nast magazine but *House & Garden*—and her second job at *Vogue,* where she had started as second assistant to the editor-in-chief.

But that career's worth of job changes had taken place in just six years since her college graduation—five if you subtracted the year she took off to live in Bermuda—and the twenty-eight-year-old veteran didn't even have her own office. Instead, Sara Foley, with perhaps the best bad job at the company's most extravagant publication, was one of the reigning queens of the legions of Condé Nast gofer girls, whose parents always knew *someone,* whose clothes and hair were always stylish, and whose overworked, underpaid tenures as "assistants" were a special kind of finishing school. They flowed into the building early in the morning and out after five like a tidal wave of conservative fashion statements: to a large degree, they were the "young people" fashion editors referred to when "discovering" new trends.

Sara Foley didn't really choose *Vogue*'s models at all. As assistant to the model editor, she did some preliminary screening, and stayed in constant contact with the agencies to book the models chosen by the editors. But most of her job was executing the career-making-and-breaking decisions arrived at by the most powerful, most particular and most peculiar staff of fashion editors and art directors in the industry. If photographer Chris von Wangenheim convinced a *Vogue* fashion editor that the *most creative and modern way* to shoot a certain shoe was to create a table scene where the shoe was tagged—along with a gun, a bloody bra and prescription pill bottles—as evidence in a murder, Sara Foley had to arrange everything. She had to rent the gun, find the bra, buy the nail polish to simulate the blood, get the pill bottles from a pharmacist, get a table, get the evidence tags from a court, and then book Von Wangenheim, a studio and a stylist. She also had to tell the photographer when his picture was later killed, not so much because it was offensive, the editors said, but because the bra they bloodied had been manufactured by a touchy *Vogue* advertiser.

It was unclear what Gia's appointment with Sara Foley really meant. It could have been that an editor at the magazine or a photographer associated with it had some interest in her. Or perhaps her booker had browbeaten Foley long enough that she agreed to take a look at Gia just to get off the phone.

Vogue was still where every model dreamed about working, even though the magazine had changed dramatically in recent years and was considered, in some corners of the industry, a shell of its former self. But *Vogue* was exactly as ephemeral as the fashion world it covered and it was *perpetually* being accused of some new emptiness. In fact, it retained more of its turn-of-the-century roots than most *fashionistas* and readers realized, because most of them never really understood what *Vogue* was. They only knew what it appeared to be.

When Condé Nast, the St. Louis–born business manager of *Collier's,* bought *Vogue* in 1909, it was a weakening sister to reigning *Harper's Bazaar.* Nast transformed it into a powerhouse that delivered coverage of national and international style events to twentieth-century America's first wave of nouveau riche. Together, *Vogue* and *Bazaar* would define what fashion magazines were: oversized, laden with artful fashion shots that redefined still photography, published for those who could afford to buy couture clothing or dreamed of buying it. Nast created the first international magazine chain by starting foreign editions of *Vogue,* and added an even higher-brow American publication, *Vanity Fair.* His company's influence was increased by each publication's power in its own country and *Vogue's* collective international presence. The Condé Nast magazines also successfully established an alternative reality for the world of high society and high fashion.

Magazines were entirely self-invented creatures. Unlike newspapers, which purported to report on the world as it was, magazines created a world within their pages, with self-proclaimed rules truly understood only by those who made them. Nast proved that if magazines were very successful, the worlds they invented could actually come to be. Many of the garments shown in *Vogue* were created only at the request of the magazine's editors. The first-ever "New York Collection," showing couture clothes designed by Americans, was organized by *Vogue* itself in 1914. In fact, many of the events written about in *Vogue,* and later in *Vanity Fair,* were arranged just to be covered by the magazines.

In creating his *Vogue* world, Nast adhered to a Keatsian code of fashion ethics—if it looked beautiful, it was true—but added a hidden Keynesian twist: Many of the vaunted flights of fashion fancy were tied to the harsh reality of advertising revenues. The magazine gave extremely preferential treatment to advertisers. *Vogue's* "editorial" pages *appeared,* to any trusting reader, to contain the unbiased fashion statements of the magazine's glamorous staff of experts. But church and state were not so neatly divided. Few garments created by non-advertisers were ever displayed, and the number of times an advertiser would be editorially "mentioned" was spelled out in the client's ad contract. There was a "Must List" of advertisers whose wares had to appear in the magazine whether aesthetically deserving or not. These practices were neither illegal nor really immoral. They were simply standard operating procedure.

Nast died in 1942, and most of his magazines weathered World War II about as well as the entire beauty–industrial complex. They all hung on by a thread, and were rescued in 1947 when Christian Dior's seminal "New Look" collection reestablished the French couture and signaled a return to women's fashion, as usual. The New Look was the fashion industry's remedy for a decade when the world had other things on its collective mind, and life had grown dangerously utilitarian and egalitarian. The natural order of fashion—the "clothing chain"—was in jeopardy. Women were working. U.S. government restrictions on garment design—banning hems over two inches, cuffs, ruffles or zippers (the latter of which caused the innovation of the wraparound skirt)—had contributed to a rise in more casual clothes and increasingly unisex designs. Americans, cut off from Europe by the war, had even begun to appreciate their own designers. The New Look helped save the civilized world from all that.

In 1959, newspaper magnate S. I. Newhouse bought a controlling interest in the Condé Nast company, but didn't initially tinker with the *Vogue* formula. In fact, it was under the Newhouse family that *Vogue* lured one of the grand doyennes of glamour and fantasy in fashion magazines, Diana Vreeland, away from her post as the very successful fashion editor of *Harper's Bazaar*. Vreeland brought along the reigning photographer of the moment, Richard Avedon, and delivered *Vogue* its first decisive victory in the decades-old battle between the two magazines.

By the late sixties, *Vogue* finally began to feel some of the pressures that could have just as easily come in the late forties—if returning soldier-husbands and postwar prosperity hadn't forced women to give up their emergency careers and retreat to suburban kitchens. Condé Nast Publications found itself faced with the shrinking wealth of the American industrial aristocracy and the rise of middle-class and even "working women's" values. The most obvious signs of a changing women's world were the explosion in more fashionable "ready-to-wear" clothes and the incredible success of *Cosmopolitan* (which was owned, like *Harper's Bazaar,* by the competing Hearst newspaper chain). *Cosmo* had found its success under Helen Gurley Brown, author of the naughtily popular book *Sex and the Single Girl,* who had taken over as editor in 1965.

At the same time, printing and mailing costs were dramatically rising, and Condé Nast brass started talking about lowering *Vogue*'s perfectly plucked brow. Former *Vogue* art director Alexander Liberman, elevated to company-wide "editorial director," was to oversee the changes, which were being fought fiercely by Diana Vreeland. Then came 1970, the year *Vogue* heartily embraced the midi-length skirt—ordering a nation to re-hem and haw, just as the women's movement successfully empowered America's fashion victims to reject the dictates of the beauty-industrial complex. Seventh Avenue suffered mightily and *Vogue*'s power in the marketplace was seriously questioned.

Vreeland was unceremoniously dumped. Her second-in-command, Grace Mirabella, was made editor. From that moment on, *Vogue* people would be identified by whose regime they had served under, and whose sensibility had been etched on their fashion tabula rasa. The magazine became gradually less exclusive as fashion became more—and the Vreelanders cringed at the term—*democratic.* The most dramatic alteration came in 1977, when *Vogue* was physically downscaled to newsstand size and offered for sale at supermarket checkout counters.

But even through all these changes, *Vogue* still stood for something in the fashion world. It was still the biggest, most extravagant and most powerful style publication in the most important market in the world. It still had its "Must Lists," which continued to be worth buying a place on. If the magazine no longer lived up to its history, at least it *had* its history. Relative to its surroundings, it was still *Vogue.*

Over the next few weeks, Gia continued the steady stream of hourly appointments and occasional tests. On Friday mornings there was usually a meeting at the agency, and on other nights they held classes on runway or makeup techniques. Gia went to castings for the Young & Rubicam advertising agency and Paramount Pictures, stopped in to be seen by several people at Revlon, Bloomingdale's, *Woman's Day* and *Bride's,* and showed her book at the studios of some of the top editorial photographers for the major American and European fashion magazines: Jimmy Moore, Anthony Barboza, John Stember, Andrea Blanche and Bob Stone. Each appointment was just a name and an address ticked off the night before by her booker. Gia scribbled down their names—or something close to their names—and checked off each appointment when she finished. If someone seemed especially pleasant or obnoxious, she might write "nice" or "creep" above their name. But most of the people were, at best, faceless photo credits.

In the evenings, Gia and Sharon would sometimes go out together—as friends. They didn't find themselves gravitating toward the gay clubs in New York because it just didn't seem necessary: the mainstream nightspots were so mixed that suddenly it was the all-gay places that seemed limiting. Besides new hangouts, they developed sources for their regular needs: groceries, for which there sometimes was so little money that they ate peanuts for dinner, and drugs, for which they could always scratch up a few dollars.

"When we first moved up there it was mostly coke," recalled Sharon Beverly. "Both of us liked to drink, but we were doing coke. There was one guy, his name was Michael. He lived on Central Park South and he had this beautiful apartment, but he was a dirty, old hippie with really long hair. He always had a lot of drugs on him, and, of course, if anyone had a lot of drugs, Gia was there. She was there *a lot* with him."

Toward the end of May, things started to happen. On May 17, Gia had a full day of go-sees and requests scheduled, including a ten A.M. with Manning, one of the few remaining fashion illustrators still working in an industry that was now mostly photographs. Posing for illustrators like Manning or Joe Eula was a classy throwback to the earlier days of modeling, when it wasn't so much a business as it was women being paid to inspire artists: that clear distinction between mannequins and muses had long since grown fuzzy.

111

At the last minute, the day's appointments were canceled. She had been booked for a newspaper ad shooting for Bloomingdale's. The photographer would be Arthur Elgort.

A bearded, thirty-eight-year-old New Yorker whose real passion had always been shooting the ballet, Elgort was clearly the fashion photographer of his moment. Both his Woody-Allenish demeanor and his informal, unpretentious, "real-life" fashion pictures were exactly what editorial and advertising clients thought of when they wanted a "modern" look. No fashion photographer had been more generously rewarded than Elgort by the recent changes at American *Vogue*, which was trying to bolster its stable of "old master" photographers—like Avedon, Hiro and Penn—with some guys who didn't take it all so seriously and understood the new corporate visual motto: less art, more fun.

Arthur Elgort specialized in street fashion pictures and studio shots with a lot of action. He often used a hand-held 35mm camera with a motor drive, and snapped personal pictures with a Minox between takes. Because his work required freezing action, he often used "fast film," which required shorter exposure times to produce a focused image but did so with a noticeable "grain," the fuzzy imprecision that had once separated "professional" photographs from those taken by everyone else.

Breaking in at *McCall's* and *Mademoiselle* in the late sixties, Elgort then made a splash in Europe at the British and Italian editions of *Vogue*—which were owned by Condé Nast but had independent editorial and art staffs—and became a fixture at American *Vogue* in 1974. Some considered his ascension to be the creative unshackling of fashion photography. Others saw it as the complete "amateurization" of an art form, or at least a bastardization of a highly specialized craft. But whatever it meant to commercial art historians, Elgort's style—or *Vogue*'s acceptance of Elgort's style—revolutionized fashion photography.

His success with American *Vogue*, however, did not mean he had carte blanche there. His most unconventional shots—the blurriest ones, the most candid ones, the ones where the breasts were too visible or the clothes not visible enough—were still only seen in the European fashion magazines, which were more willing to take chances. And when Elgort did a shooting for American *Vogue,* the art directors often didn't pick the pictures he liked best. Although photographers were allowed to edit their pictures and make suggestions, *Vogue* had the right to choose any shot taken during its session and paid a straight editorial rate of $300 per page, which was among the highest in the lowest-paying part of the industry. Elgort set the tone for the seventies by approaching magazine work as a job and rarely arguing with the boss. As he told a photography magazine, "You didn't have to be a genius to see that the seventies would be the Decade of the Client."

This new approach to photography—which Elgort certainly didn't invent, but came to personify—had given birth to a new kind of model. Because Elgort disdained conventional "posing," his style forced models to be more involved and inventive, more like actresses than mannequins. Traditional studio photography rewarded models who sat still well. Elgort's camera loved girls who could move and dance and lose themselves in a relatively controlled and totally contrived environment. He played loud music during shootings, and expected his assistants and hair and makeup people—he usually worked with his best friend, Christian, one of the few straight hairdressers in the business—to keep the shootings loose and friendly. His pictures made the clothes look exciting, and made modeling look like great, glamorous fun—more fun, in fact, than it often really was. Elgort excelled at tapping into the growing public interest in finding out what happened "behind the scenes." He created scenes with exciting behinds.

Bloomingdale's, among the hippest and most heavily promoted of the New York department stores, was one of Elgort's bread-and-butter advertising clients. The store's large advertising department generally had as much work for Elgort as he had time to do; when he wasn't out on location, he tended to shoot for them at least one day a week. Like all fashion photographers, Elgort did editorial work to stay in the public eye and generate advertising jobs, and did advertising jobs to generate cash to support his studio and his lifestyle and grant him freedom to do "personal stuff"—in his case, ballet pictures. And, like all fashion photographers, he never had as much time for the personal stuff as he wanted.

But Arthur Elgort's position in the very small world of fashion photography was an enviable one. And because honoring his many commitments required a small but dependable cast of assistants, models and stylists in and out of his studio at 300 Central Park West, Elgort was one of the people a fledgling model most wanted to impress. He didn't yet have many major American advertising clients, but he worked for every publication those clients read. Finding favor with Elgort meant that everyone who was anyone would soon know your face. If he liked you, a lot of your dues were already paid.

Both Elgort and Bloomingdale's in-house ad people were sold on Gia by Wilhelmina. Elgort used Gia in a lot of shots during the day-long session for Bloomingdale's, and liked her so much that he decided to use her again. She was funny, she was loose, she was wild. She was a hot dancer, which always came in handy at an Elgort session. She looked like a more American version of Apollonia von Ravenstein or an Italian version of Lisa Taylor, two of Elgort's favorite models. Gia could be exotic or just an ethnic, American girl-next-door. She wasn't shy about taking off her clothes—she sat around comfortably in nothing more than hair curlers and a smile, puffing away at a Marlboro and paging through a magazine.

It was May 17. Gia had been working less than three months and this was only her second real job. But she already knew everything she had to know to be Arthur Elgort's kind of model. And his nod was all she needed to leapfrog over all the other new faces at Wilhelmina and every other agency, and head for the Hollywood Board.

Several days later, the issue of *Ambiance* with Gia's pictures hit the stands. The shots weren't great, but they were good enough, and a tear sheet from a real job in a glossy magazine sometimes looked better in a model's book than all the great photos in the world. But the pictures had already been eclipsed by the news—which the agency was circulating to anyone who would listen—that Elgort was hot on Gia. And in the next three weeks there would be so many pictures taken that it would be hard to find room in her portfolio for the *Ambiance* shots. She was about to become the new darling of the Italian edition of *Harper's Bazaar,* which was every photographer's favorite magazine of the moment. There wasn't another glossy fashion book in the world that was giving photographers as much freedom; the magazine didn't seem to have any rules to break. Unlike other European magazines, Italian *Bazaar* had an office in New York, as well as Milan, and they didn't care if the pictures didn't appear to have been taken in Italy. Top photographers could work for them without leaving their Manhattan studios.

Elgort did the first pictures of Gia for *Bazaar.* Even though it was the end of May, they went outside to shoot tweed blazers and casual clothes for a fall preview story. The next day, Gia was sent to be seen by another of the magazine's regular contributors, Chris von Wangenheim, the dark prince of fashion photography. Von Wangenheim, thirty-six, had left Germany and his high social position there—he was, technically, a baron—in the mid-sixties to settle in New York and pursue photography. But he had never put aside his fascination with strong, sometimes shocking, sexually charged images: Freudian nightmares realized. He could shoot standard fashion photos. But his best work showed the clothes, told a suggestive story and—perhaps more than the work of any other fashion photographer of the day— could almost be taken seriously as art. Although he had been shooting for major magazines and advertising clients since the late sixties, he was probably best known in America for a picture he had taken in 1976 for a Christian Dior jewelry ad.

The ad was not for the Paris-based House of Dior itself. It was part of the Your Dior campaign, a way for all the various firms with licenses to manufacture Dior-label products in America to appear as one company, with a slightly more approachable image than the French couture house. Von Wangenheim had been given nearly unprecedented freedom to make whatever pictures he liked for the campaign. Adman Gene Federico would then pick an appropriate adjective to complete the campaign slogan *"Blank* is Your Dior."

The campaign had been controversial since Dior had refused to use the first ad: a Father's Day shot of then eleven-year-old Brooke Shields made up like a woman and dressed only in a man's white dress shirt, standing next to a male model cast to look like her father. They also later yanked the 1977 summer sunglasses ad with the model firing a pistol ("Explosive Is Your Dior") because of the "Son of Sam" killings: its one appearance still merited lengthy commentary in the book *Terrorist Chic*. But the jewelry ad was still the one that elicited the most photographic nostalgia. For that one, Von Wangenheim had adorned model Lisa Taylor with a diamond bracelet, ring and earrings. Then he brought in a Doberman pinscher, clamped its jaws down on her wrist, and flashed the shot so the dog's eyes glowed demonically red. "Fetching Is Your Dior."

The Your Dior campaign had established Von Wangenheim visually in America. It became known for producing very edgy shots of very big models: one of the classic photos of Patti Hansen was the Your Dior shot of her in an evening dress and a fur, standing in front of a burning car. Von Wangenheim was another photographer who could single-handedly make a model's career.

Von Wangenheim had a combined beauty and fashion feature to shoot for Italian *Bazaar* the next week. In all fashion magazines, beauty shots offered more freedom than fashion shots. With no clothes to show, just makeup products and hairstyles, there was a better chance that the magazines would accept a nude or an unorthodox pose. A beauty picture could be anything, as long as it fit someone's definition of beautiful.

A location scout had suggested to Von Wangenheim that the top of the still-uncompleted Citicorp Building might be an interesting place to shoot. An assistant was sent over to "Polaroid" the location, and then arranged with the building's management and security staff to do some shots there. After meeting her, Von Wangenheim decided to book Gia and another model, as well as bearded, Texas-born hairstylist Maury Hopson and first-name-only top makeup artist Ariella. On the first day of what turned into a tough three-day shoot, the four met at nine A.M. in the lower level of the Citicorp Building.

Upstairs, Von Wangenheim and his assistants were meeting with "the client"—twenty-seven-year-old Lizzette Kattan, Italian *Bazaar*'s one-woman fashion department and a big reason for the magazine's popularity with top photographers. Born in Honduras, where her father was in the coffee business, Lizzette was raised in New York and became a Ford model in her late teens—working mostly in Europe during the early seventies, occasionally with Von Wangenheim.

After a solid but unremarkable modeling career, Lizzette became friendly with the owner of Italian *Bazaar,* who hired her to install the most forward fashion philosophy in the glossy magazine business, and commute between Milan and Manhattan. Besides her growing importance among *fashionistas,* who respected her taste and the sheer volume of high fashion jobs she had to dole out, Lizzette had industry cachet because she was often seen in the company of designer Calvin Klein. That coupling raised eyebrows for any number of reasons. Besides bitchy questions about Lizzette's place in Klein's bisexual social life, their relationship was also sometimes blamed for a feud between designer Giorgio Armani and Italian *Bazaar.* The magazine wouldn't cover Armani's shows and the designer refused to advertise in it: the never-proven reason was that someone high in the Armani organization was convinced that Kattan was somehow spying for Klein.

While Lizzette and Chris were upstairs looking at locations, Gia was having her face put on in a makeshift dressing room. Ariella sat Gia down and began the ritualized application of the layers of creams, bases, powders and pencils required for the beyond-perfect makeup jobs expected of fashion photographs. Because the bright lights washed out so much color, it took a great deal of makeup just to make a model look, on film, clean-scrubbed rather than stone-cold dead. To get strong features onto film, the makeup artist had to prime the model's face like a canvas and paint new and improved features on top of the old ones. Because the dresses had bared shoulders and plunging necklines, the models' shoulders, chests and backs had to be made-up as well.

"That whole process is just unbelievable," recalled one

top model of the first time she was "done" by one of the top hair and makeup teams. "These people grab your hands and the next thing, they're doing this manicure, and you don't know *who* these people are. They are doing your face, they are doing your hair. You've got hands all over your body, you know. People are making up your tits and everything else you could think of."

Because the hair and makeup people had to get nearly inside the girls to do their jobs, it wasn't surprising that they were the ones who were most in touch with the gossip of the business. The world of fashion photography had no real trade paper of its own: it rarely even merited coverage in *WWD* or the new, mass-market weekly *W*. So information was circulated—with no standards of accuracy whatsoever—via magazine photo credits and morning makeup-room chatter. From there it was disseminated by telephone from photographer's assistant to fashion editor's assistant to model agency booker and back through the rest of the chat-cycle.

"It's that whole army of hair and makeup people that sort of create reputations: that's where everything is discussed, in the morning," said photographer Mike Reinhardt, often the subject of more than his share of morning gossip. "The models sit there while they're doing hair and makeup and talk about their boyfriends, about work, about the magazines, about what they're doing, where they travel, who they see, what money they have.

"And that gossip is important because the whole business is based on hot air. Because when you really get right down to it, for most jobs there are at least maybe a hundred photographers that can do an excellent job, maybe more than a hundred. Yet there are only a few who are really making it. And what really impacts their success is not really the quality of their work as much as what *surrounds* it."

After sitting through a two-hour round of shoptalk, Gia went with the rest of the crew to the top floor, where the first shot was already set up. Nobody had considered just how windy it would be up on the roof, and they were unprepared for the odd sensation of a seventy-two-story skyscraper that seemed to be swaying in the breeze. The models and the dresses they were wearing—either strapless or spaghetti-strapped—were being buffeted about. The only choices were to stand stiff against the breeze, or roll with it.

"I was wearing this really great slinky black dress ... it made me feel good," Gia would later tell an interviewer about the shooting. "And I really got into a groove and kept moving all over with it. And then one shoulder slipped, and then the other. And before I realized it, the whole top was down.

"And I went to fix it and the photographer said, 'No, that's great.' And I thought, 'Why not?' My tits looked good."

Photo sessions were generally planned so that they didn't require much spontaneity: part of being a professional photographer was knowing how to make sure a good picture ensued even if everything from the chemistry to the clothes was a disaster. But everyone hoped that events during the session would create a better image than the one they planned. Each day that took on a theme of its own, each pleasant surprise, was proof that the process of creating photographs could still be creative. In this case, Gia's bared breasts became the impromptu visual theme of the rooftop session. She posed in another dress with the top pulled down; two other low-cut dresses were photographed in more conventional poses. At the end of each day of shooting, Gia got a voucher for eighty dollars—her standard editorial rate for an eight-hour booking—and left without any idea which photographs would be used in the magazine. If the topless shots were edited out, cropped or reproduced postage-stamp size, it would be as if they had never been taken at all.

On Monday, Italian *Bazaar* booked Gia again for the day. Tuesday she did more Bloomingdale's work with Elgort—at the advertising rate of $750 a day—and finished too late to fill another *Bazaar* request. On Wednesday, she worked with Von Wangenheim for *Bazaar* again. Thursday she went to be looked over for a Bobby Brooks bathing suit ad.

The next week Von Wangenheim booked her for one of his *Vogue Patterns* assignments. While history would later enshrine pages from *Vogue* and *Bazaar*, there was probably no publication more revelatory of the true life of the fashion photographer in the late seventies than *Vogue Patterns*. The odd, hybrid publication had begun as the pattern-book magazine for those who wanted to sew the clothes they saw in *Vogue,* but it was later sold to the Butterick Company, publishers of several clothing and sewing pattern catalogs. Top photographers tried to avoid doing catalog shots, because even though the money was terrific, the pictures were, by definition, completely boring. But *Patterns* wasn't the usual catalog. Instead of a has-been or never-to-be art director, *Patterns* had hired twenty-four-year-old Marc Balet, a Rhode Island School of Design graduate who had won the Prix de Rome design competition and was earning a hundred dollars a week as the art director at *Interview,* the most visually avant-garde mass circulation publication in the country.

When Balet gave notice to take the higher-paying *Patterns* job, Warhol insisted the young designer continue art directing *Interview* as a freelancer. This double life of Balet's was a bonanza for the handful of photographers who could do both kinds of work. They had grown accustomed to shooting for Balet almost for free. Now they had *Patterns,* too. Not only did it pay well—$350 to $500 a shot for pictures that could be churned out so fast that it wasn't hard to gross $25,000 in a good week—but *Patterns* offered the kinds of trips that were usually only available from fashion magazines.

Because of the pattern book's tenuous association with *Vogue,* Pan Am would fly a *Patterns* crew anywhere in the world for free as long as the airline got a prominent plug, like a shot with a plane or pilots in the background. Hotels around the world offered rooms and meals for similar treatment. Because of this arrangement, it was actually cheaper for Balet to shoot in Bali than in a studio in New York.

The pictures in the magazine often amounted to absurd parodies of real fashion photographs. In one monthly feature, a *Patterns* reader was profiled and scenes from her life were photo-realized with a model like Patti Hansen playing her and wearing clothes made with the company's sewing patterns. The pictures Von Wangenheim shot of Gia for Balet were similarly forgettable. But work for *Vogue Patterns* wasn't for your book, it was for your pocketbook.

*　　*　　*

On June 19, Monday morning, both *Vogue* and *Harper's Bazaar* sent for Gia. This time, it wasn't a go-see her booker had fought for. The fashion czarinas had heard that their top photographers were delighted with a new girl. But not just any new girl. A new girl who was too short, too dark, too ethnic, too voluptuous, and too rebellious to be a model. But she was still perfect.

And the new girl didn't need their clothes or their makeup in order to look stunning. In her vintage store men's clothes, with her face clean-scrubbed, her long hair in her face, and a cigarette dangling from her lips, she was already a fashion statement. She was a high fashion version of those creepy New Wave rockers they were hearing so much about. She was a Beautiful Punk. She also looked completely androgynous but in a highly provocative way. She was a butch pinup girl.

Because she had an uptown-downtown quality—and what they politely called "that boy-girl thing"—Gia would be able to make things that "just weren't *Vogue*" look like they belonged in *Vogue*. So the magazine didn't waste a minute in snatching her up. They booked a shooting with Von Wangenheim on Thursday. Unfortunately, they chose for Gia's first shot the one part of her anatomy least suited to modeling—her hands, with those fingernails that had barely survived years of continual biting. Von Wangenheim and the manicurist used every trick they could think of, but the shots were killed because her nails were just too rough. But *Vogue* booked her again for the following Monday.

In the meantime, Wilhelmina realized she had a budding star on her hands. The agency canceled Gia's Friday appointments so she and Wilhelmina could have lunch and talk business. Gia had inquired several weeks before about getting a year's guarantee of $25,000 from the agency. Back then, such a commitment was out of the question. Suddenly, it was clear Gia would be making much more than that.

At lunch, Willie and Gia discussed the eighteen-year-old's future: what kind of work she wanted to do, which photographers she'd like to meet. Willie wanted Gia to meet with the people from Paris Planning, the agency that represented Wilhelmina models in France. After the meeting, Gia left town to spend the weekend with Chris von Wangenheim and a skeleton crew on Fire Island, where they went to do some testing. On Monday, she arrived at noon for her next *Vogue* try, a beauty shot by Arthur Elgort with Way Bandy doing makeup.

Even in the upper reaches of the fashion photography business, there were still some stars who shone more brightly: some because they were more talented than everyone else, others because they were simply more intriguing *characters* or more aggressively self-publicized. Way Bandy had somehow managed to become great at what he did—not just as a makeup artist, but as a peacekeeper in the most difficult work situations—and make his flamboyance and high profile work for him. He was one of the few figures in the industry who was well-known to the general public and still well-respected by his peers.

Tall and thin with thick, dark hair cut into a longish pageboy and a penchant for dramatic clothes and entrances, Bandy was a charming and mysterious figure in the business. No one knew his real name or his real age (he was thirty-seven) or who he had been before becoming Way Bandy, getting a nose job and inventing what would become the industry prototype of the uncloseted gay makeup artist. It was said that he had been an English teacher in North Carolina and had been married before coming to New York for a visit in the mid-sixties and never going back. He was hired as a makeup teacher at a modeling school and then went to Charles of the Ritz as makeup director. In 1971, he did the makeup for the Broadway show *No, No, Nanette* and left Charles the next year to freelance. His fame was established by 1974, when he and hairstylist Maury Hopson, his best friend, transformed Watergate wife Margaret Mitchell into a cover girl.

Bandy's legend had recently been marketed nationally as a slim, how-to book titled *Designing Your Face*. In an industry rife with chemical excess—the traditional, classic diet pill to keep weight down and the more fashionable, modern cocaine—Bandy was known for his vegetarianism, his obsession with nutrition and naturopathy, and his growing expertise in spiritual well-being. Very active on the downtown club scene, his indulgences were mostly sexual.

Bandy always insisted that his makeup technique was the

same as everyone else's, but he had a signature style. He used all-natural makeup from little jars with antique silver lids, which he carried in a lacquered box tied with a bandana. And he believed in heavy makeup and complete reshaping of facial features. He was a stickler for perfect eyebrows, and many models especially recalled the first time their faces were done by Way Bandy, both for the dramatic finished product and the tingly, red skin they felt beneath the surface of beige and white liquid foundations mixed with skin lotion and distilled water. Brooke Shields was one of the only models who had been spared Bandy's tweezers. Her mother, Teri, had forbidden it, but he had a standing request to be the first to pluck them.

Bandy's makeup job on Gia rendered her stunning, divine, but nearly unrecognizable as herself. The pictures were to accompany a story on the "beauty collections": the most recent of the fashion-oriented "events" created almost entirely to give *Vogue* and other magazines an excuse to "cover" cosmetics as if they were a breaking news story. The news for 1978 was that "Color Is It!" "Color and how it is used," so said the Fall Beauty Report, "is the thing to watch. In makeup, in clothes, in accessories. For day, for evening, color is the big change now ... and getting bigger all the time." In order to illustrate how "the whole attitude about color has changed," Bandy painted Gia's face several severe shades of sienna and drastically elongated her eyes.

It would be months before the results of the session were printed—*Vogue* had a much longer lead time than Italian *Bazaar,* and these pictures would run, if at all, in October. But Gia and Way Bandy forged a fast friendship that produced more immediate results. Bandy offered to help her get jobs. Since he was so closely associated with Francesco Scavullo, it was only a matter of time before Gia would be considered for one of the *Cosmopolitan* covers Scavullo's studio had churned out every month since the late sixties.

Gia worked Wednesday for a paper company, at a day rate of $500, and Thursday for Von Wangenheim for *Patterns.* Friday *Vogue* booked her again, this time with photographer Stan Malinowski to model furs.

* * *

Over the long Fourth of July weekend, which she spent in Atlantic City with Toni O'Connor, Gia decided it was time to speak with Wilhelmina about raising her daily editorial rate to $100, increasing her workload so she was modeling every day, and broadening the number of photographers using her regularly. And over the next two weeks, the variety of her work did expand. She did *Vogue* editorial shots with still-life specialist Nobu, who filled in when Irving Penn canceled at the last minute. She worked with two of the top female fashion photographers: Andrea Blanche on a *Vogue* location shot on Roosevelt Island and Jean Pagliuso on a two-day, $1,500 catalog job for Saks Fifth Avenue.

Her biweekly agency check, less commissions, was for $1,530. She put $400 into a savings account, $500 into a checking account. The rest she spent on luggage and put into traveler's checks. In four days, she was scheduled to leave for Italy. *Bazaar* fashion editor Lizzette Kattan, who seemed to be almost single-handedly launching Gia's career, had booked her for a two-and-a-half-week European trip. She would model the high fashion collections in Rome and Paris—the *alta moda* and the *haute couture*—and then double back to Milan, where *Bazaar*'s main office was, to shoot whatever was left over. The fees were negligible. But the trip was all-expenses-paid, and *Bazaar*'s September collections issue, which sometimes ran as high as 1,200 pages and came in two volumes, was one of the best opportunities in the industry for exposure.

Gia would be arriving in Rome just after the July–August issue of *Bazaar* hit the Italian newsstands. The issue included the Elgort fall fashion shooting, from which five shots of Gia were used, and the Citicorp shots by Von Wangenheim. The beauty and fashion feature opened with a shot of Gia and the other model, a "double," silhouetted against the New York skyline. On the next right-hand page—the right-hand page of a magazine spread being more important since the eye tends to seek it first—was Gia, leaning against a railing in a black Krizia dress with one breast exposed. The next spread was just Gia—looking, as one model agent put it, "achingly beautiful"—in outfits that were so low-cut that her breasts didn't really need to be further exposed. To finish the spread, the *Bazaar* art director had plucked a shot

Von Wangenheim had done of Gia and another model in the studio several days after the Citicorp session: a nude in which Gia appeared wearing only a veil and some shade of lipstick attributed to Revlon.

It wasn't uncommon at all for European fashion magazines to print nudes, but rarely were the shots so provocative and so celebratory of the face and figure of one unknown woman. Gia had "the best tits in the business," Chris von Wangenheim would later say; her figure was "unbeatable." The pictures were "page-stoppers."

"For me, a good fashion photograph makes a promise it can never keep," Von Wangenheim would explain. "By the sheer fact of being printed it appears to be an attainable truth, when, in fact, it is an individual projection of a photographer ... Fashion pictures are ephemeral. Some have great timeliness and draw the reader in, but do not hold up as photographs ... I can make a page-stopper for a magazine, let's say, by turning models upside down when all the others are upright. But it's meaningless. I say 'wow,' but when I look closely, I realize it's nonsense. It's a page-stopper, but after a moment my mind throws it away."

On such meaninglessness great modeling careers are borne.

6

Ciao for Now

Italy still had a long way to go before making good on its threat to dethrone France as the epicenter of the fashion industry. Paris had been Paris for a long time. Royalty had gone there to be outfitted for centuries before anybody ever dreamed of the so-called "collections," during which top competing couture houses (and later leading ready-to-wear manufacturers) scheduled their seasonal fashion shows so they could be conveniently viewed as one week-long event. The twice-yearly fashion horse-race was still etched onto the calendars of rich ladies, fashion editors and retailers as a reason they *had to be* in Paris. "High Fashion" still meant Yves St. Laurent and the design houses of Chanel, Givenchy and Dior.

Still, there was no disputing that the recent successes by Valentino in high fashion, as well as by Giorgio Armani and Gianni Versace in designer ready-to-wear, meant *something*. And Valentino's business partner, Giancarlo Giammetti, may have found support for his bold industry assessments before the 1978 collections: "In Paris, the couture is so old, it's ridiculous," he told *WWD*. "The French ... are so ego-centric and so damn pretentious, you can throw up ... and New York is so today, it becomes yesterday too fast. Every six months in New York, it's a new world ... the future of fashion does rest with the Italian designers."

Italy's role in the beauty–industrial complex was changing,

its lot rapidly improving. Where the country was once looked to only as a source of inspiration and fabric—both of which were used to manufacture goods elsewhere in more businesslike environments—the Italians were getting a little better at combining art and industry. They were successfully courting the rich ladies, the fashion press and the buyers from major department stores, boutiques and catalog houses. And they were using Italy as part of the sales pitch.

Twice a year in Rome, the Italian fashion world threw an extravagant affair to celebrate the resurgence of the *alta moda*—their version of the *haute couture*—and the increasing popularity of all Italian clothing exports. The Italian collections had become the playground of the fashion photographers and models themselves, who had, for some time, considered Italy the place where their talents were truly appreciated. In Italy, fashion photographers were exalted as the new visionary artists they secretly wanted to be. In Italy, fashion models—usually imported from Scandinavia or, now, America (since no self-respecting Italian girl would do such a thing)—were worshiped as goddesses of the "new womanhood."

Many photographers, models and stylists had begun their careers in Italy, where there were weekly and small monthly magazines that would take chances on new people and new ideas. This aesthetic fashion minor league had started in the late sixties, when the Italian edition of *Vogue* became the most visually imaginative magazine in the world. *Vogue Italia* was driven to new heights by freelance editor and human fashion statement Anna Piaggi, who did her first *Vogue* shots with a young Chris von Wangenheim and went on to become perhaps the most influential figure in Italian fashion with her theatrical entrances, her junk jewelry and her impetuous eye. In a way, she filled the gap left in the fashion magazine world when Diana Vreeland was dismissed by American *Vogue*.

During Gia's first weeks of immersion into the top end of the business, she had little knowledge of, or real interest in, this kind of fashion minutiae. She went where she was told to go by the agency; she worked for the clients who booked her. She had some idea of photographers she might like working with, because she had noticed their pictures in the magazines—especially Helmut Newton and Guy Bourdin, older photographers whose dark, erotic fashion photos represented a visual lineage to Chris von Wangenheim's work. She had met a few top models and hair and makeup people, who had tried to give her some pointers. And the people at the agency were doing their best to explain what was happening to her professionally.

But Gia had a short attention span. And her quick success had already shown her how far one could get in the business without knowing very much about what was going on. She knew how to get a rise out of the photographer once she got on the set. She knew how to improvise and make people laugh. She struck poses that were innovative because she really didn't care to know the more standard ones.

And she got a lot of mileage out of her relative-rags-to-relative-riches tale of "it seems like just yesterday I was working in a hoagie shop." There was a system somewhere out there, a machinery that had been "discovering" girls like Gia for decades. But the job of understanding and oiling that machinery was what she paid her agent twenty percent for. In Rome—or Roma, as the Italians and anyone trying to sound international referred to it—the machinery itself was on display.

Gia had never been out of the country before. And even though her family—when it was still together—had taken some very nice trips, including one to California, she had never traveled first class. The one-hundred-year-old Grand Hotel, off Piazza della Repubblica in the largely baroque section of Rome near the train station, was first class in the manner expected by European royalty—with exquisite ballrooms, crystal chandeliers, marble baths and a split-level bar, where afternoon tea was served daily. The Grand was where most of the imported *fashionistas* stayed: many of the fashion shows were held there and it served as the backdrop to most of the *alta moda* photographs.

On the day Gia arrived, the Grand was experiencing an Italian phenomenon as old as the Bernini sculptures that dotted the area around the hotel: a wildcat hotel worker's strike. It began only hours before Valentino unveiled his collection featuring the new "melon shape"—dresses rounded at the padded shoulders and hemline.

The strike meant that, for at least a day, Gia would be unable to take advantage of the legendary—and legendarily abused—hospitality of Italian *Bazaar* owner Giuseppe Della Schiava, known to colleagues as Peponi. Della Schiava seemed willing to do anything to get the best new models and photographers to come work for him. He had Brooke Shields signed to the only exclusive editorial contract in the modeling business. And while most American photographers would be expected to cut costs by using local hair and makeup people when shooting in Italy, Della Schiava would pay for Arthur Elgort and Chris von Wangenheim to bring in their favorite crews and run up extravagant restaurant and bar tabs. It was worth it to him. He didn't mind being an easy touch if the pictures were special and he got to meet the prettiest girls in the world.

Photographers were perpetually searching for the next easy touch: the person who would pay more than anyone else or give more freedom than ever before. Start-up magazines and companies upgrading their images were traditional easy touches. Peponi Della Schiava was a little bit of both.

Della Schiava was not a typical fashion magazine publisher and Italian *Bazaar* was not a typical fashion magazine. Fashion magazines were usually owned by companies that expected to make their money by profitably publishing magazines: profits came from advertising sales, as well as subscription and single-copy newsstand receipts. Della Schiava was a forty-year-old adman who had inherited his wife's father's textile manufacturing business, one of the largest in Italy. Before purchasing *Bazaar* in 1974, he had been one of Italian *Vogue*'s single biggest advertisers—Italian textile companies, besides taking out their own ads, often partially underwrote ads for manufacturers and designers using their fabric. In a series of events that was every magazine publisher's worst nightmare, Della Schiava had become incensed at Italian *Vogue* because he felt its editorial coverage wasn't sufficiently supportive of his advertisements. He pulled his ads, bought *Bazaar,* and set out to topple *Vogue*'s upscale hegemony in Italy. Soon after, he negotiated with Hearst International to start an Italian edition of *Cosmopolitan.*

Cosmo was meant to be profitable. But Della Schiava ran *Bazaar* like a vanity publication. He didn't really hire a staff: he oversaw much of the work himself, and Lizzette Kattan did the legwork. He didn't seem to care how much money *Bazaar* lost, as long as it brought greater glory to Italian-made fabrics and offered him an international *dolce vita* that was far more interesting than the life of a Milan-based rag merchant. He had upgraded the magazine by avoiding Italian photographers—the best of whom were already committed to Italian *Vogue*—and flying to America to round up the best young photographers in New York. He set up in a room at the Pierre and sent for all the up-and-comers. It wasn't long before his magazine was considered one of the most visually exciting in the industry. Nor was it long before he had bent beyond recognition what few rules the business had.

At Italian *Bazaar,* photographers and models often went out and shot the editorial and the ads at the same time. For special collections issues, this meant the production of what was called *groupage*—advertising sections of ten or twenty running pages, produced by the magazine's photographers and documenting designers' entire collections. The process was probably no more questionable than *Vogue*'s Must Lists and other paid editorial mentions. But it was a very foreign way of doing business and Della Schiava's detractors thought it was sleazy.

Gia spent two days getting over jet lag and adjusting to the strange new world of a country where she knew nobody, but a lot of people seemed to know her. Her pictures in *Bazaar* had preceded her, which made her even more interesting than usual to the legendary Italian playboys: a group of several dozen rich young men whose obsessions with American models were so well-established and their connections so impeccable that the Italian agencies actually alerted them when new girls were arriving so they knew which flight to meet or hotel lobby to hound. They didn't just chase the hot new models either. It wasn't uncommon for a complete unknown, making an exploratory trip to Milan, to be greeted at her cheap *pensione* by a phone message or dinner invitation by a playboy trolling for his next catch.

"That word *playboy* means a different thing in Italy," explained Giorgio Repossi, a proud member of the Milan-based fraternity, who was a marketing director for the company that published the magazine *Linnea Italiana* during the seventies. *"Playboy* is like a charming man, not a no-no. In America, playboy just wants to put himself inside something, *ta-ta-ta-ta.* The Italian playboy, we *fall in love* with the girls, not one night only. Sex in America is much more rude and cruel. Is less deep, is just fucking, people use each other. In Italy everything is more romantic. I can also be in bed with ten girls, but *I love these ten girls.*

"The *alta moda* week was the best time for picking up girls, and the Grand Hotel was the best place: it was a continuous party, every night was amusing. And being Peponi's guest was the best. It was like he was renting the whole hotel."

The highlight of the *alta moda* was generally the bash thrown by Riccardo Gay, one of the first and still one of the top model agents in Italy. It was his way of thanking the business for allowing him to book most of the *alta moda* models through his agency.

"Every season for *haute couture* we organize a big party," recalled Gay, "a *dolce vita* party, with different theme. It was really an incredible situation. We make *many* party. I can't remember which theme was which year though."

"I think that was the year with the pajama party," said Kay Mitchell. "You had to wear your pajamas and it was at the Grand Hotel—where, by that point, Eileen Ford would not stay because John Casablancas stayed there. I just remember drinking, and we were in our pajamas, hanging out and giggling—all the photographers, models and agents. Eventually the party got a little rough—rough meaning *playful,* you know. There were these goose down pillows and, anyway, it ended up with feathers from one end of this ballroom to the other, feathers covering the buffet table, everything."

But not everybody was having marvelous fun at the Grand Hotel. "When you have that amount of people there, ordering foie gras, and the magazine is paying for every penny of that," recalled Lizzette Kattan, "no, I was not having that kind of good time. I was there to work. You would hear a lot of stories, but I wasn't always really aware of what was going on. You have to realize, we're in Rome with all these people. We had to do five hundred pages in ten days, that's a lot of work. Sometimes we had ten photographers working every day, in different places, some in studio, some on the street. At that point it wasn't the money that was involved, the important thing was the result that you got."

The first shooting Gia had to do was editorial shots of Andrea Odicini's collection. According to *WWD,* the collection included "several easy-to-wear shapes ... these are clothes that women who admire the French couture will buy." According to Chris von Wangenheim, the collection ranged from passable to unwearable, so something besides the clothes would have to make the photographs interesting.

Gia had done nothing to hide her crush on Juli Foster, a rising model who had been discovered a year earlier while waiting tables in a restaurant near the Wilhelmina office, and had also been brought to Rome by *Bazaar.* Von Wangenheim, who had always been interested in homoerotic themes, decided to use the energy between the two models to his advantage. He improvised a series of photographs in a Grand Hotel suite that amounted to a lesbian seduction sequence.

In the first shot, Juli Foster looked longingly at the camera while Gia looked longingly at her: from that angle, the two dark-haired girls almost appeared to be twins. In the second, Gia washed Juli's hair—carefully, since they were both dressed in crepe tunic tops and lace skirts—in the tub of one of the Grand Hotel's exquisite bathrooms. In the third shot Juli, fully dressed and sitting on a bed, reached for a nude Gia emerging from behind a dressing screen. Gia's outfit, which all agreed looked better on a hanger than on a human being, dangled from the screen: Juli's high heel was pressed deep into Gia's naked hip. And in the last shot, Juli and Gia, wearing only high heels, appeared to be about to kiss. Juli's hand was over Gia's breast and their eyes were locked.

On Monday, the same clothes were photographed for *groupage* by Patrick Demarchelier, with Gia, Kim Alexis and several other models. Demarchelier was a bearish, bearded Frenchman who spoke little English. He was also one of the few up-and-coming New York–based photographers who was married. For that reason, among others, he had a reputation for being more businesslike than his colleagues and less experimental. Demarchelier shot the models drinking bottles and bottles of champagne, buzzily flirting and playing with the hotel waiters in the restaurant. In the evening, Gia did a series of beauty shots with Von Wangenheim.

On Tuesday, Gia was shot by Arthur Elgort for a feature that could have been called "girls of the *alta moda.*" The theme of the series was the models *Bazaar* had brought to work the collections: one picture per girl, but with her name and some biographical information in the caption. Such attention to the identities of the models was rare in fashion magazines. Models were the only major people involved in a sitting who did not regularly get a credit (except for the fashion editors, who were generally magazine staff members). For the model, the picture itself was considered the credit. But the use of the model's name (American *Vogue* and *Harper's Bazaar* occasionally gave "worn by" credits) was becoming more important as *public* recognition of models began to grow and matter: a trend that editors, photographers and art directors found somewhat disconcerting.

"I remember being in Rome with Christie Brinkley on a Chris von Wangenheim trip for *Vogue Patterns,*" recalled art director Marc Balet. "We were sitting on a hillside and these girls came up to Christie and they *knew her name.* I remember being so shocked that somebody knew a model's name. It was so *unbelievable* to me."

Bazaar ended up using Elgort shots of eleven models, most of whom were destined for major careers. Kelly Emberg graced the opening spread, followed by Nancy Donahue, one of the industry's new brassy blondes, and Shaun Casey. The next spreads included Lise Ryall, Donna Sexton, Michelle Stevens, Kim Charlton, Juli Foster and Gia—who was described in her caption as "aggressive and perfect."

On Wednesday, Gia worked with Demarchelier again, this time to produce a *groupage* for designer Andre Laug. The simple, straightforward shots were churned out quickly and efficiently, since the designer was standing right on the set watching everything, and everyone had a seven-thirty plane to catch to Paris. There they checked into the Hotel Meurice on the Rue de Rivoli, just across from the Tuileries Gardens and down the street from the Louvre. The eighteenth-century hotel, with its salons copied from Versailles, its celestial-ceilinged lounge and its historic Suite 108 (once occupied by the deposed king of Spain, Alfonso XIII, and now housing Salvador Dalí) was a gilty pleasure of French excess.

In Rome, it was easy for Italian *Bazaar* to get its pick of the clothes to photograph. Not all the magazines bothered to cover the *alta moda,* and even *WWD* only covered the Valentino show grandly: the other designers were relegated to a small, page 11 roundup story. Paris was another matter. Every magazine covered the *haute couture,* and access to the one-of-a-kind garments—some of which were hurriedly stitched together just before the model was pushed down the runway—was fiercely contested. *Bazaar* was pretty far down in the pecking order, so Lizzette Kattan and her crew of imported *fashionistas* got the clothes very late at night, if at all. This was tough on photographers like Arthur Elgort, who liked to shoot in available light, and fine with Chris von Wangenheim, who preferred to photograph late at night.

Von Wangenheim took Gia and model Regine—who bore a striking resemblance to Wilhelmina Cooper—out into the Paris night to shoot a handful of pieces from the well-received collections by Yves St. Laurent (whose "high chic" theme had set the tone for the week) and Marc Bohan for Christian Dior. Once again, Von Wangenheim chose a highly suggestive lesbian theme. The opener showed Gia and Regine in an alleyway lit from behind by car lights. Gia was playing the coquettish fem, her gown pulled down to expose one shoulder, while Regine looked the butch seductress—or as butch as one could look in a Dior blazer, slacks and a satin top. The other spreads were variations on the theme with Gia and Regine posing on the Rue di Rivoli, staring longingly into each other's eyes.

After three days in Paris, *Bazaar* brought a smaller group back to Milan to shoot what was left. With French photographer Jacques Malignon, Gia and Juli Foster spent several days doing a twelve-page *groupage* for Lancetti. In the evenings, the group went out to sample Milan, Lizzette and Peponi's home turf: to dine at fashionable restaurants like Torre di Pisa and dance at clubs like Nepentha, the Milanese version of Studio 54.

Milan was Italy's necessary evil: a crowded, cosmopolitan city where daily executive work could actually be accomplished. For that reason it was often overlooked by tourists—who, if they came at all, came for a day or two to shop and visit the Duomo and Da Vinci's crumbling "The Last Supper"—and scoffed at by those Italians who didn't need to do business there. But Milan (or *Milano*) was, much more than Rome, the place where fledgling fashion people lived. Most of Italy's magazines were based in Milan, as was its growing ready-to-wear industry: the manufacturers had recently moved their twice-yearly collections to Milan from Florence. Milan was one of Italy's most expensive cities, but it was still far cheaper than Paris or London, and offered easier train access to jobs all over Europe than Rome did.

Because of its growing popularity, Milan was developing a local economy for fledgling *fashionistas* from around the world. It had a number of *pensioni, residencias* and *albergi* (each an official Italian government designation for small places of lodging) that were becoming known as "model hotels": places where every room was filled with photographers, models, designers and stylists waiting for a big break. Among the first model hotels were Arena, where Anjelica Huston stayed, and the legendary Residence Clothilde, where everyone from Gianni Versace through Brigitte Nielsen lived while trying to break into the business. The owner of one model hotel became so familiar with her role as surrogate mother and business adviser that she opened her own agency, called Why Not?

It was while staying at the small hotels that models made friends before they had to worry if people were being nice to them just because they were famous. Milan tested a model's resolve, let her know what she was getting into. It was an experience that the last few generations of girls shared: sitting in their crowded *pensione* room, waiting for a photographer or agent to call, dreaming of a sitting for *Linnea Italiana* that might lead to a bigger Italian magazine and maybe, in a year or two, a shot at American *Vogue*.

Gia's quick rise had excluded her from that entire experience. She had come to Milan a success. The eighteen-year-old was by no means a supermodel, but she had vaulted over the barriers that held back ninety-five percent of the young women who wanted to be models. The new way of thinking in the modeling business was that this type of meteoric rise was good fortune. The old way of thinking—to which nobody dared admit lest they be branded unmodern—was that starving in Milan or Paris or New York was probably good for a model-in-training. It never hurt to know how many other "prettiest girls in town" there really were. Without taking the ladder rung by rung, it wasn't always possible to understand the modeling business for what it really was: very glamorous at the top, lucratively tedious in the middle and pathetically sleazy at the bottom.

And modeling was *extremely* bottom-heavy—perhaps even more than professional athletics, to which it was often compared. There were some other important differences between athletes and models, as well. Athletes could develop, both mentally and physically, and they could enhance performance with wisdom as some of their natural gifts faded. It was nearly impossible for a model to get much *better* at what she did, and career longevity was not only unlikely but *programmed to be impossible*. And a model's hour under the strobe wasn't the same as an athlete's moment in the sun: it lacked that essential heroism, the burst of pride in reached potential.

Even in the pony leagues, a home run was a home run and the moment could be transcendent. But even at the highest echelon of modeling, it was always a job. Because you looked the way you did, a lot of people you didn't know would do anything to sleep with you. Your job was to encourage those feelings, allow that encouragement to sell products and draw a commission from the earning power of the tease. Athletes got paid to play a game they loved: models got paid to play a game that some of them could tolerate, and the rest simply loathed. Professional athletics could be a career; modeling was, even for the top girls, almost always a *phase* to be survived.

Gia left Milan on Friday, August 4, flying to Frankfurt and changing planes for New York. Since the *Bazaar* all-expenses-paying ended with her return air ticket, she paid for the twenty-dollar cab ride from JFK to Manhattan herself, scribbling down the amount in the expense record section of her Wilhelmina datebook—a practice she had been told would help her at tax time if she paid careful attention to it. When she returned home, she also spent some time on the kind of visual bookkeeping that many models did.

In a Wilhelmina book with blank pages, she pasted some of the pictures she had collected on her trip. Most of them were Polaroids: photographers generally took a number of test Polaroids before shooting on print film, saving several for the client and distributing the others as gifts, mementos. These became the artifacts created by each job for those who actually did the work. When the shooting was over, the Polaroids were the only real evidence of the day's labor. The pictures themselves still had to be developed, and they usually were owned by the client anyway. The Polaroids were the instant gratification, and they belonged to whoever they were bestowed upon.

The more compulsive *fashionistas* pasted the Polaroids directly into the date books they carried with them everywhere: others kept separate books. For these models, stylists and editors, the pictures were a way to jog a memory that a notation like "Paris, Dior show" didn't sufficiently describe.

Italian *Bazaar*'s Lizzette Kattan put her pictures right in her regular datebook, a practice she had begun as a Ford model. For July 26, she pasted a Polaroid of Patrick Demarchelier, Gia and the crew on the Andre Laug shots. For July 28, she pasted a Polaroid of Peponi leering at the nude shots of Gia in *Bazaar,* and another of Gia holding a picture of Peponi. Gia had written "I love you both" underneath one of the shots.

Gia started pasting her Polaroids, one to a page, in a separate book. She also scribbled down, on a page further in, some of the phone numbers and addresses she had picked up in Europe. These were European agents to call the next time she was in Rome or Paris and wanted to drum up extra work. Someone at Dior wanted to see her the next time she was in for the collections. Lizzette Kattan wanted her to have her private numbers in New York and Milan, and Mr. Della Schiava's home numbers in Milan and at his island retreat on Capri. Peponi's castle was where the *Bazaar* crowd went for vacation. In the traditional European style, they took off the entire month of August.

Because they had grown fond of Gia, Lizzette and Peponi invited her to join them on Capri if her schedule allowed. The invitation would, of course, include all of her travel expenses. It all sounded a little more elaborate than what she had planned for her vacation. She was supposed to spend Labor Day week in Atlantic City with her friends from Philly. It was the traditional end-of-summer ritual for Philadelphians—topped off by the Miss America pageant—and it was being made more interesting by the recent opening of Atlantic City's first casino, Resorts International. The casino was reshaping many opinions about the shore town: Gia's father was planning to sell out his Philadelphia holdings and move his entire operation to the Boardwalk area.

The *Bazaar* invitation left Gia in an enviable bind. She had to decide between a week "down the shore" and her second free trip to Italy in as many months.

With less than a day to recover from her European trip, Gia picked up where she had left off in New York—the daily grind of appointments, jobs and chores. Since she was becoming established, the jobs were getting bigger, the appointments more important, and her time more valuable: when jobs got canceled at the last minute, she was paid for the privilege of holding her day open. During her first week back, a *Vogue* sitting with Irving Penn was canceled and paid. With the ante so increased, it was also beginning to matter more if she was late. And she was *often* late. The agency had already given her a little talk on the subject. It was unprofessional, they explained, and nobody wanted to hire someone who was unprofessional.

The agency was also a little concerned by the nudity in the shots Gia had done with Von Wangenheim. It wasn't that the pictures were inappropriate for European magazines. They just wanted Gia to understand that if she did too many nudes in Europe, it could mean problems with more conservative clients in the states. There were many American catalogs and manufacturers that worried about being associated with a young woman known for posing nude. Apparently, when a nipple or pubic hair was exposed rather than hinted at, a girl's visual virginity was spoiled. The same executives who wanted to wander onto the set in the hopes of catching a glimpse of the models dressing fretted that their company's image could be compromised by a model who took her clothes off for the camera.

And the top people at Wilhelmina knew that, besides his work for the fashion magazines, Von Wangenheim was becoming a favorite with art directors at *Playboy* and *Oui*— the European men's magazine *Playboy* was spinning off in America to compete with *Penthouse*. *Oui* especially was beginning to understand how fruitful a relationship with a photographer like Von Wangenheim or Helmut Newton could be: their kinkiest fashion concepts, rejected by their regular fashion clients, could be reborn as erotic fantasy sequences in men's magazines. It was often a particular photographer's comfortable relationship with a particular model—and not the model's deep desire to pose nude—that led to pictorials in these magazines. It was also the casualness fostered by these comfortable relationships that led models to sign releases for pictures they might later regret.

Usually, the problem wasn't the suggestive pictures so much as the "context." As Gia had to explain to her mother—like so many other models before her—nudes in European magazines were "different." Europeans had a more "sophisticated" concept of what nudity meant. Only in American men's magazines were nude pictures of women considered smut: not because they were pornographic pictures, but because they were printed with pornographic intent.

"When she first started, *Playboy* wanted her to do a spread and she wouldn't do it," recalled Kathleen Sperr. "She told me you had to be very careful. In Europe, her tits are hanging out all over. But if you do it as part of a 'fashion statement,' it's acceptable. But you can't let it hang out in a sex way."

After Gia returned from Europe, it was becoming clearer that her new life and her old life were going to have trouble coexisting. The sudden need to choose between a week in Atlantic City and a week in Capri was just the beginning.

It was easy to understand why so many of the *fashionistas* were, for all intents and purposes, runaways—people who had left their small towns for New York with no thoughts of ever coming back. The fashion world was its own huge, dysfunctional family and a very demanding one: it was a hard life to reconcile with parents and siblings and friends back home. For a while, the people from Gia's treated her like she was away at fashion boot camp and correctly assumed that she was too busy to stay in touch. But now, people were beginning to seek her out—because she was becoming successful, and because she was the only one they knew who had a place in Manhattan. Some of her old friends were jealous of her, some wanted to be closer to her than ever before. Some assumed that she would mistrust *anyone* who seemed overly friendly, so they avoided her to make sure she couldn't accuse them of fair-weather friendship. Others just had completely unrealistic ideas about what Gia's success really meant.

"I remember having lunch with Gia in a restaurant by Bloomingdale's that first summer," said John Long. "She was with this hanger-on, some Philly person trying to follow her to New York on her coattails. She kept asking, 'Can my other friends stay at your place? Can you get us on the guest list at Studio 54?'

"And Gia was trying to explain that there *was* no guest list. That sometimes you would go and the doorman would ask who you were with and then point 'You, you, and him,' and literally break up the parties anyway. Gia couldn't *guarantee* to get anybody in—except herself. But the girl kept asking and finally Gia just said, 'Tell yourself whatever you need to hear, you're the only one listening.' "

Gia's friend Toni O'Connor, growing tired of her life dealing Quaaludes in Philadelphia, decided to move to New York, encouraged by Gia's success. "She talked me into coming to New York, getting an apartment and going to acting school," O'Connor recalled, "and then she had to take all these jobs that were in Italy and I'd never get to see her. I was really lonely. She was about the only person I knew in New York.

"I'd hang out at Studio 54. Jack Nicholson tried to put the make on her at Studio and I flipped out. He was in love with Gia, he worshiped the ground she walked on. She got off on it. She was like 'I can't stand him, he's an *old man.*' She really laughed about it. We went a couple times and he really pursued her. I got more upset than anything because it was like, Jack Nicholson, *come on,* he was like *a major star.* How can I compete with Jack Nicholson?"

Gia's friendship with Sharon Beverly was also growing rockier. "We just weren't getting along," Sharon recalled. "We would just argue about everything and anything. One time we had a really big fight because she thought that I wasn't happy for her. I *was,* but I was scared for her at the same time and I just didn't want to encourage it one hundred percent. So when she would come home and she would say, 'I saw this photographer,' inside I felt 'That's really good for her because that's what she's up here for, but I'm really afraid' ... Also, she was starting to work a lot and I wasn't. She started getting good jobs and she felt funny about it, felt a little guilty."

It wasn't just that Gia had more money than she or her friends had ever had before. Her trip to Europe had been a guided tour through the many ways that money—real money—could be spent. For years, she had observed, and occasionally even lived, the high life in Philadelphia. But now she was beginning to see the difference between *regional* standards of luxury and international standards: a new sky was the limit. After her return, she started going to Studio 54 more often, occasionally even on weeknights. She also began buying herself some clothes. These were, after all, *business* expenses. There was no place to make better business contacts than at Studio 54, and she had to be able to look the part.

And the way she looked—her face, her body—would undoubtedly make a big difference in the kinds of bookings she got. So $725 for a membership to the European Health Spa seemed like a reasonable expense. Especially when she could now cover the entire fee in a day or two of catalog shootings, and still have plenty left over for a $100 gift for her agency booker and the $10 admission at Studio, where she never had to pay for drinks. Her rent was only $445 a month, an amount she was now easily clearing. On Friday, September 1, for example, she picked up an agency check for $1,382. Then she got a cab and caught her plane to Rome, where she connected for Naples and then Capri. Atlantic City could wait.

When she arrived on the bucolic island off Italy's southwestern coast, Gia was installed in one of the twenty-two bedrooms in Mr. Della Schiava's castle. She was also promptly introduced to a friend of Peponi's—an older man who apparently had been admiring her from a distance during the *alta moda* in Rome. The sixty-year-old Francesco di Siricinano was Italian royalty: like a lot of people on the buying end of the fashion world, he was from some obscure royal family with tons of money to waste and several generations waiting in line to waste it. Gia quickly dubbed him The Prince. "Everyone knew The Prince was in love with her," recalled *Bazaar* fashion editor Lizzette Kattan. "He was mesmerized by her. That first day they were going to be together, we were saying it was D-Day. He was taking her out to see the island."

By the end of the week, Gia was being made to feel one of the *Bazaar* family, a high-profile position in fashionable Italy. In the evening, after dinner, they would stroll Capri's busy streets and sometimes be photographed together by paparazzi. Gia became more affectionate around Lizzette. She began to refer to her as "Mommy." At the same time, The Prince became more affectionate around Gia. He gave her a cross to wear around her neck. She began to think he was serious when he said he wanted to marry her.

The week after she returned to the States from her whirlwind vacation, Gia got to go to Atlantic City after all. She came not as Gia Carangi, who had been going "down the shore" for years, but as Gia, top model, on assignment for *Vogue*. She and Lisa Vale, another former Philadelphian, modeled glamorous gowns in the Resorts casino, and then went out on the Boardwalk and tried to look not so much overheated as *protected from the freezing cold* by their $10,000 furs. It was a balmy September afternoon, but the shots were for December.

7

Model War Zone

With the collections and August vacation well behind it, the fashion world settled into its annual fall work marathon. But the fall of 1978 was more hectic than usual, with more than its share of peculiar plot twists.

The New York Times had been on strike for several weeks, which meant that 1.6 million copies of the crucial fall "Fashions of the Times" supplements were still sitting in a warehouse rather than tempting buyers with over 150 pages of expensive ads. The papers that were published teemed with news about a murder that doubled as a modeling business scandal. The owner of the small My Fair Lady agency, well-known horse trainer and model chaser Buddy Jacobson, was accused of shooting, bludgeoning, slicing and burning the remains of Jack Tupper, a bar owner on the Upper East Side. Tupper was supposedly having an affair with Melanie Cain, the former Ford model with whom Jacobson had opened the agency. On the same day as the murder—purely coincidentally, as it turned out—another My Fair Lady model fell to her death from the balcony of the apartment she was renting from Jacobson.

All this just made life in the upper echelons of fashion—which Gia was in the process of entering—additionally chaotic. But since the "Model Wars" were now entering their second year, the agencies had grown to expect that even normal days would have a baseline level of insanity.

*　　*　　*

The so-called model wars had officially begun in the spring of 1977, but they had their roots in the time-honored economic traditions of the beauty-industrial complex. In the history of the fashion world, many large companies had made sizable fortunes. But few so-called "creative" people had become really rich and hardly any of them really expected to. Being fabulous and living fabulously was supposed to be enough.

There had been a few exceptions to this rule. A handful of designers received handsome salaries—and sometimes even partnerships—from the manufacturers that employed them. Halston was one of the first, signing a much-publicized deal for $16 million in 1973 for the five-year-old company he had started after leaving Bergdorf Goodman. Some very commercial photographers commanded high fees; a few really hard-working models could boast annual incomes of over $100,000 during their peak years; and even some hairstylists had used their fame to build profitable salon chains or hair care product lines. Random House had reportedly paid Way Bandy a $100,000 advance for his makeup book. But most of the creative people weren't really rich, they just lived rich lifestyles during the years they worked for the top clients.

But when the designers started to become businessmen in the mid-seventies—with Ralph Lauren and Calvin Klein following Halston—their friends in fashion began to take notice. And soon photographers, models, hair and makeup people became more interested in making their own money. They wanted contracts, long-term commitments: Avedon was reported to have a lucrative one with *Vogue*—it was said that the magazine paid one million dollars a year to keep him from shooting editorial fashion for anyone else—and several models had signed with perfume companies to be the Babe girl or the Charlie girl. They wanted to know why photographers and models couldn't get residuals if pictures were reused: most fashion photographs were still shot for flat, one-time fees that included *all rights*.

And then Johnny Casablancas showed up in New York and kicked the modeling industry in its perfect butt.

Casablancas, then thirty-five, was a man with a European heart and an American brain: born in Spain, raised in Manhattan. His father had been a banker, his mother a former model for the Spanish couture house Balenciaga, and his family money came from an international textile-machine concern. After a brief first marriage and life in Brazil, he moved to Paris and fell in love with former Miss Denmark and budding model Jeanette Christiansen. Casablancas opened his own small agency, Elysee 3, and learned what he could about the arcane business of finding beautiful women and getting them paid to be photographed. While doing so, he became friendly with many young photographers, even briefly representing some of them. His photographer friends included Alex Chatelain, Arthur Elgort, Mike Reinhardt, John Stember, Patrick Demarchelier and Jacques Malignon—the core group that moved from Paris to New York in the mid-seventies and became known as the French Mafia when they began to control so much of the city's lucrative photography work.

Casablancas' first agency ran into financial trouble. He opened a second, Elite, in 1970 with Elysee's three best models. The new agency was to be smaller and more scouting-oriented than agencies had ever been. Before John Casablancas made searching for gorgeous girls a full-time job, most model agencies chose from whoever came through their doors or won their occasional contests.

With his reputation as a spotter and molder of new talent, Casablancas was prized by the top American agencies, which were run by women who did everything they could to make modeling appear to be a profession like any other. The Wilhelminas and Eileen Fords were just as happy to let someone else do the dirty work of "seasoning" young models: which often meant teaching those "valuable lessons" about what society really wanted from its beautiful women. A charming, flirtatious European man seemed a more appropriate person to supervise such instruction, far from the judging eyes of the American press or the girls' parents.

For years, Casablancas' relationship with agencies in other countries was typical of the way modeling people respected each other's turfs. Then he toppled the system he had mastered by opening an Elite office in New York in May of 1977 and going into competition with the American agencies that had once been his sister operations. Casablancas hired the two top bookers and the financial controller from Eileen

Ford: her legendary response was to send each of them copies of the New Testament with Jesus' words to Judas underlined in red. Elite lured away top models from all the agencies with promises of higher fees, lower agency commissions, guaranteed six-figure incomes and a freer working environment. And Casablancas's methods were anything but maternal: one of the only agency heads who would regularly go dancing in the top nightspots, he did business wherever the models were. Stories began circulating of Ford and Wilhelmina girls going to Studio 54 and never coming back.

The first thirteen models that jumped to Elite cost Ford $500,000 in annual billings and Wilhelmina $400,000. So Willie and Mrs. Ford promptly sued Casablancas, setting off what would forever be referred to as the model wars after *New York* magazine used that title for its cover story, subtitled "How the Top Agencies Buy and Sell the Most Beautiful Girls in the World." The article estimated that New York's model agencies were grossing a combined $15 million a year. A career breakthrough for one of *New York*'s newest writers, Anthony Haden-Guest, "Model Wars" was the first even *semi*-serious look at the industry—which had always been viewed as frivolous at best and hardly worth the attention of financial reporters.

Eileen Ford hired Roy Cohn to sue Casablancas for $7.5 million and tried to get an injunction against her former staff members. Wilhelmina took another tactic, suing Casablancas for $4 million and then suing Iman, one of the models who had defected, to see if a court would uphold the standard, and vaguely worded, letter of agency as a binding contract. (A New York court eventually ordered Iman to return to Wilhelmina—by then a moot point, since she and basketball star Spencer Haywood were expecting a child and she couldn't work.)

Besides the bruising of egos and the shifting of talent, Casablancas' immediate impact in New York was to plant the idea that anything was possible. The hard and fast rules of the business—which had, for years, largely been determined by the women and gay men who controlled modeling in America—were being challenged by a lusty heterosexual male. "Perhaps we will have to hire a pimp," Wilhelmina's husband Bruce Cooper coolly joked to *New York,* as if men who lusted after models had been unknown to him before Casablancas opened in New York.

And then, just six months after Casablancas had opened, the other high-heel dropped. If there had been any doubt before that modeling was, like everything else, about to lose its virginity (or illusion of virginity) in the seventies, the January 1978 *Sports Illustrated* swimsuit issue put an end to it. The uproar caused by one picture of Cheryl Tiegs reinforced the new truth that the way *straight men* perceived fashion models would determine the future of the business.

Tiegs, a veteran *Glamour* and *Mademoiselle* girl-next-door, posed in a one-piece fishnet suit rendered transparent when wet. And millions of American men went berserk for a shot far less risqué than those appearing regularly in the tamest of men's magazines, or even in the women's magazines purchased monthly by their wives and girlfriends. The picture became a best-selling poster and Tiegs made the cover of *Time* magazine—which confirmed her as the "girl of the moment" whether the modeling industry thought she was or not. Suddenly it seemed like prudish folly to scoff at the prurient interests of straight men toward fashion models.

To add insult to injury, the February 1978 issue of the short-lived women's magazine *Viva* included a photo-story on Casablancas and his models entitled "Invasion of the Beauty Snatcher," which doubled as a Fiorucci fashion section. Chris von Wangenheim did the pictures (the magazine's fashion editor was Anna Wintour, who, a decade later, would be editor-in-chief of British and then American *Vogue*) and the opener showed Casablancas holding an unwrapped box containing a model in a tiny bikini. On the next pages, models Christie Brinkley, Rachel Ward and Anna Anderson starred in a send-up of the industry reaction to Elite. "People want to know why every model alive wants to join one of Johnny's agencies!" read the final caption. "The parties, *mon petit chou,* the parties are not to be believed." The powers that had been were not amused.

Largely because of Casablancas, the top ad rate for models had doubled in two years, to $1,500, and then soared to $2,000 after *Time* reported that figure as Tiegs' day rate. And that day rate, which once covered all rights in perpetuity to the shots from a sitting, now bought far less: generally three months' usage in one medium, so if clients wanted to use an advertising picture longer or turn a print ad into a billboard, they paid again. One day's work could now conceivably bring in over $10,000 in billings. Because of that, model loyalty and agency cash flow were more mutually dependent than ever. The next generation of top models would be walking down a whole new runway.

The work was coming more steadily to Gia now, and the photographers who seemed like such big deals the first time around were now just regular colleagues. She had a hard time taking it all seriously. When Gia wrote down the names her booker told her over the phone, she got the spellings as close as she could. There was designer "Norman Kamali" and photographer "Chris Vongheim." And, for her first cover try at *Comopolitan* magazine—several different covers were usually shot for each issue of a women's magazine— she would be working with "Scovollo."

Francesco Scavullo was, without question, one of the most celebrated commercial photographers in America—although he was, to a large degree, best known for *being* best known. He had grown up in a working-class neighborhood of Staten Island and later in Manhattan—where his father owned the Central Park Casino supper club—and began as a photographer's assistant at *Vogue*'s studios. He worked mostly with Horst during the forties, and did his first photographs for *Seventeen* in the early fifties. He made his mark in magazine photography with certain innovative lighting techniques, pioneering an umbrella effect that created an unnaturally warm studio light and captured the look of the close-ups in old black and white films—like the Garbo movies he had been drawn to in his youth.

In the mid-fifties, Scavullo began working for *Harper's Bazaar* during its creative heyday under art director Alexey Brodovitch. Unlike Richard Avedon, who left *Bazaar* after that period with Diana Vreeland and diversified his commercial and fine art work, Scavullo had chosen a path with less diversity and a stronger signature. In his work, he turned almost completely to studio portraits: the increasingly sexy cover shots for *Cosmopolitan,* where each year a little more cleavage was visible, and elegant celebrity shots with his trademark lighting and strong hair and makeup statements. In his personal life, he became increasingly flamboyant and public. He was one of the first true fashion personalities and one of the first public men, along with Truman Capote, widely assumed to be gay.

Regardless of the freshness of his photographic eye, Scavullo had established himself as one of the first Beautiful People by positioning himself as the man one paid to be made beautiful. His unique position in the business was a combination of his considerable talent and his willingness to publicize and personify everything that went on in the making of a fashion photograph—the clothing selection, the make-over, the shooting, the pictures themselves and the gossip that filled the long waiting periods of a photographic day. He had also successfully exploited the need every magazine had to elevate its most creative talents to the status of "artist" and "genius" in its monthly world. He was the Picasso of the *Cosmopolitan* reader, his "Scavullo-ization" of subjects as distinct and significant as a cubist still life.

Scavullo was well liked among the models, even though some of the agencies (and his fellow photographers) regarded him with awe and disdain. "For *Cosmo* covers, they just take someone who already has some public acceptance, push the boobs together, fluff the hair and put on a little more makeup than usual," said one agent. "It's more of a drag queen kind of parody look rather than glamour or high fashion at all. It's more of a joke to the business. The rest of the joke is the assumption in New York that the *Cosmo* look is the look that America buys, that all the women in America would rather look like *Cosmo* than *Vogue*. And in my travels, I must admit, I find that there is some truth to that."

While editor Helen Gurley Brown made the final decisions, Scavullo had far more control over who got on *Cosmo*'s cover than any other photographer did with a major magazine. At other fashion publications, several photographers might do cover tries each month, and shots from editorial sessions sometimes became covers. At *Cosmo,* they only chose from the cover tries Scavullo did for them: he had an exclusive contract for all twelve issues.

And the magazine was only one of the ways that Scavullo's favor could lead to immediate mass exposure. He also had a wide variety of other top editorial and advertising clients, and a waiting list of people willing to pay $10,000 for private portraits. He often credited Andy Warhol for opening up his worldview during the sixties, and he had obviously learned Warhol's lessons well: he had made sure that a Scavullo portrait was the required souvenir of everyone's fifteen minutes of fame.

He did this by functioning as more than just a photographer. He really was "mad about women," in a way only someone who didn't sleep with them could be. And unlike other photographers—who felt that when a model got too big, she distracted attention from the true artists of the trade—Scavullo was perfectly happy to publicly gush over whichever model was of the minute. It was, in fact, difficult to find a major magazine story about a beautiful woman that didn't include an assessment of her appeal from Scavullo.

All his name-dropping aside, Scavullo had both the inclination to be kind and loyal when others might be brutal and the power to make that goodwill mean something. He gave second chances and, perhaps because he was operating with a less modern sensibility, he was as likely to discover a new talent as he was to rediscover someone who had reached whatever-happened-to status.

Scavullo's studio was in the first floor of a building on East Sixty-third Street: he lived on the upper floors. The studio was run by Sean Byrnes, a handsome young man who had come into Scavullo's life in 1974 and had quickly become much more than a typical photographer's assistant or studio manager. Byrnes was credited, in everything emanating from the studio, as fashion editor, styling editor, beauty editor or photo editor. It was an unusual relationship—most assistants took the demanding jobs for a year or two as stepping stones to something else—but a successful one. Since Scavullo had to take so many pictures and give more interviews than all the other photographers in New York combined, having a permanent right-hand man seemed prudent.

Scavullo was quite taken with Gia. It was his job to be quite taken on a fairly regular basis, but Gia was different.

She did not fit into any of the usual model categories that the other girls did.

"I was mad about her," Scavullo recalled. "She was very candid in front of the camera. She wasn't stylized, she didn't pose. She was like an actress in front of the camera. You got a million pictures that had her head in them. She had her own little way of modeling. She jumped around, you couldn't set your lights and you couldn't hold her still. You had to let her go, you couldn't direct her.

"When I first worked with her, I said, 'Oh, my god, this is like a new colt.' My assistant was running with the light. 'Uchh,' I said, 'this is going to be *work.*' But then I realized how to work with that and I didn't want to tame her down, I wanted her to move around. There are very few models who do that and do it well. With most models who move around, you get bad stuff. With her, you got wonderful stuff . . . it was like you got candid pictures of her and they were *divine.* There is something she had . . . no other girl has got it. I've *never* met a girl who had it. She had the perfect body for modeling: perfect eyes, mouth, hair. And, to me, the perfect attitude: 'I don't give a damn.' So she threw the clothes away, which I *loved.* It was a challenge to photograph her, to follow her."

Gia told her mother all about that first session. "I remember the first time she went to Scavullo," Kathleen Sperr said. "A lot of times they prepare lunch for you. So Scavullo had quiche and Gia said, 'Oh great, that's my favorite dish. My mom makes the best quiche in the world.' And I said, 'Gia, when somebody like *Scavullo* is serving you quiche, you don't tell him that your mom's is better.'

"And she said, 'But it *is.* I don't care. Who's he?' "

Scavullo was shooting with the team that did most of the *Cosmo* covers with him: Way Bandy, and hairstylist Harry King, who Gia hadn't met before. King had developed a reputation in his native Britain during the early seventies before moving to New York in 1974. He had quickly become one of the top cutters in Manhattan, and was working with all the top photographers. It was unclear whether King was demonstrably superior to the other top stylists whose names filled the credits in the magazines. And without those credits, it was nearly impossible to tell a Scavullo picture with a

Harry King hairstyle from one taken on a day when King was unavailable. But King had been the beneficiary of the Scavullo publicity machine just as Way Bandy had. They were the integral hair and makeup artists who comprised Francesco's team.

Gia had a toothache the day of the session, but it still went well. *Cosmo* liked the pictures and Scavullo booked her again two weeks later for another cover try. The first one had been more a test than anything else. This second one was for real. The picture had a good chance of being used, and she got a voucher for the standard *Cosmo* cover fee, which was $100.

In the meantime, the first issue of American *Vogue* with Gia's photographs in it had come out: a beauty shot by Elgort, fur shots by Stan Malinowski, and *Vogue Patterns* shots by Andrea Blanche. Any appearance in *Vogue* made an immediate impact. The magazine's monthly circulation was about one million but its "pass-along rate"—the number of people who read each issue printed—was among the highest in the industry. If a hairdresser's name was credited, his or her salon generally saw an increase in new clients asking for appointments—almost all of them wanting their hair to look just like the picture. In salons across the country, other haircutters were brought the picture and asked to duplicate the cut. A photo credit generally brought a photographer new editorial and advertising clients, many of whom were looking for something just like what they had seen in *Vogue*. If an article of clothing was shown, its sales often increased in the stores that carried it: clothes that resembled the garment were also likely to sell more briskly.

Because the captions and credits were so powerful, it was even more ironic when they were used for blatant advertiser paybacks. The pictures of Gia by Stan Malinowski, for example, ran with a feature called "The Best Furs Yet"—which was also a vehicle for the latest of *Vogue*'s creative beauty product plugs, the fragrance "beauty note," suggesting in the caption which advertiser's perfumes might wear well with the clothes. The beauty note was the compromise accepted by the beauty writing staff, who felt that its predecessor, the "fragrance credit," had violated even *Vogue*'s vague standards of truth-in-captioning. These standards included credits for products, stores and stylist associations (a stylist *of* or *for* a certain salon or manufacturer) being creatively doled out after pictures were completed.

While the credits for garments were compromised mostly by the disproportionate number of advertiser's clothes in the pictures, the beauty credits were open season on reality. Since many of the new beauty products couldn't be ready in time for early magazine deadlines, it was quite common that the beauty products used were *not* those credited. As long as the shades of makeup applied were close enough to those the magazine was going to plug, nobody was ever going to know the difference.

The fragrance credit, however, had been the most preposterous. In a fragrance credit, the caption purported to identify *the perfume the model had been wearing during the session.* At least the beauty note was a little more subtle. The $20,000 chesterfield-style coat from Maximilian that Gia was modeling would be perfect with "the dash of a new French fragrance—Capucci's Parce Que. Just what you need with sable." And Oscar de la Renta's perfume had "the same spirit in a scent" as the $12,500 reversible dyed mink cardigan from Grosvenor of Canada. The cardigan was available at—and these store credits were crucial, since current advertisers both counted on them and *counted* them— Bonwit Teller in New York and Chicago, Kramer's Furs in New Haven, Roberts Neustadter in Boston, both the Alaskan Fur Company and Saks-Jandel in Kansas City, and Frost Brothers and Meyer Epstein Furs in London, Ontario.

Since models rarely got credits, their unattributed associations with *Vogue* had to be peddled in other ways. This was usually done with a standard black and white model "composite" card—with five or six photographs, the model's vital statistics in American and European measures, and the agency's name and address. The cards were part of the massive agency print and direct mail campaign which, besides phone calls, was the only way modeling services were really promoted. The composites were a companion to the large agency posters—called headsheets—which were regularly mailed out to art directors at magazines, ad agencies, production companies and anywhere else that might need models.

For years, the headsheets had been conventional and rather plain looking, with postage-stamp size headshots of even the top girls and established hourly and day rates for each model: clients paid extra for lingerie or nudes. The composite cards were also generally plain and standardized. In fact, all the agencies used the same company in London for their cards.

The coming of Elite had overhauled the promotional aspect of the modeling business. One of the most visible changes had been prompted by Elite's controversial first headsheets, which featured a shot that showed more of one model than just her head. Her breasts were exposed, which nobody had ever done before. The headsheet was also remarkable for what it didn't show: there were no standardized rates listed for the top girls. Leaving the prices off was Casablancas' way of letting the industry know that his top rates were negotiable—*upwards*.

The bold Elite headsheet had sent a message through the industry that everyone would have to be more innovative with promotion. So when Gia's picture appeared full-page in the October *Vogue,* the agency didn't depend on the magazine itself to sell the new girl. Wilhelmina had hundreds of *full-color* cards made up with the Elgort photo and "Introducing Gia" printed across it in bold letters. You had to spend money to make money.

To fill her free time, Gia had signed up for a photography course at New York University. She regularly missed classes when photo sessions ran late, and eventually withdrew from the course because Tuesday and Thursday evenings at eight was turning into regular worktime. With paying jobs taking up more of her days, the testing and more experimental work with friends—a book someone was trying to put together, a freebie for some struggling magazine—got done in the early evening between dinnertime and club time. But Gia continued to take pictures, and told friends that she hoped modeling would lead her to a career on the other side of the camera. Since her days hanging out with Joe Petrellis and Maurice Tannenbaum in Philadelphia, she had always been more interested in what a photographer did than what a model did. Lots of models took snapshots on-set—especially now that Instamatic cameras were getting cheaper and easier to use—but Gia had something more ambitious in mind.

"She wanted to be a photographer but not a fashion photographer, more of a documentary photographer and that's what she was really working at," Sharon Beverly recalled. "She would go out and take pictures of characters on the street, the homeless. She took a lot of alkies on the street, men sitting on benches. She said she tried to talk to them. But some of them started fights with her and didn't want her to take their pictures."

She also began taking advantage of the city's many repertory cinema houses. Philadelphia had one such theater, the TLA, where she and her friends had often gone to see *A Clockwork Orange* or *The Man Who Fell to Earth,* but New York had many. The photographers Gia worked with often casually mentioned important films when they were trying to explain a certain effect or affect they were looking for. To most people in the fashion world, cinema was the closest thing they had to literature. *Fashionistas* tended to be extremely well-informed about what had been and what was being *written about*—phenomena, rages, trends—but they rarely found the need to read books or articles themselves. They were easily fascinated and quickly bored: a little bit of information went a long way, and a lot of information was usually cumbersome. "Scratch the surface," Way Bandy was known to joke about the business, "and what do you get? More surface."

For several years, Gia had made it a habit of asking people she respected to recommend books she should read or movies she should see. She jotted the lists down in her diaries, and usually just got around to the movies. John Garfield was her favorite actor. Marilyn Monroe and Greta Garbo were her favorite actresses, and she sometimes made a pilgrimage to the building Garbo lived in on East Fifty-second Street to catch a glimpse of the publicly reclusive actress. Between the Bleecker Street Cinema and the Cinema Village downtown, and the Regency uptown, Gia was finally getting a chance to see some of the movies she had heard

Stephen Fried

about: *The Grand Illusion* and *Anna Karenina,* as well as
more recent films like *Three Women, Persona, Seduction of
Mimi* and *Swept Away.* The films filled her head with visual
ideas for her own photographs. She was beginning to scrib-
ble down concepts for shots and even for short films, ideas
that were no more or less baked than the ones she watched
top photographers get thousands of dollars to execute.

Among the films she went to see was *Satyricon.* Since it
had become fashionable to describe New York City nightlife
as a series of scenes from a Fellini film, it seemed only right
that she go to *watch* one.

8
Callback

One Friday late in October, Gia's life changed. The day had not been planned as anything unusual. She was booked with Chris von Wangenheim to do a studio sitting for *Vogue,* where she was quickly becoming the new sensation. The November issue had just come out, and it included several page-stopping pictures of her. Two were street shots by Andrea Blanche. In one, Gia was shown in a St. Laurent satin top and wool skirt, fashionably reenacting a new urban ritual: in a typical example of how fashion photographers could borrow from *anything* new in their surroundings, Gia was shot with a dalmatian leashed to her one hand and a pooper-scooper in the other. In the other shot, she was posed in a black velvet Calvin Klein outfit, standing in front of a railing and a fence. To her left, waist high, was a large street sign that simply, and inexplicably, read DEAD.

But the truly stunning photo of Gia in the November *Vogue* was by Arthur Elgort, in a section on new form-fitting clothes. She posed in a Calvin Klein slip-dress that was falling off one shoulder: her hair was pulled back, and, in black sunglasses, she made beautiful-tough for the camera. The shot was buried far back in the section, but when *Vogue* later put together a book of its best fashion photographs, it chose the picture as the opener for the section on 1978. It was the ultimate visualization of radical chic.

The Von Wangenheim sitting was not to be anything quite

so interesting. The shots would be tossed into a hodgepodge generic fashion and accessory story called "Finds." There were some jackets, some tops, some skirts and some belts. The fashion editor was Kesia Keeble, one of the very few to succeed in that job as a freelancer. She worked a lot for *Vogue,* and Italian *Bazaar,* as well as many advertising clients: she had recently styled the successful Calvin Klein jeans ads that Avedon had shot with Brooke Shields.

Keeble, thirty-six, was, even by the standards of the business, a talented oddball, sort of the "good witch" of the fashion industry. Tall and strong-featured, with long, dark hair streaked with one eerie line of white, she was forever obsessed with some new spiritual pursuit or New Age cure-all. She had left her first husband and her full-time job at *Vogue* to set up a business with, and eventually marry, rhinestone jewelry designer Willie Woo. Later she was fashion editor at *Esquire,* and in 1976 she had married Paul Cavaco, who was a Brew Burger waiter when they met at a Buddhist meeting and had since become a successful freelance stylist.

Considering the myriad possibilities of a meeting of minds between Keeble and Von Wangenheim, the shot they had chosen was relatively simple. The girls would pose in front of and behind a chain link fence; they were to stand on a piece of green AstroTurf. Bob Fink was doing hair. The makeup artist was Sandy Linter, a beautiful blond woman in her late twenties who had recently become a successful freelancer after making her fame at the Manhattan salon of hairdresser Kenneth Battelle—the Kenneth who had become celebrated in the sixties for doing Jackie Kennedy's hair.

It was a very long day, with a lot of different outfits being shot. When they had what they needed for *Vogue,* Keeble left, but Von Wangenheim asked Gia and some of the others if they would stay around so he could try some other shots while he had the props. He generally did not like switching immediately from a commercial assignment to doing "personal stuff." Balancing the demands of the fashion editor, the wavering endurance of the models, and the constant fussing over the clothes was usually enough mental and physical exertion for one day. But there was still a good energy left in the studio, and Von Wangenheim had, for some time, wanted to do some real nudes of Gia, some nudes that were uncompromised by the editorial demands of even the most liberal publications.

Von Wangenheim had Gia strip down and pose behind the fence, which was being held up on either side by his assistants. Sandy Linter stayed around to help with the hair and makeup. One of these shots was to be paired with a picture Von Wangenheim had taken of his infant daughter Christine. In that shot, the child and another woman were photographed from the waist down: the baby was naked, her genitalia exposed, her face obscured by the long black skirt of the other woman, who was also wearing lace-up high-heeled boots. Von Wangenheim would later explain the shot of his child as an attempt to prove that having "babies and a stable family life doesn't exclude 'le bonheur' and eroticism. As it turned out, it deepened certain experiences. At one point I said to myself, 'If that's how I feel, if Christine is whom I love, I should be able to photograph her in the context of my photographic personality.' "

The shot of Gia was to be a "counterpoint to the baby picture, which has no fence. To me, babies are perfect and pure. They have falcon eyes that haven't yet acquired the filtration for how they perceive the world. The older you get, the more imprisoned you become."

For Gia's fenced-in nudes, Von Wangenheim began with fairly tame poses. The shot that would be paired with the baby picture showed Gia covering her pubic area with both hands, her long legs crossed and her eyes glaring into the camera. After a roll or two of poses along these lines, he asked Gia to try jumping up onto the fence and climbing on it.

"The session became amazing," recalled Sara Foley, who had come to see how the fence she had tracked down was working out. "Gia's hands were bleeding, they were bleeding from climbing up and down. Chris worked you incredibly hard. There was literally blood coming down her hands. But she loved it too, you see. It was three o'clock in the morning, and they were making amazing pictures."

But something else was going on as well. Gia had always been prone to crushes, and being in New York around so many beautiful women had just made things worse. "It almost became a joke," recalled Sharon Beverly. "One day she came home and she had been working with this makeup artist, a heavyset girl. She said, 'I don't know what's happening to me, but all the sudden I like fat women.' I can't remember the girl's name, but I remember she had an affair with her—and the girl was straight."

During the session, Gia realized that she felt something for Sandy Linter—who many in the business considered beautiful enough to model herself. Sandy and Gia had worked together before. But there was just something about the whole scene that made Gia take her own emotional pulse again.

"Years later, she could still talk about this session in such detail," recalled one friend. "She told me about the fence, and there was loud music playing and they had asked her to do these nudes. And she was up against the fence and I think she said Sandy was on the fence too, on the other side. And she said, 'I looked at her and I just fell crazy in love with her. I was listening to this music, and the more I'd jump on the fence the more excited I'd get.' It was like she kept jumping up there, nude, to impress Sandy, to turn her on.

"She thought Sandy was straight. She said Sandy had this look—she always wore real frilly things, and spandex tights, stuff like that. She said she didn't tell Sandy about how she felt then, she didn't make a pass at her."

That weekend, Gia decided to go on a diet. She scribbled the word "list" at the top of a datebook page and then wrote down all the things she needed: an enema bag, various juices, teas and vitamins, as well as a variety of fruits and vegetables, everything from turnips to black currants. She committed to taking long walks, hot and cold showers, regular enemas and regular trips to the spa.

Except for the enemas, this regimen was considered the New Age, healthier approach to weight control—very Way Bandy—especially when compared to the more traditional, more extreme route that models often took: diet pills and fasting. If Gia wanted a role model for these old-fashioned methods of weight control, she didn't have to look any farther than Wilhelmina Cooper. Willie had been blessed with marvelously long legs and arms, and a neck and head elongated like an El Greco painting—they disguised her midsection, which expanded and contracted with her weight. She had learned to rely upon diet pills as a model, and her tricks were passed on to the girls she taught. Willie did believe in starvation diets, too: it hadn't been a complete lie when she wrote in her recent how-to book *The New You* that the key to her weight control was her "Hummingbird Diet." But she also believed in pills—especially to help girls get ready for bathing suit shoots, which could come at any time.

While most women looked forward, often with dread, to one bathing suit season a year, a model could have bathing suit season sneak up at almost any time. Depending on lead times, magazines shot two to six months in advance and showed bathing suits in the spring and summer, and often again in the winter for "cruisewear" collections. Catalog swimwear shots could come any time of the year when a tropical location had sun. And then there was always a mad rush to lose weight.

"I especially remember Patti Hansen with this," said Sara Foley. "Patti was always one of those people you had to say to the agency, 'Look, this is a bathing suit trip, *please* ask her to stop drinking beer for a week before, *really*.' "

"If somebody had to lose weight fast, Willie wouldn't think anything of giving them black beauties or whatever she had," recalled Kay Mitchell. "But, then, that was the time frame when everybody was very casual about such things, you know? And Willie—well, let's just say I learned a lot about deprivation from just being around her. You deprive yourself of everything, and then go off the wagon. She would want forty sandwiches and a pizza and then we'd be on diets again."

Taking a cue from her models, Kay Mitchell, who was heavyset, tried the Dr. Feelgood of the moment. "Willie sent me to this one doctor," she recalled, "and he dished intravenous amphetamine and I had no idea in the world what I was doing ... maybe it was B-12 shots or something, but it was *like* intravenous amphetamine. At six o'clock in the morning, there would be a whole lobby full of people waiting to go in and get their injections. It was *a lot* of money per shot. I was making $120 a week as a receptionist and it was $30 a shot or something and you were supposed to go three times a week. Obviously, I'm going to get behind in my payments. It got to the point that that's what the girls would do for presents for me, pay my diet doctor bills. I would show up to pay and the nurse would say, 'Oh no, that was taken care of by so and so.'"

It would be a few days before Gia decided how to make her move on Sandy. She had just bought a $10,000 red Fiat Spider convertible—an odd choice for a first indulgence in the modeling world. The girls usually blew their first big checks on jewelry or clothes; since they lived in Manhattan and were rarely home anyway, the last thing they would consider owning was a car. But Gia was a suburban girl at heart, and a love of fast cars was in her blood. Her mother, in fact, had just received a Corvette from her stepfather. With her nest now empty, Kathleen had turned some of her attention to learning about performance cars and shopping for the perfect gold 1978.

Gia guessed that if she called Sandy up and offered her a ride in her new car, she would accept just out of curiosity. She did. "Gia told me she took her for a ride," a friend recalled. "She said they came back to the apartment and Gia seduced her."

Another friend remembered the story differently. "Gia told me that they were high and that Sandy thought that Gia was a little boy," she recalled. "So afterwards Sandy was, like, flipped out about it—that Gia wasn't a boy, you know? But they continued some relationship, although I think it was more Gia being infatuated with her and Sandy being flipped out about it."

Relationships among fashion people were rarely conventional. The marriages and really strong relationships were constantly tested by the incessant travel and the never-ending stream of young boys and girls willing to do anything to succeed. The fledgling relationships, and even the aggressive flirtations, were immediately blown out of proportion by the industry gossip circuit.

At some level, the entire industry was built on a shifting foundation of people falling in and out of love with each other, both personally and professionally. Just as voters in

Chicago were jokingly admonished to "vote early and often," so fashion people were supposed to fall in love. It had always been an occupational hazard in fashion—perhaps because it was one of the first industries to employ men and women of all sexes side by side. Or maybe it was just because every interaction required a certain flattery and flirtation. Almost every decision was made emotionally, and the chances of an "office romance" increased when people worked in so many different offices. Every photo session was a sort of simulated one-night stand: it was denying the law of averages to set off that many sparks and never expect to light any fires. Unfortunately, the best part of many of the relationships was what was captured on film and used to sell the product. Even the ugly end of a relationship could lead to a creative tension that made for strong pictures. There often wasn't much left for the participants to take home.

In the fashion business, the wide-open sexuality of the late seventies only further bent the already lax rules about relationships. There had also been an unprecedented influx of young, pretty people wanting to find a place in the glamorous professions of glamour. "It was the beginning of the Kleenex generation," recalled hairstylist Harry King, "when the business knew it could just use people up, especially models, and throw them away."

So the fact that Gia had set her sights on Sandy Linter—and some believed they had even gone to bed together—didn't necessarily mean that much. What it meant was that pretty soon people in the business would start picking up on the fact that something was going on between them. The industry was already abnormally interested in Gia's private life because she was a rising star and had been relatively public about her interest in women—even though she was also seeing men.

Although fashion had long been one of the few safe havens for openly gay men, a gay or bisexual woman was still titillating. Much attention had been paid to designer/princess Diane von Furstenberg's contention—in a 1973 *New York* magazine cover story—that she and her husband Egon, the magazine's "couple of the year," had invited another woman into their bed. When profiled in *Women's Wear Daily* in

July, 1978, Von Furstenberg was asked directly to comment on rumors that she was a lesbian: the article was titled "I Live Like a Man." Gay men were provocative only to other gay men. Gay women, apparently, were provocative to everyone *but* gay men—but not in a way that made it easy to live openly as a lesbian. Gia had once accepted a dinner invitation in New York from a man who took her to a fancy restaurant. When she told him she preferred women and had no interest in him, he got up and walked out, leaving her with the check.

Whatever the extent of their relationship, Gia and Sandy Linter would soon become linked in the eyes of their peers. But not only because of any romantic involvement. In reality, fashion people's personal lives were considered secondary to their work. Because personality clashes could be so devastating on the set—costing time and, as everyone's rates kept rising, big money—photographers and editors were constantly looking for talented people who could be consistently *teamed*. A hair-and-makeup duo like Way Bandy and Harry King. Two models who liked working together and didn't try to constantly upstage each other, like Patti Hansen and Shaun Casey. A photographer and model who were involved, like Mike Reinhardt and Janice Dickinson. And a consummate professional makeup artist who might help assure that her pal showed up on time for sessions.

The week before Thanksgiving, Gia took a short work trip to California. Chris von Wangenheim had been assigned to photograph the eveningwear from the New York collections. The twice-yearly agglomeration of American "designer ready-to-wear" shows was making an international splash because of the rise of designers like Calvin Klein, Ralph Lauren and Perry Ellis, and because jet-setters and foreign fashion folk wanted an excuse to see Studio 54 Manhattan for themselves. Von Wangenheim had conspired with *Vogue* fashion editor Jade Hobson to pack the clothes into the large, black "coffins" used for transport and take them on a little trip to Palm Springs. The shooting wouldn't be in a fancy hotel or a rich person's home, but in the middle of the flat, hard desert in the nearby Luzerne Valley. To take advantage of the variously wonderful effects of the desert sun, they shot during all the available daylight. To get to the location, they had to fly in helicopters, which Von Wangenheim would eventually incorporate into the pictures as well.

"God, I remember waking up at four or four-thirty each morning," recalled hairstylist John Sahag. He had, at the time, just relocated to New York from Paris to cash in on his professional reputation—helped along by his appearance as the stylist in the thriller *Eyes of Laura Mars*. "We had to fly up over the hills to get to the site. This guy had a helicopter, he used it the way you park your car in the garage. We'd be out there at five o'clock, so cold we were all wearing furs. By midday, we were all half-naked."

Over the next four days, the alternately freezing and perspiring crew executed a portfolio of shots that would become instant classics when they appeared in the February 1979 issue of American *Vogue*. One in particular, an overhead shot of Gia and the other two models shielding their eyes from the wind of the helicopter—which is visible only in shadow—would be collected in most of the major books on commercial photography in the seventies. The others were merely sensational studies of color and shadow, among them an opener of Gia luxuriating in the back seat of a Cadillac convertible, and a shot of Gia in a black slip-dress holding a glass of champagne, the shadows from her long legs seemingly stretching for miles.

After the shootings she returned to New York and immediately shifted gears, driving down to Bucks County to spend Thanksgiving weekend with her mother. It was the first time she had been home in several months. Although she kept in constant touch with her mother by phone—Kathleen even came to visit occasionally—she was much less actively involved with her other family and friends. Gia was good at *being there,* at making an impression during the time she spent with someone: when she was away, she was gone. Her brothers, her Aunt Nancy, her old pals from the DCA weren't forgotten, but they were gone. She spoke to them on the phone, sent a postcard from somewhere when she thought of it, but like a family member away at college, Gia was seen mostly at holidays—except for her appearances in major monthly magazines.

The course of her career was being charted by the folks back home. The women, who had grown up reading the fashion magazines, realized just how big she had become and lived vicariously through her. The men, to whom women's magazines were largely baffling, quantified her success in dollar terms and uneasily admitted how provocative some of Gia's pictures were.

Gia brought her pal John Long to Thanksgiving dinner with her, and had him pretend he was her boyfriend in New York. It was easier around her mother and brothers to concentrate on the possibly heterosexual aspects of her life in the business. She was, for example, getting a lot of laughs with her stories about The Prince. By this time in the retelling, he was threatening to kill himself if she didn't marry him.

Two weeks later Gia was off again. This time it was to London, for a week shooting with British *Vogue,* which had quietly become perhaps the most visually interesting of the *Vogue*s. Its recent success was generally attributed to former model Grace Coddington, who had become Britain's hottest fashion editor.

One of the beneficiaries of Coddington's rise was photographer Alex Chatelain, who did a lot of shooting for the magazine and, because he was based in New York—where British *Vogue* rarely shot—served as one of the publication's roving eyes for the new American models. Chatelain had been one of the first photographers to work with model Esme Marshall, dubbed "the energy girl" by *Mademoiselle* and offered up as an athletic, short-haired, bushy-browed role model to that magazine's younger readership. Chatelain had also been the first major photographer to see Gia, although he hadn't been able to book her for anything big until this London trip. They had done one small American *Vogue* shooting in his New York studio, but this was a big assignment: fourteen to sixteen color pages and probably a cover.

Chatelain did not really care for Gia personally. But he knew she was the right New York model to deliver to British

Vogue. And he knew that, whatever her attitude problems, she was a natural in front of the camera.

"She was already weird on that trip," he recalled, "already disappearing, already falling asleep, all these things people do when they're taking drugs. But she had some kind of a real presence, very strong. People say she was really beautiful, I can't say that. She didn't have a great body, didn't have great elegance intrinsically. But then something came through in the pictures. It was like Marilyn Monroe. If you looked at her unsentimentally, Marilyn didn't have a great body at the end, but when she moved or when she . . . I don't know, but Gia had that same pathetic thing that Marilyn had.

"But then, I think the way I've always reacted to girls is that I never know what's going on with them and I'm not really interested. It's just, instinctively, whether it works or not. With her, at times she annoyed me, because she was late or she was falling asleep. But I never thought of it, because then, in the picture, even without my noticing it— something was there."

Chatelain never wondered about the process of "something" turning up there until years later, when his confidence started to fade. "I guess a bigger part of it than I realized at the time was just getting swept up in the moment," he said. "I can now see that if you give a person a chance, he'll make good pictures. When I was with British *Vogue,* I got a chance to make good pictures. I had the best models, best hair, best makeup, best editors. You can't miss. You have to be a total asshole to *not* succeed. I look at Patrick Demarchelier. I don't think he's a great photographer, but he's very smart about his business and he does it well. He's being given a chance, every day, to do good pictures. So he comes out with good pictures."

The day after Gia returned from London was, as she marked in her datebook, "Mommy's Birthday." Even though she had too much work to visit Kathleen, she wanted to spoil her in the way of the fashion industry. She arranged to have flowers and champagne delivered to her.

Manhattan florists loved models and agency people, because they had made saying it with flowers their industry standard. It was not uncommon for models to send extravagant floral arrangements to their bookers, their agents or anyone they perceived as having done them a favor; nor was it uncommon for agents and photographers to send models flowers at their apartments, or even at a shooting. Almost everyone important in the business could be counted on to have some recently delivered flowers on his or her office desk or living room coffee table, and perhaps the remains of a not-so-recently-delivered arrangement as well.

Gia had always loved flowers, so she was happy to jump on the bud bandwagon. "Gia loved roses," Kathleen recalled, "and when she became a model and had all this money to spend, she sent $50-a-dozen roses like it was nothing. She brought me an orchid one time she bought with Scavullo. Her color was yellow, my color was apricot. I still can't see a yellow rose without thinking of her."

While Gia was in London, Studio 54 was raided. The Organized Crime Strike Force of the U.S. Attorney's office, seeking evidence to help them put down the disco-caine mutiny, recovered about an ounce of coke and a double set of books allegedly used to defraud the IRS. They also reportedly found a detailed list of the club's celebrity customers, cross-referenced with the drugs and other party favors purchased to insure that they remained celebrity customers.

For some, the raid came as a sign that the party was waning, that Studio (which reopened the next day) would eventually go down, and the moment of the Beautiful People would pass just like any other fashion. For others, the raid simply signaled that the party had officially moved to a new location and a new host named Steve—Steve Mass, owner of the Mudd Club, which had opened the year before in lower Manhattan.

The Mudd Club was the latest in the progression of downtown hangouts that had begun in the mid-sixties with Max's Kansas City. Max's eventually begat CBGB's, the Bowery bastion of New Wave and hardcore rock, where the Long Island band the Ramones got their start, only to see their fast, hard, gallows-funny tunes exported to England and imported back as punk rock in the form of the Sex Pistols. CBGB's had been responsible for developing acts as disparate as Blondie and the Talking Heads, Patti Smith and Wendy O. Williams' Plasmatics. These were the bands that were finally starting to reach mainstream public consciousness, collectively labeled the New Wave by enthused rock critics.

The New Wave caught on in other cities. Gia had seen some of these bands at The Hot Club in Philadelphia. It was there that she had first laid eyes on Blondie's lead singer Deborah Harry, who was replacing David Bowie as her new idol. Blondie was the most commercial of the New Wave bands, and a perfect new favorite for Gia, whose taste in music ran from rock 'n' roll to really goony pop songs her friends in Philadelphia sometimes teased her about liking—songs like "I Don't Like Spiders and Snakes." She wasn't so much drawn to music on the cutting edge as she was good at finding the next hip thing that would be reaching the mass market. Blondie, which had been kicking around for three or four years, was next. Gia's personal interest in the band grew after a guy Sharon knew in the record business arranged for them to see a Blondie show at the Tower and later meet the band at their Philadelphia hotel.

The Mudd Club cloned the sensibility of CBGB's onto Studio 54's disco with a touch of G. G. Knickerbockers—the Forty-fifth Street club where the entertainment in the main Barnum Room was transvestites flying through the air into nets above the dance floor. Club Mudd had bizarre stage shows, never-advertised live music (sometimes the fledgling U2, sometimes Shoxlumania, who dressed as Ukrainian folk dancers), and a record mix by DJ Anita Sarko that was relentlessly, even frighteningly, eclectic. Physically, the place was an even bigger dump than CBGB's, but it was more of a scene piece than a fully functional rock bar. And it reveled in its decadence—the open drug use, the sexual posturing—in a way even Studio couldn't match. Andy Warhol reportedly described the phenomenon of the Mudd Club by explaining: "In the sixties, we all had plenty to get pissed off about. Now we're too tired and jaded for that, so we come here to get pissed *on.*"

The Mudd Club was much more Gia's kind of place than Studio 54 had ever been. She could beautify *any* dance floor, but she thought of herself as a rock 'n' roll girl at heart.

And the Mudd Club certainly had both a rock sensibility and an arty edge. Downtown New Wavers mingled there with aspiring artists and performers who would become Robert Mapplethorpe and Jean-Michel Basquiat and Eric Bogosian and Ann Magnuson and Madonna. The house heroes—occasionally in residence—were Keith Richards, Marianne Faithful, Iggy Pop, Lou Reed and David Bowie, who was in town doing *The Elephant Man* on Broadway. All of this was still considered a little too dangerous for the *Vogue* world, but it was beginning to attract some uptown fascination—especially after the punk rock phenomenon produced its first front-page tragedy. On Friday October 13, Philadelphia-born Nancy Spungen was found murdered by her boyfriend, ex–Sex Pistol Sid Vicious, in their room at the Chelsea Hotel on West Twenty-third Street.

"Downtown" was still a very foreign place to the mainstream fashion world. "I remember Way Bandy had a period when he was really becoming part of the downtown scene," recalled hairstylist Maury Hopson. "He was kind of just doing it for business. He had this uptown image, and it sort of made him a little hotter and more mysterious to be seen in these clubs downtown.

"Uptown is more upscale; downtown is more real, in its phony way. The pretensions are different, basically."

The drugs were slightly different as well. Besides alcohol, which was never really dethroned as the universal intoxicant of choice, the uptown world tended to gravitate toward *ups,* the downtowners to a more mixed bag of ups and downs. The difference between the scenes was the difference between a snort of cocaine and the injected cocaine spiked with heroin known as a "speedball."

Drug use had become so casual that the biggest shock of the Studio raid was probably the realization that cocaine was, technically, still illegal. Cocaine, amphetamines and Quaaludes were casually administered. Unless a substance was cooked down and smoked as freebase, or injected, it hardly even counted. Stimulants were often being taken for practical, work-related reasons. Just like athletes drank Gatorade (to wash down the speed and steroids), nightlifers used cocaine because it was the only way that people with real jobs during the day could stay out all night. Sexual athletes, especially gay men, added poppers to the menu: the amyl nitrite capsules, used medically to counteract angina attacks, were broken under the nose on the dance floor or during orgasm for the momentary rush. This was not drug experimentation—LSD had fallen from favor along with the whole idea of acid tests for mind expansion. This was medicine: better living through chemistry.

No matter how casual drug use had become, heroin remained the last taboo. Its use had not increased along with the dramatic rise in cocaine and other drugs—at least according to government statistics. The U.S. Drug Enforcement Agency estimated that in 1978, heroin addiction had reached its lowest point in years.

But heroin use was on the rise in Europe. The worsening problem in West Germany had been humanized recently by the magazine *Stern,* which published candid interviews with a fifteen-year-old heroin addict, prostitute and "girl of the streets" referred to as "Christiane F." Her descriptions of Berlin in the mid-seventies, which later spawned a book and a film, didn't sound all that much different from what was beginning to happen in New York.

Gia had never really cared for the modeling business from the very beginning, and her overnight success hadn't changed her feeling that this was not the kind of world she would ever love. The money was suddenly pretty good and would only get better, the champagne and drugs were always the best available, and the parties were extravagant beyond belief. But the work itself, the way she spent most of her long, tiring days, was generally not very interesting to her. Modeling made her back and her brain sore. It required intense concentration on *not concentrating* on anything but moving and then *not moving*. People were always reaching out and touching her, but she wasn't supposed to touch back. People were crowding in around her, fussing over her: painting her like a Seurat so that every tiny point of color was perfect and then lighting her up like a highway billboard. She was getting really sick of it. She wanted them to stop touching her.

Certain photographers, like Chris von Wangenheim, made her feel like she was *acting* rather than just standing there

171

looking pretty (or dancing around to make the camera think she was having a good time). And she was getting a lot of mileage out of treating the whole fashion photography world like it was a big joke. For some photographers, her disdain looked and sounded a lot like that *attitude thing* that was all the rage downtown. Her lateness, lack of proper respect and other unheard-of unprofessionalism was actually working to her advantage. The photographers were just like the guys who had been coming on to her since she was a kid, their numbers geometrically increasing since her pictures started appearing in the magazines: when she told them to kiss off, they just loved her more. It was an amusing little mind-game to play, but there wasn't much to be won by winning.

Still, there was the money. There weren't a lot of other legal ways for an eighteen-year-old girl to make a hundred thousand dollars a year—which it appeared she could easily make in 1979. And there were the all-expenses-paid trips. And even though she had long ago grown tired of the masses of men and women who showered her with compliments about her beauty, there were a handful of people whose approval very much mattered to her. There were her surrogate mothers in the business, Willie and Lizzette, who were very pleased with her progress. And then there was her real mother down in Bucks County at the receiving end of all those women's magazine subscriptions. Kathleen was bursting with a kind of pride that Gia had never seen before.

"Gia would tell you all the stuff that most women want to know about the models," Kathleen recalled. "Which one had hips that went on forever. Which one had the pimples. Which one did Quaaludes to get the starry looks in her eyes. Which one was a real dog. Which one was a superbitch. Which one ran around saying 'Take my picture, take my picture,' and was just so into the whole thing.

"In the beginning, we were both sort of star-struck. She went on the most fantastic trips. She always called from where she was. She met an Italian prince in Capri. He *loved* her, he wanted a photo of her. Finally she just ripped a picture out of a magazine and wrote on it, 'Eat your heart out, Gia.' Jack Nicholson tried to get her to meet him in his room. I was in New York that week. I was making slipcovers for her sofa and she came back from this party and said, 'Can you believe it, I just turned down Jack Nicholson?' I said, 'Thank god you did that, you don't want to be involved with *him*.'

"She was in *Vogue* almost immediately—they *loved* her. She was always hard to get up in the morning, so they sent a limo for her. Whatever demand she made, she *could*. She wouldn't work with certain people. And the more of a star she got to be, the more demanding she got to be."

Many of her demands could only be fulfilled by Kathleen. The same young woman who was self-sufficient enough to live on her own as a high school student was suddenly calling on her mother, from New York, for every little thing. Gia was likely to make more money in the coming year than either her father or stepfather. But she wasn't going to miss the chance to finally have Kathleen at her beck and call.

"Gia would announce, 'I want you in New York,' and she wanted me there at her disposal, to cook for her, whatever," Kathleen recalled. "She couldn't understand that I had a life with Henry. If she had had her way I would have been up there all the time. There were weeks when I would stay the whole week, never longer than two weeks. When she came home for the weekend I would go up there and get her. She knew she could get me to do anything she wanted. She was always demanding of my time. I didn't do anything for her that I didn't really want to do. I did it. I could've said no. But she was hard to say no to. I would have done it for any of my kids."

To some of those close to Gia, the attention seemed like more than just a normal mother reveling in her daughter's success. "Kathleen was driving up there to do Gia's *laundry*," recalled Nancy Adams. "When Gia and her brothers were kids, their mother wouldn't do *anything* for them. They had to get up themselves, they had to do their own clothes. Now Gia's a model, and she's driving to New York to do her laundry for her."

More often, though, Gia would save up her laundry to bring home. And even *that* was somehow exciting to Kathleen. "She must have had two washerloads of white socks," she recalled. "When you have that kind of money, when things are dirty, you just buy more. She would just buy stuff and leave it wherever she was."

Suddenly, instead of frustration, Gia was bringing fun and excitement to her mother's life. "Gia was good to me," Kathleen said. "She was very thoughtful and took care of me. I remember one time we were driving to New York together in my '78 Corvette. We came up the Holland Tunnel and saw this cab go flying past. As we got to an intersection, he hit the curb and then he leaped in the air and dropped out of the sky onto the top of the '78 Corvette. Gia got out and started *screaming* at this cab driver. And the police are there, and she's got this knife in her hand and she's gonna knife this guy. And these New York cops are standing there watching this saying, 'If she does knife him, we'll never see it.' She was on her way to a big party at Studio 54, but she handled the whole situation. She gave me money—she said, 'Make sure you don't let them know you have the money'—and she wanted to send me home in a limousine. She looked out for Mommy that night.

"She was, really, the whole world to me. When she was home, the whole house would fill up. When she left it was empty. She had a certain way of coming through the door, like the Fourth of July and all fireworks were going off."

It was all so exciting for Kathleen that she was able to put aside any nagging doubts she had that Gia couldn't handle what was happening.

"In some ways, I realized the pressure she was under . . . I knew about the business from when I was in retailing. Even then you had to be a very particular type of person to be able to handle modeling. It's an ego trip, a lot of jealousies and backstabbing and petty stuff. It takes a certain amount of strength, and because it's such a glamorous business, everybody thinks they're better-looking than everybody else.

"I knew how beautiful she was and how fragile she was. And I had this vision of her becoming this Marilyn Monroe type and becoming a sex symbol and dying a very tragic death young."

9

This Year's Girl

The new year brought Gia's first magazine cover, the January 1979 issue of Italian *Cosmo*. When issues finally reached the few Manhattan newsstands that carried European magazines, Kathleen bought every copy she could find. The January issue of American *Vogue* included, besides six editorial shots of her, Gia's first major advertisement: a Chris von Wangenheim shot for Gianni Versace.

Over the next months, as Gia marked her first anniversary in the business, the quality and quantity of her work skyrocketed. She went to Paris to do a sitting with Helmut Newton for French *Vogue*. Newton was nearing sixty, and he had been taking fashion photographs for various *Vogue*s since the 1950s. He was raised in Berlin, but had moved to Australia during World War II and broke in at the *Vogue* edition there, eventually relocating to Paris, where he worked for all the major magazines. In the early seventies, he suffered a massive heart attack. When he recovered, his work became much more erotic, bizarre, powerful and self-consciously German. By photographing celebrities and fashion as if they were all beautified scenes from the cabarets of prewar Berlin and the lurid sex clubs on the Reeperbahn in Hamburg, he had become modern just as his contemporaries were making their final slide into classicism.

Chris von Wangenheim, over twenty years his junior, was friendly with Newton. Those who appreciated the work of both photographers, and recognized the differences in their approaches and results, usually referred to Von Wangenheim as Newton's protégé. Von Wangenheim's detractors referred to him as the "budget Helmut Newton," since they sometimes mined similar visual veins and Von Wangenheim was considerably less expensive.

Von Wangenheim believed that his taste in models was incompatible with his friend's, but Newton hired Gia for the next installment of his controversial series of cross-dressing women. He had shot women dressed in men's clothes before, but he had something more elaborate in mind. "The man-woman ambiguity has always fascinated me," he said. ". . . I had this idea in my head for some time: pictures of men and women together, only the men are women dressed up as men. But the illusion must be as perfect as possible, to try to confuse the reader." The art director at French *Vogue* had encouraged Newton to incorporate the idea into a section featuring dresses and suits by the major French designers. In an ultimate expression of man-woman ambiguity, Newton cast Gia—whose reputation in the business as an aggressive androgyne was by now firmly established—as the very feminine object of desire.

The pictures went well, although Gia told friends she believed Newton didn't really like her. She gigglingly reported his stunned expression when she referred to him to his face as "Daddy-o." While she was in Europe, she also impishly breezed through collections sittings for both Italian *Bazaar* and Italian *Vogue*. During a Paris *Bazaar* shooting with Jean Pagliuso at the glass-doored entrance to a building, she poked fun at the rivalry between the two magazines. Pagliuso shot her writing "I love you, Francois Lamy" in lipstick on the glass door. Lamy was the photographer with whom she did the Armani collection for Italian *Vogue*.

Gia was also booked to do her first trip for American *Vogue:* a swimwear excursion to Mexico. The photographer was Mike Reinhardt, and Gia was the promising rookie model tossed into the lineup with two of the most seasoned veterans: Janice Dickinson and Patti Hansen. Regardless of how the pictures turned out—like most of Reinhardt's work, they would be predictably beautiful and sexy, and would show the clothes—the trip was, in its own way, seminal. It brought together a small group that, individually, came to *define* their moment in the business.

Mike Reinhardt was always quite frank about his photographic influences. "I changed to photography when I saw *Blow Up,*" recalled the former California law student. "I thought, 'Why am I sitting here when I can be out there doing that kind of thing?' That's really why I became a photographer.

"And I always ended up going out with my favorite model and having an affair with her. It was a part of my life, and it became sort of my image after a while . . . for about fifteen years, I had this sort of business–pleasure-oriented life which was always living with my favorite model . . . one was Janice Dickinson. I lived with her for four years. And then there was another girl called Lisa Taylor. I worked with her a lot and spent some time with her. There was a girl called Barbara Minty, who ended up marrying Steve McQueen, who I also had that kind of relationship with . . . oh, Christie Brinkley, I was with her for a while. And I had been divorced once—also from a model.

"So I was known for that. I had a very bad reputation. First of all, as a womanizer, which was true. And secondly that I did much more drugs than I ever really did . . . I mostly smoked pot. I was a grassaholic for twenty years basically. I just stopped two years ago. Fortunately, I never got into cocaine in a big way and I never really liked the drug very much, although I did it for a time . . . It was great, that time, it was fabulous, but it was crazy, really crazy. I now look back at it and think, 'Jesus how did I do that?' It was a nightmare, basically."

Reinhardt's relationships with models became the standard by which all other photographers were judged. "There is always that element of a photographer taking advantage of his power and using it for sexual favors," he said. "At the time, I never saw what I was doing as taking advantage. But I realized later that it most certainly was. I would use them and they would use me. But I think that's the nature of many relationships anyway, most relationships. There's that element of . . . you could call it prostitution.

"The relationships with models happen, and they can be

a problem or not, depending on how the individual photographer handles it. To me, it became a problem toward the end of the relationship, because you'd fight so much. But I was always in a relationship, usually a four-year relationship. I don't know why, it just always ended up that way. The first two years are great, the third year you start noticing that there's a problem, and the fourth year you spend trying to figure out how the hell you're going to get out of it.''

Reinhardt and Janice Dickinson were in the fourth year of their relationship. They had met in 1975—he was thirty-seven, she was twenty—and were introduced by Reinhardt's friend Alex Chatelain. Her star rose as her new friends, the French Mafia photographers, proceeded to conquer America and the world. She became the "monster" model that everyone had told her she could never be.

Dickinson was a tall, athletically thin, former Floridian who had been repeatedly advised that her looks were too "ethnic" for top modeldom. But she had persevered nonetheless. In an industry where hardly anyone successfully worked her way to the top—most models just *happened* or not—Janice Dickinson was the exception that proved the rule. She had risen by being fearless, outrageous and smart-mouthed. She all but dared the business to reject her, and she finally enlisted some powerful supporters after struggling for more than a year. An editor at the French magazine *Marie Claire* gave her European exposure. And the top booker at the Ford agency, French-born Monique Pillard, came to believe in Janice almost as much as the model believed in herself. Monique sold Janice hard, and her eventual success as a top model was a testimony to the alliance between a model and her agency. Their relationship was one of the quintessential booker–model bonds in the industry: they were closer than any mother and daughter, or any business partners, could usually afford to be.

"The booker knows much more about the girls sometimes than their own family does," Monique said. "I used to say to Janice, 'Not only do I have my life to live but I have *your* life to live as well.' I used to go through the fights with the boyfriend, this and that, they have your phone number at home, they call you at midnight, they call you from an airport in wherever they are because they don't know which hotel to go to or they forgot. You become sort of a twenty-four-hour attendant. You are almost like the little cage where the puppy goes to spend the night."

Dickinson didn't generate a lot of American advertising work—it was hard for a brunette to get many ads, especially a brunette with such exotic, almost Oriental looks. But she made up for her lack of ads by doing an astonishing amount of editorial work. She was a constant cover girl in Europe, although she had never made the cover of American *Vogue*. It was a situation that justifiably irked her. And she dealt with the professional insult in her typically demure way.

"Janice called me one day," recalled Sara Foley, "and [Condé Nast editorial director] Mr. Liberman happened to be in my office, which rarely happened. And she said, 'Sara, do you think if I give Mr. Liberman a blow job, I can have a cover?' I said, 'Janice, can I call you back?' She said, 'No, really, do you think I should call him?' Janice really did have the foulest mouth *ever*."

Janice was also one of the first models to benefit from the new trend of using print girls on the runway. Calvin Klein was the first designer media-savvy enough to realize that if he used well-known print models for his shows—instead of runway-only girls who, with the exception of Jerry Hall, rarely got public exposure—he had a better chance of getting shots in the magazines and newspapers. Janice was a good choice because she liked working a crowd and often loudly dished with her friends the photographers and fashion editors as she came down the runway.

Janice and Mike were a formidable team. Neither of them would ever be known as the top of the top, but they might have been the hardest working model and photographer in the business, the king and queen of the commercial photography lifers. True *fashionistas*. Janice, with her rock-hard body and iron constitution, was one of the party goddesses of the working models. Her ability to drink and drug and look perfect the next morning was a constant marvel to those of weaker wills. She and her sister Debbie, also an Elite model, were nightlife queens on two continents. Mike, with his constant flirtations and endless quests for fees, was an industry standard for enlightened self-interest.

As a pair, they pushed the boundaries of what the business would tolerate. When Elite was still struggling and Janice was one of the agency's cash cows, she forced John Casablancas into an unheard of business compromise. "In this period during the model wars, models would blackmail the agents," recalled one former Elite executive. "They would say, 'I'm not paying you fifteen percent. If you want me to stay, I'll pay ten percent.' But Janice said, 'Not only won't I pay commission, but I want the commission *you* get from *your* client.' And she got it. For a period of three or four weeks, she was also getting the commission from the client. The agency was *losing money on her*. Then word got out, and John had to make another arrangement."

Patti Hansen was a different story. The youngest of six children of a Staten Island bus driver and housewife, she had dropped out of high school at the age of sixteen to sign up with Wilhelmina. She had literally grown up in the business, eventually graduating from younger magazines like *Glamour* and *Seventeen* to a more high-fashion profile.

"She did a lot of running, jumping and leaping," recalled Kay Mitchell, who was her booker at Wilhelmina and whose close relationship with her paralleled that of Janice and Monique. "She did a lot of trips and she was the little freckle-faced kid. Then she said she wanted to do more sophisticated pictures. So she went to Europe during the summer. In Italy she did photographs where she looked like the Bride of Frankenstein. Everything was dark makeup, and they allowed her to make this amazing transition in everybody's thinking. It was incredible because she could take those to *Vogue* and suddenly they didn't see her as a junior look."

By 1978, Hansen, at the age of twenty-one, was arguably the top model in the world. She was also considered perhaps the easiest to work with, the friendliest, a party girl but a professional. With her freckles covered over by heavy makeup and her comparatively zaftig figure reinvented as, in *People* magazine's words, "a sexy extra 15 pounds of lushness on the competition," she was a far bigger player in the day-in, day-out world of modeling than Cheryl Tiegs—who had become more of a disco-princess celebrity than a working girl, and had never really done much high fashion. Hansen could do the cover of *any* magazine, she was on TV hawking Revlon's Flex shampoo, and she had just finished the first Calvin Klein jeans ads with Scavullo, a billboard of which dominated Times Square.

Hansen had also recently appeared on the cover of the December 19 issue of *Esquire*, not as a faceless beauty but as herself. Her face and maillot-adorned torso were used to illustrate an article declaring 1978 "The Year of the Lusty Woman: It's all right to be a sex object again." In the cover's lower lefthand corner was Hansen's ticket out of anonymous stardom—"Model Patti Hansen: The Next Poster Queen?" The answer to the question was *no,* but her name and face had now been publicly linked. And that linkage reinforced the concept that top models were the ultimate lusty women. They were "working women" with perfect bodies and faces, "career girls" whose career was flirting.

The *Esquire* cover story was a watershed event in the debate over schizophrenic sexual roles of women—a debate the article examined, fueled and, ultimately, exploited. The piece opened with Betty Friedan asserting that "feminists all over the country ... enjoy looking pretty and dressing up." It went on to invoke the rise in popularity of jiggle TV shows, NFL cheerleaders, spandex disco clothes and million-selling pin-up posters of Farrah Fawcett and Cheryl Tiegs as proof that "women are ... clearly enjoying the new freedoms that liberation has brought, not only in equality in the office and at home but in the equality of their sexual aggressiveness. They are putting on their second-skin clothes and high heels, and they are boldly asking for what they want. Their philosophy: Everything shows, anything goes."

The article went on to quote such disparate sources as Frederick of Hollywood and feminist psychologist Dr. Phyllis Chesler, the latter of whom said, "We are living in a male homosexual culture—Wall Street, the Vatican, football teams, fashion designers ... men are separatists, and they don't want women around for longer than it takes to screw them." A slew of fashion people—Scavullo, Norma Kamali, *WWD*'s June Weir—were asked to match wits with top feminist thinkers. Between the columns were photographs of top models in really tight clothes, which could be used both to illustrate the "issues" and help *Esquire* readers to choose revealing outfits for their loved ones.

Besides good publicity for Hansen's career—and a great launch for her poster—the *Esquire* cover had another consequence. It was spied by Rolling Stones guitarist Keith Richards, who had noticed Hansen on the dance floor at Studio 54—where she often discoed late into the night in leopard tights, a leopard bra and cowboy boots. He put her lusty woman poster up on his wall.

Reinhardt, Dickinson, Hansen and Gia together in Mexico had all the makings of a beautified version of *Animal House*. And the week in Cuernavaca and Acapulco did not disappoint.

"The first thing I remember was getting a phone call at home at three in the morning from a hysterical editor telling me her toilet didn't flush," recalled Sara Foley. "They were supposed to stay with the governor of Cuernavaca or something, and the governor had been there, and his sons, too, and then the governor left and two bodyguards were left behind. Then the guards got totally drunk and they were sitting there with these machine guns and wouldn't let any of them into the house. And they were holed up in this room, and the hairdresser had to sleep in a hammock by the pool or something ..."

The trip degenerated from there. "Oh, Christ that was a tough trip," Reinhardt recalled, "between the three of them. Gia was impossible, I mean *totally* impossible. Just unfriendly, difficult, uncooperative, the works ... erratic, one day she'd be nice and then she'd be ... I wanted her to turn her back, and she said, 'I don't do back pictures.' I mean, this is somebody who's *not big yet.*

"I don't know. A lot of it, absolutely, is that the business creates monsters. They end up telling these girls, 'Oh, you're the best, you're the greatest, oh my god.' I remember one editor was making a cover with Janice and she said, 'If she looks like that again, I'm going to have to *cry*, it's so beautiful.' They're so *fake*. But then the girls begin to believe it. They're fragile, usually not greatly educated young people, who are overwhelmed by this incredible power they're suddenly given, and the money. A lot of them don't come from wealthy backgrounds and suddenly they can travel, take the Concorde, go to LA ... producers, directors, stars are after them, and it just goes to their head. They explode."

Several weeks after Mexico, Gia went on a trip for *Glamour,* a working cruise—her first time at sea—that would end on the Caribbean Island of Mustique. The photographer was British-born John Stember. He had come to America via Paris and his first wife, Charlie, had been one of the original Paris Elite models, inspiring the perfume line of the same name. But Stember was from another era in the business.

"I started as an assistant to an English photographer called John French," Stember recalled. "When John French came in the studio in the morning, the clients would stand in the shadows in the back. He would have a line of assistants. It was like a military operation. He would walk in. He would never, *ever* look through a camera himself. He had two assistants to do that. He would stand by the camera and he would say 'still' and the camera would go *plop.* He'd do that six times and he'd say, 'Thank you everybody so much,' and he would walk out and everybody would clap. And that was it. And the guy got a huge check and the clients would never approach him, except maybe feebly to say, 'Thank you very much.' It was like dealing with royalty."

Stember had gone from that rarefied experience to a far more Bohemian lifestyle, which he lived for nearly twenty years in the business. "Suddenly, 1978–79 came along and these fucking guys start coming and saying, 'Listen, come advertise our cigarettes, we'll pay you $15,000 a day,'" he recalled. "I was making $150 a page doing editorial, the most you could get was $2,500 a day for fashion ads. They started talking about $10,000, $12,000, $15,000 *a day.* So basically, I suddenly became aware of money and big studios and staff and cars and drivers and all this crap, you know. And the way the magazines were, we were living like fucking *millionaires.* It was a great time, I have to say. We did everything, and we had so much money we didn't know what to do with it. Basically the biggest problem I had during the day was to think what was the ultimate place we could go to and the ultimate thing we could do. It was fantastic, and everything we could think of just got charged to someone."

Glamour was one of Stember's regular editorial clients, and he had already done a few shots of Gia for the magazine—basically cover tries and tests in his Carnegie Hall studio. This cruise was their first major trip together. "We chartered this fucking great eighty-five-foot yacht out of St. Vincent to go sailing for two weeks and we were going to do our fashion story and beauty story," Stember recalled. "There's eight of us: Gia and Bitten, the two models, I've got a hairdresser, a makeup artist, a fashion editor, her assistant, myself and my assistant. So, first day, we don't get very much done, but we're all sort of getting used to it. Second day, okay, we've really got to get going here cause we have a lot of work to do. So I make a seven o'clock call and seven comes along and we all get up and no Gia. So eight o'clock, okay, this is getting ridiculous. I send my assistant down to get Gia up. I get the report back from the assistant that Gia doesn't *feel like* getting up. So then I go down and bang on the door, 'Gia, come on, we've got a lot of work to do, the sun is good,' so we wait and wait. Finally, about nine o'clock Gia comes up on deck in her swimming costume and I say, 'Gia, *come on,* you're supposed to be ready. What the fuck are you doing? We've got twenty pages of beauty to do, you have to get your act together.'

"Her response is 'Oh, I forgot to tell you, I meant to tell you last night, but I quit modeling.' I said, 'What do you *mean* you quit modeling? You're here on a trip. You can't just tell me you quit modeling, we're out in the middle of the fucking ocean.' So I looked at the editor and she said, 'You can't quit.' And Gia said, 'You want to fucking bet? I quit. I'm snorkeling today.' She said, 'Can you teach me how to snorkel? I might work a day if you teach me how to snorkel.' And this is what I had."

While she later deigned to cooperate on some shots, Gia continued to provoke Stember and his crew. "I was meditating at the time, you know," he recalled. "And I was sitting there on my bunk meditating and there was a little hatch above me. Suddenly I heard this sort of scuffling, but I wouldn't open my eyes. And the next thing *bang, bam, bam, bam,* she and Bitten are lowering a radio full volume on a string. I'm trying to meditate and this radio is sitting in front of my face, full volume.

"Then the next thing is they're both lying on deck, completely naked both of them, both holding sun oil, saying, 'John, please would you put some sun oil on us?' And I'm saying, 'Listen, guys, you know I'm married' [at that time to second wife, model Carrie Lowell], but they say, 'But you have to do it.' And this is the sort of games they're playing. Wearing dresses with no underwear, sitting, like, with their legs wide open. And I come out of the companionway up to dinner and here they are sitting like that, just to provoke, constant provocation.

"One night we decided to play Monopoly. So, of course, with Gia and Bitten, I have to almost punch both of them out. Gia had a knife to Bitten's throat because she thought she was cheating and had taken one of her properties. She was prepared to kill her. It took me two days to get them to stop threatening to kill each other."

Stember was going to do as many shots as possible with Bitten, to avoid Gia. "But Bitten was like this white thing from Denmark, who had never really been in the sun before," he recalled. "She blew up like a balloon. Her lips were all these heat bumps, and whatever, sores, all over her face. So I had to do everything with her looking up through about three feet of water. It was the only way I could get her face to look normal: the distortion of the water made it look alright. It was completely mad. Gia was like swimming around the boat, saying, 'Woo, woo, what are you doing, baby? Are you working?'

"We got to Mustique and we went to this bar called Basil's. Gia walked in and, at that time, her body, she just looked so amazing, all tan and everything. We walked up to this bar and she sat at the bar with her breasts kind of hanging over and this guy by the bar—a young black guy, you know—this guy didn't know *what* had arrived. He was so freaked, he went off on this spurt of poetic dissertation, every word and beautiful thing he could muster in his entire being was being presented to Gia because she was so beautiful. He was saying, 'You're the most beautiful thing that I've ever experienced in my entire life, every pore of my body is alive with your beauty' ... he went on like this for about fifteen minutes.

"After he finished, I think he thought he totally swept her away with his great tirade, and she basically just turned, lifted her head up and said, 'If I look so fucking good why don't you get me a joint?'

"That was her response to all this poetry ... all she wanted to do was get high. And then he came back with a huge pink joint, which she proceeded to smoke and she was just totally out of it."

Many photographers would not find such behavior amusing. In fact, some were already finding Gia to be a chore: she made everything harder than it needed to be. But Stember thought he saw something more behind her contentiousness than another dumb, spoiled model trying to make everyone's life miserable.

"I had a lot of fun times with her," he said. "But, basically, if you told Gia black, she would say white. If you told her to go left, she would go right. If you told her to sit there, she would stand. Whatever you told her to do, she would do the opposite and she did it to the biggest people in this business. They didn't know what hit them. They'd never seen anything like it. Normally, the girls are like 'Fuck me, fuck me, I'll do anything for you.' Gia was just 'fuck you.'

"I have never met anybody who did it in the way that she did. It was so totally self-destructive—it was the way she dealt with herself, too. But she'd put a knife to your throat if you told her that. She had this anger, you know, this tremendous anger. It took a lot of ducking and diving to put up with her. She had to see you weren't going to hit her back. I didn't need to hit her: she was doing it all for me. So I just was her friend. She would take you and *pow,* just to see what you would do. If you didn't get mad, then she'd begin to trust. But when she started to trust you, she'd feel guilty, *pow,* just for no reason.

"You see somebody like her and you become more aware of the human condition at its extreme end. Here's a girl who's extremely beautiful and in extreme pain. And you have to ask yourself: Why is someone who looks this way in so much pain?"

* * *

If her pain was obvious to everyone Gia worked with, so was her rapidly expanding appeal. She was on the cover of the April 1979 issues of American *Cosmopolitan,* British *Vogue* and French *Vogue.* Her first *Cosmo* cover sold spectacularly, as did the brown Norma Kamali unitard in which she appeared. Even though editor Helen Gurley Brown normally preferred Scavullo to shoot twelve different girls each year, another Gia cover was immediately ordered.

She was overwhelmed with attention after the covers, especially the highly visible *Cosmopolitan.* She finally knew what it meant to be "that *Cosmopolitan* girl." It meant a large percentage of the U.S. population went to bed dreaming of being *with* you or being you. And the funny thing was, the picture didn't really even look that much like her. Few of them did. For someone with such a strong, identifiable "look," it was amazing how different Gia appeared in every photograph. She had a hard time recognizing herself sometimes. The photographs took on a life of their own once they were printed and published and distributed. It was like the old Woody Allen stand-up routine that was currently being rediscovered in the wake of his wildly successful films: she saw a life passing before her eyes, but it wasn't her life.

"Gia had an interesting analogy about glamour," recalled one friend. "She said, 'You go to a movie or a play or you look at a magazine, and when you're in the audience, you see it's all glamorous. On the other side, they're lookin' out at you and they know it's *work.* And somewhere in the middle is the glamour and nobody ever really gets it.' "

The work seemed very empty but far too financially rewarding to give up. But Gia was so alone in New York: what little support she had was shaky. She and Sharon Beverly had had their last, "last fight" some time ago. The diminutive makeup artist had moved out, to an apartment on Fifty-seventh Street, and turned a chance conversation at the Fiorucci makeup counter into a partnership with the legendary Patricia Field, whose namesake boutique had made her downtown's most established fashion innovatrix. Since the early seventies, the flamboyant, openly gay Field had been among the first major retailers to merchandise a New York look that was an alternative to Seventh Avenue.

Her store became a showcase for each new pop look before it was shipped to the suburbs, and from its location on East Eighth Street—straddling the boundary between the West and East Villages—she served as the fashion commentator of the hip, the Ms. Blackwell of downtown.

In her spare time, Sharon had been ambitiously designing a makeup line and hand-customizing paint boxes for her radical colors. Field bankrolled Sharon to produce the makeup line for her store: it was eventually successfully marketed under the brand name G-Method. The partnership firmly established Sharon as part of the downtown world, and she became more involved with the Warhol crowd and the Mudd Club scene—where Gia was a frequent, friendly visitor from uptown, but still a slumming fashion type. Sharon and Gia remained friendly, but were barely involved in each other's lives.

Gia's mother came to visit, but Kathleen was becoming more fan than friend. Some of Gia's friends from Philadelphia were staying away because they thought that was what Gia wanted. Nobody understood what she was going through.

Her brother Michael was one of the few family members who visited her in New York. But he didn't take her hints that she might want him to move there. "The mistake we made was that nobody went with her," he recalled. "She could've used a friend. Of course, she said she didn't *want* anyone. But she could've used me or her mother—like Brooke Shields had her mother with her. Sometimes she would ask me to look for a job in New York. I didn't realize until later that she wanted me to be up there for her."

Karen Karuza *had* moved to New York to go to design school; she was living not far away in Brooklyn. But she always got mixed signals from Gia. "She'd phone me and want to talk about all kinds of things," she recalled. "We'd talk for hours. She told me about meeting Salvador Dalí. She said she was supposed to have dinner with him one night but she wasn't going. I asked why and she said, 'Because I'm not hungry.' That was typical Gia.

"Gia and I would be having these in-depth conversations and the operator—this is before call-waiting—kept beeping in saying someone else wanted to get through, and she was saying, 'Forget it.' She would talk about how she wasn't sure if people cared about her or Gia the girl on the cover of *Cosmo.*

"Then I would call her and she'd be very short with me. 'I'm going to England, you think it's so glamorous, it's work.' *Click.* That was Gia, you just never knew. Then she'd call and have tickets for a Valentino show for me. But we started drifting apart. People kept saying to me, 'You've got this friend, she's a big model.' She was my friend, but I didn't want to *use* that in any way, shape or form. I didn't want to push it with her. I knew the type of person she was. That conversation about the fact that it was work made me think there were enough people popping out of the woodwork."

Other people from Philadelphia needed more attention than ever. Photographer Joe Petrellis' model wife had left him and moved to New York with his assistant. "When I was going through my divorce and my pain," recalled Petrellis, "Gia would call me up and say, 'Joe, how are you? Things will look brighter for you. You're a handsome man.' She'd say, 'Stop being a baby.' This was the biggest baby in the world, telling me to stop being a baby. She cared, she took a genuine interest; sometimes she'd call every other day. Before she went to New York, we had been driving one day and that song, that 'Hop on the bus, Gus' song, came on. From then on she'd call and leave messages, 'How you doin', Gus? Let's hop on that bus.' "

In mid-April, Gia asked Italian *Bazaar*'s Lizzette Kattan if she could move in with her for a while. It was fairly common in the fashion industry to have houseguests. Some stylist-friend was always in town for a few days and didn't want to stay in a hotel, and some model, no matter how successful, was always between apartments. During her modeling career, Lizzette had certainly counted on the hospitality of colleagues around the globe. So she was happy to let Gia stay over, even though it was unclear whether Gia was really between apartments or just wanted someone to take care of her for a few days.

"Gia liked my mother a lot," Lizzette recalled. "My mother wasn't living with me in New York, but when I was there I would like her to be with me. I took her everywhere. Gia stayed with us, it was very nice. The only problem was that she was always carrying on with the cigarettes. I don't like anybody smoking around me.

"I spoke to Gia's mother on the telephone, because she called to see if Gia was living at my house and why she was there. The mother asked me blankly if I was sexually or physically involved with Gia. I told her I had no interest in Gia except trying to be a mother for her. Another time when Gia had left her own apartment, the mother called me and wanted to know where she had gone. I called Gia and said, 'Call your mother and tell her what is going on.' They didn't really have the best of relationships. Obviously, the mother was interested in how the daughter was doing, what was going on: she seemed concerned, very normal motherly concern. Gia just couldn't care less about telling her."

While Gia stayed with her, Lizzette also got a glimpse at what passed for her support system in New York. "Gia had a lot of obscure friends," she recalled. "She had a way of coming in and out of people's lives, with such speed and so briefly: I think it was hard for her to have relationships for any length of time. You would see her for four hours but you would remember those four hours. I think Sandy is the one Gia spent the most time with."

Increasingly, Gia's colleagues had come to perceive her as a very cruisy bisexual who came on to most of the women she worked with but had some kind of ongoing relationship with Sandy Linter—or, as ongoing as two full-time freelancers who worked and partied around the world could be. Those who were closer to her believed she was more flirtatious than promiscuous.

"She was definitely bisexual," said John Stember, "but she didn't have a lot of sexual relationships, I'll tell you that. She had major sexual problems, major. And for her to get into a sexual situation, it was not that easy at all. She wasn't fucking around like crazy, at all. She had real difficulty with people. She could find very, very few people that she could spend any kind of time with and she spent a lot of time by herself, a lot of time. All this stuff with her image tends to make her out to be something she wasn't. She had major problems being alive, with herself and finding any kind of ground to be with herself, which was why she was taking drugs most of the time because it alleviated the pain."

In the meantime, she was developing a coterie of fair-weather fans and first-name-only drug connections—like Raul, who worked out of an apartment in the East Village and serviced a lot of the uptown fashion people. Gia had many work friends, play friends and drug friends. But few *real* friends.

"There were a lot of hangers-on with her," said Sean Byrnes. "That happens with a lot of people, if you let it, which is why most of the top girls don't hang out anymore. If you hang out, you get a lot of not-so-nice people. I knew a lot of people who wanted her. I knew her boyfriends and her girlfriends. Just guys, kids who used to hang out at the Mudd Club. She had an affair with a girl or two but many affairs with guys. She was just young and playing around."

"She had a whole pack of little liar friends," recalled John Long, who at the time was selling lithographs through ads in the back of *Vogue* and *Philadelphia* and was writing for small magazines like *Night.* "And they all seemed to have these real *stories,* you know. One was, like, an interior decorator and a brain surgeon. It's part of being enterprising, I suppose."

Blondie's keyboard player Jimmy Destri recalled her as part of a crowd that was "an offspring of the circle I went in: you know, there's always sort of smaller gears around each person's main group." Even though Sharon Beverly remembered Destri "falling madly in love with Gia at first sight" when they had met the band in Philadelphia the year before, he had no recollection of the incident whatsoever. She was just one more pretty girl being brought around to meet him. Destri remembered meeting Gia later at Hurrah's, a pre-Studio disco on West Sixty-second that had been reborn in 1979 as the only downtown-style rock club that was uptown. No romance had ensued, but Jimmy was a pool player, and, when they were both in town, they occasionally shot a few games on the table in the backroom at CBGB's and at the bowling club around NYU.

"New York was different then," Destri recalled, "people hung out at the rock clubs because there was no scene besides the rock 'n' roll scene. In the eighties, the restaurants were hot spots. But back then, there were no dinner clubs. There was Hurrah's, CBGB's, Mudd Club, Max's, that's it. After hours, there was a place on Thirteenth or Fourteenth near Third where they used to frisk you when you went in. The Nursery. I went there once with David Bowie and they thought he was an imposter and frisked him as well." The Nursery was one of the only after-hours clubs with a pool table, but there was an entire circuit of places that didn't open until three or four in the morning—full of the people who were, in the words of one habitué, "fueled and edgy because they were still out and still hadn't gotten laid and just kept going and going until they were a step or two below psychosis."

John Long had always taken a paternal attitude with Gia, but watching out for her was getting more and more difficult. Long recalled seeing Gia stagger into the Ritz one night— before a show by former Philadelphians Hall and Oates— and confronting the guy she had come with, a fairly obvious drug date. He pulled the guy into the Ritz bathroom, and their shouting match finally led to a fight which Long, a martial arts instructor, had no trouble ending quickly. Gia called him the next day, screaming about what he had done to her friend, and their friendship cooled after that. He realized then that someone else would have to stop her from blowing a chance that few were ever afforded.

"I was trying to convince her what an opportunity she had, regardless of whether she liked the work," Long said. "Being Italian myself, I didn't like the preoccupation with the Aryan neo-Nazi look the agencies had. Here was this attractive Italian girl going into the land of the Vikings, where blondes have more fun and Jewish girls are getting nose jobs so they can look like they come from Sweden. I felt there were Italian and Jewish girls who were seeking their own standard of beauty to identify with.

"Gia was a brunette woman with full lips and big bosoms: that's *certainly* a standard of beauty. She was the first to bring that look in. It didn't exemplify the highest socioeconomic echelon. It was more of an urban American look. I said, 'Gia, there are more dark-haired girls in America than blondes, and they would look up to you.' Gia was what an Italian, Spanish, Jewish girl wants to look like.

"She just hadn't discovered what her media should be. She was convinced that photography wasn't creative, and I reinforced that. She was surrounded with photographers who were trying to convince her that they were artists. I tried to convince her that *she was the art* and they were just capturing her. There was a model around at the time who was a friend of mine and Gia's, and she was being teased by this photographer. 'He keeps saying I'm distracting his artistic temperament,' she'd say. I told her the next time he hassles you, simply say that light bounces off of me and creates what you see. If there's art in this room, it's not you, it's *me*."

10
Sustained Fabulousness

Fashion illustrator Joe Eula had, at the height of Studio 54, jumped off the Halston bandwagon to save his own life. He feared he could drug and drink and screw himself to death. By leaving the company that had become his biggest client, he found himself with a lot of bridges burned: he had blown off a very lucrative arrangement with American *Vogue,* doing fashion sketches and commentating around the country, to commit full-time to Halston. But luckily, Joe Eula was still *Joe Eula* to someone: one client's burnout was another's time-honored genius. So Italian *Bazaar* discovered Joe Eula, giving him all the magazine illustrating work he could do and covering the walls of their Milan office complex with his paintings.

The Italian *Bazaar* scene was, predictably, getting out of hand. Rumors began circulating that Peponi Della Schiava's vanity publication was becoming too vain even for the beauty-industrial complex. The drugs and drink at the photo sessions and after were becoming legendary. Stories were circulating of a model booking with no photographers, just Peponi and his pals. This was common enough at the bottom of the business: almost every model had a story about being tricked by a phony photographer or being seduced after a filmless photo session. But it wasn't supposed to happen to real, working models from major agencies. And it wasn't supposed to be done by married executives at major magazines.

"Look, I don't want to say anything because Peponi has been awfully good to me, he saved my life, really," said Joe Eula. "Let's just say he's Italian with a capital *I,* as in 'I can do whatever I want.' "

Some of the photographers who had brought *Bazaar* fame had already stopped working for the magazine. Gia wasn't doing much for *Bazaar* either, but she still did some posing for Joe Eula.

"We would just hole up in *Bazaar*'s office on Seventy-ninth Street for a weekend," recalled Eula. "Gia liked a little drink you know, so we had to get ourselves motivated. We'd try some gin. When that was done we needed some powder.

"She could be sitting there in that awful goddamn office, with this awful office furniture and we'd turn it into a modern ice palace, according to what we had to illustrate. Lizzette would be there too. 'Our job today will be furs,' she'd say, but we didn't have the furs. Just some pieces of cloth; or a photograph of something hanging on a hanger, and we had to make it become real.

"Gia would get into poses that were extraordinary. She could hold it together, maybe because she was so stoned, for what literally could be an hour. With me, Gia didn't have to make up. She didn't have to have silk stockings on—she just had to have that leg. If it was an evening gown, all she'd really need was a pair of high heels. She could have her hair all raw or tied in a kerchief and she could make it the most marvelous turban or whatever came out of her. We *talked* it. She'd get herself in the attitude and she'd feel this great luxury. She was a true actress. She really was, in front of me, the movie actress, the star, wearing 5 & 10 shit and making you think it's the greatest thing since sewing."

Gia had this impact on the people she worked with every day. It no longer mattered how well or how badly she treated them because her reputation always preceded her. And the camera generally found something in her she had trouble recognizing herself. She was a star. And when she showed up—often hours late—she was not so much delivering herself as her career, which was now an important thing to get a piece of.

Her "look" was now a presence in the business: a palpable commodity, a thing of beauty. Fashion editors and photographers referred to it when trying to tell other models what they wanted, would-be models invoked it when describing themselves. When Scavullo and Diana Ross decided to change the singer's glamorous image by slicking back her hair and dressing her down for an album cover, they thought of Gia: not the way she looked on-camera, but the way she appeared at the studio in the morning, or in the clubs at night.

"We called Gia up and said, 'Can we borrow your jeans, the ones with the hole?' " recalled Scavullo. "Those are Gia's jeans in that picture. Diana Ross said she wanted to keep them after the shooting, but Gia wouldn't let her."

Gia liked to tell a story about how photographers picked up on her style. "She told me that she would be at Sandy's and Andrea Blanche would come up," recalled one friend. "You know how when you're relaxing and you undo the top button of your pants? Gia said that sometimes she and Sandy would lounge around like that—and then next thing she knew, she would see it in *Vogue*. Andrea would pick up little things from them."

"Gia dressed street chic *way* before its time," said Scavullo's fashion editor Sean Byrnes. "And she's the one who brought that look right into *Vogue* magazine. She just gave a modern, street-smart look to photography. She made it believable yet unbelievable. She'd wear black pants and white men's shirts and black flat pumps, or a motorcycle jacket, and, of course, the beat-up jeans. And she made it so *stylish*, she looked so stunning. You could put a woman in a couture gown next to her and she looked better. She was the only one to do that in modeling at that time.

"In real life, a lot of models don't wear makeup and they don't look so hot. But Gia looked beautiful with no makeup. She also had the most beautiful breasts of any model I've ever worked with in my life, and I've been doing *Cosmo* covers for fifteen years. I dress these girls. And Gia had an incredible body. She exuded a sexuality without trying.

"She was very clever and she had a good brain. She was good at figuring out people, it was not easy to fool her. . . . You know, models are models. Models are beautiful, but very seldom do they get any element of their life in the photo. They're doing it as a job, and they do it well. But Gia brought some of what she had lived into her photos, and that's what made her really special."

In May of 1979, the pesky art-versus-commerce debate that had always hung over the world of commercial photography was settled once and for all. The news came in a *New York Times Magazine* profile of Alexander Liberman, the sixty-six-year-old Condé Nast editorial director. The first paragraph of the article would be invoked in the industry for years to come. "It's a mistake to consider fashion journalism an art," Liberman declared. "True art doesn't belong in the medium anymore. I say this to my friends, to writers and photographers: 'Do what I do in my life! Do what is necessary. Take the pictures, write the articles I need for my magazine, and then use the money you make for your private, creative purposes. Don't put your deepest soul into this kind of work!' "

Liberman pronounced that he had recently come to realize that he had been "kidding myself and the public. I know I'll get shot for this, but I don't consider photography an art." The quote appeared right next to a picture of him walking with Avedon through the photographer's recent show at the Metropolitan Museum of Art, which had received both art-world accolades and a *Newsweek* cover.

Since the Condé Nast magazines were where photography was first elevated to art, Liberman's words amounted to a weighty public attack. It didn't matter how commercial the publications seemed to be getting, and how outraged the photographers were about the monthly reader's surveys—the dreaded "Clements Reports"—that produced a score for each page in the magazine. As long as *Vogue* could still be ... *Vogue,* they could justify the way that making fashion pictures controlled their lives. But here was Liberman, in *The New York Times,* saying that what they did had no intrinsic value and that the only standard their work had to meet, or *could* meet, was that of public acceptance.

Some photographers never forgave him. "Liberman is a snake and phony of the worst order and a phony artist," said photographer Peter Beard, who had already been out of the Condé Nast fold for years and might have been the company's ultimate disgruntled former employee. "Art is like a Rorschach test. You can't pass if you don't have what it takes. Liberman is a 'designer artist': that's what I'd call it."

Right or wrong, Liberman's new approach was highly successful. *Vogue* had more than saved itself from the 1970 midi skirt disaster. The *Times* article attached numbers to the trends, and now everyone knew that *Vogue*'s circulation had risen seventy-three percent in the previous five years, to just over a million. In just the past three years, *Vogue*'s gross advertising revenues had more than doubled, to nearly $22 million.

Vogue staffers had begun to refer to their magazine as The Bible again. But this time, it was more a description of its physical density than its previous air of infallibility. It could no longer dictate fashion. Its center—the decades of creative arrogance and unmitigated gall to tell people what to wear and care about—had not held. *Vogue* now *took* pulses rather than quickening them. And its financial success was being measured in such astronomical figures—amounts no one had dreamed of a few years before—that it was easy to believe that any excesses involved in documenting this less brave, less new fashion world were being tolerated for the right reasons.

Denis Piel was American *Vogue*'s hot new find, the next underappreciated photographer in his mid-thirties to be summoned from Paris, where he was doing magazine work. The difference between Piel and the French Mafia before him was the difference in the business between 1975 and 1979: Piel was brought over with far less major magazine experience in Europe, and was almost immediately given a level of *carte blanche* that made even the regular stable of indulged *Vogue* shooters blanch.

Piel considered himself extremely lucky to have risen so quickly, and the more established *Vogue* photographers couldn't have agreed more. They ascribed his success to luck, and perhaps the innovation of his signature range of prone poses. In most of Piel's most memorable shots, the models were either sitting in a chair, leaning across a sofa, or reclining on a table or floor—often with a drink nearby, since Piel was a wine connoisseur. What could be more appropriate for this go-go time when models were so inebriated with their own success—and the inebriants that came with it—that they could barely get up in the morning? What a masterstroke for *Vogue* to find a photographer who specialized in beautiful, romantic shots of girls literally *swept off their feet*. "All the sudden Piel shows up in New York and he's doing girls lying down ready to throw up," recalled Alex Chatelain. "I hated it at the time. Now I see it as good, but I hated him then."

Piel booked Gia for his first job with *Vogue*, along with hairstylist John Sahag—who, like Piel, had come to America via Australia and then Paris. With a revolving cast of makeup artists and editors, Piel established Gia and Sahag as part of his regular team for the deluge of work that was suddenly thrown his way: especially his contracts with American *Vogue* and Christian Dior in Paris. At Dior, he was performing the same function as Chris von Wangenheim was in the United States—creating signature magazine ads for all the different boutiques and licensees the couture house had in Europe. But the European Dior Boutique ads were ten-to-twenty-page *groupages* that appeared regularly in fashion magazines in Italy, France and Britain: they were omnipresent. Gia wasn't officially "the Dior girl"—she had no contract with the company, and simply got her normal advertising day rate and residuals—but she might as well have been. Through Piel, she would be in ninety percent of the Dior Boutique shots appearing that fall in Europe.

With all due speed, Piel was given the plum assignment at *Vogue:* shooting the Paris collections. He took Nancy Donahue and Gia, whose second *Cosmo* cover, a shot of her barely contained in a yellow Giorgio Sant'Angelo bathing suit, was the focal point of America's newsstands. This was Gia's third time at the collections, but going with American *Vogue* was different from going with any other magazine. American *Vogue* had all but invented European collection coverage. While the world's other fashion magazines tried to outdo each other, *Vogue* was above the throng trying to outdo itself. *Vogue* was like *The New York Times* or CBS News and the Paris collections were its equivalent of the presidential elections: when the organization's creativity and professional efficiency were put to their ultimate tests.

The Walter Cronkite of the Paris collections was *Vogue*'s fashion editor, Polly Mellen— *"Mrs.* Mellen" to all but those few who could address her informally. Even though her boss, *Vogue* editor Grace Mirabella, was clearly the ranking member of the entourage that always got the prime seats along the Paris runways, Paris was Polly Mellen's show. The editors-in-chief at Condé Nast magazines had too many corporate and ceremonial responsibilities to get involved in all the detail work that went into running the magazines. At the collections, Grace Mirabella would select her favorite pieces, meet with the designers, and decide what "directions" were "important." But the fashion editors were the ones who sat in the studios and oversaw the photo sessions. They were the ones who primed the girls for the camera and screeched if they noticed an errant thread on a dress while surveying the scene through their opera glasses. They were the ones who alternately drove the photographers crazy with their minutiae and contributed the One Idea—a tilt of a hat, a suggestion to a model about what to think about, an invocation of a mood—that made the picture work. They were the ones in the trenches, making sure their whims were properly executed.

And fifty-three-year-old Polly Mellen was their archetype. She was the last of the true Vreelanders still working full-time for *Vogue*. And she was the one who carried the "anything for a great picture" ethos into the era when "anything" and "great picture" were being drastically redefined. Her first *Vogue* sitting had been in the mid-sixties: five weeks in Japan with Avedon and top model Veruschka, producing landmark fashion photos. And she maintained the vestiges of the old *Vogue* as it tried to respond better to working girls: "Working girls, *working* girls," she said, "look, I have great respect for the working girl, but she does not have to be so boring, boring, *boring.*"

Polly Mellen's fashion free association was legendary, and many of *Vogue*'s actual fashion statements—the headlines, the trios of descriptive adjectives, "The New Allure: Soft, Spirited and Leggy!"—went from her mouth to her assistant's notepad to the typesetter. Her ability to look at a garment, describe its relevance in the universe and riff on its practical applications was often parodied—like in the standing *Vogue* joke about space travel, "Zero gravity ... *I see scarves!*"

But Polly Mellen's brainstorming was also the standard by which other fashion editors were judged. How else was one to properly execute the job of choosing clothes for a living and putting them on beautiful girls than to exaggerate the importance of every detail? If millions of American women were going to make major wardrobe decisions because of the photos in *Vogue,* didn't they deserve someone who took the mission of channeling their fashion energy seriously? If zero gravity didn't make you see scarves, what was the point of being a fashion editor?

But for the first time in years, Polly Mellen wasn't coming to Paris. Just before the collections, she had a personal catastrophe. During a party she and her husband were giving at the summer home they rented in Connecticut, the deck, which was built out over a rock ledge, separated from the house and sent Polly and many of her sixty guests toppling fifteen feet down. One woman died of a heart attack, and there were many other serious injuries—including Polly's sister-in-law, who broke both legs and her pelvis. Polly herself escaped with two hematomas on her arms, and considered herself fortunate because "a nail missed my spinal column by *that much.*" Because of her injuries, she decided to skip the collections, even though it meant missing Denis Piel's couture debut.

It also meant missing one of the most talked-about runway shows of the decade. The fashion press had been quietly grumbling for years that the couture was dead—that it had become nothing more than an expensive public relations spectacle to increase awareness of certain fashion *names* and increase the value of lucrative licensing deals being made by the couture houses. But then Yves St. Laurent had hidden away for six months and created a collection that inspired everyone. In his show—which, as always, was the grand finale of the collections—he offered some fashion direction *and* he included some clothes that humans could wear.

St. Laurent also brilliantly co-opted the resurging interest in Picasso. As the collections were underway in Paris, the Museum of Modern Art in New York was holding a massive retrospective of the painter's work, as important in its artistic scope as its hype. The demand for tickets to the show was unprecedented, as was the viewing policy: for the first time in major museum history, tickets had to be purchased in advance for a certain day and a certain two-hour time period. With its restrictive pricing and excessive hype of a marketable brand name, the Picasso show was the first "designer" art exhibit. St. Laurent had chosen an economically convenient time to be inspired by the late painter's work.

But Polly Mellen would miss out on all the excitement. Which meant there would be even more pressure than usual during Gia's first Paris collections sittings for American *Vogue*. The magazine had a full-time editor in Paris and had hired a young American student, Charla Carter, to act as a bilingual gofer and assist the incoming editors during the collections. Robert Turner, *Vogue*'s only male fashion editor, was assigned, at the last minute, to do the sitting.

And then Denis Piel announced that his photographic innovation would be to shoot the collections in available daylight *only*. *Vogue* had never shot collections during the day. Couturiers wanted the clothes during the day so they could be sold, and, since the earliest days of transatlantic travel, *Vogue* editors had always stayed on New York time while in Paris—to minimize boat, and later, jet lag. Besides the daylight, Piel also wanted more than just the simple props usually used for the hotel room shots. Among other things, he required the two little boys St. Laurent had dressed as harlequins from a Picasso painting to add a theatrical flair to his runway show.

"Denis loved the *mise en scène* and he wanted props," recalled Charla Carter. "We had to bring in special armchairs and couches. On the desk had to be a Hermès pigskin agenda, nothing else. He was quite extravagant. His bills at the Hotel Crillon . . . breakfast omelet with truffles, $50, five bottles of red wine at dinner.

"That was just added to the normal extravagance, which made the *Vogue* collections pictures a bigger deal than everyone else's. They had photographers shooting the shows themselves, and the pictures were then immediately developed. All the editors who had been sitting in the front row would be driven back to the office, this beautiful room in the Place du Palais Bourbon. They spent hours poring over the slides and cutting down the choices. There was a whole security system for the clothes, since you were getting these garments worth $30,000 and they had to be returned or *Vogue* paid. There was this whole stable of *Vogue* chauffeurs. And you knew that after the pictures were shot, they had to be developed *immediately,* so they could be sent to New York on the Concorde to be on Mr. Liberman's desk. So they had a whole complicated system worked out.

"Like, we always had kimonos for the models. And each girl, when she arrived, even if she didn't want to, had to put on one of these navy and white cotton kimonos. If they weren't dressed like that when having hair and makeup done, it was a *scandal.* . . . We'd always have coffee pots, rented refrigerators filled with juices, huge bowls of dried fruits, cookies, big plates of cheese, goat cheese, little white round chevre. I'd have to go out and buy from markets, they didn't have services in Paris then, nobody delivered. So I had to buy the food, and make sure I had Polly's pins when she called. She had this little stuffed tomato on a leather cord around her neck with straight pins and T-pins. And I had to make sure the prop kit was stocked—the metallic suitcases with everything in them. Belt-hole punchers, falsies, tampons, pins, malaria tablets. Double-edge tape. If Polly was on set and she screamed 'double-edge tape!' well, you better have it. It's the single most useful stylist's tool."

Even by *Vogue*'s standards for Paris craziness, July 1979 was madness. "I had difficulty with the editor there," recalled John Sahag. "He was a son of a bitch. The situation is, we're in Paris to shoot the collections. It's a big fucking deal. Everybody from New York is panicking. Denis has his own thing also. He was a little bit of an *arriviste,* that's what we call them. He's in a battle. He wants to shoot the clothes the way he wants them. But at the same time he's nervous about what they'll say in New York. For me, I want to be able to get another assignment, but I'm looking to score some really unbelievable-looking hair. No matter who's in my way, I'm going to do what I want to do. And for every shot, I have to do the hair differently."

After being told for the umpteenth time what was wrong with the way he had styled Gia's hair, Sahag decided to have a temper tantrum of his own. He marched Gia to the hotel bathroom, screamed "Get the fuck out of here," and slammed the door behind them. "Gia was on the bathroom floor, laughing hysterically," Sahag recalled. "She was just so pleased to see something like that. I was so upset. I was red. And then I started to laugh like her. She goes, 'Yeah, he's a son of a bitch.' She was trying to calm *me* down."

The sessions might have been crazed, but the pictures were a huge success. The stunner was a photo of Gia, in a lace evening dress, lying down with the two harlequin boys from the runway show on either side, holding tight bouquets of flowers. All the effort to locate and redress the little boys had been well worth it. St. Laurent himself later used the picture for his own book as the shot that summed up the collection. American *Vogue* used twelve shots of Gia in all. Alternate versions of the same pictures appeared in the new German edition of *Vogue,* which had just started publishing out of Munich the month before and wasn't yet able to do its own collection coverage.

Gia was becoming a big enough model that taking extraordinary measures on her behalf became ordinary. "We usually just booked a backup model for any session we used Gia," recalled photographer Albert Watson. "She was beautiful enough that if she showed up, it was worth doing it that way." Such a businesslike attitude was typical of Watson, a thirty-seven-year-old from Scotland who had begun his commercial photography career in the then-unlikely locale of Los Angeles before relocating to New York in the late seventies. He was known as a glossy, commercial photographer with an extremely *professional* operation. Photography wasn't his lifestyle, it was his job. His work "team" wasn't his "family." He had his own family, a wife, Elizabeth, and two sons: Liz Watson ran his business, and was branching out into representing hair and makeup people.

"One time I shot with Gia the entire day," Watson recalled, "and on the very end of the shooting we needed one more shot. We were outside, and there was a Hell's Angel guy on a motorbike. The guy had stopped at a traffic light and I asked if he would be used for the shot. I wanted to put Gia on the back of the motorbike with him. She was wearing a leather outfit—Montana I think. So he agreed and he made about five or six passes past the camera. I went up to her and said, 'That was terrific.' She said, 'Have you got the shot?' I said yeah. She said, 'So that's it?' I said, 'That's it.'

"She turned to the guy and said, 'Let's go.' So, still wearing the clothes, she hopped on his bike and they just split. It took about three days to get the outfit back."

But Watson's favorite Gia story took place in Paris during an advertising session for St. Laurent during the *haute couture*. "We were shooting these dresses that were each $60,000, $70,000, $80,000," recalled Watson, "and when Gia put on the first one, she was chewing bubble gum and snapping it. There were all these ladies there from St. Laurent to dress her. The head dresser had been with St. Laurent since the beginning—and had been at Dior with him before. She came in and she tied the bow on one of the black evening dresses a certain way. So Gia was kind of looking at this, chewing gum at the same time, and the first thing she did was untie the bow. She said, 'No, no, no, no, it should be more like *this*,' and she retied the bow.

"Of course, the expression on this dresser's face was just incredible, with Gia retying the bow and snapping her gum. So eventually they retied it four or five times and they agreed it was all right. So that was fine. Gia came downstairs wearing the outfit and she saw that dinner had arrived. It was a night shooting, and there was a roast chicken there. So she walked over to the film table, picked up the film scissors, and went—in the St. Laurent dress and the bow, with the makeup and the hair—and picked up the chicken, put the scissors in and proceeded to cut the chicken in half. I must say, she didn't get anything on the dress. Then she peeled off a leg of the chicken and just ate it. When she was done, they redid the lips and she looked beautiful."

Gia was doing more than sustaining professional fabulousness. To the lower echelon of *fashionistas*—the assistants who did all the drudge work for fashion editors and photographers, the models who coveted her position—Gia was becoming something of a hero.

"God, I don't want to turn Gia into something mythological," said Helen Murray, one of the reigning *Vogue* assistants in the late seventies, "but I would hear these stories, and I'm sure I'm not the only one who lived vicariously through them. She was doing stuff we all wanted to do but were too afraid to. This spectacular-looking girl who didn't give a shit—I greatly admired the stories I heard about her."

Murray worked for Polly Mellen in the mid-seventies, but also became professionally friendly with Frances Stein, the mercurial *Vogue* fashion editor who was "much scarier than Mrs. Mellen." Stein left the magazine in 1979 to become a vice president and designer with Calvin Klein—whose exploding company was grossing over $100 million a year—and soon convinced Murray to leave for Calvin as well. She languished there in the fragrance division and received continual *Vogue* updates on the phone.

"Gia just wasn't gonna kiss anybody's ass, and there was *so much* ass-kissing going on," Murray recalled. "The first really famous story I heard about her—and this was when I was still at the magazine—well, Gia at one point refused to do lingerie shots for *Vogue*. She had an extraordinary body, but I don't think she was comfortable being booked for lingerie, hanging around in a bra and panties all day. And she was in her rights to refuse that kind of work. It's one thing if you want to do it for advertising—fine, then she would do it for the money. But for $150 a day for *Vogue?* I can understand turning that down.

"Anyway, they had a sitting organized at Westbury Gardens out on Long Island. They had a location van, and everybody was supposed to meet at Condé Nast and go out together. At the last minute the booker called and said Gia had her own car and she wanted to drive out herself. She *swore* she would be there on time. And she was. She drives up, on time, gets out of her car, walks up and sees that there's all this underwear hanging in the van. *Vogue* had not told her that they wanted to do lingerie: they got her out there under false pretenses.

"So, she just calmly says to the editor, 'I forgot something in my car,' and she drives back to New York, leaving them all there. I thought that was spectacular."

Murray had come to her attitude toward model behavior through a series of eye-opening experiences in the business. "When I started and these models were my age," she recalled, "I felt, at times, that I would have traded places with *any* of them. Not long after I started, this model Paola killed herself, just a couple months after she was on the cover of *Vogue*. I thought, 'How could a girl who got the cover of *Vogue* kill herself?' It was inconceivable.

"Then there was a girl I had known since I was a teenager who became a top model—her name was Lisa Taylor. We weren't, like, close friends, but I had done some growing up with her and I thought she had the most perfect life in the world. We were supposed to have dinner one night, and I couldn't find her. I called her booker, and she said Lisa was in the hospital because she tried to kill herself. Then I started to *get* it, I started to understand. I was stupid. I thought that it would be a hell of a job to be traveling and young and beautiful and hanging out with all these glamorous people and having men beat your door down. What more could a girl want? Lisa was not alone. There were *many* who needed a hell of a lot more than to be told how beautiful they were. A lot of them didn't feel that beautiful. They didn't understand, they didn't get it; they couldn't make the distinction. The *only thing it was about* was what they looked like. It was only how they looked."

The bottom line was the picture. And as Polly Mellen's assistant, Murray got a taste of what would be tolerated in the name of beauty. "If it meant an assistant had to run fifteen blocks to get a pomegranate, it was done," she recalled. "One day I had to organize a dinner party for Janice Dickinson. Janice arrived at the studio and had had a fight with Mike and she was upset and so Mrs. Mellen—instead of having me iron or do the things I normally had to do—gave me the job of finding out everything Janice needed for her party and ordering it. Janice was crying, and it was a picture for Ralph Lauren. Mr. Penn was the photographer, and he was going in close and he couldn't photograph Janice's eyes if she was crying.

"So I was calling stores and if they didn't have the cheese

she wanted I had to go into the dressing room and ask, 'Janice, they don't have Asiago, would this be okay?' And I'm just thinking, 'What the fuck am I doing?' In fairness to Mrs. Mellen, what was she going to do? The only way to get control of the situation was to not let Janice talk to Mike for the rest of the day—when he called he was *not* put through—and have me do all the work.

"So, you can understand why I so relished the Gia stories. It might make me look like an idiot now, but I honestly felt at the time that there was something terribly *right* about her rebellion. To me, she was just a sweet girl who had this streak in her, and I greatly admired her rebellion."

Gia, her look, and her attitude had moved to a new place on Fourth Avenue, in a low-rise apartment building near Union Square, on the uptown fringe of downtown. The one-bedroom apartment had plain white walls, hardwood floors and a pass-through from a small kitchen: it was $600 a month plus another $85 a month for garage space for her car. Gia furnished the apartment sparsely, as was the fashion among fashion people, since they weren't home much. The living room was decorated with an upholstered, tiger-striped corner section from a jungle-theme conversation pit (on which sat a pillow in the shape of the Frosted Flakes mascot, Tony the Tiger), a lamp in the shape of the Eiffel Tower, a massive gilt-framed mirror waiting to be hung, a stool covered with Fiorucci stickers, a TV and a framed photograph of Debbie Harry. On the black, smoked-glass coffee table was a small, white plastic spaceship toy with a green alien sticking out. Along the wall that led to the tiny bedroom was a plastic strip full of pictures of Batman and Superman and some Polaroids from recent sittings tacked together.

Gia could rarely be found in her apartment. Her mother often kept up with her professional whereabouts through the credits on her published editorial photos and through her postcards. Her private life could be pieced together by the growing stack of New York City parking summonses—many from tickets written near Sandy Linter's building—that were being delivered to Richboro, where Gia's car was registered.

The agency kept track of her by having her call in. It was

easier than trying to hunt her down. In most cases, a big girl like Gia would have been long-attached to a particular booker who would know her haunts, her habits and even when her menstrual period was due so big bookings weren't made on bloaty, uncomfortable days. But Gia had never become particularly close with any of her bookers. Her main relationship at the agency was with Wilhelmina herself.

Willie was guiding Gia through her career—which was exploding. In America, she had just premiered in her first cosmetics campaign, for Maybelline's new Super Shiny Automatic Lip Color. Maybelline wasn't as high fashion as Revlon or Estée Lauder, the two companies that dominated the high end of retail cosmetics. So the print ads, shot at Regine's, appeared in *Glamour* rather than *Vogue*. And Gia's picture—in which she was applying "Melonshine" with the Super Shiny trademark wand—was plastered over counter cards and other point-of-purchase materials in drugstores rather than department stores.

In Europe, even though Gia's editorial work for Italian *Bazaar* and the various *Vogues* was limited, her public recognition was high—the Dior Boutiques ads were everywhere—and about to get higher. She had been chosen as the sole model for a large portfolio of Giorgio Armani ads, shot by Florentine art photographer Aldo Fallai, that would appear all over Europe. She had no contract—Italian manufacturers rarely paid top market prices for models—but she would certainly appear, to the international fashion world, to be the "Giorgio Armani girl." In the photos, her hair was pulled back to appear short. In fact, it was just growing back after a haircut that had been done for a *Vogue* pictorial with Irving Penn, who had documented the process and the finished product. Gia hated the haircut so much that she canceled all her bookings for two weeks. She only emerged from her apartment for a *Vogue* sitting with Richard Avedon.

Avedon was the last of the major New York fashion photographers to come around to booking Gia. "She was not an Avedon girl," said Francesco Scavullo, "Avedon wouldn't have found her that divine." It was amazing that Avedon, at the age of fifty-six, found *anything* in fashion photography divine anymore. He had been the most influential eye in the industry for nearly thirty years, had been discovered and rediscovered by every client in fashion, had inspired the Hollywood musical *Funny Face* and had basically done it all, nine or ten times.

Avedon had surfaced when the fashion industry resurfaced after World War II. A star-struck autograph hound and high school dropout from the Bronx, whose father had owned a Fifth Avenue clothing store until the Depression, Avedon had spent the war as a Merchant Marine taking identification pictures. After the war, he enrolled in a New School for Social Research design course being taught by *Harper's Bazaar* art director Alexey Brodovitch, and then began hounding Brodovitch to give him work. He eventually did—when Avedon stopped trying to take grand, elegant photographs, and began shooting more casual pictures of his own girlfriend and her friends. Those pictures launched his career, and he soon began shooting fashion and portraits for *Bazaar* as well as advertising work. From that point on, he was *Avedon,* and he had been skimming the cream off the top of commercial photography ever since: taking the fashion photographs, celebrity portraits, movie stills and advertising shots that defined several eras.

Since coming to Condé Nast in the mid-sixties just after Diana Vreeland, Avedon had been given an extraordinarily large percentage of the company's editorial work—there were periods during which he shot close to ninety percent of all Condé Nast covers. But Vreeland's departure coincided with Avedon's new choice of aperture: he began working with an old-fashioned Deardorff camera, which shot 8 × 10-inch negatives, because, he said, his standard Rolleiflex "was beginning to take the picture . . . I wanted nothing to help the photograph except what I could draw out of the sitter." The new camera—and a new insistence on shooting with seamless backgrounds—gave Avedon a new signature look and photographs of uncharacteristic clarity and richness of detail.

But the Deardorff also hampered Avedon's usefulness to *Vogue.* Its very slow shutter locked Avedon into very controlled studio settings—even his outdoor art pictures were being shot on seamless—just as *Vogue* wanted its power photographer shooting fast on the street. Avedon was dooming himself to pre-modernism. No matter how much that disappointed the Polly Mellens, it all seemed part of the plan. He wouldn't be asked to travel as much, and his sittings would become even more exclusive, his talents valued even higher. Now clients would hire him when they wanted the best of the best, when money was no object. Whenever the ante was raised on fees, or creative control, Avedon would be there to rake in the pot.

His latest such triumph was a high-profile ad campaign for Italian designer Gianni Versace. Now that Versace was designing his own line and looking to make a huge splash in America and Europe—in men's clothes, for which he was better known, as well as women's—he wanted to follow in the well-publicized footsteps of Calvin Klein, who had realized that the public's fascination with the fashion business and with modeling could be used to make the *campaign itself* an event. Klein hired the most visible models in the world—first Patti Hansen and then, when Patti wanted $60,000 to reprise her Times Square billboard, Brooke Shields—and had them shot by the photographers with the highest name recognition. Then he hired well-connected fashion publicists and let celebrity turn advertising into news.

Knowing all this, Versace decided to out-Klein Calvin. He and Avedon decided that the spring 1980 Versace campaign would employ not one but *all* of the top high-fashion girls in New York, in groups and singles. The top male models of the day would be hired strictly as "props" for the shots. And instead of letting an art director or stylist control the sittings, Avedon would do it himself, assisted by the models and the crew sent over with Versace's instructions: Gianni's sister, Donatella, and his protégé, Paul Beck, a young American who had joined the Versace organization after modeling in the company's first-ever men's campaign. It would be an unusual group effort to make unusual group pictures, the need for a camaraderie exacerbated by Avedon's slow 8 × 10 camera, which required longer-than-average poses and took ten minutes just to produce a Polaroid. The models would get to decide which of the clothes they wanted to wear and be asked to move and improvise. Then they would hold the improvised poses for excruciatingly long periods.

The campaign was so prestigious that even though the rates were hardly extravagant (for Gia, $1,250 a day) and included no residuals or extras, they could not be refused. Balking at the day rate meant losing one's spot in the campaign that, by design, defined who the top high-fashion girls were. They were Patti Hansen, Gia, Janice Dickinson, Renee Russo, Beverly Johnson, Kelly LeBrock and Jerry Hall. The pictures were done on simple colored backgrounds, lit and shot so they had an other-worldly richness. And the posing had an unusual flow to it: the models were hanging on each other, leaning on each other, somehow moving without moving. Instead of one or two signature shots to drive home the image of the campaign, there were dozens, to appear in magazines, catalogs and point-of-purchase material all over Europe and America.

Gia was the central figure in many of the shots, perhaps because she interacted more with the male models. Renee Russo sat on one model like he was a chair and Patti Hansen stood a little stiffly even among the unclothed men. But Gia's shots looked like she and the guys were actually grabbing at each other, toying with each other. In several shots, she pulled the male models' hair as they held her: in one, her hand was curled inside the waistband of the man's pants. Gia was also the model called upon to wear most of the bathing suits and revealing tops: having "the best tits in the business" was working to her advantage.

The Versace campaign was an international sensation and it sold a lot of clothes. But Avedon's most modern pictures in years were memorable for other reasons as well. They succeeded in capturing a rare moment. They were snapshots of the beauty-industrial complex and New York City at their peak of craziness and creativity and camaraderie and promise—when everyone seemed happy and healthy and wealthy enough, and it looked as if the hip, not the meek, would inherit the earth.

And they were shot only days after the Ayatollah Khomeini seized power in Iran and took both the American Embassy and the high-minded presidency of Jimmy Carter hostage. There wasn't yet a hint that the event could provide the media-savvy campaign of Ronald Reagan with the rhetorical "hook" it needed to promote the teleprompted conservative like a pair of designer jeans. It was still inconceivable that the techniques the beauty-industrial complex taught Madison Avenue could be used to sell the country its first spokesmodel president—a body-double leader who would then go to war against life in the fast lane as inconsistent with American values.

11

Life During Wartime

A few days after the Versace shoot, a handful of the top models came together again for a different kind of sitting: an editorial shot for *Interview* to plug Sandy Linter's book. Sandy had written or, rather, had been packaged into a how-to manual on "the new nighttime makeup" called *Disco Beauty*. The book featured photos of most of the top models of the day. Each picture was accompanied by a paint-by-number schematic drawing, detailing how "a good face—one that has been properly colored and contoured—creates an excitement, a magic and an evanescence that symbolizes the blinking, slinking, frantic fantasy world of an all-night disco." The book had a cover shot of Bitten and opened to a picture of Juli Foster—topless and looking faux orgasmic. Then came a portrait of Sandy, the "most exciting new makeup artist in the country," peering out through a soft-focus haze as part angel, part bleary-eyed, pouty-lipped disco queen. The rest was a hodgepodge of pictures culled from various editorial and test sessions Linter had done.

Photographer Michael Tighe had been assigned by *Interview* to take a picture of Linter with some of her model pals: Gia, Juli Foster and Patti Hansen. Under normal conditions, the shot would have taken no time at all. Tighe was known for his quick, controlled sessions and, besides, nobody was being paid. But normal conditions were no longer in vogue.

Gia's mother, Kathleen Sperr, in her den decorated with magazine covers (1); Gia as a Brownie (2); brother Michael Carangi at the Altantic City luncheonette of his late father, Joe Carangi (3); Kathleen and Joe with Joe, Jr. in 1958 (4)

Bowie Kids

The locker Gia shared at Lincoln High (5); Bowie apostles camped out at Philly's Sigma Sound Studio (Joey Bowie, *far right*) hoping to be invited into sessions for *Young Americans* (6); Nancy Adams, Gia's aunt and peer (7); Northeast girls Karen Karuza and Gia (8)

One of Gia's first modeling test shots (9) by Joe Petrellis (10): a photo (11) from the portfolio of Maurice Tannerbaum (Mr. Maurice, 12) that first got Gia noticed at Wilhelmina; Gimbels ad (13)

Soft on sweater dressing: Gimbels special purchase 5.99

The "Hollywood Board" at Wilhelmina Models, adorned with posters of founder Wilhelmina Cooper—Gia's first surrogate mother in New York—and her discovery (14); a candid Polaroid (15); the first promotional card for Gia (16); *(opposite page)* the Lance Staedler shot that first opened doors for Gia in New York (17), and a Staedler private photo (18)

17

18

Ciao, Gia

(*opposite page*) Rooftop shot at the Citicorp Building for Italian *Bazaar* (19); *Bazaar* fashion director Lizzette ...attan, who gave Gia her first ...ajor jobs (20); from Lizzette's diary ...age (21); Chris von Wangenheim, ...e dark prince of fashion photo- ...aphy (22); (this page) ...hotographer Patrick Demarchelier ...d Gia during the 1978 *alta moda* ...3); Gia and *Bazaar* publisher ...poni Della Schiava in Capri (24); ...a with a Polaroid of Lizzette and ...poni (25)

Model War Zone

New York magazine declaring the model wars (26); a decision in one of many lawsuits (27); top makeup artist Sandy Linter (28), who became closer with Gia after the Von Wangenheim session that produced a *Vogue* fashion page (29) and a powerful art photograph (30)

Beautiful Punk

Gia mugs with her Italian *Cosmo* poster (31) and lounges in her downtown apartment (32); street chic and stoned again in New York (33)

Sustained Fabulousness

Local-girl-made-good Gia on the cover of *Philadelphia Magazine* (34); being made up by friend Way Bandy during *Vogue* shoot on St. Barts (35); photographer Francesco Scavullo (36); on the boat to St. Barts (37)

Bubblegum Habit

Designer Perry Ellis (38), whose breakthrough collection Gia modeled on the runway (39–40) and for American *Vogue*; Gia's datebook entry just before Wilhelmina's death from cancer, reminding herself, in her usual sloppy spelling, to "get herion" (41); the Scavullo shot for American *Vogue* in which Gia's needle marks were visible even after airbrushing (42)

Gia and her lover Rochelle with the red Fiat Gia bought with her first big modeling fees (43); mug shots from Gia's two arrests (44–45); a Polaroid self-portrait (46)

Comeback

lite's Monique Pillard, who directed Gia's return and was her last
mother figure in New York (47); the 1982 American *Cosmo* cover
that Scavullo "gave" Gia (48); Gia's page in *Scavullo: Women* in
which she discussed the end of her drug use, even though she was
using again by the time it was published (49)

"There's a lot more to being good-
looking than makeup and prettiness
... there's a lot more to being a
woman than that. When I look in the
mirror, I just want to like myself ...
And if I like myself, then I look
good."

Rehab

A therapeutic self-portrait Gia did during her months at Eagleville Hospital (50), and her certificate for completing the first part of the rigorous program (51)

EAGLEVILLE HOSPITAL

Eagleville, Pennsylvania

Presents this Certificate to

GIA CARANGI

FOR HAVING COMPLETED THE

INPATIENT PHASE OF THE PROGRAM

On This __26th__ Day of __March__ 19 __85__

Martha L. Waters
President

52

53

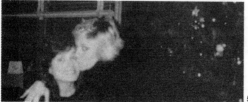

54

Gia with rehab friends Dawn Phillips (52), with whom she briefly lived after being diagnosed with AIDS, and Rob Fay (53); her last Christmas with Rochelle (54)

Gia after rehab (55); the Joe Eula painting of Gia winking that hangs in Lizzette Kattan's living room (56); Kathleen and Gia in late 1985 (57); Cindy Crawford—whose looks earned her the nickname "Baby Gia" in the modeling world until she made her own fame—in a Scavullo shot for which she was deliberately made up to resemble Gia (58)

"Everyone was outloonying each other in one way or another," recalled Marc Balet, then *Interview* art director. "Everyone was strange or stoned or drunk. The picture could have taken forty-five minutes to an hour. Instead, the makeup alone took an hour, and it took about six hours to take this picture. This is around when everything became very crazy in the business."

Kay Mitchell, who came along with Hansen, recalled the session as the first time she realized Gia's feelings for Sandy were romantic. "The two of them were obsessive," she said, "and that became, really, pretty awkward. It seemed like quite a romance, you know, and it was the first time I had really actually *been there.*"

"They all kind of showed up," recalled Tighe. "I especially remember Gia. They had all put on their *Interview* T-shirts. Then Gia took off her shirt and was naked for a while and, well, it was an extraordinary figure she had. I was just quite taken with her beauty. Sandy took her shirt off too. The idea was to shoot them from overhead, all circled around Sandy. I ended up climbing on a ladder, and they were all sort of curled up with each other on the floor, just being very sexy with each other.

"I was trying to direct them, and they were rather rude to me. They just wanted to play with each other and have fun. I remember looking at Marc very frustrated and he got the clue I was having problems with them. He tried to direct them as much as he could.

"They were all very intimate with each other, but it's easy for girls to be like that. I'd never really known Sandy. I remember the first time I met her, it was in Studio. A friend introduced me to her, and she gave me this big kiss because she was very impressed with my work. But we hadn't worked together. Gia, I had only worked with occasionally; Juli, I had worked with quite a bit. They were all hugging each other, and being very silly and very crazy. I remember when we wrapped it up, Patti came up and gave me one of the greatest kisses of my life. But it wasn't fun. They were very loud and girly and obnoxious.

"On the other hand, I'm sure I was stoned. I didn't feel quite in control and my confidence probably wasn't what it would have been a year before. I don't know what was known of *my* problems at that point. I felt so obvious at times, I'm surprised some people didn't know what was happening. I had lost my studio: that picture was shot in the loft of a guy who had been my assistant. I had really pretty much lost my business. And, I don't know that I was really trying to save my career. I was still more interested in shooting dope."

Tighe was in the midst of a professional free-fall. He had been discovered by *Interview* in 1976 and quickly became a regular there—even though he was nineteen and still living with his parents. Within a year, he had a rep and a regular weekly gig shooting ads for Saks Fifth Avenue: having never worked as an assistant, he suddenly *had* an assistant and a studio at Eighteenth and Broadway. He also had a girlfriend who was a junkie, and while all his friends at Studio 54 were doing cocaine, he was right along with them, shooting heroin. He became a regular at the abandoned clubs on the Lower East Side, where heroin users from Manhattan and Long Island, too fearful to venture into Harlem, had created their own drug mall.

One round of New York *fashionistas* had already been totaled by cocaine, but falling fashion victim to heroin was still fairly avant-garde. Just as he had been professionally precocious, Tighe was ahead of his time in booting his life for heroin.

While Gia hadn't tried heroin, she was deeply immersed in the drug culture herself. "I saw Gia and Sandy together one night and my heart broke," recalled Sharon Beverly. "It was at some book party being held at one of the clubs. I hadn't seen Gia in a long while and that was the first time I realized how many drugs she was taking. She was really high and I was, like, sick to my stomach to see her that way.

"I looked at her and I was trying to speak to her and she wasn't making any sense, you know, she was so high. I said 'Gia, what's the *matter with you?*' And she said, 'What are you talking about, nothing's wrong.' And I said, 'I don't know what's *going on* with you. You don't seem like yourself.' All she wanted to do was party. She said, 'I don't know what you're talking about,' and she ran away from me. Then I knew something wasn't right."

*　*　*

Drugs were cyclical, just like fashion. About every ten years, drug enforcement officials noticed a small increase in heroin use, and the public was predictably surprised. At the end of the fifties, it was the jazz players and the beatniks. At the end of the sixties, it was the college overexperimenters and the Vietnam vets. New York was large enough to have a small permanent junkie class—the far edge of life in Greenwich Village and Harlem—but it was prone to trends, too. The downtown art scene had never really given up on the sixties, or on heroin. The Velvet Underground had made its fame on Lou Reed's song "Heroin" and that downtown anesthetic aesthetic always had a place in the popular mythology. The mythos was packaged in the early seventies by Bowie. It was licensed in the mid-seventies when *Interview* grew from an in-house organ to a widely distributed art tabloid. And it was mass consumed in 1977 when *Rolling Stone* moved from San Francisco to New York in time to turn the *Saturday Night Live* crew, the *Interview* crowd and anyone else too raw for *People* into a generation's new rock stars.

In the process, New York became the epicenter of what was coming to be seen as a new "mass hip," a kind of universal exclusivity where everyone felt they were in on the ground floor. "It was like everything John Lennon was doing in 1965 was working its way down to J.C. Penney," said photographer John Stember. There were more people than ever looking for the next big thing: a curious combination of global events were conspiring to make it heroin.

The opium poppy crop in 1979 was the largest in recorded history: the fall of the tough-on-drugs Shah of Iran and the Soviet invasion of Afghanistan assured a virtual heroin free-for-all in areas where raw opium was usually stopped. The harvest was remarkable for its volume and its purity. Street heroin was commonly three to fifteen percent pure, which was why it had to be cooked down and injected to produce the desired effect. But heroin was beginning to appear at purities *starting* at twenty percent under a variety of street names like "Bang Bang" and "Casa Boom."

"China Brown" became almost a brand name for heroin so pure that it didn't need to be injected. It was presented to the Beautiful People as something to smoke or snort when cocaine was no longer a thrill—or so much of a thrill that an industrial strength "down" was necessary. The assumption was that China Brown was "safe" as long as there were no needles involved. This was, of course, preposterous. So a new group of accidental junkies was being born. Newspaper articles about China Brown and an "Iranian Connection" further piqued interest. Drug-related deaths and emergency room episodes began to slowly rise.

Heroin business boomed. Dealers in one abandoned social club on Eldridge Street were reportedly selling $300,000 worth of heroin a day. "It was so out in the open that we used to hang out on the street and wait in line," Michael Tighe recalled. "Each place had its own name. The Red Club was a place I went to a lot, 99X; they had wild names just to ID the heroin. At lunchtime on Eldridge Street there would literally be *hundreds* of people on the street copping heroin. There were so many of them that it became a crowd control problem. There were these little abandoned storefronts, and what they'd do is there was a parking lot on the street, and hundreds of people would line up. They'd let twenty, thirty people in, lock the door, everybody would buy their dope, let them out and let in twenty or thirty more. The heavies would stand outside the club with baseball bats because there was such a rush of people trying to get in.

"Back then, on the Lower East Side, there weren't really any white people living there. If you were there and white, you were there to buy drugs. For me, it was all very exciting. It was the real underbelly of the city, very decadent and crazy. And, you know, in the seventies, as long as you did your work, nobody cared about drugs. Not even heroin. I was about twenty years old when I started shooting dope. You're young and making a lot of money. Who's gonna stop you, as long as you're doing good work?

"After a while, I was buying in larger quantities. There was one guy I used to cop from a lot. I met him through this girl junkie I knew, this rock 'n' roll groupie, just a girl from Brooklyn who used to travel with Keith Richards. She introduced me to this guy; you had to spend several hundred dollars to see him. Downtown, you didn't have to spend anything. To walk in this guy's door, you had to *spend* ... he was not gonna deal with people with fifty-dollar buys.

For a while, he was the only guy I went to. He lived on Eighteenth Street and Eighth Avenue. Keith used to cop from him, Debbie Harry too.

"There was also a while when I was going to Harlem a lot. It was very dangerous. It was all black, your life was much more in danger going up there. It was so obvious what a white person was doing there."

The Mudd Club was often singled out as one center of the downtown drug trade. "Those days everyone had this idea that being a junkie was very glamorous," Anita Sarko, the club's top DJ, would later say. "That's why you don't see too many people from the Mudd Club around anymore—they're either back in the Midwest or they're dead."

The modeling business knew full well how drugs and alcohol were affecting the girls. But awareness didn't mean they knew what to do about it. Several years earlier, when they still had some control over their girls, the agencies could make good on threats of blackballing. But intoxicants were now so common that it seemed almost hypocritical to suggest that models "just didn't do that" or that a model's reputation could be "ruined." Some models would assert that they needed cocaine to keep up with the bookings the agency was making for them. It had reached the point where some of the more wholesome top girls, like Kim Alexis, were being jeered behind their backs for being too straight and goody-goody.

The industry had its ongoing fears about drug use among its top models. The Fellini movie had been going on a little too long, even for a Fellini fan. "Those girls did a *lot* of drugs," recalled photographer Mike Reinhardt. "It got to be a really, really weird scene. For about six months, Janice, my best friend Pierre Roulez, who later died, another top model and I sort of lived together and became very, very close and sort of binged on cocaine. Janice was ... well, that was out of hand. And that's why it ended basically. I couldn't take it anymore and she left me. Janice was literally at a point of no return.

"And Patti [Hansen], well, Patti always was great. Somehow she always had her feet on the ground no matter how far she went. And I know she went far, drug-wise. We always somehow knew that she would find her way back.

Whereas with Janice, and of course Gia, you had the impression that, well . . ."

Just before Christmas, 1979, a chill went through the Wilhelmina agency: Keith Richards summoned Patti Hansen to his thirty-fifth birthday party at the Roxy. Richards might have been the free world's most famous substance abuser. He had been atop rock music's "most likely to expire" list for nearly a decade, and had been an admitted heroin user since the late sixties, when songs with unveiled junk references like "Sister Morphine" began to show up on Stones albums. Richards had lived on the edge for so long that the edge was now defined by where he lived.

Patti Hansen prepared for their arranged meeting—set up through Mick Jagger's girlfriend Jerry Hall—by drinking a lot of vodka. She and Richards hit it off, even though he had come to the party with a girlfriend *and* Anita Pallenberg, his longtime heroin pal and the mother of his two children. Keith and Patti went back to his place and listened to some music. A few days later, she was at her apartment with friends when Keith called at three A.M. and asked her to come to another Manhattan club, Tramps. Her friends feared for her, especially when she disappeared for five days, which she later said was spent cruising Manhattan in Keith's limo listening to reggae. Patti was taken by how skinny and lost he seemed, how defenseless. They spent New Year's Eve partying with Robin Williams, and then she was off to Paris for the collections.

None of this was good news at the Wilhelmina agency. They had spent the better part of the previous year trying to make sure that Hansen, their workhorse, was happy. They had even sent her favorite booker, Kay Mitchell, out to open a Wilhelmina office in LA. Patti had begun making the inevitable model noises about branching out into acting, which meant her full-time modeling days were probably numbered. Wilhelmina had already lost Pam Dawber to theatrical agents, and wasn't about to let the same thing happen again.

The news about Hansen and Richards also came at a personally inopportune moment for Wilhelmina Cooper, who was still basking in what was perhaps the most powerful public recognition of her career. She had appeared on the cover of the December 3, 1979, edition of *Fortune* magazine: not as a model, but as the head of a successful business. She was one of the first women to ever grace the cover of a business magazine by herself, instead of on some successful man's arm. She considered the cover an incredible honor. It was also likely to be a boost for business. The cover shot illustrated the first major magazine business story ever done on the modeling industry. The shot also represented one of the first times that anyone had written about modeling without referring first to Eileen Ford, or to a current Ford model.

The article portrayed Ford and Wilhelmina as basically neck and neck: Ford with $11.8 million in billings, Willie with just under $11 million, and John Casablancas's Elite tallying just under $5 million to pull ahead of the heavily male Zoli agency. But Elite was clearly coming up fast. Nine of the past twelve *Vogue* covers had been Elite models, and Casablancas reportedly had the highest average earnings per model.

Casablancas also used the article as a way to announce the direction his business would be taking. He no longer saw the need for regional agencies in America or Europe. He had opened a modeling school in San Francisco and an office in Los Angeles for print work. He had also purchased minority shares in a rival agency in Paris and in London's Models One. "I aim to be autonomous," he explained, "I no longer want to deal with two-faced agents who promise me a model they also promise to six of my competitors." To make good on that threat, he would eventually have to buy out—or stab in the back—almost every friend he had in the business.

In late December, 1979, Gia got her own magazine story. She was on the cover of the new *Cosmopolitan,* but she was also on the cover of *Philadelphia* magazine's annual "Hot People to Watch" issue. "Meet Gia," the headline said, below the Denis Piel outtake from the *Vogue* collections shot, "South Philly soda jerk to New York's hottest model." Executive Editor Maury Z. Levy had gone to New York to spend an afternoon with Gia: she invited Levy and a photographer into her apartment, popped open a can of Colt 45, and said whatever came into her head. She didn't even bother to turn down her stereo, which was playing the B-side of Blondie's new *Eat to the Beat* record. Levy probably could not have made up a better opening scene—although he might have tried—than Gia listening to Debbie Harry sing "Die Young Stay Pretty": "Deteriorate in your own time, leave only the best behind, you gotta live fast cause it won't last."

"The bad thing about New York," Gia told Levy, "is that they don't have steak sandwiches here. You know, I really miss Pat's [South Philly's legendary steak shop]. It's funny, people think I worry about my weight. Well, I don't. Sometimes I even like to get pudgy. I think it's cute. I don't like to be real thin. Sometimes I see these other models, they take their clothes off and I think, 'God, give this girl some beef.' They're usually real bony, like chickens. They're always ordering health food. I hate it. I order a hamburger. I mean, I get off on food, you know. I'd rather do food than any drug." When asked about the appeal of her *Cosmo* covers, she joked, "It's all in the lungs," and proceeded to take a deep breath that dramatically expanded her tight stretch top, "and I have very big lungs."

Wilhelmina Cooper told the magazine that she expected Gia would earn close to $500,000 in 1980. "She can be really sophisticated in one shooting, and be a real Lolita type in another," Willie said, "and this will give her a long life span." Gia said that sometimes she just sat back and laughed when she thought about all the money she was making. She claimed to have an accountant—a reference to her stepfather, who was trying to get her to pay attention to her bookkeeping—and said he was "dying to get me into real estate, like, I'm gonna buy a townhouse and stuff. You know, you have to invest because no matter how much money I make, the government's gonna take half of it away from me. And, like, that ain't fair. The government takes all this money away from me, and what are they doing for me? I consider myself a pretty good citizen and all. I'm nineteen years old and I'm makin' myself a hell of a lot of money and what am I getting for it? They're just taking it away. I don't even know where it's going. It's a real drag. I'm really pissed off at the government."

While looking around Gia's apartment, Levy noted that

she had two nude Polaroids of herself hung on the wall and several others wedged into the bathroom mirror. When he asked her about them, she just shrugged her shoulders like it was no big deal. She explained that she was not worried about the short professional life span of most models. "I'm gonna get out before that happens," she said, "because I feel satisfied already from modeling. I did it, you know what I mean? I made it." She also said she had a twenty-seven-year-old boyfriend. Levy had been told by people who knew her in Philadelphia that she was gay, but he ran her quotes about the boyfriend anyway. She answered most of his questions in monosyllables, so he took whatever he could get. What did this boyfriend do for a living? "Nothing," she laughed, "he's a bum. Most models I know, they really have these rich boyfriends, but I'm not into a guy's money. I'm not impressed by somebody who's got a Lear Jet and who's going to take me to Florida every weekend . . . and all Studio 54 is is a bunch of guys in three-piece suits who want to give you cocaine.

"I just want a body, like a nice hot body and some big lips. Forget everything else."

The *Philadelphia* story ended the same way as the interview did—with Gia sitting on her couch listening to one of the few Blondie songs written by her pool-playing buddy Jimmy Destri. "Every day you've got to wake up," Debbie Harry sang, "and disappear behind your makeup . . . hey I'm living in a magazine, page to page in my teenage dream, Cause I'm not living in the real world, No I'm not living in the real world, no more."

When the article came out, just as she was getting home for Christmas, Gia was stunned. "She did not want to do that article," recalled Kathleen Sperr. "She got very upset about the whole thing. She didn't like the people that came to visit her, so she put them on, told them a lot of stuff just to answer them. She didn't want to tell them anything that was the truth. Then when the article came out, she couldn't believe it. She felt they had ripped her apartment apart unmercifully. She was totally upset. She talked to her different friends, to Harry King and Way Bandy, and they told her not to worry about it. They said, 'If they spelled your name right, don't worry about it.' But, she was mad. She was fit to be tied."

The article was not very flattering. Nor were the letters to the editor it spawned. "Your interview with Gia," one reader wrote, "if it didn't show us anything else, reinforced the statement, 'beauty is only skin deep.' "

"If I was a parent," wrote another, "after reading your story on Gia Carangi, modeling would be the last thing that I would allow my daughter to become involved in."

"Admittedly, I am more accustomed to writing this kind of letter to *other* magazines that begin with the letter 'P,' " panted a third reader. "Gia is the most beautiful girl I have ever seen. Can you show us more? (or less would be even better)."

Flattering or not, the article did serve to link Gia's name with her face, at least in her home town. In all the gay and straight clubs in Philadelphia, where stories had been circulating about a local girl who was now this big-time model, the legend had become real.

And the article served another purpose. Gia had told Levy that the main reason she agreed to the interview was because "my mom will think it's neat." And now, nobody could doubt that Kathleen Sperr's daughter really was the one on all those *Cosmo* covers. The ones she had framed and hung over the couch in the family room. The ones that made Gia wonder if her mother hadn't gone a little overboard in living vicariously through the model fantasy.

Gia was no longer playing along with her mother quite as readily as she had for the first year or so. "At the beginning she told me everything," Kathleen recalled. "Later, she wouldn't answer questions. She would say, 'You don't ask Michael or Joey how many hoagies they made. Why ask me? It's *a job!*' We would ask when pictures were coming out, and she got all like that about it. She would tell you stories, but you wouldn't know they were about a particular picture. I was interested in everything she did, and she knew that. But if you got too wrapped up in the magazines or particular pictures, then she felt that was taking something away from her. It was like, you were interested in the magazines and her work and not in her.

"She couldn't understand how great everybody felt about

somebody in their family being a big model. She simply could not deal with it. She got paranoid about people staring at her. If she was home and we had people here, she would stay in her room. You could be walking down the street with her and suddenly she would jump into a cab because she was convinced everyone was looking at her. She would get hyper if we were walking down the street and a limo went by and I was looking at it. She said, 'You don't know what it's like if you're in a limo and they're gawking at you.' She'd see famous people on the street and she'd tell you who they were, but then duck down. She didn't want me popping my eyeballs because of who they were. But at the same time she was thrilled to point them out to you.

"What happened to me and Henry one time—and if Gia were with us, she would have killed me—we were in Bloomingdales' fine giftware department and they had a whole series of picture frames on display and they had cut pictures of girls out of magazines, like they do. And I saw Gia's picture. I got all excited. And Henry was starting to get embarrassed, he was telling me to calm down. I was walking back around to see if people were looking at it. I guess I did overreact. But it was my daughter!"

In early January, Gia took a ten-day trip to a spa in Pompano Beach, Florida, for German *Vogue*. John Stember was the photographer. Frances Stein, who still did some freelance fashion editing, was in charge of the trip. Kim Alexis was the other model.

"Gia was with us, because Frances *loved* Gia—the way Gia *looked*, that is," Stember recalled. "So Frances immediately took one look at Kim Alexis and said, 'This girl looks completely stupid and I don't want to use her. She doesn't look like she's got a brain in her body.' Frances' whole thing was, if the girl didn't look intelligent, she wasn't and, therefore, she didn't want any part of it 'cause she thought that was an insult to women.

"Frances Stein is a wonderful woman, completely mad, and great taste, best taste of anyone I've ever met probably. But she has a low boiling point and she will not take any shit from anybody. She just goes crazy. So we had Gia, and Frances had arrived with about twenty coffins full of clothes and jewelry—she had a number of slaves carrying this stuff. And she would come with pages and pages of Xeroxes of images, she did tremendous preparation so you knew where you were going.

"So, this thing immediately became, like, here's Frances and here's Gia. Gia won't take any crap and Frances won't take any crap."

Gia's wake-up call for hair and makeup was six A.M. She missed it, but they were finally able to get her ready by ten-thirty or so. The first shots were to be at poolside on a chaise lounge, and Stember was making the final preparations—moving the camera tripod back and forth, checking the light meter readings and the focus, doing Polaroids of the scene. When everything was ready, Gia was brought from the shaded area where she had been made up and was carefully arranged on the chaise.

"I looked through the camera," Stember recalled, "and I was just about focused on her face, when I saw her move off to the side of the frame. The next thing I heard was a splash. She was in the pool. And she just laughed. This is the kind of thing she did. So, of course, Frances got into an outrage and this is how the whole thing went.

"The funniest thing of all was that, at the end of the trip, Frances was so pissed off with Gia that she decided that we were leaving without her. Gia had no money, and no ticket, and we were in Florida. I had everybody in the rental van. At Frances' insistence, nobody told Gia. So we're driving away and I see Gia running out of the front door of the hotel. I'm driving the thing, right, and I've got Gia with her case in hand running behind the van—white, she's ashen white in the face—and I can see all this in the rearview mirror. Frances is saying, *'Drive, drive, drive,'* and I'm saying, 'Frances, I just can't drive and leave her there.' And she's putting her foot on *my foot* on the accelerator. *'Drive, drive, drive,* leave that fucking bitch, *drive!'*

"And I said, 'No, no, no, I can't *do* this.' So I brake, and the next thing, the door is wrenched open. And Gia knows it's not me, it's Frances. So the two of them are rolling out of the van, punching each other. They literally got into a fistfight. But this was Gia."

* * *

Back in New York, a fight of another sort was just ending. Steve Rubell and Ian Schrager, the co-owners of Studio 54, were about to be sentenced in Federal District Court after pleading guilty to evading almost $500,000 in corporate income taxes.

The sentencing was the culmination of a year-long drama that began after the December 1978 raid on the club. The highlight of the legal maneuvering—which began in earnest after Studio's third (and least public) co-owner, Jack Dushey, pleaded out and gave the government enough information to indict his partners—came when Rubell and Schrager tried to save themselves by throwing White House chief of staff Hamilton Jordan under the bus. They offered the government proof that the high-ranking Carter aide used cocaine twice, in 1977, at the club. The gambit didn't help their defense, but it did set off a five-month, federal grand jury investigation of Jordan. He was later cleared of wrongdoing—prosecutors intimated that Schrager failed a lie detector test—but the Jordan scandal was another blemish on the Carter reelection campaign and may very well have laid the groundwork for Republican antidrug scapegoating during the eighties. It was certainly the first time candidates Reagan and Bush came to realize the political usefulness of drug charges.

The night before Rubell and Schrager were to be sentenced, they were feted one last time at Studio 54. More than two thousand people reportedly showed up for the farewell party, which was hosted by Halston, guested by Liza Minnelli, Richard Gere, Reggie Jackson, Bianca Jagger and Andy Warhol, and highlighted by Diana Ross singing from the DJ booth.

On Friday, January 18, 1980, Rubell and Schrager were sentenced to three and a half years in prison and fines of $20,000 each. The party was over. "Steve Rubell was responsible for some of the last good times in New York City," said photographer Peter Beard. "They had to put him in jail to stop them."

When she returned from Florida, Gia sensed immediately that something was very wrong at the agency. Wilhelmina was sick. It had begun with a miserable cold that became a persistent cough. Antibiotics weren't helping. As Gia was leaving for Paris to do the collections for *Vogue* with Andrea Blanche, the consensus was that Willie probably had bronchitis.

The shots in Paris didn't go well. Gia was there for four days, including her twentieth birthday on January 29, but *Vogue* ended up with only one usable shot of her. "I remember being out at two A.M. looking for her all over Paris," recalled Edward Tricomi, who did hair for the sitting. "I finally dragged her back to the hotel and she went to sleep, but she was still crazed. She had a huge fight with Andrea the next day and just walked out and flew back to New York." When Gia returned, with just a free weekend before leaving on another *Vogue* trip, she found out that Wilhelmina had been admitted to a hospital for observation.

On Tuesday, February 5, Gia left JFK for a week on the Caribbean island of St. Barthélemy—or St. Barts, as it was known—which was quickly becoming the fashion industry standard for paradise. The former French colony had been discovered by some of the French Mafia photographers, who were trying to buy houses there. The *Vogue* sitting, with Polly Mellen, was one of the Scavullo crew's infrequent road trips. Scavullo didn't especially like working outside his studio anymore—too much could go wrong—but he "did it because of Gia," recalled Sean Byrnes. Gia could now pick the jobs she wanted to do, and she had made it known that there was a better chance she would accept a booking if it involved working outdoors on a sunny island.

On the boat ride from St. Martin to St. Barts, Harry King snapped pictures of Way Bandy and the models: Gia, Kim Alexis and Jeff Aquilon. King, who hoped to one day make the leap from hair to photography, had begun doing some test shots privately with Gia to put together a portfolio. "I was inspired by her beauty and her body," he recalled, "and all I wanted to do was shoot those titties of hers."

Everybody was very relaxed on the ride over until Sean Byrnes found something that had dropped out of Gia's bag. "She dropped her drugs and I found them and threw them overboard," Byrnes recalled. "And she got hysterical." Byrnes was no stranger to drugs himself, but he knew the effect they could have on an outdoor shooting, where so many extra things could go wrong—things that would likely be blamed on him. "Francesco loves the morning light," he said, "and if the girls are taking drugs all night there's no way they're going to get up and look good at five in the morning.

"Gia didn't know that I did it, and, at first, she was ready to leave. I thought it was coke, but it wasn't."

Polly Mellen saw that there were going to be behind-the-scenes problems with the trip. But she also saw how beautifully the pictures were going, and how well Gia worked with Scavullo, Bandy and King. "I don't consider whether a girl is difficult or not difficult," Mellen recalled. "If she's good, I work with the difficulty. Gia was very vulnerable, it was part of the beauty of her photographs. She gave you back something wonderful. There's never been anyone that had what she had. And she was just at the right time. She had that boy-girl thing, and it was sexy—it was *everything*. She was absolutely dynamite.

"Gia had a very brilliant future in modeling. And that isn't true of every girl who gets into *Vogue*. Some models will never make it, they just aren't big-time, but they can work for a certain picture, a certain situation, and then that situation passes. For example, there was a girl, her name was Katherine Redding. We were looking for a redhead and Dick [Avedon] called and said, 'I think I found one.' We used her and we did ten pages on her and never used her again. She was used by other people, but I didn't use her again because she didn't appeal to me anymore ... it's a whim ... That's terrible, don't you think? Terribly hard on a girl. A girl can *work* for you for a moment and then ... I think that's terribly hard.

"But that wasn't Gia's situation. Gia was really dynamite ... even though she was really sick in a lot of ways. I knew her background was difficult, but I didn't know she was a lesbian for a long time, until the St. Barts trip. And it was really a problem. In other words, she couldn't satisfy herself ... and she was very, very aggressive. You couldn't room her with another girl. If you did, she made advances and the other girls would come and speak to me. You had to keep her away from other beautiful girls and you had to watch her very carefully if she went out at night—if you were going to see her again the next day."

No matter how difficult Gia's behavior, the pictures were exceptional. Scavullo considered one shot of her being tackled, nude, in the surf by Jeff Aquilon, to be one of the best shots he had taken in his career: natural, alive, unpretentious. *Vogue* didn't use the shot. It finally ran, *very* small, in an unrelated, generic sunskin story months after the other St. Barts pictures were published. But Scavullo had the photograph blown up and framed. It would forever dominate the southern wall of his Manhattan studio.

Gia was frantic to leave St. Barts as soon as she could, but anxious and frightened about what she would find out when she got back home: "I wish & I don't wish I was in NY," she wrote in her datebook. By the time she returned, Wilhelmina's condition had worsened. The doctors were no longer talking about bronchitis. Even though Willie had always been a heavy smoker, the diagnosis was still shocking: she had lung cancer. The malignancy had reached an advanced stage—it was inoperable, and it was unclear whether any treatment at all was possible. She could die very soon. She was only forty years old. She had a twelve-year-old daughter and a five-year-old son. She also had an agency of 285 women and 85 men who looked to her as a professional role model. But few of those models had as much invested in their relationship with their boss as Gia did. Gia was one of the only models whose professional and personal welfare had never truly been delegated to one of Wilhelmina's employees. She had always been one of Willie's pet projects.

"That was an unusual situation," recalled Kay Mitchell, "because the Patti Hansens and Shaun Caseys *liked* Willie, but I was the one that spent most of the time with them. But Gia related to Willie and Willie related to Gia. Willie, I think, felt how fragile she was and that she needed special attention. When Gia had problems, she would go right to Willie. Gia became a softer, sweeter person when she was with Willie."

On her first day back in New York, Gia did errands to try to get her mind off Willie's condition. "See about flowers," she wrote in her datebook. "Mail rent, tel., Con Ed. . . . Take clothes to cleaners ... call Sandy ... call Mommy ... buy incense and beautiful burner ... read 'Her Majesty's Secret Service' ... Get Heroin." Over the next week, she didn't really work. She tried to get her apartment in order and played around with the drugs she bought.

She would later tell several different stories about how she had come to try heroin—which she was still only snorting. In one version, she had first snorted it socially. In another version, somebody had sneaked up and "needle-popped" her at a party: shot the heroin quickly into a muscle in her arm. In both versions, she had been absolutely overwhelmed by the quality of the high. It was like everything she had ever loved about Quaaludes, but better. It was the greatest feeling, or lack of feeling, she had ever had in her life.

After one of her first completely idle weeks in over a year, Gia took a booking in Boston for Jordan Marsh. She was so out of it that she missed the first two Eastern Shuttles and then was nearly arrested trying to get through the metal detector to board the third. She was carrying a switchblade. And when security wouldn't let her take it on the plane, she made a scene and called the agency screaming, "He took my knife, he took my fucking knife!" Karen Hilton was finally able to calm her down: the agency, she assured her, would be happy to replace the knife if she just got on the plane. Gia finally went to Boston to make her $1,250.

The knife episode convinced top people at Wilhelmina that Gia was out of control—even for a pampered top model. In between her four appointments the next day, Gia was asked to come in and speak with Karen Hilton, who suggested she get some help. Hilton recommended her husband Robert, a part-time actor and drug counselor who was trying to decide which was a more realistic career. Since the Hiltons had moved to New York, he had been doing soap operas and informally counseling some of the lesser-known models who were buckling under the pressure. Bob Hilton was a recovering heroin addict himself, so the girls knew he more than understood what they were going through.

Gia succeeded in deflecting Karen Hilton's suggestions. "She was great at promising, 'Yes, yes, yes,' " recalled Wilhelmina executive Fran Rothschild. "She had some cute, cunning ways about her. She crawled underneath your skin, with just a smile. Professionally, she was in trouble from day one. Willie tried to tame her like we all did."

Under normal circumstances, the agency might have tried to be more insistent—even though "tough love" was becoming an increasingly risky managerial technique as girls learned how easy it was to switch agencies. But Gia's drug use, no matter how menacing it suddenly appeared, was not high on anyone's priority list. Willie's health was everyone's main concern—Willie's health and, of course, the business ramifications.

The doctors did not expect the model agent to live much longer. Behind the scenes—in whispers outside her hospital room and in hushed tones on the office telephones—the battle for succession at Wilhelmina Models was already on. Even though Willie and her husband had been romantically estranged for some time, Bruce Cooper was legally supposed to inherit majority ownership of the agency if its namesake died. Everyone's place in the agency would then depend on personal relationships with Cooper and perceived ability to retain the services of the top girls after Willie was gone. Kay Mitchell, just shipped off to California, found herself out of the loop. Karen Hilton was vying for power along with Fran Rothschild and Bill Weinberg. Rumors circulated that Willie was being urged to change her will on her deathbed to assure that her husband would be bought out by someone who actually knew how to run Wilhelmina Models and might be able to preserve some semblance of what she had built.

While all this went on, Gia found herself with plenty of free time on her hands to sit and brood. On Monday, February 25, she had only a half-hour meeting with some people for Timex about a TV ad with Avedon, nothing at all on Tuesday, and a small morning job on Wednesday, giving her nearly twelve hours to kill before going to Studio 54 to see Chuck Berry. On Thursday she had nothing but another half-hour TV job audition—this one for French Body Lotion—and on Friday, there was just a midday sunglasses ad sitting.

On Saturday, March 1, 1980, Wilhelmina Cooper died in Greenwich Hospital in Connecticut. The next day, New

York's Channel 7 went ahead with its airing of a pretaped interview with Willie on its *Kids Are People Too* program. She answered questions about skin problems and what it was like to be a model.

Gia was devastated by Willie's death. "She was crushed by it," recalled Kathleen Sperr. "It was the first time she ever had to really deal with someone close to her dying, someone young." Besides the loss, Gia also felt abandonment. It was almost as if her own mother was leaving all over again. And there was no way for her real mother to really comfort her. In Richboro, Pennsylvania, Kathleen was still her mother. But in New York City, where Gia had been living on her own for over two years, Willie was her mother: Kathleen had all but abdicated her maternal role to become Gia's biggest groupie. "Gia and I had a way of switching roles, one played the mother, the other played the daughter," Kathleen recalled. "I guess when she was up in New York, I was the daughter."

Gia was also unpleasantly surprised by the industry's reaction to Willie's demise: people seemed callous, almost completely uncaring, interested only in how the death affected their careers. It made her feel that life in the fashion business was even cheaper than she had thought. "She told me that when Willie died, a lot of people didn't feel it," recalled one friend. "A lot of people just took it like it was nothing. She didn't think it meant enough to them."

A memorial service was held three days after Wilhelmina's death at the Riverside Memorial Chapel. To some, the grief at the early evening event seemed barely skin deep.

"The memorial service on the Upper West Side was so typical of the way this game was going to go," recalled Kay Mitchell. "And I was so *totally* naive about it. I went with Karen and Bob Hilton. Karen said, 'Kay, why don't you find a seat and I'll be in in a minute.' About fifteen, twenty minutes later, she's still not there. I'm inside talking to a few people and I said, 'Where's Hilton?' and someone said, 'Oh, she's outside *greeting* everybody.'

"I mean, *this is my girlfriend, okay?* And she's outside stealing the thunder. People are coming in saying, 'What are you doing in here, people are asking for you?' It was very much the one-upsmanship thing. And there were rumors circulating that John Casablancas was outside the memorial service talking with people, and that before Willie had died he was already talking with some of the girls: 'She has cancer, the whole agency's going to be a mess, come with us.' There was going to be no time for grieving: you either got in line or not."

But even with all the infighting, it was unclear if there even *was* a company without Willie. "I remember a girl saying she was thinking of going to Wilhelmina," recalled Harry King, "and Way said, 'Why on earth would you want to go to a dead woman's agency?'"

Gia told friends that she and Sandy had a scene after the memorial service. "I remember her telling me that when Wilhelmina died," recalled one friend, "Sandy was flipped out because Gia had gone dressed in this real nice, tight black dress with silk stockings and black high heels. And afterwards, she went back to Sandy's apartment and waited for her in this dress. She said that Sandy had so much trouble dealing with her in these clothes because she thought of Gia as a boy.

"Gia said that after Willie died was the first time she really did heroin. She had snorted it—especially in Europe, where it was more popular and easier to get than cocaine. But after that she started shooting it."

The heroin initially made her quite sick. Three days after one long night at the Mudd Club—where heroin use was quite open, especially in the upstairs lounge—Gia still felt so sick that she barely made it to a *Cosmo* cover try and a party at Diane von Furstenberg's apartment. The next day she was forced to cancel the Timex TV ad with Avedon that had taken three different meetings to set up. She began to frequently "book out"—the term used when a model wants to be absolutely unavailable—and was often waking up ill. Each time, she wrote "sick" across the top of a datebook page.

She worked less frequently. To anyone who didn't really understand what was going on, it might have seemed that she was giving herself some downtime and being "more selective." Any model reaching the point she had in her career might be encouraged by her agency to cut back somewhat on editorial work and concentrate on generating more big money advertising assignments for print and television.

If you were doing long editorial trips or three or four sittings a day in New York, it was hard to find time to work the people who gave out the precious few yearly or multi-year modeling and personal-service contracts. Garment manufacturers rarely made those kinds of deals. It was mostly cosmetics or perfume companies, which marketed absolutely nothing but image and a few cents' worth of chemicals, and therefore placed a much higher value on the selling power of one face, one body, one look. Long-term deals with such companies came through more than just a model's reputation in the fashion magazines or the devotion of a few big photographers or editors. This was business, the dating process in what could be a long professional marriage. It involved endless meetings, auditions and tests with the types of people *fashionistas* generally loathed: ad agency functionaries, art directors, executive types, folks with real jobs. It took time and the kind of patience and forethought that few models could be bothered with.

So to some, Gia probably appeared positively prudent for cutting back on editorial work. But she was actually just beginning to buckle under the pressure of the business and the drugs. Years later, those who survived the time period would look back at 1980 as the year the world they had created stopped taking orders from them.

For Gia, the downward spiral began just as she was making the connection that could possibly boost her to the next best thing to a cosmetics contract—a signature relationship with a booming American manufacturer. Her work in the Armani and Versace campaigns was making an impact worldwide.

The next major American designer to hit the jackpot was assuredly going to be Perry Ellis. The Virginia-born department store sportswear buyer had worked his way up in Manhattan Industries' Vera company until, in 1978, they let him design his own sportswear line under the Portfolio label. After three successful collections—highlighting his interest in casual-looking clothes made with expensive natural fibers—Manhattan gave Ellis his own namesake line, and soon Bloomingdale's gave him his own shop. By April, it was abundantly clear to everyone, including the media-savvy designer, that Perry Ellis was going to be the first great fashion statement of the eighties.

Vogue planned to make that statement in its August 1980 issue, offering major coverage of Ellis's fall collection, retrospective shots of his previous collections and a profile of the designer. Gia was booked as the sole model for an Ellis sitting with Avedon. On Monday, April 21, the day before the shoot, Gia did a half-day for *Vogue* with Scavullo and went over to Perry Ellis' Seventh Avenue offices for a fitting. On Tuesday, she did the Avedon editorial shots and on Thursday, she did a *Vogue* cover try with Avedon and Polly Mellen. On Friday, Gia was booked for another fitting, this time for Perry Ellis' fashion show. She had not really done much runway, because she was considered too short and curvy for the work, and a less-than-elegant walker. But Ellis could see that his fall collection was going to be inextricably linked with Gia. In a way it made perfect sense, because her look was high fashion but unpretentious, European but American, just like his clothes.

Gia never showed up for the early evening Ellis fitting, so she did it over the weekend. On Monday morning, she did the show. According to *WWD,* the affair was packed "with enough photographers, buyers, foreign press and Fashion Groupies to rival a European collection." During most of the show, Gia mimicked the other models as they happily bounded down the runway in Ellis' bleacher-lined Seventh Avenue showroom. But, occasionally, the cameras would capture a grimace on her face.

12
Bubblegum Habit

Three days after the Perry Ellis show, Gia called Eileen Ford. She wanted to talk about changing agencies.

The battle at Wilhelmina was over, and Bruce Cooper had lost. Bill Weinberg and Fran Rothschild were going to take over the agency, keep the name, and buy him out. Kay Mitchell was still there, but her loyalties had always been with the Coopers: she was being kept on largely to provide introductions and smooth the way with her decade's worth of contacts. Keeping Wilhelmina Models strong was going to be a difficult task. When it was just Ford and Wilhelmina, the differences were clear: conservative versus liberal, the mom's agency and the daughter's agency. Now Ford and Elite were at opposite ends of the spectrum, and without the overpowering presence of Willie herself, Wilhelmina seemed destined to be lost in that growing middle ground of the professional but lesser agencies: everything from Zoli and Stewart to the seamier companies set up by other Johnnies-come-lately.

Willie's girls were looking around and many of the other top models were trying to assess where they wanted to be in the eighties. Like Gia, many of the models weren't making these assessments with the clearest of heads. While they were all pretty well versed on the short-term effects of whatever they were using, little was known about the longer-term impact of the chemically enhanced highs and lows. For most, it wasn't really a question of physical addiction so much as personality changes: irritability, depression, paranoia, compulsive behavior. The simple truth was that while many of the Beautiful People drank a lot and took a lot of drugs, few of them were very good at it.

"This might sound a little crazy," explained photographer Michael Tighe, "but by the time you learn enough about drugs and what they do to you, it's too late to do anything about it. Sometimes when I look back and see what I was doing with the drugs ... if I knew then what I know now, I think I could have done great as a junkie. I know the whole notion is probably ridiculous, but I think I could have functioned for years as a drug addict. I didn't know what drugs did to you, or could do to you. By the time they consumed me, to where I didn't want to know about anything else, it was too late to make it work in my life."

Although it was unclear if she would end up at Ford or somewhere else, Gia began assembling pictures for a new model card and portfolio. In the meantime, she was falling apart, breaking even the very lax rules she had set for herself—and the industry had accepted—as she rose to fame. Instead of making people money, she was costing people money, including herself: if a booking was ruined by her nonperformance, she often had to pay the other models' fees. She showed up six hours late for a Bruce Weber sitting for German *Vogue*. She stopped working for weeks at a time, and turned up a mess when she did show up. She did a Christian Dior fur ad with Chris von Wangenheim in which she and Patti Hansen looked like ghouls in mink. Von Wangenheim couldn't have looked much better—his own career was beginning to fall apart because of existential angst, cocaine and the breakup of his marriage.

Gia was spending a lot of her time with Sandy Linter. Their relationship no longer appeared playful and outrageous to their colleagues. The industry's soft-core porn fantasy was beginning to look like a scary series of Von Wangenheim outtakes.

Gia and Sandy would take the seaplane out to Fire Island or drive to Jones Beach for the weekend, or just for the day, working through what had become of their relationship.

Since Sandy had many more real friends in the business than Gia, most viewed what was happening to them as Gia dragging Sandy off the deep end with her.

"Gia explained this all to me later, and said she felt like she was a game to Sandy, an amusement," Kathleen Sperr recalled. "I don't know whether it's because I don't know how a woman feels about another woman, but when she explained some of these things to me, about these relationships, I just couldn't comprehend it all. I just can't comprehend that kind of relationship. I don't know the feelings, how they come about. I can't really relate to them. I could understand what she was saying . . . like who wanted what more. From what I knew, Gia had to be highly motivated on her own to want to spend that much time with Sandy. And the number of parking tickets she got . . . her car was parked there a lot and towed from in front of Sandy's several times."

"I just think Sandy wasn't interested in having a relationship and Gia was," recalled Nancy Adams. "I think it was over and Gia just kept coming back. Gia would call me and ask me to write her poems to give to Sandy. I remember telling Gia about a guy who wanted to go out with me. He was sending me all these letters and then he threw me this towel, and he said, 'Here's my towel, I'm not throwing it in yet.' Well, don't you know, Gia buys a pink towel and does the same thing to Sandy. But I got the impression that Sandy was just much more career-oriented than Gia, and was no longer willing to let whatever was between them hurt her professionally."

Diane von Furstenberg, who Gia had met when they did an eleven-page *Vogue* ad section for Saks the year before, invited her and Sandy for a weekend at Calvin Klein's beach house on Fire Island. "Gia was very sweet," said Von Furstenberg. "She brought me this little toy, a little cat—my daughter always remembered that. There was some connection at that time between me and her—I don't recall it now—but I wanted to help her. I recall going into her room and finding her sitting in the closet, looking into her bag. Much later, when I realized she was shooting up, I realized that's what she was doing."

Before and after the weekend, Gia called Von Furstenberg often: she would later suggest to friends that she and the designer had a brief affair. Gia was also constantly calling her remaining friends at Wilhelmina—her booker Lucy Cobb and Karen Hilton. To try to help ease her pain, Gia went to the SPCA and arranged to adopt a cat, which she planned to name Pokey.

Soon, Gia was skipping bookings altogether. Or showing up high to the sittings. Or shooting up in the bathroom during sessions. She was booked to go up to the Italian collections over the July 4 weekend: the *alta moda* at the Grand Hotel, just as she had done two summers before on her first-ever modeling trip. This time she took a cab to Kennedy Airport, saw that there was only a one-way ticket waiting for her and decided there was something wrong with the booking. So she turned around and took a cab home, vowing to get all her Wilhelmina vouchers paid off the next day so she could switch agencies.

"I called Wilhelmina's [and] told them what happened," she wrote in her datebook, where she usually only reported her business and personal appointments. "They thought I should have went . . . it seemed like a strange deal. Everyone at the agency kept saying I was to be paid $5,000, which is the right price for the trip. But at the end I would get $3,000.

"I don't know what is happening in my life. Nothing seem[s] or feels right to me. I want to live so bad. But I am so terribly sad. I wish Wilhelmina didn't die. She was so wonderful to talk to about work. I cry every day for a little while. I wish I knew what to do. I almost bought a beautiful cat today. But it had ring worm. I pray that things fall into place."

Three days later, Gia was on the cover of American *Vogue*. She had been on the cover of *Cosmo* the previous month, and was also on the cover of the new French *Vogue*. But the cover of American *Vogue* was the Carnegie Hall of modeling. It was also, if she was still able to recall, the only thing she had ever wanted out of modeling.

"I think maybe the parents didn't understand what was going on," said Sean Byrnes. "I mean, you see your daughter on the cover of a magazine, great, what could be going wrong?"

In fact, nobody had really tried to tell Gia's parents anything was wrong. Even when Willie was alive, the agency had never perceived Gia's relationship with either of her parents as strong enough to be of help if there was a problem. Gia would occasionally send her mother in to turn in vouchers or pick up checks if she was in New York, but she was not thought of as one of the girls with an omnipresent, all-protective "model-mom." Kathleen would have been only too happy to take on that role: Gia had never let her.

Willie had been the only person at the agency with any inkling about Gia's relationship with her mother. When Karen Hilton took Willie's place, she accepted Gia's version of her life situation: that she was estranged from her broken family and her parents could not be counted upon to get involved. Karen did not take Gia's drug use lightly; she just didn't consider the family an option. So Gia's problems were dealt with internally.

"Wilhelmina's agency never called me about *any* drug problems," said Kathleen Sperr. "I think they denied it. They were making big bucks off of her. It's amazed me as more time has gone by that they never did contact me. They would have known what was happening. They knew they were working with very young impressionable girls. I mean, if they had her best interests at heart . . ."

But Gia's agents weren't the only ones in denial. Kathleen had been disregarding clues for months, perhaps even longer. "I think Gia was trying to tell me, had I not been so blind to it," Kathleen recalled. "I remember one night she took me out to dinner in New York. She wasn't right. All through dinner she was trying to tell me something. She kept telling me, 'I have this big, big problem.' And I kept saying, 'Well, Gia, you're a survivor like me. Whatever this problem is, you'll work it out. You'll get over it.'

"She was trying to tell me this big story—something with a job that had happened that week. But she was very vague about the whole thing. That's what she would do. The first time she unloaded something, she'd skirt all around it. Later she would talk to you about it as if she had already told you. And the way she explained it all, I didn't realize how really important what she was trying to tell me was.

"Maybe as her mother I was not ready to face it. It's only

because I've been through as much therapy as I have since, that I realize I probably failed her at that moment. She probably didn't want to let me down and let me know what was really wrong. Maybe she didn't think I could handle it—because I thought she was so wonderful."

The structure of the modeling business could work for or against a model with personal problems. Because so many jobs were contracted at the last minute—based on past performance, recent photographs and a hunch—a disparaging rumor about a model could be enough to make a client choose someone else. One bad day in a model's career could really resonate: especially if she had two or three bookings that day, or annoyed a particularly influential client. But everyone also knew that one client's nightmare girl was another's Princess Charming. Some girls were even more attractive to photographers when they were high than when they were straight: certain drugs produced certain faraway looks or stoked certain inner fires that worked for certain pictures. And certain girls had looks that were so specific— and, at that moment, essential—that it was worth risking a session in which the model couldn't perform on the chance that she could, if only for a moment. They only needed one perfect picture: if it was perfect, it didn't matter if it had been the first (and only) shot, or the last of thousands.

And when Gia showed up straight to sessions—or showed up at all—some remarkable pictures were taken. The best of them even had a certain quality that earlier photographs of her lacked: the shots were actually beginning to look like Gia. The girl in the magazine was beginning to more closely resemble the girl who slumped into the chair in front of the makeup mirror each morning—the girl who, on "bad days," showed up so wrecked that someone had to hold her head up while the makeup was applied.

The change in the pictures was partially attributable to new directions in makeup. Less drastic, more naturalistic looks were coming into style—it was becoming less fashionable to just repaint the girls' faces. But it also appeared that Gia's looks were growing stronger, more defined, more loved by the camera, even as she was ravaging her body with drugs. And photographers seemed to have an increasing fascination with shooting a more "real Gia" as she grew from a spoiled pretty girl into a beautiful riddle—the answer to which people feared knowing.

"She scared me a little bit," recalled Harry King. "There was something about her that made me feel uneasy. I used to say it to Way: 'She has a demon inside of her.' "

Just as Gia's *Vogue* cover hit the stands, the model wars went nuclear. Patti Hansen and her $300,000 annual billings left Wilhelmina Models for John Casablancas' Elite. She claimed the reason was that the Wilhelmina executives had discouraged her from pursuing film projects, but some thought otherwise. "Hansen left the agency because of a personal falling out between she and my wife Karen," recalled Bob Hilton. "For some reason, Patti decided that Karen didn't support her relationship with Keith [Richards], even though I thought we both communicated very well with Keith and both liked him a lot.

"And I never saw any kind of direct relationship between the tremendous increase in the drug use and her relationship with Keith that everyone seemed afraid of. Patti just used a lot of coke, but no more than anybody else around that time. Keith was actually a lot cleaner at that time than people gave him credit for. He was a hell of a lot cleaner than *a lot* of the people in the fashion business. He was always drinking bourbon and doing coke and stuff, but he was in remarkably good shape as far as I could tell."

After Hansen's switch, Esme Marshall and her $200,000 annual billings left Elite. Over the past months, Esme had let her trademark short hair grow out and let her professional guard down. She, like Gia, was showing up late and missing bookings. Her problems were rumored to be more boyfriend-related than drug-related, although she vigorously denied having any problems at all. "Let me tell you something," Janice Dickinson would later recall, "if Esme didn't show up for work, it's probably because she was covered in bruises and didn't want people to see her like that. Esme was getting the shit kicked out of her. She just entered into this Svengali relationship. When someone is not showing up for bookings, it's a cry for help."

Esme fled Elite, which she said was "getting too big," to

become the sole client of a new agency called Fame, run by forty-one-year-old salsa record producer Jerry Masucci, and co-owned by the Fords. She brought her Elite booker along with her, and her boyfriend as well. "It was beyond my control," Esme would later admit. "He used to not let me go to bookings. It was very weird. He tried to run me over once. He was jealous of my booker 'controlling' me. I think he was totally jealous, or believed the woman should stay at home. But then he was proud! When ads would come out, he'd say, 'That's my beautiful girlfriend.' He was Jekyll and Hyde."

While all this was going on, Beverly Johnson, the industry's top black model, set a land-speed record by moving from Elite to Ford and back to Elite in one week. Not long afterwards, she and Hansen were photographed on the dance floor at Xenon with John Casablancas. The club was where Elite threw its frequent parties, mailing agency T-shirts out as invitations and waiting to see how suggestively the models could tie or tear them. One night Casablancas even had a pool put onto the dance floor so the T-shirts could be properly wetted.

Turning down the agency's suggestion that she seek drug counseling with Robert Hilton, Gia instead took the suggestion of Scavullo and others in seeing Park Avenue nutritionist Dr. Robert Giller. She went in late July, after a hellish two-week stretch during which the combination of the heroin, her period and her desire to keep working nearly did her in. She lost ten pounds very rapidly, barely made it through a lingerie shooting for Diane von Furstenberg, and somehow bluffed her way through a party her mother threw for her brother Joey's wedding. Joey's first marriage had ended in divorce; his daughter had gone to live with her mother in California. Of the three Carangi children, Joey had always been the most estranged from his mother, so Kathleen was trying to make everything perfect. She had been noticing that something was not right about Gia, but there hadn't been much time to talk. Especially after Gia cut short the week's vacation she had planned by returning to New York after two days.

Giller was the latest of the Dr. Feelgoods, the next in a long line of medical professionals employing hair tests, nutritional analyses and vitamin injections. The difference between Giller and his predecessors was that he not only had the requisite celebrity clients, but he hung out with them. It was no wonder that his B-12 shots were the morning jump-start of choice for the Studio 54 crowd: he was one of the crowd. He would later write a best-selling fitness book, *Medical Makeover,* which featured many celebrity endorsements and Giller's "No-Will-power Program for Lifetime Health" that allowed a reader to "kick all your bad habits for good—in eight weeks or less!" Giller charged her $140 for the initial visit and sold her $61 worth of vitamin supplements. Gia felt assured that the doctor could help her kick drugs with his approach.

The day after Gia's first visit with Giller, she was taken to lunch at the Oyster Bar by her booker at Wilhelmina, Lucy Cobb, and *Vogue* model editor Sara Foley. They hoped that by ganging up on her, they might impress upon her just exactly what she was throwing away. "People were, at this point, bending over backwards for her," recalled Lucy Cobb. "Gia was not showing up for bookings, costing them a lot of money. Even under those circumstances—which usually would assure the girl would *never* be booked again—the magazine would give Gia another chance. She had already blown it with them, I don't know how many times. Sara and I both wanted her to work for *Vogue.* We were just like, 'C'mon, Gia, get it together, be a *little bit* responsible.' She always meant well. She tried. It was just really hard for her."

The magazine was willing to give her one more chance, even though she had pulled the ultimate stunt, creating one of the fastest-traveling anecdotes in the history of fashion: she had walked out on Dick Avedon.

"She used to tell me that story herself, she thought it was great," recalled John Stember. "She went to do a cover for *Vogue.* They did all the hair and makeup and spent all those fucking hours getting her ready and getting her dressed and the editor was flitting around saying, 'Wonderful, wonderful, she's the most gorgeous thing in the world,' screaming at the assistants, you know. So Avedon goes *click,* one click. And Gia says, 'Hold on a second, I've got to go to the bathroom.' So she goes to the bathroom to have a pee. She climbs out the window, gets in a cab and goes home."

* * *

Even after that, Gia continued working for *Vogue,* where her cover had been doing extremely well on the newsstands. She managed to stay clean for several weeks—at least during working hours—and did sittings with Denis Piel, Chris von Wangenheim and Arthur Elgort. Then *Vogue* sent her on a week-long trip to Southampton with Scavullo. Harry King was doing hair, Sandy Linter makeup. Instead of going with the others, Gia insisted on driving her own car out to Scavullo's house, after first stopping off at Dr. Giller's for a vitamin shot.

Vogue was hoping for a replay of Gia and Scavullo's highly successful trip to St. Barts. Instead, the trip turned out to be a nightmare.

It began when one of Scavullo's assistants pushed Gia into the pool. "The poor guy just didn't realize you don't push top models into pools," recalled Harry King. "I think she found it difficult to be around a lot of people anyway. And she had pulled herself together to come down and hang out with an editor, her assistant, makeup, hair, two photographer's assistants, three other models. She had pulled it together to come do that, and she's there two seconds and this guy was, like, 'Oh, I'm going to push you in the *pool.'* And in she went. She tried to make light of it. She was smoking a cigarette at the time, and I remember she came up with the cigarette in her mouth."

"She was so upset, she started to cry," recalled Scavullo. "I fired the assistant on the spot. She hated that kind of guy."

From that point on, the trip degenerated. "She would drive off," recalled Harry King. "We assumed she was looking for drugs." They also assumed that she found drugs. And when the pictures were finally delivered to *Vogue,* so did the magazine's fashion department. In a number of the shots—which were of bathing suits and summerwear—there were visible, red bumps in the crooks of her elbows, track marks. "I remember when those pictures came in," said Sara Foley, "there was a big scene in the art department." The shots were edited and airbrushed to minimize the obvious, but several pictures eventually ran in the November 1980 issue where the needle marks were visible.

Gia did one more sitting for *Vogue* the day she returned

from Southampton, with Denis Piel and Polly Mellen. The shot, a beauty picture for an article on the "fragrance collections," was one of Piel's best, a seemingly stolen moment of Gia, sitting in a wooden chair, tugging at the front of her spaghetti-strap dress and peering down at herself. The session was Gia's last major work for the magazine, because it was finally clear that she could not go on—or she had at last violated even *Vogue*'s standards for indulgence.

"At one shoot, she had fallen asleep and we had to wait and leave her in the chair until she woke up," recalled Polly Mellen. "And this other time—it was *shocking,* this incident. We were shooting her in a very bare dress and the photographer said, 'Polly, could you come here and look through the camera.' And there was blood coming down her arm, from where she injected herself while we were shooting."

But *Vogue* was just one of many clients. Two days after her last *Vogue* session, Gia had a full day that hardly suggested her career was in jeopardy. She had a morning screen test for Peter Bogdanovich's new film, which she missed because of a Perry Ellis fitting and another catalog shot. Late in the afternoon, she went to Scavullo's studio to be interviewed for the coffee-table beauty book *Scavullo Women* he and Sean Byrnes were preparing for publication in 1982. And in the evening she met with director Franco Zeffirelli, who also wanted to see her about a film. Several days later she took a late afternoon flight from New York to Los Angeles, did a four-and-a-half-hour lingerie sitting, picked up a voucher for $1,575 and caught the red-eye back to New York.

But not long after, the work began to dry up, and her professional friends fled for their own lives. Sandy Linter refused to even take her phone calls: one night, in desperation, Gia had climbed up the outside of Sandy's apartment building to try to break into one of her windows so they could talk.

"You know, there are hardly any girls who disappear when they're reaching their height," said Scavullo. "They usually stay around until you can't photograph them any longer. There were lots of girls who were victims of those times—the nightlife, Studio 54, dancing, having fun. There were girls who took a lot of coke and destroyed their beauty.

But I don't think Gia was one of those. I think she was a victim of herself ... she was too smart for the world she had come into. I don't mean the fashion world. I mean *this* world."

In early November, Gia moved back uptown, to East Fifty-third Street, to put some distance between herself and the Lower East Side, and try to get a handle on her life. She also agreed to move to Eileen Ford, the agent least likely to tolerate her drug use. To the untrained eye, it looked like one more big model switching agencies in a power play. But the agencies knew better. They knew that Gia's drug problem was the one that everyone else in the industry judged theirs against. They also knew that any agency that succeeded in helping her clean up would find itself with a valuable commodity. The business was still waiting to forgive her. She was still poised for that half-million-dollar-a-year career that Willie had talked about in *Philadelphia* magazine.

The day before she was supposed to sign the papers to switch to Ford, Gia finally met with Robert Hilton—who was being paid by Wilhelmina Models to counsel her. To break the ice, Hilton told her some war stories about his experiences as a heroin addict in San Francisco in the late sixties. The tale that affected her the most was about a foiled apartment robbery attempt in which his junkie partner got stabbed in the chest with an ice pick. Hilton told Gia that all he could think, as his friend died in his arms, was that if he followed through and stole something he could at least get high.

"That story really got to her," Hilton recalled. "You get a bunch of dopers sitting around and there's going to be a large aspect of death talk, because somebody is always overdosing, being dumped in an emergency room. So she started telling me about the shit she had done on the Lower East Side. You know, it's funny, but I didn't think the Lower East Side was anything peculiar at the time. Now I realize it was just outrageous, but, at the time ... New York was in the middle of some kind of wacky cultural explosion, some convergence of music and fashion and art and literature and everything just kind of . . . life just kind of *opened*. That kind of selling of heroin just seemed part of it.

"Gia spent an awful lot of time down there. She went through an awful lot of money, you know. For a heroin addict to go downtown and spend $100, that's ten bags of dope: that's a nice hit. Gia had no problem going down and spending $2,000, $3,000 *a day*. I don't know how the hell she did it. I mean, her anecdotal stories of drug use was the thing that I couldn't quite get. She wasn't that big a girl. But I guess her tolerance must have been ridiculous, because some other people who knew her said she had, in fact, run through that kind of money.

"She had had a couple of overdoses, in the shooting galleries. Do you know what happens to drug addicts when they overdose? What drug addicts do to other drug addicts? They throw them into a tub full of ice cold water or inject them with milk or saltwater. She was a regular at the shooting galleries down in the Lower East Side.

"It was actually ridiculous how many times she overdosed. She was a real pig for heroin, a real glutton. She had a definite love affair with the stuff, she was crazy about it. Gia was the perfect candidate to be a heroin addict. Because, left to her own devices, she really had an awful, awful lot of self-loathing. And heroin does not kick you into overdrive the way cocaine does. Heroin has the effect of making the whole universe a real friendly place and it was almost as though she had found a perfect prescription for her personality. Because she was one kid that was in a *lot of pain*, and there was just something about the way her pain resonated. I felt it a lot."

She never really explained to him where the pain came from. "The only way I could paraphrase what she was saying," he recalled, "was that she felt like a fraud. She said 'fake' or 'phony,' like a prom queen. Whenever Gia got dressed up and stood in front of the camera, with the makeup and the hair and all that, the distance between that and her inner life made her feel like a fake.

"She also talked a lot about having her heart broken by Sandy. That was a very significant relationship to her. A big part of this, I think, was about her sexuality.

"And then, of course, there was the modeling business

itself. With the way Gia felt about herself, I could never figure out how, of all the careers on the face of the earth, this kid could end up modeling. It was only because she had this ability to kick into this childlike overdrive and let herself play in front of the camera that she could do it. 'Cause, man, real deep down, she didn't like herself at all. Sometimes she felt good when she was in front of the camera, but it was only temporary, and she knew that. I don't know, a lot of people never thought Gia was too bright. I never felt that way. I thought she was a real smart kid and part of the problem with her was that everything good about modeling was only temporary and it only made things feel better for a while.

"The worst thing that happened to Gia was that she became successful. The last thing in the world that girl needed was to be indulged and she was indulged constantly. She could show up three days late and be in the most absolutely despicable condition and that *minute* she was forgiven—for having that face and looking that way. And boy, she was *real beautiful*. There was just this quality about her, almost impossible to describe ... and I don't think that kind of beauty can ever be *just* physical, that kind of feeling that somebody gives us. She just had a rich, sensual look to her face that was, well, it was *staggering*.

"And a lot of people's careers and fortunes and futures rode on her. They didn't care about her, they put up with her. And the only reason they did was because it affected *their* lives. She wasn't well-spoken, she wasn't articulate. These fucking people had no use or love for her except for the fact that she made money for them and they put up with her as though they loved her, as though they cared for her. Everybody talked about how they loved her. Bull*shit*. She wasn't that easy to be around."

Hilton never forgot a story he was told by Gerald Marie, who was the head of Elite in Paris (and later married model Linda Evangelista). "I remember one time I was over there and he took me by this place—it was a girls' school," he recalled. "And he said when Gia first started coming to Paris, he would take her and drop her off there in front of the school and leave her there. It was like a treat for her. I mean, at the time, I laughed like hell. But later I really thought that was so exploitative and sick.''

While he understood a lot of what Gia was telling him—more than her parents, family or friends could possibly have—Hilton didn't have a lot of training in actual therapeutic techniques. He was an experienced peer counselor and knew how to use the "I've been there" routine to form a bond. But he had yet to learn what to do if finding someone to talk to wasn't enough.

"There were a lot of things about Gia's pain that I had difficulty with. I now know a lot more about why, since I've been to graduate school and don't *only* do the ex-addict-to-addict stuff. These things were difficult for me then because, basically . . . there was no way to say to her, 'Don't deal with the pain,' and there was no way to even *begin* to diminish it. She would say, 'This makes it go away.' And I would say, 'Well it's killing you.' But, to her, that was real secondary shit. I mean, first of all, it's never real for people in that situation, they're always invincible. But, really, she didn't *care* if it was killing her. All that mattered to her was that, for a little while, she didn't feel that pain.

"Gia was the first model who had really made it, who had a tremendous name, and whose drug problems had to be dealt with in any profound way. Everyone else, for the most part, was still working, still doing what they were supposed to be doing: it got worse for some of them later. But Gia does not stand as a testament to my abilities as a therapist *at all*. She did try to get cleaned up. I've got to give her credit, she tried. She did make an effort.''

Hilton tried to convince Gia that she should call him or come see him whenever she felt the urge to head to Eldridge Street was growing too strong. "She called me from shoots and stuff, running out the door," he recalled. "But I didn't have any way to stop her. She'd call and say, 'I can't take it, I'm going to go out and do it.' What was real clear to me was that there was no way in the world that some counselor, or outpatient clinic, was going to help her. Certainly not me, unless she was going to come and live with me and I was going to watch her twenty-four hours a day. And even at that, she was so unbelievably manipulative. I finally said,

'Listen, this girl needs a therapeutic community.' A suggestion like that, of course, was not an option."

It was not an option because Gia had already left Wilhelmina. She had signed with Ford, where she lasted a couple of weeks.

In mid-November, Kathleen Sperr came to New York to help Gia set up her new uptown apartment. She still did not know for certain about Gia's drug problems—or she wouldn't let herself know. She continued to see Gia's out-of-control lifestyle as part of the glamour of being a top model. She continued to see whatever setbacks Gia seemed to be having as the petty jealousies of a glamorous industry. She even saw the fact that Gia needed her help setting up a new place because she had simply *left* many of her things in her last apartment—the clothes, some of the guitars she bought even though she couldn't play—as part of the twenty-year-old's prerogative as a famous person.

"I had had my suspicions before," Kathleen recalled. "Suddenly, I couldn't get her on the phone: I had *always* been able to get her on the phone, we spoke daily when she was in the country. Then I started seeing the bank statements, seeing the money walk out of the bank. But, like anything else, you can *suspect* something, and as long as you don't actually know for sure, there's still a chance that it's not the problem.

"The clues had been there. She was talking about getting in situations where she lost her fee and had to pay the other models. I had found a hypodermic needle in her things before. But I just couldn't believe it because, as a child, if you took Gia to the doctor for a shot she'd scream bloody murder."

Finally, when Gia returned one night from a drug shopping spree, Kathleen confronted her. "I was waiting for her when she came back," Kathleen recalled. "That's when we got down to the truth ... and, once I finally put it all together and confronted her, it was hell from then on. That first winter, when I found out that she was into heroin, was when she was the worst about being found. I would go to New York, go to the apartment. Sometimes she would know I was coming up, other times I could get the doorman to let me in. Sometimes I would drive up, write out the Lord's Prayer, slip it under the door, sign it, 'Love, Mom,' and drive back to Richboro. There were times when Henry thought I was being unreasonable. But he knew that there was going to be no living with me if he didn't let me do what I had to do. There was no way he was going to come between me and Gia.

"She was trying to get it together. She was at Ford's for a couple of weeks, that didn't work out. Then she just decided to come home and clean up."

Gia moved back to Philadelphia on February 11, 1981. It was two weeks after her twenty-first birthday, and almost three years to the day since she had begun modeling. She moved into her mother and stepfather's house in suburban Richboro, where she couldn't get from her small bedroom to the kitchen without passing the family room wall that was *covered* with framed copies of her magazine covers and *Cosmo* calendar posters. Gia wanted her mother to take them down, but she wouldn't. "Gia liked the *idea* that the covers were on the wall, but she couldn't stand to be in the room with them," Kathleen recalled, with the kind of solipsistic logic and maternal cluelessness that often frustrated her daughter.

The week Gia left New York, *Time* magazine ran a cover story on modeling. In a bit of corporate backslapping, the cover just happened to appear the week before the annual *Sports Illustrated* swimsuit issue, which was published by the same parent company and was riding the swelling wave of model-oriented publicity to ever-growing newsstand sales. The *Time* story highlighted Brooke Shields on the cover, and inside had pictures of Christie Brinkley (who was about to appear on the *SI* swimsuit cover), Janice Dickinson, Carol Alt, Rachel Ward and Apollonia. Most conspicuous by their absence in the article—their names were not even mentioned—were Patti Hansen, Esme and Gia.

13
Bad Girls

Rochelle Rosen* was aggressively ambivalent. She wasn't sure if she loved or hated her family, so she did both. She wasn't sure what gender she preferred, so she slept with a lot of men and a lot of women. She wasn't sure which drugs she liked best, so she did a lot of everything. She wasn't sure if she was basically good or basically bad. Those who knew her weren't sure either.

Rochelle Rosen was a smart-mouthed Philadelphia college student, petite with dirty-blonde hair, who came from money and had always been the one in any group who was in the most trouble. Her mother had given birth to her at age seventeen, with her father still an undergraduate in college, and they had lived with the Rosens' wealthy grandparents for Rochelle's first five years. When she began getting into trouble in high school—eventually being sent for a short stay in a rehab hospital, which she recalled as "more a way of getting away from my parents than anything else"—she was sent back to live with her grandmother. Her younger sister, who fulfilled enough of her parents' expectations for both daughters, remained at home. The move had not changed Rochelle's lifestyle much, and she fondly remembered being caught laying out several thousand Quaaludes on the Persian rug in her bedroom in her grandmother's apartment: "She looked in and said, 'Clean this stuff up and vacuum that carpet.' I loved my grandmother."

As a student at Temple University, Rochelle had become a regular in both the gay and straight dance clubs, traveling easily between the sons of Philadelphia's rich and powerful and the daughters of the sexual revolution. The club of the moment was called Second Story, a city church that been converted and now fancied itself the Studio 54 of Philadelphia. A number of the guys Rochelle knew from Second Story had famous fathers, written up in *The Philadelphia Inquirer* business section or the Pennsylvania State Crime Commission Report. Such a combo-platter peer group was a common situation for a girl on the Philadelphia club scene. Just like in New York, where preppies slummed in the same places where the strivers strove and the hip looked down their perfect noses, Philadelphia nightlife had become a real melting pot. WASP kids and ethnic kids, rich kids and poor kids found that, unlike their parents, they had something in common: they were all queued up for the same lines of cocaine. Since everyone was, technically, breaking the law, the lines between "good" and "bad" people became—like everything else—awfully blurry.

"Without getting into any names, okay, let's just say I knew some people from South Philadelphia and Cherry Hill who were involved with organized crime," Rochelle recalled. "There was this one guy ... he's dead now, so, what can he do? He used to pay me to round up girls from Second Story and bring them back to his house to have parties. The club would let out about four and I would go in just before that. I used to take his Mercedes and go downtown and pick them out of there and bring them back to the house. He knew that I wouldn't be involved with him, but I would get him the girls and he would give me, like, a hundred dollars for each girl I could get back there. And they were free-basing. He was into that. In fact, he had boats that came to Florida and he'd go there and bring *so much coke back*.

"It was mostly just drugs. Well, no, they were into all that, like, weird sex, group sex, too. But, well, I never got really into it because I was really gay, so I didn't even want to be with *one* guy, let alone six. So I always got my drugs and got out. Oh, my god, I was so *bad,* then. I was so *young!*"

Gia had met Rochelle very casually in Philadelphia the

previous summer. "We were introduced by a friend of mine who had modeled with her at Gimbels," Rochelle recalled. "She walked in with Gia, who was wearing a black motorcycle jacket, a white T-shirt, blue Levis and white hi-top Cons—that was before that was stylish—and she had a Heineken in her hand. I almost passed out. I was going through the dilemma of sex at that time, and I had never come into contact with anybody who was that stereotypically homosexual. Then, after meeting her, I walked into Green's Drug Store and there was a stack of *Cosmopolitan*s and I looked, and it was that girl who was in my house. You could see it was her face. The whole thing just turned my head, and I'm not the kind of person who's easily awed.

"When we met she had already been taking heroin and had been through twenty-one-day detox. She had what they call a 'bubblegum habit' because she was able to detox in twenty-one days. She was getting Percodans or Percocets from some dentist. If you try to stop doing heroin, you can take Percodan and it'll give you the same high and won't hurt you. Then the dentist cut her off and she went to the vitamin shot guy—she *loved* those mainlined vitamins—I think he gave her Percocets and Valiums, too. She was trying to stay clean."

When Gia moved back to her mother's house in Richboro, she started seeing more of Rochelle—who bore some physical resemblance to Sandy Linter. Kathleen was unconcerned about Gia and Rochelle at first, believing that they were just friends. Then she began to realize that they were lovers. And she also suspected that Rochelle was not a likely candidate for the role of the strong, level-headed companion who would inspire Gia to stay clean and help her get back to the modeling career waiting in New York.

The fashion world was going on without Gia. She was one of the few girls with a look that was considered irreplaceable: there were a lot more blondes waiting on deck than brunettes who could do high fashion. But being irreplaceable didn't mean you wouldn't be replaced—it wasn't as if the collections were going to halt if she was unavailable, or *Vogue* would run blank pages. No one person was ever that important in the *fashionista* world. The jobs were more important than the people who did them: the decision to create something—a photograph, an advertisement, a garment, a perfume, a career—was more important than what was actually created.

Still, individual players did matter—to each other. Each person was just a cog in the machinery, but it took only one or two connections to get inside the machine and a few more to stay inside it. Gia had already lost her first mentor in New York when Wilhelmina died. But that was more a personal loss than a professional one. A top model could always get another agent, and a lot of what an agent gave a model came in the beginning of her career.

But losing favor with a top photographer who liked working with you and generated a lot of jobs could cost a model a lot of money. If the photographer was a friend, it could cost the model even more. Gia had already burned bridges with a lot of New York's top photographers. Professionally and personally, she couldn't really afford to lose any of her remaining fashion business friends. Her chances for a comeback were directly related to how many of the same people who had encouraged her rise were still in place to rejoice in her second coming.

Chris von Wangenheim went on vacation to St. Martin with his girlfriend in early March, a trip meant to put the last grueling year of his life behind him. He had been going through a divorce that had become messy both emotionally and professionally. He was a fairly traditional European man and did not really believe in divorce, especially since there was a child involved. He had also been working on a book for St. Martin's Press for years—a project that might finally elevate him above the throng of high-paid commercial shutterbugs—but his wife, retired Ford model Regine Jaffey, was refusing to let him use some of his best photographs. Regine had been Von Wangenheim's favorite model, but he had never bothered to get releases from her for pictures of herself or their child.

The emotional strain, and Von Wangenheim's increasing use of cocaine, had decimated his career. He had lost ad clients—first Versace, and now Dior was about to give the American licensee campaign to Avedon. And his edgier editorial clients were abandoning him. He had even parted company with the *dolce vita* crew at Italian *Bazaar,* after spending a few paid weeks in Capri and then proclaiming himself unable to take even one picture. "By that time he was snorting cocaine every five minutes," said Lizzette Kattan.

"I've never seen anybody so totally undone," recalled fine art photographer Ralph Gibson, a friend of Von Wangenheim's who had also copublished, in 1980, the art book *Fashion: Theory,* which included essays and photographs by Von Wangenheim and seven other top fashion photographers. "I just watched the unraveling, the unfurling of a great person. He had moments of brilliance, but he was totally cynical about the commercial world, in a German aristocratic way. I mean, it was something he scraped off the bottom of his shoe most of the time. But he was running such a big overhead, he had to keep scraping.

"What happens is that fashion photographers make it solely on their inspiration, which is then leeched out of them. Very few of them stay inspired. When you're really hot, you make this particular photograph for yourself, whether anybody would buy it or not. And that's how they all get their foot in the door, and get their names known— because it's inspired work. We all know what inspired everything is. It has a peculiar perfume about it. It is instantly scented. Well, then what happens is that people come along and start to dampen the enthusiasm through rejection: the work gets rejected, gets cut in half, it gets abused and then it's purely a survival situation. And many photographers don't continue to grow under that.

"Once you're established, you can coast for a long time. I know for a fact that Von Wangenheim was definitely in need of a major resurgence of inspiration. And his divorce was fucking him up terribly."

Von Wangenheim and his wife had reached an unhappy but final arrangement. He had brainstormed a new approach for his book with Marc Balet, the third art director to try to make the project work. They would use the theme *Women Alone* and Von Wangenheim would take lots of new pictures to mix in with the best of the past—including several shots of Gia. The photographer had gone to St. Martin with renewed hope for his life and his photographic career: he was going to take pictures down there, and recharge.

But he had also left a makeshift will. He scribbled it down in twenty minutes and handed it to his flabbergasted friend, downtown fine art photographer John Flattau. He gave it to him along with the key to his loft/studio, since Flattau had agreed to check Von Wangenheim's mail while he was away.

On March 10, Flattau went over to his friend's place to sort the mail. After finishing, he went to lock the loft's heavy double door. The key snapped off in the lock. When Flattau returned to his own apartment, he received a phone call. Chris von Wangenheim had been killed in a single-car crash on St. Martin. His girlfriend had survived.

"It was a total shock, but in no way mysterious," recalled Ralph Gibson. "And when he died, *everything* he did died with him. Some guys are better set up for posterity than Von Wangenheim was, absolutely. He hadn't set up his archives or anything like that, because as young as he was, he didn't think he needed one. I, on the other hand, have long since set mine up. I could be dead ten years and people will still think I'm alive, the way I could leak work out."

Von Wangenheim's death was another tragedy for the business and a terrible personal loss for Gia. But it did not seem like an isolated incident—just a particularly gruesome symptom of a socioeconomic disease that was turning the glitzy, Studio 54 disco-world of the *fashionistas* into an endless night of decadence at the Mudd Club. The week after the photographer's death, *New York* magazine did another of its semiannual Anthony Haden-Guest cover stories on the modeling business. "The Spoiled Supermodels" detailed a purported client and photographer revolt over rising model prices and power. The agencies were compared to OPEC and photographers were encouraged to vent about the outrage of sessions being canceled because a certain *model* (rather than a certain *photographer*) was unavailable. The article also delivered to the general public the litany of model horror stories that had been privately circulating through the industry for the past year.

Since the author was using pseudonyms, composite characters, and probably apocryphal stories, the identities of the two most prominently portrayed offenders, "Leandra" and "Cleo," were unclear. Cleo was identified as a heroin addict with a "model-chaser boyfriend" who left shoots to meet her drug dealer and jumped into the Grand Canal in Venice during a TV commercial shooting. Leandra reportedly arrived to a sitting "grumpy and extremely late ... [with] filthy feet and bitten nails" and proceeded to sweep the makeup jars, brushes and tubes onto the floor and tear a designer dress "in half." When Haden-Guest said that the last time he had seen Cleo was "in one of those after-hours joints that open at about five, after the rock clubs have started shutting down ... her skin was blueish-pale like milk in a dark pantry," he left little doubt that Gia was at least part of his composite character of the model from hell.

The New York *Daily News* was also about to publish a week-long series on "the dark side of modeling" called "Night Face Day Face." Its highlights were a thorough accounting of Esme's rise and fall—about which only Esme herself seemed unaware—and a heartbreaking profile of Lisa Taylor, whose wrist had been so beautifully bitten by Chris von Wangenheim's Doberman. At twenty-eight, Taylor was going public about why her career was in shambles, destroyed by substance abuse and what she said was a self-destructive relationship with actor Tommy Lee Jones, whom she had met during the filming of *Eyes of Laura Mars.* Taylor said that cocaine was the main culprit: it made her paranoid and she would often be sitting in her apartment all alone when "suddenly, I'd think there were five thousand people standing around me trying to take my picture. I'd actually look around to see if they were there."

She went from cocaine to drinking a lot of martinis. Her weight fell nearly ten pounds and she was terribly depressed, but she found that her editorial work actually picked up during that awful period. "There was one photograph that Helmut Newton did of me for *Vogue* that I begged them not to use but they used it anyway," she said. "It was me in a sauna with just a towel over my lap, holding a huge ladle with the water dripping into my mouth. I looked *awful,* but it was beautiful, you know, as a photograph. I wasn't smiling, my hair was standing straight out and was all greasy, but it was beautiful."

*   *   *

Gia was busy generating her own horror stories in semi-retirement. Just after midnight on Sunday, March 22, a suburban Philadelphia police officer in a marked Jeep was staking out an apartment complex when he saw a little red sports car come barreling down a divided, tree-lined street. The car collided with the dead-end fence, backed up, jumped the traffic island, and zoomed off. The officer turned on his siren and began a high-speed chase through the residential neighborhood and into another township, calling officers in both jurisdictions for backup. When the careening car finally stalled, the officer got out of his Jeep and got close enough to see the female driver before she started her engine again and drove away.

The officer jumped back into his Jeep and finally pulled even with the sports car, trying to force it off the road. The driver instead turned toward him and played bumper cars until he backed off. By that time, other officers had come from the opposite direction and blocked off the next intersection. Gia was taken into custody.

She had a strong scent of alcohol on her breath and fresh track marks on her arms. A doctor's exam showed her blood alcohol to be within an acceptable range: she was under the influence of cocaine. "She was upset, pretty mouthy and obnoxious," recalled the arresting officer. "She did say that she was a model, and at one point she was saying how much she made as a model and that we were only cops and peons, whatever. She was a rather attractive girl, just screwed up on whatever she was screwed up on."

The arrest was just the beginning of a nightmarish summer at "The Hacienda"—the name Gia's friends had given to the Spanish-style Sperr residence. In early June, Kathleen and Henry went to Bloomington, Indiana, to get their 1978 gold Corvette certified. "I was real into Corvettes that year," Kathleen recalled. When they got home, they found every surface in the house covered with a thin layer of soot. "Gia almost burned the house down," Kathleen said. "She put something in the fireplace and didn't open the flue, and then she fell asleep because she was so high on heroin. I screamed about that for three days."

Gia had also developed a frightening abscess on the top

of her hand—the very sight of which made her mother ill. "At that time, her hand started getting really infected, because she was shooting into it," Kathleen said. "How she ever kept that arm, I don't know. The infection was absolutely horrible. I said, 'Gia, if you die, people will say to me *where were you?*'"

Gia spent the summer trying to kick drugs and periodically taking jobs. She was based in Bucks County and occasionally went down to Atlantic City. Her brothers and father now lived permanently at the Shore, only ninety miles away—less than an hour the way Gia drove—but far enough that they weren't much a part of her day-to-day life. In fact, as they opened two Hoagie City locations—one around the corner from Resorts and a second a block from Caesars—they were only vaguely aware of how bad her drug problems had become, and Gia did her best to keep it that way. Only Michael even had an inkling, but he had a life (and some drug problems) of his own.

Gia's aunt Nancy couldn't really help. She still lived in Philadelphia, but she found herself unable to deal with Gia's drug problems. It was too painful and hopeless a situation for her to be around, so she increasingly distanced herself from her troubled niece.

Gia was represented, however momentarily, by a new agency called Legends, which Kay Mitchell had opened after finally parting ways with what was left of Wilhelmina. One of the jobs Legends arranged for Gia fell during the same week in early August as her scheduled criminal court date. John Duffy, the prominent local defense attorney her parents had borrowed money to hire (he had represented a defendant in the recent Abscam trials) had planned for Gia to get into the state's Accelerated Rehabilitative Disposition (ARD) program for first offenders. ARD offered a second chance without a guilty plea and, eventually, a clean criminal record for staying out of trouble. The strategy backfired when Gia failed to show up and act contrite. "When it came time for her to appear for her ARD hearing, she was in, like, Egypt," recalled Duffy. "I called for her, and didn't get any reaction. My secretary called and talked to her stepfather and they said she was in Egypt, doing a shoot, there was a yacht involved. And then I didn't hear from her." A bench warrant was issued for her arrest.

Several weeks later, Gia robbed her mother. Early one morning—about five A.M.—Kathleen woke up with a premonition that she should take a look at her well-hidden stash of jewelry. When she checked, she saw that much of it was gone, including several family heirlooms.

Gia had even stolen Kathleen's wedding ring from her marriage to Joe Carangi. Kathleen never found out whether Gia pawned the wedding ring for drug money or kept it as a tragic memento, because their confrontation about the robbery was brief. When Kathleen came banging on her daughter's bedroom door just before dawn, Gia seemed to know precisely what she was enraged about and exactly what had to happen next. She hurriedly gathered together a few things and, without saying a word, sprinted out of the house. It was days before she called to let anyone know where she was.

In the meantime, Kathleen and Henry went to the local magistrate in Bucks County to swear out a criminal complaint against Gia. They hoped that an arrest, *another* arrest, might be a way to force her into rehabilitation. "It was the only suggestion that made any sense," Kathleen recalled. "Any other authority I talked to told me to wash my hands of her. Nobody wanted to touch a heroin addict." The medical world often had a hard time dealing with heroin addiction. The attitude bubbled up from the hospital emergency rooms, where doctors saw and treated all kinds, but found their Hippocratic oaths most heavily tested by junkies— whose problems seemed utterly self-inflicted, and whose personal strength and integrity seemed as minimal as their chances for recovery. Even in the growing drug and alcohol rehab establishment, junkies were often viewed as untouchables—not "diseased" like those psychologically addicted to substances, but physically dependent and doomed.

"I wanted to get her committed," Kathleen recalled, "but because of her age and the fact that she was out of my household, I could have gone through the legal process and spent all this money and she could still be out on the street again in twenty-four hours." The judge issued the warrant, but Gia was never actively pursued. Only a major criminal in a major city would actually be stalked down in such a situation.

Gia sought refuge with her old Bowie-buddy Toni O'Connor. She moved into Toni's small apartment in Philadelphia's Roxborough section—a strongly ethnic neighborhood that had also developed an enclave of working-class lesbians. Toni was working part-time doing quality control for a tool and die company, mostly as a way to cover up her drug dealing, which had switched from Quaaludes—which were now nearly impossible to get—to cocaine. The job was a more comfortable cover than telling people she was a prostitute.

"I was really starting to get hooked on drugs myself at that point," Toni recalled, "doing a lot of downs to escape reality. I had just met my real dad, who had left when I was five. After not seeing him for years, I saw him at the DCA, screwing around with men friends of mine.

"Gia had nowhere to go, so I let her live with me. She was in bad shape. She had these big lumps from those calluses where she shot up. Plus, her spine had, like, really bad deposits because of drugs—like, cysts coming out on the base of her spine from impurities in the heroin. Rochelle wasn't around at this point: I guess they had broken up, for a change. Gia was taking methadone. She was in a program in a place in West Philadelphia and she had a counselor and everything. But she was still doing dope. She would go out and lie to me and tell me she wasn't getting high anymore.

"It was a weird situation because, on the one hand, it was like Gia and I were back together again. We used to go down to this women's bar, Rainbows, during that time and it was like we were back on top again. But she was fucked up, and not like when we were on Quaaludes in high school. This was different. She just wasn't herself. When you're on downs, it's like, the next morning, you wake up and you're back to normal. When you're sticking a needle in your arm, you 'jones' for another fix. You're not gonna kill someone to get another friggin' Quaalude."

In a way, their reunion was a return to old Bowie-kid escapades. But every situation had a rougher edge than before: fewer of the stories ended with everyone living happily ever after. One afternoon in August, Gia and Toni went for a swerving joyride through Center City in Gia's little red car and were pulled over by police at four-thirty in the afternoon. When Gia's name was run through police computers her outstanding warrants came up: since she had already posted a thousand dollars bail in her other case, she was released on her own recognizance, pending trials.

And their drug friends were experiencing more than just monumental hangovers. "She was running with a friend of mine, Shelly, a gay guy who used to be the doorman at Catacombs, a mixed, after-hours club under Second Story," Toni recalled. "They would go over to Camden together to buy heroin. He went over there one time by himself and got shot and killed."

Toni and Gia bumped into an old friend of Toni's one night at the East Side Club: it was the woman's first glimpse of the fabled lesbian model from Philadelphia. "She sure didn't look like she looked in the magazines," the woman recalled. "I was so shocked. She had put on some weight and she just looked out of it. She was smoking a cigarette and it was burned down to the filter; she was still holding it and the ashes were dangling. I took the butt from between her fingers, because she was going to burn herself. Toni was just, 'I'm back with Gia.' She always thought it was meant to be."

But Toni knew something was very wrong. "Gia was selling her belongings to buy drugs," Toni said. "She sold a camera, she sold clothes. She had a bunch of leather clothes from when she was modeling, and I bought them from her. One jacket she had was this beautiful white leather, I gave her two hundred forty dollars for it. But finally, I was supporting her.

"She would come over to a friend's apartment and lock herself in the bathroom and shoot up, and my friends would get mad. She would shoot the heroin, then she would suck it back out and push it back in and suck it back out. It was like she was having sex with the friggin' needle. I couldn't compete with this drug. She had a love affair with the needle.

"She wasn't happy. She said she had been doing what Kathy wanted her to do. She always felt that her mother was trying to live her life through her, and she couldn't allow it to happen anymore. And it's not that I'm trying to blame Kathy—this is just the way Gia saw it.

"She would say, 'No one ever asked me what *I* wanted to do! I never wanted to be a *model*. I wanted to be a *rock star*—like Jim Morrison.' Everybody always thought it was Bowie with her, but it was the Doors."

Like many of the hardcore Bowie fans from the early seventies, Gia had tired of the changeling as his work got more commercial and then positively weird. The final straw for a generation weaned on Ziggy had been Bowie's pronouncement in a *Rolling Stone* interview that he wasn't gay and never had been: it was the ultimate betrayal of the faith his fans had placed in him. By moving on from Bowie to Blondie to the Doors, Gia was again surfing the wave of mass hip. The LA band, which succumbed with its leader in 1971, was being rediscovered by teenagers as the first classic rock act, prompting the memorable 1981 *Rolling Stone* cover "Jim Morrison: He's Hot, He's Sexy, He's Dead."

"She was obsessed with the Doors: 'LA Woman,' 'Love Her Madly,' that was Gia," Toni recalled. "We would lay in bed and she would write out the lyrics to their songs. Basically we would eat and go to bed and that was about it. She was addicted to sausage at that time: eleven o'clock at night she would have to make sausage, breakfast sausage. She could be so funny. Or she'd want to go down to Jim's for a steak sandwich.

"Finally what happened was I came home one night and she had fallen asleep twisted up in my quilt. It was a new quilt, I had just paid $500 for it, and she fell asleep with a cigarette in her mouth and burned a hole in it. I got really mad and said, 'I'm not baby-sitting you anymore!' I was paying for food, clothing and shelter for her. She didn't even care about taking care of herself. She just made me so angry, I just snapped that night. I ended up throwing her in the shower and being really mad at her.

"And I told her to leave. She wouldn't. And I was so infuriated, and so out of it on 'ludes myself, that I reached in my purse and pulled out my Mace and *sprayed her in the face*. She cried so bad when I did that, she was like a little kid. I don't think I could ever forgive myself for doing that," she said, beginning to cry. "She didn't leave until the next morning. She packed her bag, took all her clothes, and disappeared."

In the fall of 1981, Gia went back to New York to lay the groundwork for her comeback. She went to see Monique Pillard at Elite's offices on East Fifty-eighth Street. In the four years since the model wars broke out, thirty-eight-year-old Monique had far transcended whatever power might have accrued to her had she remained Eileen Ford's top booker. A year and a half after Wilhelmina's death, Elite was now running neck and neck with Ford in billings, and Casablancas had all but turned the day-to-day relationships with the girls over to Monique. He was still the visible name and the head talent scout, but he had an empire to build and young models to bed and pajama parties to throw at Xenon. Casablancas' job was to channel the lustful drives of the world's male population and get paid for it. Monique was Elite's Eileen Ford, completing a rise that had begun in the early seventies when the original Eileen Ford had plucked her from the Revlon beauty salon on Fifth Avenue, where Monique had worked since emigrating from France at age fifteen after her parents divorced.

The matronly, round Frenchwoman—who had done little in her years in New York to lose her heavy accent—was settling into her role as the industry's new power-mom, a time-honored position with some interesting new twists. Monique's maternal and commercial instincts had to be carefully balanced, sometimes even entangled. When confronted with the possibility of signing Gia, who had already been blacklisted by all the other major agencies, Monique had to consider two questions. Was *she* the one who could save this poor girl, and her multimillion-dollar look? And was the incredible risk worth taking, in light of the recent defections of Kim Alexis, Christie Brinkley and Anna Anderson, and the near-defection of Carol Alt?

"Everyone knew about the problems Gia had," said Monique. "I had heard all about her from the other girls. What she was looking for was the mother image that she lost with Wilhelmina. I understood she went to Ford and missed a couple of bookings and Eileen threw her out. When I first met her, she wasn't looking that great. But she was so beautiful. She was sitting in this little cubicle office, and I could not take my eyes off that face. I knew all the things she had done, all the stunts she had pulled. But I was still thinking, 'I can't believe she's sitting next to me, this really incredible-looking girl, this really special girl.'

"I said, 'John, I want to take this girl.' He said there was no doubt about her beauty, but did I really want to take her on? My assistant, Oscar, who was at Wilhelmina when Gia started there, said, 'Monique, *she's a legend.'*

"She always wore long sleeves. The first day she came in here I asked her to roll up her sleeve and show me her arm, and she wouldn't. But I loved her look and I thought I could make her work."

Unlike some of the other agencies, Elite wasn't even pretending to confront models about their drug problems: after all, Casablancas was fond of saying he preferred models who partied a little too much to those who didn't party enough. "We didn't know much about drugs then," recalled Elite controller Jo Zagami, who had come from Ford with Monique and also had an underlined Bible somewhere in her desk. "Unfortunately, we learned a lot from Gia. We tried to help her, and she always said, 'Why are you taking this time with me?' She couldn't accept that people cared for her. I recall reaching out my hand to Gia once, to get her to take my hand. She just looked at it, and then slapped it.

"The mother, I recall, didn't want to know what was going on. It was just us." Even after all that had taken place, Kathleen still trusted that the agency probably knew best when it came to Gia's welfare in New York. And Gia would only be in New York to work, because she was going to stay around Philadelphia and commute up only when she had a job. The arrangement was a way to keep her away from the temptations of the New York drug scene, but still get her modeling career back on track. Kathleen was certain that if Gia could reclaim her position as a supermodel, everything else would work itself out.

Elite's signing of Gia raised a few eyebrows. "I shouldn't think that a modeling agency would take a girl on if they knew she was using heroin," said Harry King. "They knew? They took her on knowing that she was a heroin addict?

Oh, that's marvelous. Well, they're businessmen up there. I'm sure they thought, 'This girl could make money for us.' It's not a rehabilitation center, you know."

"The thing about Gia was that, if she showed up and she was in one piece, the pictures that came out were still incredible," recalled Monique. And the few pictures that had been published in 1981 certainly bore out that opinion: a stunning Italian *Vogue* cover, Albert Watson shots in French and German *Vogue,* and the last remaining Your Dior shot. Also lingering in the magazines during her hiatus was a shot for a one-third-page ad for a North Jersey company called Royal Silk, which sold silk T-shirts and lingerie through magazine coupons and a catalog. They had hired Gia after seeing several of her *Cosmo* covers, because they knew that "anyone who worked for *Cosmo* would work for us." The more fashionable catalogs like Spiegel—for which Gia had worked—usually took new pictures each season, repeating only a handful of photos of long-selling items. A company like Royal Silk, with a fairly stable product line, didn't have or need that luxury: a successful photo session could produce pictures that would work season after season. The strip ad with Gia wearing their green silk T-shirt would run in *Vogue* and *Cosmo* for years.

In mid-December, Toni O'Connor got a call from Gia. She was living with her mother again: Kathleen had taken her back and, because she seemed to be doing better, didn't notify the authorities. Gia and Toni spoke a couple of times on the phone, and finally made plans to get together for New Year's Eve. Gia would be bringing Rochelle, who Toni knew only by sight and reputation from the clubs. Toni went out to Plage Tahiti, a chic women's store around the corner from her new apartment in a Center City high rise, and bought an expensive black tuxedo dress just for the occasion.

Gia and Rochelle arrived in the early evening, and the three began to party. Toni thought the plan was to get high and go over to Second Story to dance. But besides the plan, there was also a plot.

"So she and Gia came over and we were drinking a bottle of wine," Toni recalled. "I gave them Quaaludes and we did some coke. I was really high. If you pushed me, I'd fall down. And before I knew it, Rochelle had punched me out and tied me up. I was wearing a dress with a cummerbund: she tied up my hands with that. She cut my telephone cords, put this school bag over my head with a drawstring and tried to choke me to death.

"Then she started sticking her hand up my dress and like, without being explicit, she started sticking her finger up me until I bled. And she just kept punching me in the face, 'til I had a lump the size of an egg.

"Gia was just sitting there watching. Rochelle kept saying, 'Oh, Gia, let's throw her out the window,' and Gia just said, 'No, I can't.' I think Gia was in shock; she didn't know what to do. Rochelle had such control over her. They ended up stealing, like, two hundred dollars from me—gold, jewelry, leather, the leather stuff I had bought from Gia. Then they left me there, with my stereo blasting a Go-Go's record. I finally got myself out of the bed and called the police. I just remember being in a catatonic position, just rocking back and forth and crying, sitting on my living room floor, like I can't believe someone did this to me. It was the most devastating experience I ever went through in my life."

Toni eventually decided not to press charges because she feared retribution from Gia's father—who she mistakenly believed had Mafia connections because he was Italian and in the food business. But she did make sure that everyone she knew found out about what had happened.

"Everybody heard the story because I took the dress back to Plage the next week and exchanged it for a leather jacket," she recalled. "I felt I had to get rid of the dress. I knew the people that worked there and I told them why I wanted to trade it in. I wanted people to know the story, because I wanted people to know how evil Rochelle was. She's possessed by the devil. I feel sorry for her: people who do things like that don't get away with it. She's a sick woman. The cruelest thing I ever did in my life was spray Gia in the face; maybe she was trying to pay me back for that."

Rochelle remembered the incident a little differently. "Toni O'Connor had kept Gia's clothes and we went there to get them," she said. "Gia and I went up on New Year's Eve, and we packed a bag with socks and ropes and hand ties and all kinds of things. We planned this whole thing. Gia had told Toni she was going to go out with her, only Gia brought me over with her. We went up and we got her high and we tied her up and took all her clothes off and stuffed socks in her mouth and stole all of Gia's clothes back, the leathers and all the stuff that Toni wouldn't let Gia have back. We took all that stuff out and we left her there tied up. It was pretty funny.

"And we left the music playing. 'Our Lips Are Sealed' by the Go-Go's, and it kept playing and playing. Every time I hear that song now I think, Oh my God! I think of what we did that night. It was wild. We did some wild things."

14
The Conquered Heroine

In January, Elite's 1982 headsheets and cards came out. In the war of the agency promo materials, they now came in an elaborately printed softbound book. Gia took her place on the roster of Elite's 1982 stars: Carol Alt, Andie (Mac-Dowell), Bitten, Kim Charelton, Janice and Debbie Dickinson, Nancy Donahue, Kelly Emberg, Iman, Lena Kansbod, Paulina (Porizkova), Phoebe (Cates), Joan Severance and Tara Shannon. Among Elite's lesser girls in their "Model Management" division were Kim Delaney, Kathy Ireland, Kelly Lynch and Sela Ward.

Gia was determined to remake a name for herself in modeling. She was met in New York by both the people who had never succumbed to the drug and drinking culture, and those who had already reached their own personal bottoms, disappeared to gather themselves and returned to see just how many bridges they had burned.

Predictably, the industry was most forgiving of those furthest behind-the-camera, whose problems had been best hidden from the public eye. The national economy would also help many *fashionistas* in their attempts to reenlist. The model wars and the boom in the designer ready-to-wear business had never fallen victim to the Carter recession—asking prices had continued to escalate through difficult financial times. As Reagan's voodoo economics waived rules for the wealthy and unfunded the impoverished, the rich got richer and a generation of young professionals were re-warded for voting (and living) their pocketbooks. The U.S. economy began to come back, the dollar became stronger against European currencies, and businesses grew with the rising fortunes of the American fortunate. There would be more magazines, more boutiques, more brand names, more ad campaigns, more job descriptions. There would also be more work for those who could compete in a bigger-money fashion world where someone like Calvin Klein was no longer a *fashionista*-made-good but the leader of a multinational corporation, a rich industrialist.

But it was hardest for the models to come back—if they still only wanted to be models. They were expendable to begin with, their obsolescence planned for by everyone but themselves. Their contacts and track records were significant, but too much experience could reinforce the easily formed impression that a girl was past her prime. When Gia came to see Sara Foley—who had "gone away" herself and reemerged in the agency of Patrick Demarchelier's rep Bryan Bantry—the old pictures in her new Elite book only reminded the agent how amazing one of her favorite models *used to* look.

"I remember when Gia tried to make a comeback, she used to carry that nude behind the fence around in her portfolio," said Foley. "She came up to see me, and there was something very sad about it. She had this portfolio, and the picture, and she was so proud of it ..."

But for every person who proclaimed Gia "over," there was another thrilled by the prospect of working with someone of her stature. It would not be easy for her to generate a lot of tony, high-fashion work. Clients who were once thrilled to take whatever time she had free now wanted her to come by so they could see her first, or even take a few Polaroids. In some ways, Gia was being put through the rigors of rejection that she had avoided during her initial rise. But, as Monique had guessed, there were still many clients willing to book her, sight unseen, because she was Gia. And now that she was joining the Screen Actors Guild and trying to get more TV commercial work, other things besides her beauty and her reputation as a print model would affect her success. If she could charm ad agency representatives during the numerous call-backs required for each TV commercial, her slightly faded beauty would not hold her back.

One of her first jobs after returning to active duty was generously provided by Scavullo. He agreed to give her a *Cosmo* cover-try. "He did that because he was a very kind man and he felt sorry for her," recalled Harry King. "Scavullo had had people very close to him be involved with drugs before."

She was shot stuffed into a strapless Fabrice party dress, her hands tucked beneath her. Way Bandy did the best he could with Gia's makeup, Harry King did the same with her hair. The camera angle was meant to minimize the bloating caused by the methadone and the weight gain from the sweets junkies often crave. The pose was designed to cover the gory abscess on her hand—an actual tunnel leading directly into her bloodstream—about which she still hadn't seen a doctor. "That thing on her hand" quickly became an industry metaphor for what Gia had done to herself. It was a self-inflicted stigmata that she continually picked back open, like a child unable to keep her hands off a scab on a scraped knee.

Scavullo convinced *Cosmo* to use the shot of Gia for the cover of the April 1982 issue. She was also interviewed for the magazine's "This Month's *Cosmo* Cover Girl" feature, recently created to respond to the growing public interest in fashion models. Gia told the interviewer that "a model has to *create* moods. You have to be careful not to get stuck in a mood—emotions have trends just like fashion." She noted the difficulty of staying in the mood. "How am I supposed to *feel* beautiful if they give me an ugly dress, plastic jewelry, and an atrocious hairdo so tight it could cause brain damage? ... sometimes I've felt like *running* out of a shoot—I had to contain myself—but the pictures turned out nice. Often, the idea that you don't look good is all in your head."

Gia talked about the difficulties of delivering on the promises fashion photographs appeared to make. "[People] see you as an ideal of fashion," she explained, "it's hard to live up to that image. When I get out of work, I throw on a T-shirt, jeans and my sneaks just to get back down to earth." And she said she envisioned herself in "a job where I can be *out* of the limelight making things happen, possibly cinematography. Modeling is a short gig—unless you want to be jumping out of washing machines when you're thirty!"

The cover photo itself suggested that she would be wise to begin laying groundwork quickly for that next career. "What she was doing to herself finally showed in the pictures," recalled Sean Byrnes. "It was kind of sad. We got her on the cover, but I could see the change in her beauty. There was an emptiness in her eyes."

Albert Watson also continued to use Gia. Because his work and his work style were so much more commercial than many of his high fashion contemporaries, Watson still wasn't as well-known as some of the French Mafia photographers. But as the fashion world began appreciating business acumen, his dependable talents were becoming more recognized and his pictures were actually growing *more* interesting. Once criticized for being a jack-of-all-visual-trades, Watson was now being recast as a good influence on a fashion world gone mad. Although he was known for not getting mixed up in people's personal lives, Watson knew as much about Gia's problems as almost anyone in the business did. Besides doing a good bit of work with her over the years, Watson and his wife were professionally close to Sandy Linter. Gia still wasn't completely over Sandy: she occasionally relapsed into calling and wooing the makeup artist.

During her comeback, Gia worked with Watson more than almost any other photographer. And, for a while, his work habits appeared to be rubbing off on her. Gia was doing her best to be extremely businesslike about modeling—showing up on time, sending flowers to anyone who did her a favor. Avedon called her in for a look and booked her for the upcoming round of Gianni Versace ads—the fall '82 campaign would be shot around Easter. There wasn't much high fashion editorial work, but she had a steady stream of catalog and department store ad requests. Besides the regular print clients, she was meeting with casting directors for commercials and movies. On a typical day, she was now mixing go-sees and callbacks with jobs—not unlike the beginning of her career, except the jobs were for top money and the callbacks for campaigns. On April 5, she worked all day for Avedon, earning $2,500, and then left the studio for a second callback for a Silkience shampoo ad.

After several months of commuting, Gia started looking for a new apartment in New York. She found one she liked in Greenwich Village, in the same Horatio Street building where Harry King lived, and made an application on April 8. That evening, she went to Scavullo's studio for an important television taping.

The ABC program *20/20* was putting together a report on the modeling business. They had asked Gia, through Monique at Elite, if she would agree to be interviewed for the segment. It was a difficult decision, because it was clear that the reporter had some knowledge of Gia's drug problem and would probably ask her about it. Monique told Gia that if she wasn't afraid of exposing the fact that she took drugs, the show might be a good opportunity for publicity. Her true confession might even help someone.

The evening went as smoothly as possible, considering that Scavullo booked Sandy Linter to do the makeup and Gia didn't get on well with the crew. They first wanted to film her walking down the street toward the studio. When she did, they asked her to walk differently, slower. "This is the pace I walk at," she explained, but they insisted on documenting her walking the way *they* wanted.

The crew filmed Gia being made up by Sandy, having her hair done by Harry King and being photographed by Scavullo. Then they sat her down for an interview. The reporter began by waxing rhapsodic about the way she seemed to change her very being when in front of the camera. "I have to," Gia said. "I become whatever your eye wants to see. It's my job. I'm a fashion model, that's how I do my job." Without any more warm-up than that, he jumped to the delicate subject of how Wilhelmina's death had affected her. "I felt very close to Wilhelmina," Gia explained, in a pained voice. "It was a great loss for me . . ."

"Cut!" the cameraman yelled. "She's licking her lips!"

The reporter asked her to answer the emotional question about Wilhelmina again. "She helped me when I had just started," Gia explained, "as a friend she helped me. She was extremely intelligent, she was just a great person to have in my life . . . her death was a terrible loss to me . . ."

When the interview came around to her recent career problems, the reporter phrased his questions in a way that made Gia feel like she had been ambushed. "At one point you got kind of into the drug scene, didn't you?" he asked. After she awkwardly answered, he followed up with another leading question: "It almost destroyed you, didn't it? You thought more than once about packing it in, didn't you?"

"Yes, you could say that I did," she admitted. "But I thought about that [suicide] also without drugs. Now I have a great lust for life, you could say, and I love life and it's a wonderful feeling and I think I had to go through [that] in order to have this feeling I have for life right now." The interviewer even set her up to seek audience absolution for her drug use by asking, "You're free of it, aren't you, now?" But it was too late: she was already completely frazzled. Then she paused after being asked if she was happy with her career, and he made a big thing out of it. The whole interview hadn't gone the way she planned at all.

The next day, a Friday, Gia was doing Versace ads with Avedon. The campaign was expanding to larger group shots that had to be done on a stage rather than in Avedon's studio. The series culminated with an extravagant shot of twelve top models draped over each other in an orgy of gold lamé and black leather. Gia was at the very front of the quivering mass, closest to the camera, a fallen angel in spaghetti-straps. "It was the most significant photo of the whole period of our company," recalled Versace's Paul Beck.

But the successful Avedon shooting didn't help Gia get over the feeling that the *20/20* interview had been a big mistake. She called Monique and the segment's producer Bob Wallace on Monday to see if *20/20* could be pressured into eliminating her section. "I yelled at that person," recalled Monique, "I said, 'You sorta tricked her.'" But, no matter how often the agency or Gia called, the *20/20* producers refused to withhold the interview.

Otto wanted a make-over. Like the rest of the German fashion industry, the gigantic, Hamburg-based Otto Versand catalog company—the Spiegel of Deutschland—was trying to upgrade its dowdy image. Otto had added a new higher-end catalog called Apart and was trying to attract some of the top American high fashion models whose faces were slowly becoming known to German women because of the new German *Vogue*. But the international fashion world had little respect for German aesthetics. "Working for German clients" was becoming an industry catchphrase for earning quick money making mediocre pictures of really bad clothes.

Germany had one internationally legitimate fashion designer, Jil Sander, one resident photographic legend, F. C. Gundlach, the so-called Avedon of Germany, and several other major women's magazines, like *Petra* and *Brigitte*, that covered higher fashion. But German women were still very dependent on catalog shopping: they had helped turn catalog companies Otto Versand and Neckerman into massive operations and had recently embraced the new upscale Escada catalog, with a line designed by former top German model Margarithe Lieberson. Because German magazines had far less cachet than their European counterparts—and the powerful German catalogs were, after all, still catalogs—German clients often had to pay more than anyone else when they decided it was time to use the top American models and photographers. These high rates were especially attractive because Germany did not tax freelance wages like France, where the government took a huge bite out of foreigners' fees and were somewhat more strict about reporting.

European jobs had always been a good way to generate cash. The American girls could demand that the local agencies pay them in full before they returned home, and it was entirely up to the models to report their European earnings to the American IRS—which many of them didn't bother to do.

But Germany was becoming an especially soft touch. Many German magazines still paid models and photographers directly, in cash, although German *Vogue* and some of the bigger catalogs now paid through the agents.

In the great German tradition of efficiency, these high-paid catalog jobs were also booked months in advance: the catalog clients paid for "options" on the girls' time to assure their shootings went according to schedule. But even with the higher fees and options, it wasn't easy for German clients to book the top girls, especially if they wanted them to actually come to Germany. German fashion quickly became known as the pinnacle of European open-mindedness: a refuge for models who were slightly past their peak, or had problems.

It came as no surprise to the industry that Gia became one of the first top American models to work for Otto Versand. She had done work for German *Vogue,* and she was no longer in a position to turn down $10,000 for twelve days' work, even if half the clothes had decorative piping like couture lederhosen. Otto Versand did shootings all over the world. The exotic locations were not chosen for scenery— the backgrounds were never included in the catalog shots— but for the intensity of the sunlight, which, according to company research, improved the appearance of the garments. Her first sitting for the company began April 16, in Newport Beach, California.

When Gia left for the West Coast, the *20/20* situation still hadn't been resolved, and she had started calling Sandy again. She wrote "last time I will call her" in her datebook and hoped that a trip away would distract her attention.

Gia had a handful of friends in Los Angeles that she was hoping to see. A small part of the modeling business had shifted to the West Coast when Wilhelmina and Elite set up offices there, joining the traditional flow of actors, directors and writers from New York to LA. One favorite hangout for the younger Beautiful People was the Roxy Theater on the Sunset Strip. The private club above the Roxy, On the Rox, was an epicenter of the LA sex, drugs and rock 'n' roll scene—which was still in shock over the March 5 death of John Belushi, the king of its party animals. Gia had become friendly with Elmer Valentine, a co-owner of the Roxy as well as co-owner of the fabled Whisky-A-Go-Go down the Strip. The first important rock club in LA during the sixties, the Whisky had spawned groups like the Byrds, the Doors, Buffalo Springfield and Frank Zappa's Mothers of Invention, and grew into a major music-celebrity gathering place, the Cotton Club of Southern California.

Valentine was a middle-aged ex-Chicago vice cop with a reputation for always showing up with a gorgeous girl or two on his arm, but he generally remained behind the scenes at his clubs. Most of what the general public knew about Valentine came from his cameo appearance in the 1980 hagiography of Jim Morrison, *No One Here Gets Out Alive*. During the Doors' formative years, Valentine continually booked the band as an opening act and continually fired them for swearing on-stage and playing so loud that they blew away the headliners. In a drunken rage, Morrison was known to hop up on-stage between sets and yell, "Fuck Elmer, fuck the Whisky!"

Gia made plans to drive up to LA from Newport to see Elmer during her free time. He always treated her well, showed her the town, took her out, made her feel protected. "She was unhappy," Valentine recalled. "She didn't like people coming on to her all the time. She couldn't handle the bullshit and the model-fuckers. She stayed with me a few times over the years. I gave her money when she asked for it: typical junkie stuff."

The Otto Versand sittings were considerably less glamorous than doing the Paris collections for *Vogue,* and Gia was having a difficult time. On the second day of the shooting, Gia got her period and, after hours standing in the hot sun, nearly blacked out. Then four of the other models were canceled when they arrived at the booking, so Gia had to wait a day while replacements were ordered. At the end of the long days Gia shopped—buying clothes and books by Hermann Hesse and Nietzsche—or went to LA to see Elmer. As the shootings continued, the other models were making Gia increasingly uncomfortable.

"The other models seem to resent me," she wrote in her datebook. "Is it jealousy or [are] all girls just like that ... I get the feeling a few of them would like to pull my hair out. Why don't I get those feelings toward other girls ... sometimes they say things that are quite nasty and rude. I think it is a terrible part of the human race, a real flaw. I thought we all were suppose[d] to love one another ..."

The day before she went home, Gia went to LA. "Hung out at On The Rox," she scribbled, "went up to Elmer's pad, got totaled, then went to Whiskey A-Go-Go to see the Motels. Got Elizabeth [another model] and her three boyfriends in ... she gave me a pink rose (I like her) turned them on to C. Me and Elmer had fun."

The Conquered Heroine

On her last day in LA, Elmer took Gia shopping, buying her three jackets and a couple of books. They had lunch at The Palm and he showed her around Hollywood. "I have to go back to LA to work out of Elite and get to know the town," she wrote in her datebook on the plane trip back. "I think it could very easily be a favorite city of mine.

"Here I sit in my new but old Marine sergeant's jacket ... feeling very set apart from the other humans. But I am finally really starting to dig being different. Maybe I am discovering who I am. Or maybe I am just stoned again Ha Ha Ha Ha."

Even though she had just earned $10,000 and could certainly afford a limo back to Bucks County, she had her parents come pick her up at the airport. "Henry will meet me at JFK," she wrote on the plane, "and hopefully Mommy will be with him."

On May 3, Gia moved back to New York, her comeback certain enough that signing a lease on an apartment seemed justified. Henry helped her move her things. "Think I am going to love it here," she wrote. "Cool out from the dope pal." Life in the West Village was different than uptown or the just-emerging East Village. It was a friendly place to walk around, window shop, get coffee. It was more like the areas of Center City Philadelphia she had always liked. The buildings, and the people, seemed to be on a more human scale. In the Village she always seemed to bump into someone on the way to wherever she was going.

Gia got in touch with Sharon Beverly and began spending time with her. Sometimes they would hang out at Patricia Field's store on East Eighth Street, or just go out for dinner. On the way to Sharon's apartment one evening, Gia ran into some people she knew who took her over to the Ritz to see a band. "We went into the semiprivate lounge," she wrote, "while waiting to pee I met a cute little Italian boy who offered me some coke. Then I danced by myself. It was a good dance."

After her first few weeks of living in the Village, Gia returned home for her mother's birthday. "Got up about six, Snort," she wrote in her datebook about the day. "Bought some beautiful pink and purple flowers and a card with poppies on the cover. On the inside, wrote a little letter to Mom, having to do with our personalities and getting along and the special love I have for my mother. She is a *real* sweetheart. Definitely.

"Went to dinner with Mom and Henry. He is, as usual, grossing me out. He is so cheap. When the bill came he was going to figure out how much my share was. After I had taken him out to dinner in NY at a more expensive place. Boy. Man."

While Gia was at home, she finally had the abscess on her hand taken care of. "The fellow I took her to," recalled Kathleen, "looked at her and said there was a tunnel in her hand. He was horror-stricken, and it's *something* when you see a doctor who has been deeply moved. He said, 'You never told me it was that bad.' But that was the reaction we always got. Nobody would ever believe her drug problems were as bad as they were, because people don't realize that people who look clean and well-to-do and knowledgeable could have that much of a problem."

Since she had the surgery done as an outpatient, she was able to return to New York the same day. She went out for a walk in the spring air with her shooting gallery pal Raul, and ran into Ariella, a makeup artist she had worked with many times, and a hairdresser she had worked with once. "I don't know why," she wrote, "but Ariella was being very rude and crass towards me. So was the hairdresser whom I don't even know. They were actually laughing at me. All I said was my apartment gave me the feeling of seclusion. They asked me all sorts of caddy [catty] questions. I don't understand why they're so nice to me when I work with them. Well, I knew they weren't my friends. But they don't have to be my enemies either. Raul slept over—I think he is my friend."

Several days later, Gia went out with friends to one of the newer downtown clubs, Danceteria, and then over to the Continental, an after-hours club in an old garage on the far West Side, where she bumped into makeup artist Lesley Browning.* "Lesley started to tell me that Thomas stood her up," Gia wrote, "she had brought her bag with her overnight things. She said she didn't have a place to stay. I told her she could stay at my place. We went to breakfast and then to my home. Watched TV and smoked some dope. She is so beautiful, her skin is so white. I think I am falling in love. I wished I could have stayed in bed with her all day. But I had to go to Germany. I waited till the last minute to tell her which I think was wrong on my part. I want to take care of her so much. I hope that she comes and stays with me. I need her and I think she needs me. I hope she lets me help her."

When she got to her hotel room in Munich, Gia started to cry. She hadn't really wanted to do the trip for German *Vogue,* the flight had been grueling and she was still getting over her sleepless night with Lesley, who she already missed terribly. Since she didn't have Lesley's phone number, Gia called several people back in New York to try to get it. When that was unsuccessful, she got the number of the makeup artist's agent and called unsuccessfully several times. The next morning, as Gia ate breakfast in the hotel before the sitting with Bill King, Lesley called and was patched through to the house phone in the lobby. "She is such a sweetheart," Gia wrote. "I can't stop thinking of her. She better not be sleeping with anyone else but me cause she is really going to upset me if she does. I am such a sucker for a pretty girl that I like."

From that point on, Gia worked sporadically for her few established clients. Her last photographs in American *Vogue*—only her fourth appearance in the two years since the disastrous Scavullo sitting in Southampton—appeared in the September 1982 issue, just a few pages before the excerpt from Bert Stern's upcoming book *The Last Sitting*. For the September 1962 issue of American *Vogue,* Stern had done what became the last photo sessions with Marilyn Monroe, at the Bel-Air Hotel in Beverly Hills. Only a handful of the photos had been published at the time: before she died, Monroe had vetoed many of the contact sheets and physically destroyed some of the color slides sent for her approval. On the twentieth anniversary of the sitting, Stern put together a book of the photographs and his memories of the sessions. Most of his recollections concerned getting Monroe drunk on Dom Pérignon and Château-Lafite-Rothschild, getting her to take her clothes off and, during the last session, when she was nearly unconscious, passing up his opportunity to have sex with her. "She nestled closer," he wrote. "The energy between us was pure magic. We were inches away from pure erotic pleasure. She wanted to make love. She was ready. I was the one who stopped."

Gia was booked for the spring 1983 round of Versace ads—which were being shot in the fall of 1982, just as the last batch were making their predictable sensation. But she left the session before any usable pictures could be taken of her. "I forget what the problem was exactly," recalled Versace's Paul Beck. "The clothes were for the following summer, they showed a lot of skin and everything. She was very thin. The clothes didn't fit, or she didn't feel well or something."

From then on Gia worked mostly for German clients. She was joined in the German catalog shoots by other top models like Janice Dickinson, Andie MacDowell and Carol Alt—often in outfits, hairstyles and poses so preposterous that even Otto Versand booker Heinke Thomsen had to chuckle, "I'm glad sometimes the models don't see the catalog."

Through the jobs for the German clients, Gia became friendlier with Janice Dickinson. "I know Janice was very much friendly with Gia," recalled Monique Pillard, "because I know they sent a lot of messages back and forth through me and they did trips together." Janice was going through her own model craziness. She was having drug problems, for which she would eventually go through several rehab programs. But she was also going through "this sex thing" as many of her colleagues called it. After she broke up with Reinhardt, she got involved with a male model and regularly regaled friends and acquaintances alike with diatribes about his sexual prowess—how she "never had sex like that before."

She also veered into what fellow *fashionistas* referred to as "Janice's nude period," when she began posing naked even when she wasn't asked to. "I remember during her serious nudity phase," said Lizzette Kattan, "we were at the *alta moda* and suddenly the police came and asked for my help. Janice had taken all her clothes off and jumped into the fountain at the Grand Hotel and the traffic was stopping for people to see."

While Janice was more flamboyant with her problems than most top models, she was hardly alone with them. "These models have a very big sex problem," said Monique Pillard. "They are made like the goddesses of the world. I mean, oh my God, can you *imagine?* And all of a sudden they have hang-ups about themselves, very anti-men hang-ups, and what happens is they go crazy half of the time, because they don't feel intimately at home within themselves. They're afraid they can't perform as the picture makes them [appear to] perform ... you get these girls who look *wow,* you know. And this girl feels thoroughly inadequate in her private intimate life."

Bob Hilton would later write a graduate school paper on the psychology of beautiful women—based solely on his experiences with models. His theory was that if women were rewarded for nothing except for having good looks, they turned "self-indulgent, willful and nasty."

Gia got the chance to do an armchair psychoanalysis of herself as her contribution to *Scavullo Women.* The handsome coffee table book was finally published in early November of 1982, and included photos and interviews with dozens of women but prominently showcased color before-and-after photos of only five: Elizabeth Taylor, Patti Hansen, Kim Alexis, Beverly Johnson and Gia. Unlike the others, who looked surprisingly plain without makeup and glamorous with, Gia looked naturally stunning in her "before" shot, but terribly overdone and almost fearful in the "after."

Scavullo had edited out some of Gia's most candid comments, for fear they would hurt her career, and he gave her the benefit of considerable doubt by insisting that her drug problems were far behind her. "It wasn't just a matter of stopping," she said.

It was a matter of wanting to live in the world that I live in and making it work for me instead of against me. I think the reason someone gets into something like that is because—for me, anyway—there were a lot of unanswered questions in my mind about work and about life. Money didn't interest me. I got to a point where I had all this money. I had everything I ever wanted in life—or thought that I wanted—and I said, "What the hell is this all for?" I mean, I need money to survive. But I think people value it too much. The world seems to be based on money and sex. And I'm looking for better things than that, like happiness and love and caring.

I was really down on society, but then I found that I was part of society too, and for me to be doing drugs made me just as bad as I thought society was. I think maybe society is kind of what I make myself. And that makes me happy, happier than being high. If anything, I'm high on being straight because now I can feel my body, I can feel my head. Before, I was like numb. It's just really selfish. I don't care if you're on Quaaludes or you're a nice housewife hooked on diet pills and Valium, it's just a selfish way to live. I learned a lot from my experience, so I don't regret it. It was good for me, like a slap in the face . . . I'm an extremist, you know. I had to go all the way.

[Now] I'm disciplining myself. If I have a booking, I plan for it the day before, I have to. If I didn't, and if I were late or didn't show up or something, they'd think I was goofing off, so the thing is to make sure I'm together and that I get enough sleep. I'm basically a night person, so it's hard for me to go to bed at a normal hour. Then, in the morning, I just want to keep sleeping. I don't want to get out of that bed because I'm hiding in that bed; it's so nice and warm. I've had this problem all my life. It's why I was always late . . . I was really spoiled, you know. I was a brat. And that stays with you. It's a hard thing to change. But once you know these things about yourself, you have to try to discipline yourself, because after a certain age nobody else is going to do it for you.

When you're in demand, and people are saying "I want you, I want you," it isn't easy to say no. I don't like to disappoint people. I'm basically a satisfier. So you find yourself working a lot—a lot. And if you want to take a day off, because you need a day to rest or to get yourself together and have your energy for the next day, it's hard. Models are never supposed to be down or be tired or have a headache. They've got to be up all the time.

You know, I thank God that I'm good-looking, or that people think I'm good-looking. But there's a lot more to it than makeup and prettiness and all that stuff . . . there's a lot more to being a woman than that. When I look in the mirror, I just want to like myself, that's all. And if I like myself, then I look good.

Scavullo then finished the Gia section of the book with his own editorial comment. When he had penned the words almost a year before, they seemed like hopeful encouragement. Now they were sad, almost mocking. "Gia has got to be liking herself a lot these days," he wrote.

Even though her career was deteriorating, she was still making enough money to live in New York and carry on a long-distance relationship with Rochelle—in between her occasional crushes, like Lesley, which usually ended up as one-night or one-week stands. Gia had her German clients, and residuals from work she had done with Elite and Wilhelmina. "She'd hide in her apartment and stay home to be with me," Rochelle recalled. "It wasn't always because of drugs that she missed jobs. It just didn't mean that much to her. If it was a sunny day and she was supposed to be somewhere, she would just decide we were going to Fire Island. She would tell me that she had called and canceled her booking, and then we were up in a helicopter going to Fire Island. We'd come back at night and go out to have a drink somewhere and somebody would come up to Gia and say, 'Where the hell were you?' And then I realized she hadn't ever called. But I'd look at her and she'd look at me through her hair—which was always over her eyes—and what could I do?

"Sometimes, of course, drugs were the problem. One Christmas we were in New York and I had about $50 on me and Gia was getting sick. I was feeling bad, so I figured I'd give her money to get straight. We drove down and parked on Avenue C and Fourth Street and she disappeared, she slipped away. I went back to the apartment and she showed up later. We had a horrible fight. She wanted to sell the TV to get more heroin. She didn't want to work for the money. She was always worried that people she worked for would know she was high. She wouldn't go near there if she didn't feel she looked good—and she became paranoid. So then we would stay in for three days and drink grape soda and watch cartoons or movies.

"When Gia's mom would come up to New York, which she did frequently, I would have something else to do that day. I knew they wanted to spend time together and that Gia didn't really want her mom to know about me. Later I would come home with her on holidays, and her mom's attitude toward me depended on how well Gia's modeling was going. When she was doing good, they were thrilled she was there, happy to see us. 'Look at my baby,' her mother would say. If Gia was down, it was almost like we weren't welcome to join into what was going on. We'd spend the whole day in Gia's room.

"This is about when Gia started wanting to see me more, getting all nuts about me moving in with her. Before that, I had things balanced. I was seeing this guy in Philadelphia, Ken, who was married, and I was seeing Gia. Gia was away a lot, and I'd only see her on weekends; Ken was married, so I'd see him, like, in the morning or, like, on Sunday. Then, all of a sudden, Ken leaves his wife, Gia leaves modeling and I'm stuck in the middle because I always had time to do both of them before. Nobody knew I was gay. My parents, who lived in North Jersey, certainly didn't. But Gia took care of that. They really liked Gia; they thought we were friends. Then when I was staying with my parents, and Gia couldn't get me on the phone, she used to call, starting at like midnight. By like, two, three in the morning, she'd start asking my mother where I was, who I went out with. Then my mother would say, 'She went with Mark' or this or that, and then Gia would have a fit."

Rochelle was taking her share of drugs at the time as well, but she was coming to appreciate the difference between her drug use and Gia's. "I guess you could have called me a functional addict at that time," she recalled, "I was using drugs more than recreationally. To me, if I have my own supply and I'm offering it to other friends of mine or I'm going out at night and I have some in my pocket, that's not recreational. But it was under control because I still went to college, I still got nice grades, I was still accepted to X-ray technician's school, and I still handled that and went on with my life."

Rochelle would recall one incident that crystallized in her mind the difference between her drug use and Gia's. "We were at a New Jersey Turnpike rest stop," she recalled. "Gia went into the bathroom and she was in the stall and I was going to throw some water on her from the next stall. And I looked over the top and she had the syringe in her hand and she had drawn it up. I said, 'You put that down or I'm leaving you here!' And she had it in her hand, and I crawled under the stall and I said, 'If you don't put that down, I'm leaving and I'm never speaking to you again.'

"And, believe me, at that time Gia was madly in love with me. She would do *anything* for me. But she would not give me that syringe. And that's when I knew."

Even with her prodigious drug intake, Rochelle was amazed by Gia's voracious drug appetites. "Gia spent an unbelievable amount of money on drugs," she said. "She could do four bags of heroin at a time. A normal person could do a half a bag and be totally fucked up. She did four bags in one shot, that's $40, and she'd do a couple shots in an hour. She was spending hundreds a day. She told me that she once spent $40,000 on drugs in a week or two. It had to be coke—nobody could take that much heroin. But I would find bank statements and she would withdraw $1,000, then $3,000, then $5,000, then $10,000—all in the same day.

"Gia had this thing about money. She'd go around with $10,000 in her sock or her shoe, to the point where you could see it if she pulled up her jeans. She'd go down to the shooting galleries like that. When we were in New York, she wouldn't think twice about spending a couple hundred dollars on dinner. She'd buy three guitars even though she didn't know how to play them. She'd send me roses—for a while I got roses every day. She was not tight with her money, but she wanted to hold it: she didn't even like to have it in the bank. She'd buy me clothes, but she always had to be the one holding the money. She felt that if she gave me money, that would give me power.

"In fact, sometimes when she worried about me leaving her, she used to take the money out of my jeans and hide it from me. I'd say, 'Gia, where's the money?' She'd say, 'I don't want you to go anywhere.' She thought I was powerless without money. I'd say, 'Gia, I'm leaving, give me the money, I need it to buy gas,' and she'd say, 'No, you're not leaving,' and physically stop me, hold me to the floor or sit on me."

While she was trying to keep what was left of her career afloat in New York, Gia had quietly enrolled in an outpatient methadone program in West Philadelphia. "She came in and said she was a top model and *nobody* believed that," recalled one of her counselors from the program. "Clients *always* fabricated stories of being wealthy, they always wanted you to think they were a lot better as people than the image they were portraying that day. The first day you come in, you're there most of the day, with lab tests, seeing different people, being evaluated. We all went out to lunch that day and saw she was on the cover of a magazine, in a gown that showed her arms—and she was in our office with track marks on those arms that were unbelievable.

"She indicated that she had been missing job appointments, and that her manager was covering up for her. We didn't talk much about the career because there was more need to focus on the abuse, but she spoke about how her career caused her problems, how people were still offering her drugs. She knew she would get drugs in return for her work. Usually you try to get a patient to separate themselves from the people they associate with drugs. For her, that was difficult because so many people involved in helping her sustain her heroin problem were in modeling, but she didn't want to give up her career because it was the only thing she was proud of.

"She came with a young lady—blond hair and short [Rochelle]. They looked like they both could have been into rock, dressed punkish, in black, with little boots on. Gia had an oversized sweater on. They seemed like they were both coming down off a high. The girl seemed really loyal to Gia. She might have been the motivating factor for her coming in.

"I can remember a conversation amongst us, that we felt that the girl was either a committed friend, or someone who was there because of Gia's fame and was attempting to be a loyal friend—because Gia seemed to be very freehearted with money or whatever else she had. She seemed to have poor family support, so this was somebody who showed her some sort of caring."

Her "poor family support" was more like complete family confusion, bafflement and powerlessness. And Gia was, in fact, not the only Carangi kid with drug problems. Her brother Michael had never completely separated from his high school drug culture either. His experimentation had recently climaxed with him going crazy after smoking sensimillan pot laced with PCP. When his mother came to try to calm him down, he pushed her—hard. Unsure of what to do, Kathleen called the police, and swore out an assault charge on her son so he might cool off in jail. Gia was in New York the night this all took place, but was summoned by the family to come and help reason with Michael.

"I was messed up on drugs," Michael Carangi recalled, "I had a memory loss, I was out of it, out of control. My mother had put me in jail, so, obviously, I didn't want to hear from her. Gia came down from New York, and when I saw her, I straightened up. It was a bad time for me, but Gia helped me overcome it."

In the early winter of 1982, Rochelle got into trouble herself. She was living in Philadelphia but commuting to North Jersey, where her parents lived, to log time in a hospital there toward her license as an X-ray technician. One of the characters she knew from Second Story had a proposition for her. He and some friends were making counterfeit money with plates that they had smuggled in from Europe. He wanted her to deliver the plates to someone in Atlantic City. She would be paid, of course, in cash.

"The guy showed me, like, *stacks* of hundreds," Rochelle recalled. "And he gave me a stack and said, 'Here, you can have it.' So, I take the money and I'm really nervous and everything. I mean, there was a *lot* of money. I called a friend of mine and he came over to my apartment. I had the money and the plates in shoe boxes in the bottom of my closet. We counted it, and there was a quarter of a million dollars there, in fake hundreds. It looked real good. In fact, we spent most of it. We took the money and the plates to Atlantic City and gambled with it. What you do is, you throw the money on the craps table and they don't look at it, they just push it down the slot and give you chips. So I'm throwing down five hundred dollars a shot, no big deal. You gamble it, you have the chips, you cash them in and then you have cash, real cash.

"Well, I made a mistake. I mixed up a bad hundred-dollar bill with a real hundred-dollar bill and gave it to the teller to get change. Well, the teller checked it and called security. They came running after me, through the casino. I had a red silk outfit on: it was the day before New Year's Eve and the place was packed. I *ran* out front, got a cab. This was a scene out of a *movie*. I'm trying to shut the door, six security guards coming after me, and I'm yelling at the cab driver, '*Go, go, go!*' And the cab is going and stopping and going and stopping because they're all yelling, 'Stop, stop!' I got a security guard, this big fat woman, hanging around my waist. We're still moving, I'm not letting go, right?

"Finally she did yank me out. And the cab driver takes off. So they *get* me, they grabbed my friend, too, and they want to know where the plates are. And I said, 'Oh, the cab driver got them.' Of course, I don't know the cab driver from nothing, but they're like, 'Shit, the cab driver!'

"The plates were in the trunk of my friend's car. I was in jail, just for a night until I got my parents to come and get me. I called somebody from jail and told them where the car was and that somebody should do something. I don't know exactly what went on, but all I know is that before the Feds got to the trunk, it had already been broken into and I think they got the plates out.

"Gia's idea was that she was going to take me to Rome to live so I didn't have to go to jail. She still had some money, and she knew she could work there."

A week later, the *20/20* segment on modeling finally aired. Across the nation, people knew that Gia was "a virtual symbol of the bright side and the dark side of modeling" and an admitted drug abuser. But because the program had not been specific about what kind of drug she was admitting to abusing, most viewers assumed it was cocaine—the drug most other models and celebrities admitted to using.

The show didn't really hurt her career because, in the States, there was little left of her reputation to tarnish. In New York, many of her clients had stopped doing business with her. A handful of people, most notably Scavullo, had yet to be burned by Gia not showing up or showing up high: she decided it was better to keep it that way. She did work one last time with Italian *Bazaar*. "She disappeared for a while," Lizzette Kattan recalled, "and then one evening the phone rings about midnight and she wants to come over. She came over and that was the first and only time I saw her out of it. Her arms were all marked, she was trying to cover herself. She didn't want me to see her like that. The day after, I was doing a shooting and asked if she wanted to work. She said yes and she slept over. I knew she was completely destroyed, but we didn't talk about it. During the shooting, she was trembling so terribly that she couldn't work. She said, 'I can't make it,' and she left, she disappeared. That was the last time I saw her."

Gia called Diane von Furstenberg one day, desperate for cash. "She asked me for a hundred dollars," she recalled. "She was in bad shape then. I just gave it to her. What else was I going to do?"

She had a handful of German clients left. But, by that time, in the opinion of her drug counselors, she was working only to support her habit. And she could support it well: two or three trips could yield $20,000 to $30,000, and the German payments were tax-free. Other fringy New York clients bypassed Elite altogether to pay in cash or in drugs.

She did well enough during the Otto Versand trip to the Canary Islands in the fall that they immediately booked her for the spring trip to Tunisia. Monique expected problems, so she insisted that Gia come directly to the Elite office from Philadelphia, without *any* detours. She planned to have someone from Elite escort her to the airport. "I realized that New York was like a total relapse for this girl," Monique recalled, "so I thought this would work. She was sitting here in the office and she looked gorgeous. *All we had to do was get her to the airport.* But she disappeared, and I knew that she wouldn't make it. She called from the airport and said she was okay, but then she got sent home. I don't know why."

"We had to send people out to *buy her stuff* in Tunisia," recalled Heinke Thomsen. "Of course, we didn't book her again after that."

Sitting in the airport in Casablanca after being asked to leave the booking, Gia wrote postcards to Monique and Elite controller Jo Zagami.

"Dear Monique, the planes are as slow as the camels. I am waiting for my plane in Casablanca. Otto thinks I'm a fat camel. I hope things are okay! Always, Gia (Sorry, but I don't think I am fat or unable to concentrate, just confused and jet lagged.)."

"Dear Jo, I hope everything is going well there because I'm coming. They think I am fat. They wish they were as fat as me. What the hell? Always, Gia."

Monique had been doing what she could to try to set Gia straight. "I'd call her into the office," she recalled, "and I'd say, 'What did you do that the client sent you home?'

" 'You tell me,' she'd say, 'the client talked to you.'

" 'Well, you fell asleep with a lit cigarette in your hand. What caused that?'

" 'Is that what the client said?'

"You know, like that. She was not nasty. She was tough. But not 'Go fuck yourself' tough. She just drew the line and you couldn't get her to move it. She was a tough little cookie. She didn't come in and say, 'Oh yeah, I screwed up.' "

Throughout her time with Elite, Gia was encouraged to seek professional help for her drug problems. Former model Jack Scalia had had particular success at the Hazelden clinic in Minnesota, and many models were being sent there to dry out, away from the gossip columnists in New York. Gia, however, refused to go, or even to admit that she had a problem.

"I felt that I could've been stronger," recalled Monique. "I'm not going to say I was the *cause* of Gia doing drugs, but I feel like I should've said, 'Sit down over here and I'm going to get it out of you, today!' I've been working with other people here who got involved with drugs. All it takes is for them to get married, to have a baby or meet a nice guy and realize that this is a job and tomorrow there's something else. But with her, I never knew."

In the spring of 1983, Gia left New York for the last time. She went first to her mother's house, but the situation was very uncomfortable. Kathleen feared for Gia's life and was profoundly disappointed over the fall of Gia's career: the increasingly tempestuous relationship between Gia and Rochelle just fanned the emotional flames.

The living situation came to a head after a string of events that would be played out again and again in the coming years. The previous spring, Gia's mother and stepfather had dragged her to a pool party for their Corvette Club in the hope that she would meet a nice young man. She was introduced to, among others, Gayton Goffredo. "After the splash party," recalled Gayton, "the mom came up and said, 'What do you think of Gia? Do you know who she is? She's one of the hottest models on *Cosmo* and *Vogue* and so on.' I don't really think she was gay. I thought she was bisexual, maybe, because she did seem to have an interest in me. Kathy tried to get us together. The impression I got was that she didn't want her daughter to be gay, and thought I could possibly straighten her out."

They went out once, an afternoon at a car show which Gayton vividly remembered more for the ride over than the actual event. As they approached a turnpike toll booth, Gia asked if he liked the shirt she was wearing, then said *she* didn't and proceeded to remove it—with nothing on underneath—and put on another. Then she asked him to pull over to a rest stop, disappeared into the bathroom for fifteen minutes, and came back "whacked." Almost a year passed before he heard from her again.

In May of 1983, Gia called to see if he wanted to come to a John Cougar concert with her: she liked the singer because of his music and because he sort of looked like her. When Gayton arrived to pick Gia up, she told him that a friend of hers would be coming as well and instructed him to drive to Rochelle's grandmother's apartment in Jenkintown to pick her up. Once at the concert, after an appropriate amount of Valiums and mushrooms had been consumed, the three wandered around until Gia disappeared. When the concert ended and Gia still couldn't be found, Rochelle and Gayton waited in the parking lot and then returned to Jenkintown to wait for a call.

In the meantime, Rochelle made Gayton something to eat. Rochelle remembered nothing at all happening between them, but Gayton recalled, "I started getting intimate with Rochelle, it got pretty far and then that was it. I saw I wouldn't get anywhere, so I left." Early the next morning, Gayton was awakened by his mother, who said Gia was on the phone: she was screaming that she had been left at the arena and had to take a $30 cab ride home and she wanted the $30 from him, *immediately*. He went over, gave her the money, and as he was about to leave, Rochelle pulled up. The girls had a terrible fight in the driveway, with Gia accusing Rochelle of sleeping with Gayton.

In Rochelle's mind, she and Gia had just broken up. So she got together with her married friend, Ken, and they decided to move to Atlantic City together and make a go of it. They packed up his car, drove down and took a suite at the Kentucky Hotel until they could find a place. As they were moving things from the car into the hotel room, Gia pulled up—Rochelle's grandmother, who didn't approve of Ken because he was married, had told her where they'd gone. Gia was dressed up in men's sharkskin pants, cowboy boots, a yellow cashmere sweater. She asked Rochelle if she could talk to her in her car for a second. When Rochelle got into the red Fiat, Gia slammed down the gas and drove her away, eventually losing Ken, who gave chase.

"She had this all set up," recalled Rochelle. "She had the Rolling Stones' 'Tell Me You're Coming Back to Me' cued up on her tape deck, she had bought a rose. She said, 'Here—is that what you want?' Then she looked at me and grabbed my hand and said, 'If you want to stay with him, you can stay with him,' and then she lowered her voice and said, 'but you're gonna break my heart.' That's the way I like to remember Gia, because she looked great, she sounded great, she wasn't high, she was real sincere and sweet and romantic. She said, 'Do you love him or me?' I said, 'I love you, but he's better for me.'

"I made her take me back to the hotel. My whole life was in the back of Ken's car. We went back, he was sitting there in his car. She walked up and told him to roll down his window. He did, and she punched him in the face.

"Then I got in Ken's car and told him what I wanted and *he* took off with me. Gia chased after us through Atlantic City. The cops finally pulled her over. She didn't have any license or anything. They put her in jail and her new sister-in-law, who lived down there with her brother Joey, went down and got her. I went back to the hotel with Ken, waited for him to fall asleep, and went down, got my stuff, and met them. We stayed with a friend of Gia's father's, and then we decided to get a place in Philly."

Kathleen had wanted Gia to leave anyway, because she couldn't handle the pressure. "I was having cataract surgery done," she recalled, "and the doctor said I shouldn't have any kind of excitement. By that point I just couldn't deal with her and I decided it was time to look out for *me*." But, in the kind of emotional flip-flop that was becoming typical of the relationship between mother and daughter, Kathleen then tried to stop Gia from moving.

"I remember being in the middle of those two," said Rochelle, "and literally holding them apart from swinging at each other. Gia wanted to leave her mother's house, and Kathleen tried to stop her from taking her own things—her guitar, her clothes. Her mother would not let her take the stuff."

Gia rented a trinity house—the traditional Philadelphia small home with three stacked rooms and a basement kitchen—in a gentrified courtyard on Bainbridge Street. The house was a block off of South Street, which had become, since the mid-seventies, the pop-cultural heir to Sansom Village. The cornerstones of what was called South Street's renaissance were the TLA (a former experimental theater, once under the direction of Andre Gregory, that had been converted into a rep cinema), music clubs like J. C. Dobb's and Grendel's Lair and a number of funky shops and restaurants. South Street now truly was, like the words of the

1963 Orlons' hit, "the hippest street in town." On weekend evenings, it was overrun by teenagers from across the Delaware Valley. As the disco club culture began to subside, South Street also became one of the easiest places in town to buy drugs.

Gia was still in a methadone program. But she continued to use heroin. And when money from modeling residuals was low, she was forced to hit up everyone she knew for cash, or to take items of hers—or anyone else's—to the pawn shop at Seventh and South.

"I gave her money," said photographer Joe Petrellis, "I sent messengers to her house. I did the wrong thing. But I didn't know what else to do. I always had a little guilt that if I had talked to her mother and gotten them together ... I regret the fact that we didn't all get together and get her into somewhere good, so she could work with a good psychiatrist.

"But, I could've helped her. I know if I had, if I took her out and spent time with her and showed a genuine caring twenty-four hours a day, she might've come around a little bit. When you get into that pit, it's the hardest thing in the world to climb out.

"And she always said, 'I'm not hurtin' anybody.' And she could be as high as a kite and she could talk to you just like I'm talking to you, you wouldn't always know. I never saw her cry, she would always bounce back and start to *laugh*. I told her about a friend that died and she laughed, she said, 'They're better off.' "

"Those years were just unbelievable," Kathleen recalled. "I just told my ex-husband that he should be prepared for any news because she was capable of anything. People in that situation will do anything for drugs—hook, steal, I've had people tell me they've seen what amount to smoker films of Gia. I just tried to prepare myself. I knew that any day I could get a call and she'd be dead."

"She didn't talk about her family very much, which we found very unusual," recalled one of her counselors at the methadone program. "But in her circumstance, we didn't have a lot of time. I would have a session with her once a week, twice when it was necessary. And a lot of the time when a client was doing that poorly, the family distanced

themselves. Families were being taught that whole tough
love approach; we believed the family had disassociated with
her. We certainly weren't ready to try to introduce the family into treatment. But, remember, there is only so much
these programs can do."

Few of the patients who used the center in West Philadelphia were actually there to stop taking drugs. And patients
were mixing drugs in new and different ways, creating highs
that were confounding to counselors trained to treat old-
fashioned junkies. The only way to be sure if someone was
using was to force them to take a urine test. But failing a
"urine" didn't really mean anything. Counselors couldn't legally withhold methadone, the primary drug used to help
junkies kick heroin, because a patient tested positive for
drugs. A failed urine test usually meant that the methadone
dose would be *increased,* on the assumption that drugs were
used because the dosage was too low and wasn't "holding"
the patient. This made many counselors uncomfortable, because they knew that clients became dependent on methadone just as easily as heroin. And clients felt less pressure
to stop using methadone, which cost, at this facility, $20 to
$50 a week on a sliding scale, and was often even covered
by medical insurance.

Recent federal budget cuts—from a Reagan White House
that believed in just saying "just say no" instead of preven-
tion *or* treatment—even further scaled back what could be
accomplished. Professional medical and psychological staff
were laid off, hours were scaled back: the seven-day-a-week
facility was cut back to six, with Saturdays only for dispens-
ing methadone. And the state of Pennsylvania added to the
problem by overhauling its archaic mental health laws and
making involuntary commitments nearly impossible. Self-
destructive patients couldn't be committed for treatment unless they tried to kill themselves, and no drug addictions
were considered suicidal behavior.

"Gia was not our client with the most need," recalled the
counselor. "We had females selling their bodies. I had a guy
who tried to 'take off'—take off means to shoot—in his
temple and on the inside of his eye. I had a patient who
came in, she had a hole in her arm that was as big as a
coffee cup. Gia wasn't homeless. I had patients who came

in with no home, hadn't eaten in days, had children who were hungry, were in abuse situations. These were the kinds of cases that made you go home and want to cry. Especially when there were children involved. Gia had a lot more than a lot of others. That young lady who came with her? Sure, we tried to discourage that association, at least until she got a grip on what her real problem was. But a lot of people didn't have anyone to come in with them *at all.*"

Gia wasn't considered a difficult client. She seemed to listen and try to follow advice—although her counselors heard from other clients that she was using, and even "tricking" for drugs. She just wasn't really improving. The staff did have one brainstorm about how to help her. They wanted to fix her up with the only other famous person in their program. David Uosikkinen was the drummer with the local rock band, the Hooters, who were finally getting some national recognition. Uosikkinen was also a longtime heroin addict, who was still several years from cleaning up (which he finally did). The staff felt that Gia and David, both in the public spotlight, might understand each other.

But the match never got made, and it wasn't long before Gia stopped coming around the program altogether. Her counselors never heard from her again.

15
Under
the Boardwalk

As Gia's condition deteriorated, there was more finger-pointing over who was to blame for this tragedy. As the cycle of her cleaning up and using again continued—borrowing money, apologizing, then stealing, apologizing—the people who Gia's life touched went through cycles of their own. They blamed themselves, feeling guilty they hadn't done more to help her. They blamed others. Kathleen largely blamed Rochelle for corrupting her daughter. She said Rochelle kept Gia on drugs as a way to keep control of her. Rochelle blamed Gia's mother for not giving Gia the love and attention she needed as a child, and for writing Gia off as hopeless after her modeling career had been ruined.

"Kathleen really did just ignore the drug thing like it wasn't happening," Rochelle said. "I came *after* the problem. Yeah, the mother was convinced that I was the problem. But that's because she has a problem in her head believing that *she* caused Gia to be the way she was. I mean, when Gia was really bad, she would cry, 'Why did my mother leave me when I was eleven? She was my best friend, why did she leave me?' I know I didn't have any answer for her."

Gia wasn't sure who or what to blame anymore. "She told me once that she thought she was possessed," said John

Long. "Gia was obsessed with *The Exorcist,* which she had
seen when she was thirteen or fourteen. She wasn't a Catholic, but she had been raised Catholic enough that when she
saw *The Exorcist* she was really scared and really traumatized. She said that she thought she might be possessed, and
that was what was wrong with her—why she couldn't fall in
love with the right person, of the right sex, why she had this
desire for things that weren't good for her."

The cycles of addiction were maddening: the hours of lu-
cidity, the hours of panic and desperation, and then, the
stunned euphoria. It was far too easy to write off the junkie
as the victim of some self-imposed terminal illness. The frustration was that each day, each hour, offered a hope for a
complete recovery, a hope dashed so often that even the
loyal began not to bother. "Dope ain't no joke," Gia wrote
in her journal, "after one too many pokes, where's the
laughter, insane passion, why is my face so ashen? Living
without dreams."

Gia was not set on modeling as her only way out of drug
dependency. She was looking into schools in Philadelphia
for filmmaking and was considering enlisting in the armed
forces, most likely in the Air Force. "She wanted to do
something she could be proud of," recalled Rochelle. "We
looked in career books and I said, 'How would you like to
be a paramedic?' She was real into wearing a uniform and
driving an ambulance. She'd say, 'Gia Carangi, Emergency
Medical Technician, *yeah* ... they won't laugh at me *then,*
will they?' "

And there were times when she could be very sensible
about what had to be done: making checklists, even doing
simple written biofeedback exercises given to her at the
clinic to try to identify her true feelings. "Detached," she
wrote one day, "I feel detached misunderstood confused &
scared. Agitation will find relief in the exercise of *simple*
memories. Look not around, nor forward—but back (specu-
lative philosophy of the day)?" She also maintained her
dream of someday becoming a musician and incessantly
wrote song lyrics, with explanations at the top of the page
of the meter and instrumentation.

But then something would happen, and she would need
heroin again. She would check every counter and drawer for

loose money, empty every pocket of every garment in the house, make a few calls to see if anyone else would loan her a few bucks to fix her car or some other such lie, scan the room to see what might be left to pawn at the upscale Society Hill Loan or the grungier place at Twelfth and Bainbridge, a block from the projects. If all else failed she could go shoplift something on South Street and sell it to one of the neighborhood's twenty-four-hour-a-day denizens. Then she would go out to cop: hop in the car and make the quick drive over the Ben Franklin Bridge to Camden or head up Broad Street for the laborious nightmare of driving into North Philadelphia. If she was really desperate, she could buy retail from one of the other junkies in the neighborhood, who had already invested the time and energy to go to Camden or North Philly or even New York.

After she copped, she came home and took out her works. She cooked the heroin down in a spoon, tied off her arm above the elbow, and shot, "booting" the drug mixed with her own blood in and out of the syringe until the danger gave way to euphoria. Sometimes when she was high, she would write, and all that flowed into the stream of her consciousness was diverted into her journal. Personal pep talks had a way of degenerating into Miss America acceptance speeches gone awry.

Gia began writing in her Fiorucci journal, a note to herself to call her Elite booker:

> *Call Patty tomorrow and tell her that your very or so sorry that I haven't been calling in and I haven't made my appointements. But I have a problem, which I was try to figure out a solution for. I always try to get rid of a problem on my own, any problem I have I probably caused myself, usually by not being itellingent. I never tell anybody my problems, they're my problems and everybody seems to have their own, but I remember Monique telling me that should let the I work with at the agency know even if nobody solved my problems for me. You would at least now how I was feeling and what I was doing or what was going on in my life ... hopefully if I can fill in all those Blank Charts.*

Monquie gave me the idea ... it finally snuck in. So going to have a wole new concept of handling my business. The problem trying to straighten out I came up with an ingeneous idel that I don't know any model who has conceptual plan to try to increase any business. I already have try to have a pleasant disposition, which I usually am. But I going try always to to thinking it's going to be a wonderful job. And isn't life great. Because if I am bad mood I know just the working makes me crink. These some of my worst as working person and lot of trouble it makes late which usually hour at least which really disturbs and embarasses me which think people realize how bad I feel, even friend at Elite I did dumb things, I think late is dum. Not showing up all it always my fault I was Vogue.

I never told anybody the truth about why I just wouldn't show up some days. Which some think was funny. But I didn't it was fun at all. It was impossible for me to cancel at the last minute and try to bow out gracefully. I couldn't, I tried to be courteous which I should, any client you're hired or confirmed (as oppose cancel) This is a model point of no return ...

... While is the life unfair? Because people make it that and I haven't which People been dead 100 yrs laws I really off the track, I want get my plan attaction on paper and finishes So I can get to rebuilding Roman Empire ... Let I Like fall. I think besides pains teenage are going through the most important in Life I felt lost with my idinti And didn't understand anyone else. I really thought I was sucure and indenpent Which make me aceptible in Society eyes and my only link with Society But otherwise I look down on Society It lyed I hate any lies It really make me think people have turn into rats and Government want do cause people run U.S.A. people have to change moral majority for America We are proud successful plain people or we try to be and most so do people forget is honest I know I feel bad if have lie about things. because if everyone would lieing if the US could exterminate lies and people

would be lies there out of are read and contaminating the hontess way. When everyone know that everyone is honest people start trusting each other I know it would peace and a sence of triquility from that people could not help but be happy. People could friends anybody ...

But it A Good Dreams for American to set Goal for it and do. I have enough faith Americans have special for country America the pround and Beautiful Most America are prod to so everyone is taking advantage of country we doing to own home. I know God American straight country Please start at begining ...

this is cry someone can understand that we all live on this plot of Earth but you can't survival on Bad America's soil Horrable the thowth Maybe know in Govement of such horrable because country is important it is are bread and butter And America At least I have & butter. I am will help preserve my Greatest Nation I would sweat hours work on Land if I knew what do. I sure Americans we aren't what Earth the most Land of Beatiful I believe in my country I don't believe the Government People are the heart & soul of coutry Its out country we the people of U.S. We must different of Sevice Pubic Health Sevice, Review CIA More then we want to Amit you would have to be brainless or live in a cave no relize that present way we run is Eternity ...

We are powerful but we allways we never let U.S. weak It rate very high ... some hate tha and people. Weid tourstist funny people out U.S. don't care who you they look down not visit evenually return to their country Lets US ALIVE CARE FOR LAND WE LOVED MOVE.

If you are the type a guy gal who down getting dirty okay I have job investigate junk waste factory Envorment Mandatory safety you know are the people lot own places the air are we breathe and water that a little color will remian blue clear fresh clean All as american's cleanness is next to Godlyness and to be close is an honor why because if only as that could touch him look right into his eyes and strife and work to close them you would feel ashamed and that worth cause to touch our God without Man I would very mean not the Guy you would mother Religion the humane race resoures its power of peace and love is holding right now & has many kept people killing made the love turn evil into good Our Gave us everyone a priceless Beside being and trying to warn men mustin man & abong our father of unervise. See it is so silly for people to go war for reason god says thou salt not no people aren't suppos kill or go war—is ALot killing for nothing war is meanless Wjay was do for country Americans won against Nazi's & Hitler and it finish Veisiam but the Had some Idea wanted so think German Back Hitler that he could war . . .

On the facing page, most likely on another day, she wrote: "Friday Night Videos, Gia Carangi Sweepstakes, PO Box 4502, Blair Nebraska."

In the fall of 1983, Gia decided to move to the Jersey Shore—in part because her mother still wouldn't let her come back home. Atlantic City was a far different scene than New York or Philadelphia. Its traditional position as a seasonal party town with a year-round seamy underbelly had mutated, with the coming of legalized gambling, into something far more formidable. Amid the increasingly visible poverty of the resident have-nots and the steady flow of tourists unburdening themselves of their cash, a new, young, big-living middle class had emerged.

Fueled by high-paying, low-training jobs in the casinos— and the companies servicing the casinos' customers—the now-endless summer had developed its own fast lane, rivaling the *dolce vita* in the world's major cities in some ways, and mocking it in others. Atlantic City had become, in a few short years, a sort of Manhattan stripped of its cultural pretensions, its high commerce and its media-fueled sense of time and space. It was just one big Times Square. What most major cities considered their garish underside was Atlantic City's *only* side. Unlike New York, where people worked hard and played hard, the whole of Atlantic City society was devoted to playing hard. Fantasy, hedonism and depravity were not trendy subject matter for fashion photographs or club themes in Atlantic City. They were the bulwark of the economy, the region's only natural resources.

Gia's father, who she still referred to as "Daddy," had successfully relocated near the Boardwalk. Joe ran the second Hoagie City; his son Joey ran a pizza parlor on the Boardwalk itself. Between the two of them, Gia's brother Michael and her uncle Dan, the family was still managing the original shop near Resorts and looking into others.

The Atlantic City side of Gia's family had been spared most of the first few years of her drug problems—they saw her only on holidays and during infrequent visits. Only Michael, with whom she had grown even closer since his own rehab experience, had really seen the depths to which Gia was now capable of sinking. They had once even traveled together. After he got out of the hospital, she took him away to St. Barts, to see the island paradise she had found. "She wanted me to experience that," Michael recalled. "She had some Valiums and stuff, but no arm work—I would look for it by this time. She got fucked up, started drinking, you party when you're away. She went out a couple nights with this girl from France. I never saw any needles around, but she was fucked up. And she was no fun when she was fucked up. She got pretty nasty if things didn't go her way. She fell—we had rented mopeds and she had an accident on one, cut her hip up. We went in town to the medical center and she demanded more Valium because she was in pain. They gave her a bunch. It was pretty much like that."

When Gia came to Atlantic City, she moved in with her father and Michael, taking a bedroom in the apartment they shared near Hoagie City—at Tennessee and Pacific, just above Caesar's. She then set out to convince Rochelle to join her. By this time Rochelle's court case had been settled. "I never told, I never turned evidence," she recalled. "My parents wanted me to tell and I wouldn't do it. I got five years' probation because I had an excellent lawyer, lots of thousands of dollars later. They got my X-ray technician's license revoked and got me thrown out of the hospital.

"My parents wanted me to stay with them after that. For a while I did. I got a job in Short Hills working in this real exclusive skin salon. I would go see Gia on the weekends. But she wanted me to move down there, and I finally did.''

Gia's plan was that she and Rochelle would have the kind of stable, homey life that she had wanted with many women, but had never been able to experience. "Gia was like an Italian guy from the old school," Rochelle recalled. "For a while she really even dressed like a guy, even wearing boxer shorts. And she wanted a sort of old-fashioned relationship. She wanted to make me a 'nice girl'—and I *wasn't*. I never knew what love was, or good sex was. Gia was a great lover. And she wanted to live together in a husband and wife type of thing. I was the wife. She was the dominant one. She was the man. I mean, it was really, just pretend. I mean, *I* was pretending. Maybe she was serious.

"But she was also just like a child. She called me 'Doodie-kins,' I was Mrs. Doodiekins, she was Mr. Doodiekins. I'd boss her around and she'd say, 'Yes, King Doo-doo.' 'Gia, go get me some tea, get me a coke.' Any hour of the morning, she'd go. She'd just wait on me, she was good like that. But, like a child. She'd get all excited about things like Dairy Queen. I'd say, 'You want some ice cream?' and she got all excited. 'Can we really go to Dairy Queen, really?' ''

But the chemistry between Gia and Rochelle wasn't conducive to a quiet home off the range. Gia wanted the kind of emotionally ambitious relationship that only the stablest people were able to pull off. But she had no idea how far she was from being mature enough to rudder such a commitment, nor how unlikely a choice Rochelle was for such a union.

"That's very typical of the way Gia was," Kathleen said. "She was the same way about children. When she was modeling she would say she wanted to buy a farm and have all these animals and all these children. She could picture herself there playing with the kids and reading them stories and doing all the things that a little kid does. But never once did it cross her mind all the work she'd have to do, what it was really about. It's just like when she was in high school, she could never understand why people didn't ask her to baby-sit. But you just *knew*.''

To the surprise of no one, Gia's relationship with Rochelle, based on so many unspoken, unshared assumptions, was an emotional three-ring circus. "She was always accusing me of being involved with other people," Rochelle recalled. "She always thought I was cheating on her. And I wasn't cheating on her, at first. I think part of it was that she was more comfortable being gay and out than me. She never cared. She liked being gay. She loved women and cars, that's what she told me. 'Blondes,' she would say, 'I love blondes.' She used to say she never really thought a woman was a woman unless she was a blonde.

"She was blatantly homosexual and proud of it. Me, I didn't say it so much, I was more bisexual I guess. I didn't let everybody in the straight community know like she would, only the gay community, and only when I went out with her. And, you know, since she was 'Gia the model,' people used to try and be friendly to me to get to her. So I was quite satisfied to stay in the house. We really had a good relationship when we were just with each other. But we would go out to the gay clubs and restaurants down on New York Avenue: the Saratoga, Studio 6, The Brass Rail.

"Gia didn't really understand men. She never really did understand the man/woman relationship and the way men think—maybe because she just thought of herself as a guy, too. She would talk about men, like, they were her buddies. I'd say, 'Gia, *no,* they're not your buddies.' When I met her, she claimed she had never had sex with a man. I said she should just do it so she knew what it was. She called me up one night—she was in New York modeling, I was in Philly in school—and she called and said, 'I did it!' And I said, 'Did what?' And she said, 'Well, I could'a done *that* with a German shepherd.' Now that I look back, though, maybe that whole thing wasn't true. Maybe she wanted me to see her as a certain kind of gay woman to set a standard for me."

Rochelle got a job doing nails at Salon Samuel, the well-known coif shop in the Tropicana casino owned by the flamboyant Samuel Posner. Sam, as he was known by all, had made a professional reputation by doing over both celebrity clients and the truckloads of new cocktail waitresses pouring into the casinos. If there were ever any truly beautiful people in Atlantic City, they knew the charming, chatty hairdresser.

Gia was still doing some modeling, but mostly she worked for her father. "We settled into a routine," Rochelle said. "Every morning at six o'clock, I'd feel somebody pokin' me 'C'mon, the clinic, the methadone,' she'd say. It opened at six. She'd poke until I'd tell her to take my car and go, although she really wanted company. Then she'd come back and say, 'McDonald's.' She'd go there and come back and wave Egg McMuffin in my face and then the methadone would kick in and she'd feel good. Then she wanted to have sex.

"Some mornings she liked to eat breakfast at the Cup and Saucer, this little diner. She always had creamed chipped beef on toast and she'd lean across the table and tell me she loved me. She was really open and aggressive. I'd be working and she would come and bring my lunch. One time my boss saw her and said, 'Hey, that's Gia!' And I said, 'Yeah, she's my roommate.'

"She used to wait for me outside of work, call me up there fifteen times, any excuse she could get. If I was doing a guy's nails, she'd come in and accuse me of getting a date with him. She was so possessive, overpowering—so jealous, it was amazing. She had a bad temper. I was in the car with this guy friend of mine and I wouldn't roll the window down. I knew that one, 'Roll the window down.' She jumped *through* the windshield of my car feet first, right through it.

"Did I cheat on her? Once in a while. Once in a while, men, once in a while, women. But it was only when she did something that made me think it was over with her. I wouldn't take it as cheating. I guess I only did that stuff to piss her off."

Their fights became legendary among their small circle of friends. Gia's father never claimed to really understand the relationship, but grew to accept it and to expect the periodic battles.

"Rochelle came into the store one day," recalled Dan Carangi, "and she said, 'Look what Gia did to me!' She said Gia beat her up. I guess they had a little lover's quarrel. I said, 'Look, Rochelle, nobody said you had to live with her.' "

"When I heard them back there crackin' heads, I didn't get involved," explained Michael Carangi. "It's like two cats.

You're gonna get hurt if you pull a girl off another girl. Y'know, women are just different. There's, like, a girl I used to go out with, and she used to feel that if she was with a girl she wasn't cheatin' on me, y'know? I said, 'Well, if you're sleeping with her, what's the difference if it's a guy or not?' But women have their own way of thinking."

Gia's modeling career finally came to an end that fall while she was living in Atlantic City. "I remember one time the people from that Elite place were calling at Hoagie City," recalled Dan Carangi. "Gia was supposed to be on a plane for Germany and they called and talked to my brother. Said Gia never showed up. The woman said, 'We love Gia and we want to give her all the chances we can, see if you can get in touch with her.' Another time Gia told me she was supposed to be making some lipstick ads that were never finished because they dropped her when they found out about the drug addiction. She'd get herself all together, look really great, get ready to work again, and then something would always happen." During one of her last trips to Germany, she had been stopped at the airport at Hamburg and searched by local authorities, who found works in her luggage and threatened to send her home.

Finally, Elite used a behind-the-scenes pact between the agencies as an excuse to freeze Gia from working. The International Model Management Association—which existed mostly for the regional modeling agencies to communicate and had no power over New York agencies whatsoever—made an agreement about drug use. "They said that if somebody had a drug problem nobody would represent them," recalled Jo Zagami. "At that point I froze Gia and said you can come back when you can." Elite's decision seemed justifiable, but at the same time, somewhat hypocritical in its lateness. There was nothing very humanitarian about representing an admitted junkie for over a year and then cutting her off for her own good after her earning power had sunk below acceptable levels. But it was, after all, as it always had been, just business.

One of her last jobs was a fur and leather supplement for German *Vogue,* shot by Albert Watson. Fashion editor Suzanne Kolmel came to New York to do the sittings. One of the shots was a singularly sad close-up of Gia's face, swathed in fur, the camera flash reflected perfectly in her weary eyes. But a cover try was less successful. "Albert booked her again to help her and to give her another cover," Kolmel recalled. "But, she was completely in heroin . . . she was *shivering,* she couldn't stop. She was so pathetic. And here, she had been the *biggest* girl."

Several months after Gia moved to Atlantic City, Kathleen came to visit. It was the first time mother and daughter had seen each other in over six months, probably the longest they had ever been apart in their lives. "She was kind of huffy with me, still upset that I hadn't let her move back in," Kathleen recalled. "And I said, 'Don't you understand that I *had to say no?*'"

"Maybe you should've done it before," Gia said. "This is the first time you ever said no to me."

Kathleen hoped that the conversation would prove to be cathartic—that it could be a first step toward Gia turning her life around, and perhaps even returning to her life's work in modeling. But the conversation did little to change the situation.

"Parents can do so much more if they really want to, if they don't ignore situations," said Gia's aunt Nancy Adams, who, at the time, was living in Philadelphia and still watching the situation from afar herself. "Kathleen just ignored this, she could've been more of a help. Rochelle struggled with it. If Gia came to me and asked me for money for drugs, I would give it to her—because I knew what the alternative was. The problem was really too big for everyone. But the denial of this problem on Kathleen's part was just unbelievable.

"It was just part of the way she had always dealt with Gia. I remember at one point, Gia was maybe nineteen and Kathy was telling my sister Barbara and me how undeveloped Gia was and that she was still a virgin. And my sister dropped a plate. She looked at me and just mouthed, 'She's lost her mind.' Gia would *never* tell her mother the truth, that's true, but her mother dealt with her on such a crazy level. Rochelle and I, and a lot of people, tried to help her, but she wanted her mother. This poor girl, she had so much to deal with, and it always came down to 'Why did my mother leave me when I was eleven?' I never had an answer for this. What can you say? What is the answer? I'm not saying my sister is responsible, but ... it was *Rochelle* over the years who was keeping Gia out of alleys and trash cans and all the other things that could've happened."

It was never exactly clear what kinds of things did happen to Gia when her desperation for drugs overcame her street smarts. The stories always came out later, in bits and pieces. "I know one time she was raped by a black guy in Atlantic City," recalled Rochelle. "She had gone to get Valiums in one of the ghetto neighborhoods because the methadone wasn't holding her. She said she went to this guy's apartment and he locked the door, threw her down and raped her. And then he kept coming into Hoagie City when she was working and bothering her.

"Besides that, I don't think she ever turned tricks for drugs. I know she promised people sex and *tricked* them. She would give them, like, an apartment key and tell them, 'Okay, go to my apartment,' and not be there. I do remember one time I came home from work and she was there with this guy—she told this guy that she was going to do him, or whatever, and he gave her the drugs and she was all high. So when I came home it was like, 'Get the fuck out,' and the guy left, like he was afraid.

"But sex was very special to her. She'd knock somebody on their head and take their wallet before she'd do that. She'd go into somebody's apartment and wait 'til they were asleep and steal their stuff.

"Although, well, she did tell me she was embarrassed about a lot of things that she had done. She never said what they were, you know. I guess they could have been sexual. And maybe she didn't tell me because she knows how I think about things. I would never, I mean there is no way I would have sex for drugs. Gia knew me well enough to know that I would think that was scummy and low."

In March of 1984, Patty Stewart was looking for subjects for an assignment from her photography class at the Philadelphia College for the Arts. A compact, dark-haired twenty-two-year-old who had become friendly with Toni O'Connor and some of the other girls at the DCA after Gia left town, Stewart mostly knew about the supermannequin from Philadelphia by legend. She had met Gia only once, at a huge, outdoor concert by the Police and the Go-Go's at Liberty Bell Racetrack in the Northeast, but the meeting had made quite an impression. Years later she could still describe in detail the mystical drugged glow of Gia's face behind mirrored sunglasses, and her leather pants with a *V* ripped into the backside, revealing underpants that said Dior all over them.

Patty and Gia had a mutual friend Vicky,* who worked in her parents' flower shop in South Philadelphia but often visited Atlantic City, where her family had a home. She was an ex-lover of Patty's, and an enamored friend of Gia's who had loaned the model money about five times too often. When Patty let it be known that she needed test subjects, Vicky suggested that Gia might do the budding photographer a favor. A tentative meeting was set up, but then Vicky had a little too much to drink the night of the rendezvous and wasn't able to act as intermediary. Gia arranged to meet Patty at the Saratoga herself.

"She was straight that night, wasn't high or anything, and she looked great," Patty recalled. "We talked, I told her about my thesis. She had been nervous around me initially but she got more comfortable. It was getting late, and she made a pass at me—we were sitting there kissing. Now, I'm not very forward to begin with: she made the pass. I went to call Vicky, and she didn't answer the phone. We walked over to Vicky's parents' house, where I was supposed to stay, and she didn't answer the door. So Gia invited me to stay at her place, above the hoagie shop. We just stayed up all night and ended up spending, like, four or five days with each other. We never took the pictures, but other things happened. She started spilling her guts to me.

"She told me a little bit about Rochelle—she said they were just friends, which I knew was a lie. She talked a lot about Sandy. She said people sort of knew she and Sandy were an item and would book them together to see what went on—but that they would act real professional. She said Sandy was the last girl that she really loved, and that I reminded her of Sandy. We got pretty intimate. She started filling my head with all kinds of ideas. 'You're such a nice girl and you're into photography ... after you graduate, move down here with me ... when I get better, I'm going back to New York ...' She wanted to get a video camera and open a little studio to take videos of people: it was starting to be popular then for actresses to have a video portfolio.

"She was telling me all this stuff. I started falling for her. I told her I hadn't gone out with anyone for a while. When you're a lesbian in Philadelphia and don't fit the stereotypical image, it's not easy. Gia was butch in a fashionable way. When she went out, she wore cowboy boots and dungarees instead of Reeboks and khaki pants. With lesbians, ninety percent of them have sneakers on, white sneakers, and little Lacoste shirts. It's rare you meet someone who's feminine and who doesn't fit the image.

"She kept saying, 'I can't believe how nice you are.' She thought I was very naive about the drug scene, about the addict thing, about how hard it can be to break away from it. A lot of times she'd tell me something and I'd say 'What?' She wanted me to be her guardian angel, because she knew I wasn't part of that world."

As part of their whirlwind romance, Patty was treated to an abridged oral history of what had happened to Gia in New York. "She talked about modeling," Patty recalled. "She said that, when they were on the islands, all the models referred to her as 'Sister Morphine.' They would all come to her and say, 'Gia, find us drugs,' because she could find drugs *anywhere*. She told me about Janice Dickinson. She said one time they were on a shoot, Janice Dickinson was missing her boyfriend and said, 'Come over here, Gia.' Gia said, 'I wasn't gonna be her fling.'

"She said she would show up for a shoot and all the models were in their furs and diamonds, all the big names, and she'd walk in with dungarees and a leather jacket and they'd all look. 'I blew them away,' she said. She didn't like having to play glamorous. She didn't like modeling that much, although she explained that being in front of the camera was some magical thing with her: your body goes into a different phase. She knew how to be on. But she didn't like it.

"There was one thing, though. Those Calvin Klein underwear ads had just started coming out, the ones with the women's stuff that looked like men's stuff. We were reading a magazine and we came to that ad. She said, 'See this? I should have this ad.' She was mad that she wasn't the Calvin Klein underwear girl."

Her envy of the Calvin Klein underwear girl was more than just a feeling that someone else had successfully copped her attitude. The modeling world was buzzing over the unprecedented exclusive contract Klein was signing with South African model Jose Borain to be the signature face and body for all the products with the Klein name. She would do Avedon-directed TV ads for clothes and perfume, Bruce Weber still photographs, runway work, everything. For a hundred days of work per year, Borain would be paid $1 million over three years. For that fee, she wasn't allowed to model for anyone else, and couldn't even leave New York for more than a weekend without the designer's permission. It was the biggest modeling deal since Carol Alt's contract with Lancôme, and far more important. The Klein contract was a whole new concept, born of the incredible marketability of a designer's name and visual signature.

"Gia talked about Wilhelmina and about some of the photographers, which I loved to hear," Stewart recalled. "She talked about Chris and his wife, about Scavullo, Helmut Newton. Chris and Scavullo were the photographers she seemed to really like. Andrea Blanche she mentioned. She told me about walking out on Avedon. She said they were doing the Versace campaign with the big camera and it took so long to shoot everything—like shooting a still life with people. She said all the models were dressed and he was taking a long time because he couldn't get one set-up right and she was just sitting around and he didn't even have the courtesy to come back and say, 'Look, girls, I'm sorry for the delay.' She was there for so long, she had just had it. So she went to the bank or to get cigarettes or something and just didn't come back. She said he had no respect for people that way and a lot of people in the business applauded her because it was about time somebody put him in his place.

"Gia and I liked a lot of the same music. She told me some story about Mick Jagger. She was *obsessed* with Keith Richards, obsessed. But she said she was at a Stones concert and she was backstage with Mick Jagger and he wanted to kiss her, or he *did* kiss her, and she was so frightened that

Jerry Hall would walk in. She said he wanted to get it on with her but she didn't want any part of it. If it was me, I would've kissed him just for the sake of kissing Mick Jagger.

"She talked about the guys from Blondie, about hanging out and playing pool with Jimmy Destri. She was a *big* Debbie Harry fan. She was in the 'Eat to the Beat' video. There's one scene where everyone's dancing in this club, the camera goes by her. She liked them a lot. She said she met Bowie at somebody's apartment. She said it was a very ordinary meeting. He wasn't a jerk. He was more friendly than she expected and seemed to want to get to know her better."

Gia's father would occasionally come upstairs to knock on her door and see if she was all right. "He brought up some sheets," she recalled. "He said, 'Here, Gia, put these on your bed.' They were satin sheets, black. She said, 'You know why he gave me these? Because he knows you're up here and he's happy when I'm with somebody because he knows I'm not doing drugs.' He thought she couldn't have sex when she was doing drugs.

"At one point, I had to be somewhere to take pictures for a friend and I said I had to go home. She didn't want me to leave. She made me stay. How? She, um, jumped on the bed and took all her clothes off and practically threw herself at me. There are a lot of women that are just pretty, but Gia wasn't pretty, it was so much deeper than that. It was very deep. And she was a great manipulator of people. I stayed. When I finally did leave, I had to go to my parents' house and she came with me. She met my parents. My mother said, 'She's very beautiful and very sad.'

"I collected old toys from the fifties. I had a little red toy VW and rubbery kinds of monsters: she was fascinated by them. She sat on my bed and, for about an hour, we played. She said, 'This one is me,' and she put them in the little car. 'Let's go to Camden to get drugs!' Later that day, when I took her back to her apartment, she gave me this little figurine, green and fangs and pointy ears, it had a cape and a *G* on it. She said, 'This is me when I'm not on my medications.' She also gave me this friendship ring—two clasping hands with a heart—and a picture of her and her cat that lived at her mother's house.

"That last day she started getting really weird. Right before we left her apartment, she went into the bathroom and was in there for a while. When she came out she said, 'What did you think? I was shooting up?' When she gave me the picture, she said, 'Don't lose this picture,' and I just had a real strange feeling. She was giggling and giggling. I now think that she got high."

Even though their week together had ended on such an odd note, Patty had high hopes for something lasting with Gia. But, the romance ended as soon as Patty left Gia's sight. They had made tentative plans to get together the next weekend, but Gia wouldn't return Patty's calls to firm things up. Gia's father or brother had to make apologetic phone excuses: Gia wasn't home, she was sleeping.

"After calling her about ten times over the next couple days," Patty recalled, "it finally clicked that she didn't want to have anything to do with me. Then she said to my friend Vicky, 'That girl Patty is really a pest.' Finally, she told Vicky what had happened, and told her to tell me she wanted the picture back. Vicky had already been through some disappointments with Gia herself, so she had sorta warned me. But I was heartbroken. I was a sucker.

"I called Gia again, but her father said she wasn't in. So I took the picture over to Vicky's place at the Shore. After dropping it off, I'm walking to my car, and in the shadows there's Gia. And she runs up to me crying Patty, Patty. She wants to borrow twenty dollars from me. She did too much heroin and she had to get coke to combat it. She was crying and sobbing on my lap. She said, 'I'll do *anything!*' Oh, it was so hard to witness that. She was talking real slow. She didn't sound right, like she had had a lobotomy or something. I just felt so sad and sorry for her. I gave her the twenty dollars and I said, 'I'm coming with you, I'll bring you back home.' I took her to a *really* horrible part of town. She got the drugs. I brought her back home. She said, 'I'm not ready for a relationship, I'm not ready to get involved with anybody.'

"I said, 'So, what was it, tell me that, what was going on, was it a fling, what? I mean, it boggled me too. I hadn't planned on falling in love in five days.' She said, 'I changed my mind, can't we just be friends?'

"I said she had no reason to shut me out of her life. She didn't know too many people who didn't do drugs. She thought I was too straight, I guess. I remember at one point, I started crying and I told her about one of my best friends from school. 'They just found her dead. She went scuba diving, she was high. She reminded me a lot of you, Gia.' I told her I didn't want something like that to happen to her. She just looked at me and said, 'It's not gonna happen to me, any doctor will tell you that you have to take coke when you do too much heroin.' I just ended up leaving . . ."

In New York, Gia had become one of the biggest "whatever happened to" stories in the modeling industry. She would join the "where are they now" queens like Ann Simonton, the former Ford model and 1974 *Sports Illustrated* cover girl who left the business in 1979, cut off her trademark long red hair and became one of the most fervent feminist activists in the country. Based in Southern California, Simonton became part of what previously had been a small annual protest against the Miss California contest, held every June in Santa Cruz. The month was an especially significant one for Simonton; she had been gang-raped at knifepoint in Manhattan on the way to a modeling job in June of 1971, and decided to quit the business after seeing herself in a department store ad, peeking provocatively from under the comforter that was on sale. "The connection between what I was doing and the rape hit me full force," she said.

Her tactics against the pageant and other exploitation of women had slowly escalated. She and other feminists founded the "Myth Kalifornia" pageant and protested by wearing dresses made of meat; an anti–*Hustler* magazine poster was made of Simonton lying down nude as three men, holding a sign reading "We Stand On Our First Amendment Rights," planted their feet on her. But it wasn't until Simonton's past as a top model was revealed in 1983—by another member of the group—that the story of her protest became national. That's when she also began telling specific tales of degradation from her career, like the lingerie shooting during which the agency people analyzed her anatomy. "I found myself bent over in a girdle," she said, "with a grown man and woman studying my derriere, saying, 'What do you think' ... 'I'm not sure, what do you think.' " Her exposure would allow her to become a one-woman national protest against modeling and pornography. She founded the organization Media Watch and lectured nationally.

A model-fights-back story of another sort had just unfolded in Italy. In late June of 1984, a troubled, twenty-six-year-old aspiring model named Terry Broome fulfilled the *other* fantasy of every young girl who came to Milan to build a portfolio. She gunned down one of the city's most prominent playboys, Francesco D'Alessio. Broome would later tell an Italian reporter that the first time she met D'Alessio he "walked up to her, suggested they have sex and, opening his fly, extracted his erect penis and began manipulating it vigorously." On the night in question, D'Alessio had asked the coked-up Broome if she wanted to go to bed, mentioning he would be happy to call some friends if "one man wasn't enough" for her, whereupon she pulled a pistol from the pocket of her black Fiorucci jacket and shot him four times. Broome was sitting in a Milan jail awaiting trial, but her feat was already being viewed, in more ways than one, as *the* seminal event in the social life of the Milanese modeling world. "The story of Milano ends with Terry Broome," lamented playboy Giorgio Repossi. "We suddenly realize that it is playing with fire. And it is sad, because this girl wasn't really a model, and this guy she kill, I not like him, he always belong to the group that was less clean. My group was more of a pure group. He was a strange person. He was gambling. He was a ball-breaker alive and a ball-breaker when he died."

But Gia's professional demise hadn't been quite so newsworthy. Like Chris von Wangenheim, Gia and her career simply disappeared one day. All that was left were a dusty portfolio stored in the basement at Elite, and the eight 5 × 7 cards in the *Vogue* library model file, detailing her appearances in the magazine. No other fashion magazine bothered to keep track of which models had appeared on their pages, and only a few libraries kept back issues of the publications. Gia's work was most easily found in the salons and boutiques and doctor's offices that were less diligent about updating the magazines in their waiting areas.

Only the *fashionistas* who had worked with her still told

the Gia stories, as the young man from the Northeast who had once called himself Joey Bowie found out. After his years of Bowie craziness, Joe McDevit went to New York as well, working with Larry Cannon, who did all the wigs for the Metropolitan Opera. After seven years with the opera, McDevit moved to Paris and then Milan in 1983 to break in as a makeup artist. By 1984, he was doing good European editorial work, and meeting some of the people who had worked with Gia. A mention of his childhood association with her brought many stories.

"I remember [hairdresser] Howard Fugler told me Gia would come to the studio with pockets full of candy bars," McDevit recalled. "She'd be stoned and needed something sweet. He'd try and do her hair and she'd keep dropping her head. He had to pick it up. I did the collections with Janice Dickinson in 1984 at the Grand Hotel. She had already pinnacled. She was on her way down, but she hadn't gone to rehab yet. We were doing nude photos, of course, all these obscure poses. I remember walking into the studio the first time and she was sitting in a chair, naked. Janice was some incredible woman. The first thing she said to me was 'Hey, boy, want a blowjob?' Pure shock value, Janice. But she could still put on the tightest red dress, slither across the floor and the Italians went crazy for her. Someone in heaven loved her to still look like that after all the years of abuse she put herself through. She had been one of Gia's get-high buddies. She talked about that. She said they'd lock themselves into the studio bathrooms for an hour at a time, get stoned and then stumble around the studio. Janice would say it was all a big joke."

Gia's disappearance brought a tear to a handful of fashion people, a sigh of relief to many others. Those who had bumped into her recently prayed for her. And those who knew her only during the first few years speculated on what had led her to destroy her beauty, her career, her life. In one of his many moments of indecision about staying in photography, Lance Staedler even wrote a film treatment about her. He had to piece together tales he had heard from other models over the years because, even though he had taken the first great test shot of Gia, they had never done an assignment together.

* * *

Gia would take shelter with any number of different people in Atlantic City during breakups with Rochelle. One couple whose lives she slipped in and out of was Ted Catrana,* a waiter at one of the bigger Atlantic City restaurants, and his wife Sherry.*

"I met Rochelle and Gia the same night," recalled Ted Catrana. "The salon people came over and we were partying. It wasn't real loud or anything, because our little son stayed asleep, but it got into a little mess. The first night was just one of them things, I'm a little embarrassed to tell. Gia went into the bedroom to lay down. We had been drinking. Gia wasn't, she was all methadoned out. My wife noticed she went into the bedroom. Rochelle came in and checked up a couple times, then she left with the rest of them. Gia stayed with us.

"Gia was in the bed, in her underwear and a T-shirt. She was just being sexy. My wife seemed very turned on. They made a move and started kissing. If you want to know the truth, I was gonna leave. I had heard all about Gia, about her and other girls, it was very common. When I was getting ready to go, she said, 'Don't leave.'

"I never wanted to take advantage. She was whacked, and I didn't want it to be a thing of me taking advantage of a whacked girl. But a man is a man and you can only go so far, and she initiated it. Gia seemed very fresh the next morning. My wife was very edgy, but Gia had a way of just smoothing everything over. Gia got into the shower. I asked my wife if she was all right, I started to feel guilty. I asked her how it was for her: she said it was different. At first I worried whether it was going to hurt us as a couple. When Gia was in bed, she was like a little baby, like a warm kid. She was sexual in her own way; she was very warm and sensitive. Once you met her, you were touched forever."

Gia stayed with the Catranas on and off over the next few months, periodically returning to Rochelle. "One night me and Gia went out and got home really late," he recalled. "And Rochelle was there with my wife and it didn't look like friendly talk. Gia and Rochelle started to go at it, fistfight. Rochelle got into the car and drove off. Gia took off after her, all upset. They went to the apartment. I sort of felt bad that it was my fault, so I went over to try and break it up. I never saw two women fight like that, it was crazier than you'd think. Finally the cops came, everybody calmed down. Then they pretty much were back together, being lovey-dovey, so I got out of there.

"To me, Rochelle was Gia's downfall. Rochelle is Bonnie—she's worse than Bonnie, she's Bonnie and Nancy Vicious put together. Rochelle would stab you in the back in a *minute*. Her mentality is pretty much the mentality of Atlantic City: Kick 'em when they're down and discard them. It's a rough, crazy town.

"But Rochelle was just bad for Gia. One day she'd be helping her out and the next day I'd see them and they were strung out. Rochelle was always good at her job, good at doing nails. She's vicious and all, but she had some qualities. I'm just saying, for Gia, she was Satan. Gia's mother, of course, was a big problem for her, but she wasn't even in the picture. Gia said, 'She doesn't talk to me.' I don't think the mother helped her the least bit.

"Gia and Rochelle told me they did some smokers in Philly. They joked about it, 'Remember that guy we did.' Maybe they were just saying it to excite me, but when you have habits like that, anything is possible. One night I was at their apartment and Rochelle said she was going to put on a videotape of them, and Gia said, 'No, no, no.' They spoke of it openly, that they were turning tricks. Or maybe, yeah, it was that they performed for them, just to get them off. That was one of the things that was stressed: 'No, we wouldn't sleep with them.' "

Ted was not exactly a Boy Scout himself. "I'm not saying I was an angel," he said. "I did *a lot* of cocaine at that time and over the next couple years. I did a lot of coke with Rochelle. I'd say Rochelle and I shot up cocaine at least fifty times. We'd sit in her kitchen and do cocaine for hours at a time. I later went away for rehab in North Jersey for cocaine. But Rochelle . . .

"Eventually what happened with this little love triangle with my wife and I and Gia was that Gia started to turn more toward my wife than me. I always told her she didn't have to do anything for me, but I didn't want her to continue just with my wife. I knew I would get too jealous myself. I had feelings for Gia too, and I didn't want her to sleep with me to be with my wife. I didn't want her to use me. A couple of times I came home from work and they were together. My wife worried that she was in love with Gia, and felt a little deeper than she should have. And every time that happened, something would happen with Rochelle, and Gia would go somewhere.

"But, basically, Rochelle was just flooded with girls and guys and Gia was looking for that one-on-one. She wasn't getting it from Rochelle, and it was driving her crazy. She wanted an exclusive relationship. And, believe me, she would do *anything* to get it. I remember going to their apartment one night and they were just going at it. Clothes were ripped off. Rochelle was sitting in a corner and Gia had her by the throat and was going down on her, like, trying to force sex on her. Gia's shirt was off, Rochelle's pants were off, and she was screaming. When I opened the door to the apartment, she was screaming, 'Get me outta here!' Gia gave me the look of death. She was in a rage. Of course, the next day, they could get back together."

It was an endless cycle, Gia and Rochelle, but each time around left Gia a little more depleted, a little more desperate.

"I remember one night," Rochelle said, "I was staying with this guy, the one whose window Gia had jumped through. He was out, I was just home watching TV in my robe. All of a sudden, Gia comes climbing through his window in a Ralph Lauren tuxedo and black cowboy boots, fully made up with her hair long. She said, 'C'mon, I want to take you out to dinner.' I looked at her in this tuxedo and I just said, 'Gia, you're out of your mind, it's done, it's *over.*' She said c'mon, c'mon. She talked me into it."

Kathleen was almost completely out of the picture, feeling there was little she could do but wait for a call from the police about the last of her daughter's nine lives. She was beyond crisis mode. The emergency had been going on for nearly four years. There had been too many last straws. And with Gia in Atlantic City, someone closer by would be called to put out the emotional brush fires. It was her ex-husband's turn. He had jurisdiction.

Gia's father wasn't sure exactly what to do. He gave his

daughter a place to sleep. He gave her a job, which she sometimes even *did*. He gave her extra money when she hit him up for it, which was often, even though he had a pretty good idea where it was going. And he gave her a place to cry.

"I can't tell you how many times he helped her out," recalled Dan Carangi. "Gia *broke* my brother. Sometimes I'd walk upstairs and she would be on his lap and with her head on his shoulders for hours. She was close with her Dad, much closer to her father than her mother."

It was true that Joe Carangi had great affection for his daughter. He was, as he always had been, willing to do anything for her. But they were the any*things* of a man who believed that he had always spoiled his daughter—with no clue that she felt, at some essential level, that he had never really given her the time of day. It wasn't that he didn't love her or indulge her or hold her when she came to him. He just didn't *get it*. He didn't understand girls, and most of what he knew about junkies came from his observations of the ones who wandered into his new luncheonette, Joe's Place, for breakfast after getting their methadone at Atlantic City's main clinic—which was located just around the corner. The ones who were up on their luck and had a little money paid easily. The real goners emptied their pockets onto the table or the long Formica counter, picking out linty coins and perhaps a crumpled bill or two from among the pawn tickets and keys. But they all had that stunned-stoned look in their eyes, the narcotic glow on their otherwise disheveled faces. His contribution was to feed them—sometimes for free if someone was particularly pathetic and he was feeling particularly sympathetic. If you came to his place, Joe Carangi would give certain kinds of sustenance. But you had to pick from what was on his limited luncheonette menu.

There was no longer the slightest doubt that methadone wasn't going to solve Gia's problems. She was in her fourth program in as many years, and she was showing no signs of improvement. "I saw her down there one time," recalled Kathleen, "and it was like she was epileptic or something. She had the shakes. Gia had always stood very straight, and held her shoulders beautifully. The longer she was on that program in Atlantic City, the worse her shoulders got."

Pressure from her family and Rochelle finally convinced Gia that she needed inpatient care. "Gia had agreed to go into rehab after I threatened to leave her, to *really* leave her," Rochelle recalled. "I called Kathleen and asked her to come get her. She was like, 'Well, I have a Corvette Club meeting tonight. Of all nights, does she have to pick tonight? I would come tomorrow.' I said, 'Kathleen, you have to come *now!*' I *begged* the woman. She did not come until two or three days later. Gia's mother cared more about her Corvette Club meeting than Gia. The only time she would come for Gia was when Gia was at the top.

"I knew all along that if it hadn't been for me, Gia would be living on the street. And I also knew what was going to happen if she went into rehab. I knew they'd say I was her 'enabler' and that they would have to turn her against me. That's how rehab works; they try to break the pattern of drug use by getting you away from the life that led you to it. I knew I was taking a chance that I would lose her. But I was twenty-five years old by then, I had grown up a lot. And I knew there wasn't any choice."

16
Rehab

Gia's lawyer John Duffy was stunned when he heard his client had checked into Eagleville. A recovering alcoholic himself, Duffy was pleased that she was finally seeking inpatient treatment. He just couldn't imagine someone like Gia in a place like Eagleville. "It's a bare-knuckle joint," he said. "It's the last bead on the rosary. I do a lot of intervention work, and I never send *anyone* to Eagleville. I don't want a patient in a place where they're going to learn *more* about violating the law. I wanted to help her get into a better program. But Gia called me and said she wanted to stay there."

Eagleville Hospital was not the Betty Ford Center. The inpatient rehab center in Philadelphia's northern suburbs had been created to insure against the very thing that Betty Ford and other exclusive treatment centers stood for: class and economic distinctions determining quality of care. Located in a rural area just outside of Norristown, Eagleville had been created by local Jewish philanthropists at the turn of the century to treat indigent tuberculosis patients of all religions. In 1967, Eagleville shifted direction and became one of the country's first therapeutic communities for the treatment of alcoholism. Drug rehab was later added, and Eagleville became known as one of the few facilities in the country to embrace the radical notion of "combined treatment" for the broader problems of addiction rather than the traditional substance-specific approach.

Through these changes, Eagleville maintained its commitment to indigent patients and court-urged, voluntary commitments. It was designed to be the top of the bottom: the last best chance for the worst cases to save their lives. And that altruistic mission was even surviving the financial difficulties that had come with the Reagan years—treatment money was increasingly being redirected into Nancy Reagan's "Just Say No" ad campaign. The funding drought had forced cutbacks, a financial reorganization and a reorientation as primarily a hospital rather than a therapeutic community. Eagleville had been forced to advertise on television for a few patients who might actually have health coverage.

But the hospital was still racially integrated, maintained a separate women's unit, and refused to shy away from the most hopeless cases—which was the way heroin addicts were viewed by a public health system increasingly concentrating its efforts on more fashionable, more insurable addictions like cocaine and alcohol. Most of Eagleville's 126 short-term detox and rehab patients, and its 70 long-term patients in the ambitious Candidates Program, were on public assistance. Many had come to Eagleville after living on the streets, more than a few had criminal records. The facility's dedicated staff knew the value of serious care for the most serious patients. Some of them had begun their careers in counseling, social work and even medicine after saving themselves at Eagleville.

Gia had about $2,500 remaining of the hundreds of thousands of dollars she had made modeling—as well as a stack of debts and outstanding warrants. She gave Rochelle the money to hold onto, and had herself declared indigent so that welfare would pay for her treatment. In December of 1984, she entered the detoxification program at Eagleville, which lasted days or weeks—however long it took clients to rid their bodies of whatever they had taken, to get over the worst of their physical withdrawal symptoms and to recover from any emergency physical damage from suicide attempts or accidents. After detox, patients who wanted to stay drug-and-alcohol-free were admitted into Eagleville's month-long inpatient program of classes, group therapy and individual counseling. The average patient was at Eagleville for forty-five days.

But Gia didn't make it that long. Two weeks into her stay, her aunt Barbara was killed in a pre-Christmas auto accident on the Atlantic City Expressway. Barbara had been Gia's baby-sitter as a child and, even though she hadn't spent as much time with her as a teenager as with her aunt Nancy, Barbara had a very special place in Gia's heart. Barbara was another of the mothers Gia never had, but she had also served a pivotal role in the Adams family. She had always been a sort of buffer between Kathleen and Nancy, spanning the generation gap between the two and enabling them to have some semblance of sisterly interaction. Only if Barbara was there as charming peacemaker could Kathleen, Nancy and Gia spend an afternoon together shopping. Barbara was free-spirited and had a way of bringing people together. The week before her death, she had taken one of the casino buses to Atlantic City rather than driving. As the bus tooled down the expressway, Barbara had suddenly found herself leading all the passengers in a round of Christmas carols. That was just the kind of thing that could happen whenever she was around.

The Adams family was in shock. Barbara had left the teenage son from her first marriage—who had been raised by his maternal grandmother—and a huge emotional vacancy where her bright spirit had been. In her grief, Gia checked herself out of Eagleville to be with her family and attend the funeral. She stayed with her mother for ten days, and then disappeared. She turned up in Atlantic City with Rochelle, using heroin again and pawning anything she could get her hands on. And this time, Rochelle wasn't so insistent that Gia go back to rehab. The line between being part of the problem and part of the solution, so clear to her only weeks before, was now very fuzzy.

With Rochelle no longer so insistent that Gia return to inpatient treatment, it was up to Kathleen and Nancy to pressure her. But with Barbara gone, there was nothing to temper the acrimony between the sisters. Everyone seemed to have been suddenly transported back to 1971, when Kathleen first left Joe and everyone started pointing fingers. Kathleen saw Nancy as Gia's corruptor. "Nancy has always done everything to keep Gia and I at each other's throats," said Kathleen. "She tried to destroy me to Gia. For some reason Nancy was either extremely jealous of us or, I don't know, it's hard to figure out why a person does the things they do. I don't know if she wanted to be me or wanted all the things I had—the nice, huge single home and lots of money—or what. Maybe she wanted to be Gia. Whenever Gia had a friend, pretty soon Nancy tried to get in on it.

"But, I think that she's basically a very trashy person. Scum, in my opinion."

Nancy saw herself as trying to stay out of her older sister's way as much as possible, to make sure none of Kathleen's mood swings connected. "I always wanted to have some kind of amicable relationship with Kathleen," Nancy recalled, "in the hope that there could be some peace between her and Gia. The bitterness between Kathleen and I has been rampant at different times, but she's paid. She's the sorry figure in this. She has lost more than anyone."

Nancy's relationship with Kathleen had only worsened over the course of Gia's drug dependence. In her belief that Kathleen was ignoring Gia's drug problems—or selfishly refusing to do what needed to be done to improve the situation—Nancy would sometimes call their mother and try to convince *her* to pressure Kathleen into action.

But, despite their differences, Nancy and Kathleen finally agreed in early February that they should go to Atlantic City together and refuse to leave unless Gia came back with them to reenter Eagleville. Their first job in Atlantic City was *finding* Gia, since she had disappeared again and even Rochelle didn't seem to know where she was. They camped out at Rochelle's apartment for the weekend. To kill some time, and break some of the obvious tension in the fragile coalition of three women who could *barely* tolerate each other, Rochelle did artificial nails for Nancy. Finally, Gia showed up.

"I went into that room and Gia was so *broken*," Nancy recalled, "like she didn't have any spirit left for anything. She had been to New York, probably to pick up money and get drugs. I confronted her and she started again about her mother leaving her when she was eleven, and it was really hard for me to be strong for her. I told her that she couldn't think like that. Like, *big deal* if she blamed her mother for everything. It didn't matter. Her mother wasn't responsible.

"As soon as you say that you are *aware* that you blame your mother for everything, okay, it's not her fault anymore. Now you *know* about it. What are *you* going to do about it? It's your life, and you have to live it. Come on, you know, *life goes on.* Mommy left you. But you're a big girl now. What do you want? You're a heroin addict and living on the street and making Rochelle crazy and your mother is *sick* and you need to go into the hospital and this *can't keep happening!* All that sadness, that intensity—it was like somebody putting their hand in my heart and taking a big yank at it."

Several days later, Gia was back in detox.

Eagleville was everything that Gia's methadone programs had not been. The program was relentlessly aggressive and generally unforgiving—especially since patients were so active in each other's therapy and so many of the professional staff were themselves recovering.

But Eagleville was also caught at a theoretical impasse. There had always been two models for rehab: a psychological model and a disease model. "The field was in a raging battle then over whether addiction was the result of a personality problem or whether the personality dynamics were the result of the addiction," recalled Charles Folks, a senior clinical staff member at Eagleville. The old-time, recovering alcoholics—who committed to twelve-step programs for life—believed in the disease model. Many of the academically trained people embraced the psychological approach that therapy or a therapeutic community could ostensibly *cure*. The debate had been largely theoretical until the federal funding cutbacks, which assured that *neither* theory could be adequately implemented. The crunch was especially difficult on Eagleville, which had prided itself on offering high-minded treatment to low-income patients—the most successful of whom could spend seven or eight months in an ambitious therapeutic community, looking at the issues themselves. Gia joined what would become the next-to-last group to be offered such options. After that, the disease model would win by default.

"Goals were becoming very different when a person might spend a month in inpatient and *that's all*," recalled Folks. "All you can do is get through whatever denial of the problem might exist and say 'Go into a twelve-step program.' "

At the level of the daily therapy sessions Gia attended, the theoretical debate translated into very concrete questions. Who ran the facility, the professionals or the inmates? Who decided what a patient's "real problems" were, the therapists or a jury of one's addicted peers? These questions didn't apply just to the group therapy sessions, which tended to become very confrontational and emotional. There was also a system of "tabs," in which patients accused other patients of sneaking drugs, breaking house rules or otherwise violating the codes of rehab honor by "tabbing" them to the professional staff. After a certain number of tabs—whether for suspicion of substance abuse or not throwing away a paper cup—patients could be discharged. Like points on a driver's license, there were ways to reduce your tabs. It was a harsh system, but inordinately real: why pretend that in the outside world everyone who made decisions affecting your life knew what they were doing?

For the first forty-five days of treatment, Gia was in an all-women's program. The women were housed in a separate building—the original sanitarium structure, which was physically charming compared to the institutional buildings that had been added later on—and all their therapy was single-sex. The rehab world was coming to understand that women were being done a disservice if immediately mixed with men for therapy. Women seemed less likely to confront underlying issues if men were around. Women also seemed less responsive to very confrontational therapy, which was often used to penetrate what professionals saw as a heightened system of denial among males.

"Women come in with a denial system, but it's not as rigidly expressed," said Gloria Zankowski, former director of Eagleville's women's program. "Women's needs are more in assisting them to develop trust, make them feel they're in a safe environment. Many are victims of sexual abuse and incest and are unable to handle something highly confrontational." Gia was told that her goals in the program were to overcome denial of her drug problems and recognize the underlying issues that led her to substance abuse. She was supposed to identify both her "enablers" and the circumstances that usually led her to use drugs.

After completing her inpatient phase, Gia applied for and was accepted into the Candidates Program, a more selective, rigorous, long-term program that had space for twenty women at any given time. The first phase of the program was designed to be a sort of psychological boot camp. Patients got up at six-thirty every morning, had breakfast in the central cafeteria and went through three-hour group therapy sessions. They were assigned co-ed or single-sex groups. The small, all-women's group, to which Gia was assigned, was often referred to as "The Barracudas" by those in the mixed groups. After lunch, there was more individual therapy, three hours of work, some free time and then dinner. Gia was given a job in the cafeteria. "Gia worked the food line, putting out all the desserts," recalled one former Eagleville patient. "You always knew when Gia was in the kitchen because the dishes were backed up to the ceiling. 'Miss Ca*rang*i,' they called her." In the evening, there were often house meetings on the women's unit, and patients were encouraged to attend AA meetings on the campus.

Patients were asked to choose a "role model" from among the professional staff. Gia chose one of her evening counselors, who was also recovering and, because she was attractive and had a warm personality, was a favorite of many Eagleville patients. "Gia was in love with her," recalled another former patient in the women's program, "but, then, a lot of us, women and men, were in love with her."

Romantic or sexual relationships of any kind were strictly forbidden during the Candidates Program: they could result in an immediate discharge. Patients were supposed to be working on *themselves,* and even the most normal human drives were redefined as "avoidance behaviors." Inside Eagleville, sexual attraction wasn't sexual attraction: it was social anxiety and fear of rejection being misinterpreted as love or lust. Sexual preference was also heavily scrutinized. Much to her frustration, Gia found that her avowed homosexuality was considered a major problem by her group. She felt that being gay was the least of her problems, while her group continually harped on it as one of the roots of her difficulties.

Homosexuality was a difficult issue generally at Eagleville. The professional staff recognized that there was a difference between "healthy" homosexual lifestyles and unhealthy, ego-dystonic homosexuality. But no one was precisely sure how to tell the difference. Eagleville's one openly gay staff member, a man, had become the facility's de facto "gay expert." He began a separate sexuality group to try to address the problems of homosexuals in a system that looked judgmentally at even the most socially acceptable sexual behavior. Patients had to learn to separate whether they were *capable* of having same-sex romantic attachments from the bigger question: Did they *personally* have no choice but to live as homosexuals, with a full understanding of the consequences of that commitment?

Many of her fellow patients believed Gia's truthful answer to that question would be no. They harped on her gender-related issues as the prime example of her avoidance behavior. But Gia's main therapists saw her problems quite differently. "There's no question she had a lot of unresolved issues about her sexuality," recalled one of her counselors, who is no longer associated with Eagleville. "She didn't know where she fit, she was very confused about all of that. She felt real bad that she had no children. She really loved children and talked a lot about her older brother's kids and said having kids was something she wanted but didn't know if she could have.

"A lot of what I tried to talk to her about was not making that kind of decision when she was in recovery. When people are in recovery, you try to have them put things that are very difficult to deal with on the side, so they can stay sober long enough to have a healthier foundation and maybe then deal with other things in their lives.

"But, really, the bigger issues for her had to do with her deep depression. She was at Eagleville because she didn't want to use drugs anymore. But once she was off drugs and in the therapy, her depression was immense. I thought her depression was mostly situational. She felt real overwhelmed about her family situation, the modeling thing, that woman Wilhelmina dying—she had never really resolved that. But Gia's major discussions with me were about the relationship with the mom. I think she loved her father very much and felt connected to him and had a lot of issues with him. But she wasn't really dealing with him as much.

"I don't think she or Mom could separate each other out. They were sort of enmeshed and Gia was very unhappy with that, but also couldn't detach herself. I think the mom was really controlling of Gia. I don't know if the mother was purposely doing that, but I know that was Gia's perception. Gia felt real guilty about things, especially the things she did to please other people instead of herself. A lot of the modeling she did for other people. Getting sober, trying to get her life together, hiding this relationship with the girl in New Jersey, she did a lot of things to please her mom.

"And she would cry about her mom. Usually, when you're in therapy with somebody and they start crying, the therapist can hold it together. Gia's crying . . . was almost like it could click off other people's crying. It was a deep, sobbing-type cry. She would cry in group and the other women would cry. It was just this immense pain that would just sort of come out, and it would leave a lot of her peers feeling real helpless, like there was nothing you could do to take away all of this. It was like she had tons of bricks on her."

Besides the pains Gia had carried with her all her life, the situations she had just left in Atlantic City and Richboro seemed to loom larger with each passing day. No truce had been arranged in the war between Kathleen, Nancy and Rochelle when Gia went into rehab. In fact, it had escalated.

The fighting had begun again before Gia left Rochelle's to go back to Eagleville. A dispute over how much money was left in Gia and Rochelle's joint account led to accusations from Kathleen that Rochelle had robbed Gia. After Gia checked into Eagleville, she wasn't supposed to have phone contact with anyone. But she soon sneaked calls out to Kathleen and Rochelle anyway, subtly pushing and pulling on each of them.

Then Nancy Adams threw her own wrench into the works. She decided that she would move to Atlantic City and replace Gia as Rochelle's roommate. Gia assumed this meant that Nancy would also be replacing her as Rochelle's lover. Nancy denied it, but Gia became insanely jealous anyway. She convinced Kathleen, who didn't need much convincing, that Nancy was conspiring to destroy her life. "When Gia got into Eagleville, whatever she did, Nancy jumped in and picked up," Kathleen recalled. "It was sick."

Nancy was unable to make Gia or Kathleen listen to her version of what had happened. Nancy had been so pleased with the way Rochelle had done her nails during the Gia vigil that she had come back to the shore a week later for another manicure. This one took place at Salon Samuel, where Nancy ran into owner Sam Posner—who she knew from working at the Shore doing makeup several years earlier. Sam offered Nancy a job at the salon. Sharing a place with Rochelle was a convenient afterthought because, in fact, Nancy had started dating Sam. But Kathleen had strong opinions about him as well. "The *stories* I've heard about him," she said. "I know what he is. He's a lowlife of the earth who takes out girls and does things he's not supposed to do—takes pictures of them and shows them around. Nancy uses him and he uses her. It's sick. Yet I can't get my family to wake up and see that this is the world Nancy lives in."

It was almost as if Gia's therapists had four patients in one. "Gia had a very pressured kind of relationship with these three women who seemed to be the most important people in her life—her mother, her aunt, and her lover," recalled the former Eagleville therapist. "These were three very aggressive women trying to get Gia to do what they wanted. It was a lot of women fighting about her, all these people arguing over who's going to get Gia's affection. The mom was real afraid of the aunt's involvement with Gia. Gia's perception was that the mom was jealous of their relationship. They were apparently pretty tight.

"It didn't seem like they were fighting over Gia because she was a star or anything. I think it was because she was so much like a baby. She wasn't like an adult, she was like a child. She would deal with things in her life and take care of herself as best she could, but emotionally she was a little girl and I think that elicited from a lot of people this 'I want to take care of her' thing. It's inappropriate, given that this woman was an adult, she was addicted and she was killing herself—and all these people *knew* this."

The pain that Gia felt about Kathleen would eventually be mirrored by the Eagleville staff. "The mother called up a lot and wanted to know what was going on," one therapist recalled. "I didn't find it odd at all. I heard people complain about the mother, like she was really wild. I've worked with a lot of borderline people and a lot of women who are dysfunctional. To me, this mother and daughter were not that odd. The mother didn't stick out in my mind as a bizarre person. This is a woman who loved her daughter, who didn't quite know how to deal with what was going on. It's true of any family with an addicted member. Now, she's certainly a *very* pushy woman, and some people had a hard time with her. And Gia was completely the opposite—I could imagine Gia sitting there quietly and her mother pushing her around. The mother would question me—'Who are you? What do you want?' But if it was my daughter addicted and living on the street, I'd want to know, too.

"A lot of parents get like that. They panic. I wasn't angry or upset with the mother. I just thought she was panicking. When a parent has a child in treatment, they go through their own stuff—was it my fault, what did I do, was I a bad mother? Her mom couldn't deal with her *own* life. She had her own issues to deal with—her husband, her first husband, the sons, Gia, and whatever her own personality was.

"I mean, any woman who leaves her husband and her kids is going through *something*. I don't know how long that takes to deal with. The mother left, from what Gia reported to me, because of abuse from her dad. I doubt very much if her mother had been through therapy or anything like that, so it was probably hard for her in her own life. When her mother left, Gia never resolved any of those issues.

"Interestingly enough, we had in the chart about abuse between her and her father, from her reporting about being abused by her dad. She never talked about it. The way she talked about her relationship with her dad was that she stayed very masculine to get approval from him, and that was part of trying to keep a relationship with him after she matured. It wasn't anything that he wanted her to do, that came from her. She thought it was her way of being one of the family, which she saw as being all male figures. She said that her mother really wasn't that involved with her when she was growing up.

"On the women's unit, we did a lot of work on mothers. I think Gia's tears were about not having what she wanted from her mother, feeling abandoned by her mother. What we tried to talk about in group was, given that time in our society when her mother left, and she was being abused by the dad, women didn't really have very many options, there weren't very many services provided. What I tried to do with people is get them to understand the other person's position. But she was still 'Why did this happen *to me?*' I think Gia was caught in loving her mother and having a lot of hate for her mother for leaving her as a child. She was able to cognitively understand that her father would not have allowed her mother to take her and her brothers. I believe Gia did know that. But she was still stuck with that feeling, 'Why did you leave me there?' and more of the emotional stuff of being the only girl."

Sessions with family or friends were not a routine part of treatment at Eagleville, and there continued to be times when Gia's therapists forbade outside contact with anyone. But Gia always bent those rules. She sneaked a call to Rochelle and Nancy urging them to come visit on Easter Sunday, and then pretended she didn't know why they were at the front desk, confused that their names weren't on the visitors' list. (Nancy made things worse by offering to bribe one of the staff members to be taken to Gia's building.) For a period, Gia was even barred from contact with her mother. But later on, Kathleen began attending some therapy sessions with Gia on the hospital grounds.

"Everybody who dealt with us thought we were very tied together," Kathleen said. "One therapist used the way I let her serve me coffee one day as an example of the way we were tied together, constantly switching mother and daughter roles. I arrived early for an appointment and they asked if I wanted coffee. I said no. Then Gia comes in with this coffee and she hands it to me—and it's light. I drink my coffee black. But I sat there like an obedient child and drank it that way."

The therapy did not remain so benign for very long. Kathleen felt herself being analyzed and attacked, a process she never recalled agreeing to. "The therapy is really intense over there, they know how to get at you," Kathleen recalled. "You say it looks like it's going to rain out, it becomes a big issue. You don't even want to open your mouth because you know you're going to hang yourself.

"The intense sessions started to bring up all these things inside of me. *Everything,* all the reasons why I thought I needed help in my own life: things that had happened, the religion, my mother, my sisters. One night I started seeing all these little file cards popping up with all these sentences on them, things that I thought I had dealt with and buried and gotten rid of years ago and here they were. And somewhere inside of me, this voice says, 'Yo, Kathleen, if you don't cut this shit out, you're gonna be like Norman at the end of *Psycho* watching a fly on the wall, you're not gonna know who's who.' So I put a stop to it. My mother said, 'You don't have to do this.' I said, 'Thank you, Mother. Finally, after all these years of my married adult life you tell me something I can do.'

"By the time I went back over there, I became enraged. I went back there and said, 'I'm not the druggie, I'm not going to be ripped apart like this anymore.' I had sense enough to realize: you've buried this, don't let somebody rake it up and grind you through it again.

"I guess Gia really did expect too much from me. I always felt she was never going to be happy until she had me totally, one hundred percent for herself. She always created situations where I had to devote it all to her. But there were times when she took care of me and I took care of her. It switched back and forth. There were times when each of us tried to break away—there is a separation you should make from parents to become an adult—and the other always blocked them. She would tell me what to do, she gave me a reason to pull myself together. She would have a way of making me get mad and pull my act together if I felt I wasn't getting the credit I deserved ... she just kept me stirred.

"But the therapy was hard for me. She'd say, 'Mom, we really had a good session today,' and I'd say, 'Gia, what did you get out of this?'

"Our relationship has been compared to *Fatal Attraction,* too. But I had a different way of looking at it—it's probably the whole thing really. I just *wanted* her. When the boys were born, one of the first trips they had to the doctor for their regular checkups, he said to me, 'Kiss them good-bye now, eventually you'll lose them to another woman or to the service.' When Gia was born, she was to be the last child, the girl. She was the one I could put it all into because she was a girl, I wouldn't [be accused of making] a sissy out of her, or whatever. Maybe I held on to her too tightly so I was able to let go of the boys a little bit.

"And she might have been all right, but then, I don't know, maybe if I hadn't left her father, it could've worked out all right. I only know what went on in my mind. When I left, she held on to being that eleven-year-old girl emotionally. That's what came out at Eagleville, and she agreed with that. She was this eleven-year-old girl finally finding herself as a twenty-five-year-old. That's another reason why she didn't know if she truly wanted to be a lesbian. After she was done with all that soul searching and therapy she went through, added to the fact that she had been on drugs all that time, she didn't know."

On Memorial Day weekend, a lanky, tough-talking auto mechanic named Rob Fay stole a car from his job and went on a drive from which he didn't plan to return. He was twenty-five years old, addicted to free-base cocaine and alcohol, and his father, from whom he was estranged, had died three weeks earlier. "I said, 'Where's that big emotional outpouring like they have on TV?'" Rob Fay recalled. "I didn't have it, so I continued to party my brains out. I brought the car back, but there were cops all around so I ditched the car. I attempted suicide—put a belt around my neck, but I put it on too tight and passed out before I could hang myself. I woke up. I was, like, 'How low can you be?' Totally hopeless, totally alone, with nothing, and I decided, well, let me give it one more try—I went to turn myself in to the police.

"I went to the police station, told them who I was and they said no, they didn't have any warrants for me. Here I am, I just tried to kill myself, turned myself in and *even the cops won't take me*. It's raining, it's eleven at night. I slept outside under a bridge and went back. The cops *still* couldn't find any paperwork. When I was hitchhiking the night before, a guy had picked me up who worked at Eagleville and told me about it. So I went to Eagleville figuring, 'If they don't take me, I can kill myself and it'll be justified.'"

Rob Fay was quickly detoxed at Eagleville and entered the thirty-day inpatient program. He met Gia, who had already been there for over four months, on the hospital's bucolic grounds. "She was different from the other people I met there," he recalled, "she didn't take any shit off nobody. If they were wrong, she had no problem standing up for what she believed in.

"We had a love of Bowie in common. She had a lot of pictures of him and Angela—some pictures her friends took on that movie set. I mean, we both were freaked out over him. I always liked him because he was different and he had the balls to be different. David Bowie had this song, 'All the Young Dudes.' We used to talk about this song because we were both the same age and I had tried to commit suicide when I was twenty-five and he talks about 'kicking it in the head when you're twenty-five.' I didn't think I'd live past twenty-five. And she was convinced that there was no way you could maintain this type of lifestyle and be twenty-six.

"She told me right away that she was gay. She was fighting that, she said, 'I am, but' ... she had a rough time with a lot of men in her life. There were times in New York when people just took advantage of her. I guess you wouldn't really call it rape because she wasn't screaming, but there were a lot of times when that happened when she didn't want it to happen. But being as high as she was, you can't argue, you don't even know what planet you're on. Something like that happens, it's just, 'Oh, well, it's part of the scene.' She had been raped a few times. Date rape, or whatever you want to call it. She had a lot of anger about that.

"A lot of things made her angry, she was an angry person. She stuffed a lot of things down. Nobody took her seriously for a long time, because she was Gia—*Gia*, like a china doll or something to a lot of people. Even at Eagleville, Gia was this fragile little thing. I said bullshit on this—that's the thing they *created* for her, this little world where Gia was mommy's girl."

When Rob met Gia, Kathleen wasn't allowed to visit—mother and daughter only saw each other during therapy. During one session, Kathleen brought Gia a kite. It was bright yellow—Gia's favorite color—and shaped like a butterfly. The therapist told Gia afterwards that she should give some thought to the life cycle of the butterfly.

"I remember one time we were flying kites," recalled Rob Fay, "and her kite was a yellow butterfly. I said, 'I really like your kite.' And she said, 'Oh yeah?' and just took the string and let it go. I'm like, 'What are you doing?' She said, 'I was just thinking about my mom. This is what I have to do with her. I gotta let her go.'

"She and I got in trouble at Eagleville. Before I even knew she had been a model, I always thought she was beautiful. I was playing tennis with her and she just looked real . . . I don't know, *European* to me one day. And I turned to a friend of mine, who happened to be in my group, and I said, 'Isn't she beautiful, she looks like she's chiseled from stone or something.' And he looked at me and he brought it to my therapist, who immediately declared us in love and fucking. They even restricted us from each other at one point. Everybody thinks everybody else is trying to fall in love, but it wasn't really like that. I got accused of it, in group. But Gia, to me, was like a buddy, a sister or something. She was just real special. All these accusations just infuriated me and made me work against the place. I think it stifled my openness, you know? Gia was just as pissed. She thought it was ridiculous. I mean, for one, she was gay and that was like, well, that's as far as it was going to go. One of the things that attracted me to her was that she was gay and I knew I didn't have to put out or nothing.

"I mean, they tell you, 'Don't have any relationships,' which means 'Don't get laid.' And, you know, the AIDS scare was there and all of that. For the first time in my life, I was doing something right, doing what I was told to do. Hanging around with gay women seemed like a good solution. And I still got shit for it."

Gia and Rob became friendly with one other Eagleville patient. Cheryl Paczkoski had grown up in Philadelphia's working-class Fairmount section and, in her late teens, got heavily involved with coke and methamphetamines—the so-called "poor man's cocaine," which was considered a regional specialty because so much was produced in labs in Bucks County. Gia, Rob and Cheryl thought of themselves as The Three Musketeers.

"People in Eagleville really gave Gia a hard time," Cheryl recalled. "For one thing, they could never believe the amount of drugs she had consumed. They would say she couldn't have shot that much. But Gia didn't have any reason to lie. Her life was too exciting to have to lie. A lot of people were against her. They felt she was so closed. And she would always get calls from friends and her mother after she was told not to. They used to drill her, scream and yell at her. They were hard on her. They always felt she didn't open up, said she was lying. They were harder on her than anybody else. I guess that was to help her grow.

"They would accuse her of using. One time I remember they had her tested because her face looked all puffy. Here it was, she had been up the night before crying. Her roommate had told me she was crying.

"I remember, she did a skit about wanting to break up with this woman—you had to do these skits about stuff in your life. She wanted to break up with the woman in the skit. She wanted to end it, and when she felt that, she would go into the bathroom and get high. She went off to the side and set up everything and tied off and got high and then went back and she was all happy and high. At the end of the skit, patients could get up and give you feedback on it. You couldn't talk back. You had to give them your attention."

The skit was part of a web of exercises that included written biofeedbacks, frustrations being punched out on the plastic "anger mats," drawings and the creation of a "lifeline" to pinpoint which events led to others. She was told to create a physical representation of the specific issues in her life, a self-portrait of constructive criticism. She drew a large mural depicting herself carrying a cross, her body floating somewhere between the earth and the sun. Although she was a good enough artist to do a fairly realistic, detailed rendering of human faces and forms, she chose more abstract imagery—just an outline of a body, with features more symbolic than literal.

Her face had one weeping eye, a Bowie-esque lightning bolt, a question mark and stitches on her skull. In her chest was a broken heart, black lungs and a small black swastika. On her arms were needle marks. On her genital area were male and female stick figures. On the drawing she listed the themes that her therapy sought to address: "Confusion, Hate, Separation, Frust[r]ation, Growing Pains, Sexual Abuse, Mental Abuse, Helplessness, Love."

There were also "tasks" that could be given by therapists to make certain points. Because Gia so actively downplayed her beauty and was so aggressively nonfeminine, she was once given a task of putting on makeup and doing her hair. It was an exercise that her counselors thought might drive home the point that even though Gia was an untraditional woman, she was still a woman—a concept she didn't always seem to grasp.

The grand finale of these exercises was called the "self-disclosure," a presentation that often lasted a half hour, put on in the small auditorium for the entire Candidates Program. Dawn Phillips, one of the few openly gay women in the program, was outraged by the reaction after Gia's self-disclosure.

"I remember her talking, you had to speak into a microphone and she did it," Dawn recalled. "She was more confident than I would have been. She didn't stutter the whole time. At the end of these exercises, patients could get up and give you feedback on it. And you couldn't talk back—you had to give them your attention. *Every single person* mentioned her being gay, that being gay was her basic problem. They didn't think she was as okay with it as she claimed to be. Or, well, they tried to make her not okay with it—that's how I felt. And I think it was because of her looks—the fact that she was a model and the way she looked, that she didn't look like the stereotype of a lesbian.

"I was getting so outraged I was about to get up and yell. I wanted to attack everyone in there, but I was too frightened to do that. Finally, Gia had to leave to go to work. That night, she came into the kitchen and I was sitting there. I just started talking to her and told her how I felt. I thought what they had done to her in there stunk, she didn't deserve it, and I didn't see her gayness as being the issue. She was elated that somebody was saying this to her, could understand her. It was like a shock to her."

After the first three months of the Candidates Program, patients had to get jobs off-grounds, although they still lived at the hospital. They could also get passes to socialize, but they had to make out a pass plan of who they would see and what they would do. Therapists could veto plans to socialize with suspected enablers, and patients were routinely discharged from Eagleville for not following their pass plans.

Gia was never caught, but she was beginning to sneak visits with Rochelle. "She'd get a pass to come out, she'd go to the mall and I'd pick her up," recalled Rochelle. "She wasn't using when she was in there. She was straight, she was being good.

"She had been sneaking phone calls to me all along. She would write me letters from Eagleville saying she didn't want to see me anymore, and then she would call me and say, 'Don't take those letters seriously, they made me write them.' Gia was upset that Nancy was living with me. When Gia would call me, sometimes I would tell her to listen to that song 'Don't You Forget About Me.' [The song, by Simple Minds, had been popularized in the recent hit, teen-angst movie *The Breakfast Club*.] I was worried that after her treatment she would not come back to me. I thought she would disregard me because she was being programmed to forget people, places and things in her past. I just kept saying, 'Listen to this song.' "

In September, Gia completed the inpatient part of her program at Eagleville, a milestone which only thirty percent of the Candidates actually reached before being discharged prematurely or simply dropping out. In the third phase of the program, patients took apartments off-grounds—often with recent Eagleville patients—and got full-time jobs in the community. They returned to Eagleville at least once a week for counseling, although many continued to come to the hospital every night for twelve-step meetings. Others went to the various meetings held in the Norristown area. Economically depressed since the ebb of its manufacturing sector in the seventies but still the Montgomery County seat, Norristown had developed a significant population of recovering people. There was, at any given time, a small group trying desperately to stay clean, another group that had been clean long enough to be counseling others, and a much larger third group of former Eagleville people who had returned to their addictions and found themselves geographically trapped in this hard-luck urbanized suburb.

Although her mother begged her to move home, Gia followed her therapists' advice and moved in with recovering people in Norristown. She shared a fairly depressing apartment—on an unpaved alley just off Norristown's main street—with two other recovering women from Eagleville, one of whom had lost an arm to an abscess.

Now that she was out in the real world, there were things that had to be taken care of. Gia pulled out the blank-page book that she had received during her first weeks at Wilhelmina—the one in which she once had pasted the Polaroids from her first major sittings—and turned it upside down. Starting from what was the back, she drew a little cat and then made a list: to call the dentist, to go by the welfare office and to check on her insurance. Then she started combing the want ads for jobs. On the other side of the book were the scribbled phone numbers of the contacts she made during her first trip to Europe, addresses for Paris hotels and "The Prince," notes to herself—"while in Paris if Christian Dior is shooting . . . while in Rome call Riccardo Gay." But, as she was growing accustomed to saying, "that was before." So she wrote: "counter & warehouse, $5.25/hr . . . Philly Steaks, apply in person . . . office cleaners, $4/hr . . . cook deli & dessert, $4.50/hr."

Through Eagleville networking, she finally got a job, at just above minimum wage, as a sales clerk at Designs—a store that sold Levi Strauss products in the new wing of the King of Prussia Mall. She also had tried to start dating men, although she wasn't supposed to get involved, on orders from her counselors. Sascha Brodelin—a Rasputinesque, Russian-born fashion photographer she had been friendly with since her early days in New York, but whose career had never taken off like hers—was coming down to take her on dates. But privately, she was still holding on to a crush she had developed on her role model at Eagleville. "Here you are, not supposed to be attracted to anybody," recalled Dawn Phillips, "and here's Gia, real blatant about the whole thing. This counselor was getting roses and poems via this anonymous person. I think it started while Gia was still inpatient, the poems at least."

The counselor tried to downplay Gia's gestures without alienating her. "Gia mistook caring as sexual," recalled the counselor. "That was pretty much how she looked at relationships. She needed people and in the process would push people away, by needing them so much that she put an expectation on them that they couldn't meet."

The people Gia knew from Eagleville were aware of her past and her recent recovery. In a small therapeutic community, gossip and even tidbits from confidential group sessions traveled fast. The people she worked with at Designs were the first on whom she could try out the "new Gia," the result of seven months of sobriety and intense therapy.

"I have to say, she acted like everything you ever hear about someone affected by drugs," recalled Stephan Sammartino, who was also a salesman at Designs and, because it was on his way, would often drive Gia to work. "She talked very slow, like she had to think about what she was saying. She talked like an elderly person or like she was wasted, but she wasn't. She was very funny, but like an older person would be. She'd talk loud, get carried away telling stories until all the customers were listening in. She would just tell us this off-the-wall stuff, totally out of the blue.

"She was a little self-conscious about having been at Eagleville, but she always joked around about all the things she wasn't allowed to do. Supposedly, she wasn't permitted to have a relationship with anyone. She would always jokingly complain about not being allowed to go on a date. Then it was, 'Oh, I went on a date and we kissed and that's all I was allowed to do.' This went on and on. So one day we were standing around—supposedly watching the dressing rooms—and we started telling stories.

"Gia said, 'I went on a date last night and something happened.' So we all gather around, and she starts out talking real low. 'So, we went here,' she led us to believe that this was a guy—she always referred to her boyfriend—'and we didn't want to do anything, I didn't want to have sex with him. So, we went out for ice cream, I got rum raisin, and brought it back to the house ...' And she said she put it between her legs or whatever, and he ate it. She put in more details, and her voice was getting louder. And then the best part was, she said, 'But those *raisins* were something else!' Just the way she said it, it was so great. We would always joke about rum raisin after that."

Gia talked a lot about her mother and emphasized how important the split-up of her family had been. It was as if the fourteen-year-old trauma were still a fresh, open wound, or perhaps a bone that had broken long ago and had never been set properly—requiring a painful rebreaking and reset-ting to be made right. She said she still wanted to get her family back together. "If her mother was coming to visit," Sammartino recalled, "she'd tell me, 'My mom's coming, but the guy she's with, it's not my dad. He's nice, but he's not my dad.' The first time her mom came, I remember, she came striding in and, well, you get customers in the store, the minute they walk in it's like 'Here we go,' your eye goes right to them. We were just about to start on her and Gia said, 'That's my mom, don't say anything.'

"Her mother was very, like, sturdy, husky, like a real strong nun. You wouldn't want to play with her. And she'd come in and walk right to the back of the store to the man-ager: 'I'm Gia's mother, Mrs. So-and-so, and can she go to lunch right now, we're going to go.' She wouldn't go to Gia and ask if she could go on break. She went right to the back. The mother wasn't rude, and she seemed affectionate with Gia. She'd give her a big kiss and hold her hand as they walked through the mall. Gia would go like a little kid with her head down."

Although she acted dopey and slow at times, glimpses of the old, mischievous Gia were beginning to emerge.

"When Gia was around, we always had some running joke," recalled Sammartino. "I remember there was this ad on TV—'Gee, your hair smells good.' Every time we saw her, we'd say, 'Gia, your hair smells good,' and she'd finally stop waiting on the customer and start talking to us.

"Every now and then we would talk about drugs. We were all fairly young and we were interested, like, what did you do that made you have to go to Eagleville? She would tell about how she did all these drugs, that she'd shoot up. Everything you could imagine to take, she would take. She said that's why she was blackballed from modeling. She said she had been a model. She said she used to be rich. I can't remember if I believed her or not. She said she was a model. She never said she was a big famous model. We figured, oh, like some rinky-dink place. When she first said it, she said, 'Oh yeah, you'd be surprised. I've gained a little weight, but I used to be like this and really beautiful.' Her hair was really short, and she said she looked better with makeup, but she didn't like doing that, it wasn't *her*. The other girls in the store would say, 'She is pretty, very *plain* but pretty.' She said she would bring in the pictures but she never did."

17

Beyond Your
Wildest Dreams

Rob Fay went into the last phase of the Candidates Program several weeks after Gia did. They would meet up at the nightly meeting at St. Paul's church in Norristown—an "open" meeting that encouraged newcomers and, like Eagleville itself, tended to put all addicted people together rather than separating by substances.

Sometimes they hung out together during the day. "It seemed like she was really enjoying sobriety," Fay recalled. "We would go places and that girl taught me how to enjoy *everything*. I mean, a bee coming at you, she would enjoy it. She had this sense of how important things are: snowin' out, rainin' out, leaves, stuff like that. The sound of traffic. Things like that, things I was just beginning to notice because I could see and hear again. I just thought, wow, this girl's pretty cool to hang with. Look at the shit she's teaching me, stuff that I should've learned when I was a kid. She was appreciating it again. It was a new beginning.

"Jesus, I never had that much fun before or since. She was just nuts. We went into a department store one time, and they got those little courtesy desks there with the manager standing behind. I'm just walking in, and she says, 'Keep your hands in your pockets, I'm not bailing you out again for shoplifting.' So I played right into it, I said, 'I'll be in the ladies' lingerie department,' and then we would just bust out laughing.

"We talked about making movies together. We'd see something in real life, like an old couple driving with the wife sittin' real close to the husband—I mean, like, seventy years old or something. That kinda stuff really hit her. She said, 'I could really use that, that would be nice on film.'

"We were having an amazing time. They have a saying in the recovery program: 'Beyond your wildest dreams.' That's really what it was."

When Gia spoke about the future, she seemed most interested in children. She didn't talk about getting married and being a mother so much as she dreamed about having children around.

"She *loved* kids," Fay said. "She'd see kids in the malls and she'd go over to them. She didn't give a shit what the parents thought. Kids would come over to her, too. This cute adorable kid comes walking right over to Gia—the mother's saying, 'She's never done this before with anyone.'

"She wanted to have a kid. Kids could make her laugh. Little kids in the neighborhood would be yellin' and screamin' and you or I would say, 'God*damn* I wish them kids would shut up.' She'd say, 'Listen to that, let's go out and talk to those kids.' And she would. She used to talk about how they got all their life ahead of them ..."

Easing patients out of the Eagleville nest was one of the most harrowing parts of the rehab process. No matter how long a patient had been sober and working hard in therapy, a huge percentage returned to substance abuse in a very short amount of time—sometimes the same *day* they left. The patients who went on to get their lives together and keep their addictive behavior checked were often the ones who went out on a bender just after release and scared themselves. They either scared themselves to death, or scared themselves straight. The difference was often the purity of the drugs or pure luck.

"I remember when they threw me out of the outpatient part of the program," said Rob Fay, "as I was leaving, they said, 'You'll be high in a week, and dead in a month.' I remember those guys standing in a circle telling me that.

Today, two of them are alive. One is sober, but he's only been sober for four weeks. Four of them are dead. Two killed themselves, and two others were drug-related situations."

The fear of returning to the life of an addict hovered over every decision. The rarely subtle advice of the counselors—who Gia saw during the day as a client, and in the evening at meetings as a peer in sobriety—was meant to reverberate in the brain at moments of weakness. One of the things Gia's therapists had agreed upon was that she should not move back in with her mother. But what they didn't tell her was how difficult it would be to live in Norristown, with recovering people, users and dealers everywhere, and the Eagleville gossip network crowded with stories of inpatient breakthroughs and outpatient tragedies.

Inside Eagleville, everyone was pushing for you to get better. Outside, many people seemed to be taking bets on when you would fall off the wagon. The people who were your best friends inside—because they had nothing else to do but support you—now had better things to do with their time. Norristown was comforting because you could see just how many other people were in your same predicament, but it was frightening to see just how poorly some of those peers were faring.

In November of 1985, against the wishes of her counselors and friends, Gia moved back in with her mother in Richboro. "When she moved back to her mom's, I told her she would start using again," recalled Rob Fay. "I told her it's the worst thing you can do."

"Hello Book," Gia wrote in her journal, "It is now Nov. 16. I am at my Mom's again and feeling fuck-up. You see a quite odd thing happen . . . I fell in love with my counselor and I think she just feels sorry for me I hate anyone to pity me it so degrading. Well, I won't be talking to her, it's hopeless and I must move on I've been stuck for to long. I have a girl Rochelle who loves me and I her I am just not ready for tieing up. Girls have always been a problem for me I really don't know why I bother with them."

Gia quit her job at the mall—one day she just didn't show up for work, and was never heard from again—and tried to concentrate on moving forward. She contacted Elite and

Scavullo's studio to let them know she was alive, out of rehab, drug-free and thinking about doing some modeling in the coming year. She even called Lizzette Kattan, who had married well in 1983, left *Bazaar* and the business to start a family, and was living in Milan.

The modeling business might very well have been happy to have Gia back, if she were ready to work and back in shape. Most of the models she broke in with had either disappeared or risen to the newly created status of "supermodel." This was achieved by combining traditional fashion magazine and advertising work with *Sports Illustrated* swimsuit issue appearances and relationships with rock stars, athletes or other "real" celebrities. This path could lead to attention from newer media outlets with lowered, or at least *different* standards of celebrity. *USA Today* was the new national newspaper with an inexhaustible appetite for fame and near-fame. Music video now had its first twenty-four-hour cable network, MTV, and its first prime-time program, *Miami Vice*. And there were new daytime and late night talk shows where models were suddenly considered worth talking to.

Even with this new attention available, many of the top models didn't seem that interested in modeling anymore. Kelly Emberg had all but given up her career to cohabit with singer Rod Stewart, Iman had followed husband Spencer Haywood to Italy when his NBA career ended, Patti Hansen had been in a few bad movies before marrying Keith Richards and becoming a full-time mom, Christie Brinkley was beginning her very public romance with Billy Joel, as was Carol Alt with hockey star Ron Greschner. Since 1980, Cheryl Tiegs had been designing women's sportswear for Sears.

The cresting model of the moment was twenty-year-old Paulina Porizkova, who had been an Elite model since her mid-teens: her pictures began appearing in places like French *Elle* as early as 1980. Paulina had combined her years of print work in clothes and cosmetics, consecutive *SI* covers in 1984 and 1985, and an appearance in a music video for the Cars (whose lead singer, Rick Ocasek, became her boyfriend) into a formidable visual résumé. Then she began making talk show appearances and proclaiming, in heavily accented English, that modeling was boring and she hated it but she was making a lot of money. The complaining only increased her celebrity status. It was impossible for even a top girl to convince a model-mad America that it was fascinated by a wonderful world of modeling that didn't really exist.

Paulina was showing the same healthy disrespect for the industry that Gia had been famous for. The difference was that Paulina always showed up for her jobs. So her attitude did not prevent her from winning a contract with Estée Lauder.

As the modeling industry expanded—Elite had now copied Ford by sponsoring its own international competition with a guaranteed contract as first prize—it needed as many of its elder statesgirls in place as possible. The agencies needed Christie Brinkley to attract the next crop of girls who wanted to *be* Christie Brinkley. Even though modeling had been through many changes in the past five years, there were still only ten or fifteen girls since the mid-seventies who had ever made it to Gia's level. It was what they *did* with that recognizable beauty after modeling that made a difference. Many of those who worked with her thought Gia would make the transition from supermodel to actress far better than most—because she had such a strong personality and was as stunning in motion as frozen on film. She certainly seemed as likely a prospect as another former Philadelphian, Veronica Hamel, who was finishing up a long successful run on *Hill Street Blues,* or Andie MacDowell, whose voice was dubbed over (by actress Glenn Close) in an attempt to save her appearance as Jane in the Tarzan movie *Greystoke.*

Gia spoke with her lawyer, who had come to visit her at Eagleville, to try to get some of her legal matters taken care of. Besides modeling, she looked into a writing course at the community college and a photography course in Philadelphia. Just before Christmas, she even went to Atlantic City to see Rochelle. Both were working hard to be on their best behavior. "We were together for that Christmas," recalled Rochelle, "and she wouldn't even drink the egg nog. She was completely straight. She said, 'I don't want to do it. I don't want to die.' "

"Right after Christmas, Gia came into my room one night," recalled Kathleen. "She said, 'Mommy'—she was still calling me Mommy, even though they tried to get her to stop at Eagleville—'Mommy, look at my ear.' I looked into her ear and it looked like big flakes. It looked like the stuff on her feet. All the time she was in rehab, she had some problem with her toes, like a rot. I mixed up a solution and flushed out her ear and the stuff that came out was unbelievable. Her skin was also bad. Her skin had always been very clear and translucent. She had never worn makeup before going to New York, and her skin had reacted badly to all the makeup then, but it had cleared up after she stopped modeling. But now she had what looked like teenage acne. She also started saying she just didn't feel right."

AIDS was just beginning to seep into the mass-market consciousness, after years of being whispered about. Actor Rock Hudson's public admission during the previous summer that he had contracted the disease—and had traveled to France for treatments unavailable in America—was followed by his highly publicized death on October 2, 1985. The chain of events finally gave the general media an excuse to cover what was still being referred to as "the gay plague."

In the fashion business, all eyes were on Perry Ellis, whose thirty-seven-year-old lover, Laughlin Barker—also the president of Ellis's company—was dying of AIDS. Ellis, so much the image of the robust American man that he was often the best model for his own clothes, was, himself, looking ill. Rumors began circulating after Ellis fell against Bill Blass in the receiving line at a December party at the Metropolitan Museum, and the incident was reported in *The New York Times*. When he appeared in January at the Council of Fashion Designers Awards—just after Barker's death—the widely circulated paparazzi photographs told the story that no one in the industry dared to publicly utter. Ellis, too, was wasting away from AIDS.

The fashion industry had been quietly noting for a year or two that a lot of the young, partying kids they counted upon for influxes of raw energy were disappearing with greater regularity. Nightlife burnout was common and drug use was taking its victims, but this was something else. These people were "going away" and never coming back. Fate had chosen Perry Ellis to be the fashion industry's first poster child for the AIDS epidemic. He would deny the rumors. Rock Hudson's death had done little to ease public acceptance of AIDS or homosexuality. And in the image-conscious fashion industry, homosexuality, once a hallmark of a higher fashion sense, was now associated with the plague. Makeup artists and hairdressers, who had once regaled models in the mornings with stories of sexual exploits, now found it prudent to announce their monogamy, or even celibacy. The rumor mills added "Did you hear who's sick?" to the list of standard questions to be addressed, just as they had added "Did you hear who's gone away?" when rehab visits began in the late seventies.

Gia clipped whatever articles she could find in the newspapers and magazines about AIDS. She was convinced that there was something wrong with her. She had never been tested for exposure to the AIDS virus. Eagleville did frequent in-service presentations for staff about precautions in taking urine and blood samples. Everyone in the rehab community knew that intravenous drug users were a high-risk group, both because of shared needles and sexual habits. Drug rehabbers had been one of the first medical groups to decide it was safer to assume that every patient *had* been exposed than find out test results too late.

Besides, new patients were not routinely given AIDS tests anyway. The tests still gave too many false positives, and Eagleville wouldn't refuse treatment even if exposure to the HTLV-III virus could be proved. If patients had symptoms of AIDS-related disease, they were put in the hospital like anyone else with medical problems. If they were asymptomatic, it was considered almost better that they didn't know. It was hard enough to convince a recovering person to give life a second chance when they actually had a second chance.

Gia began having her suspicions throughout the winter and spring that she might have AIDS, but she did not display any other symptoms. She wasn't quite ready to go back to New York and try modeling again, so she worked several different local jobs: first as a checkout clerk at the Acme, and later in the cafeteria of a nursing home.

At some point during the winter, Gia began using drugs again. She called her counselor from Eagleville, with whom she was still doing a weekly group session, and informed her that she wouldn't be coming anymore. Before each group session, patients had to give a urine sample. Gia knew that hers would be "hot." She was discharged and her Eagleville case closed out. Although it was not commonly done—or recommended, for various security reasons—the counselor gave Gia her home phone number so they could keep up an informal contact.

Although she was living with her mother in Richboro, Gia started occasionally sneaking out to visit Rochelle in Atlantic City. "When she first came back from Eagleville," recalled Rochelle, "I stopped using drugs completely so there would be nothing in the house for her to get into. But I had to work from noon till ten at night some nights and I had to leave her alone. I came home for dinner one day and there's a guy in my living room and there's a pile of coke on the glass table. I walked in and Gia's saying, 'I didn't do any, I didn't do any.' I said, 'You, shut up, you, get your stuff and get out.' I was threatening her. I told her, 'If it happens again I'll call your mother,' and she freaked, she said, 'No, no don't call my mother.' Two weeks later I came home, made dinner and she's eating and I saw a bruise on her arm. I said, 'What is *this?*' She said, 'I tried it, and now I know I don't like it anymore. I hate it.' And I sincerely thought that she meant it. But after that, she was obviously doing drugs again and she got worse and worse.

"This is how I figured out what she's doing. I look in her books—with all her checks and withdrawals—and I see she has *receipts from the turnpike*. She had written checks to get through the tolls and then she spent every dime she had on dope in New York. The receipts showed that she was up and back in a matter of hours. Writing bad checks for the tolls—she had balls, I'll tell you. Who the hell would even *think* of writing a check for the tolls on the turnpike?"

During the winter and spring, Gia would sometimes drive to the Shore during the day, use her extra key to get into

Rochelle's apartment, take something to pawn, get high, and go back to Richboro without coming by the salon to let Rochelle or Nancy know she was in town. Rochelle thought she was losing her mind. Things were just disappearing from her place, a mysterious glass with melted ice cubes in it would be sitting on the table when she returned from work. But then Nancy spotted Gia walking into the apartment building with a glazed gaze and a druggy-looking guy during an afternoon she was supposed to be in Richboro.

"I went back to the salon and called my sister," Nancy recalled. "I told her I had just seen Gia on the street down here and she looked like she was on drugs. Kathleen started freaking out on me. She said I was a fucking liar, and Gia was home and doing really good, and all I ever did was make up stories about Gia. I said, 'I'm not trying to bad-mouth Gia, she's in trouble again.' She hung up on me."

"The next time I saw her, I said, 'Gia, what happened to the cassette player?'" Rochelle recalled. "And she wouldn't lie to you. She wore her hair on her face and she'd sorta look up through her bangs at ya. And I said, 'Did you sell the cassette player?' And she said yeah. And I said, 'How am I supposed to listen to my music?' And she said, 'Well, you still got the turntable.' You just couldn't stay mad at her, because she was like a bad little child. This went on until she had gotten really bad and sold jewelry of mine. It wasn't the value of the jewelry so much as it was that my grandmother had given it to me. At that point I threw her out and told her to go back to her mother, which was, of course, the worst thing you could say to her."

Gia did what she was told and went back to Richboro. She was, by then, convinced she had AIDS. She tried to tell her mother that she was ill, but Kathleen didn't believe her. "On Memorial Day, she came to me and said, 'Mommy, I really have something wrong with me,'" Kathleen recalled. "You could tell she was disturbed. And it still bothers me that I just went ahead about my business. I was working at Spiegel then, and I just went to work. But that's what you would have done—she didn't seem any different. So I went to work, she and Henry had dinner together and she headed to the Shore."

Gia went first to her brother Michael's place, to get all her things together. Then she pawned everything she could get her hands on. She also sold her car, for a bargain $1,700. Her mother had always held the title to the Fiat because it was registered at her Richboro home for tax purposes. Through all the years of Gia's addiction, Kathleen had always refused to transfer the title, but she had recently relented and signed the car over. With the money—well over $2,000—Gia bought all the heroin she could afford and checked into one of the cheap hotels she and Rochelle would go to when they were living with Joe Carangi and needed a few days by themselves. Gia did her best to overdose on heroin, but was unsuccessful. When she regained consciousness, she went out to a restaurant, but found that she couldn't bear to eat any of the food she ordered. She fed the food to a dog she saw outside the hotel, stayed in the room for a couple days, and finally sneaked into Rochelle's apartment.

Rochelle hadn't heard from Gia for about a week. "I came home from work and went in the apartment," she recalled. "I had my friend Steven staying with me and I laid down and I heard breathing. I told him, 'There's somebody in this room.' He's a cute little gay guy: he put his hand on his hip and said, 'There's nobody in here.' Then I heard a cough. I looked, and Gia was under the bed. She crawled out and I said, 'What are you doing here?' She said, 'I'm sleeping and didn't have anywhere to go. I'm sick, I don't feel good, I don't have anywhere to go.'

"I cleaned her up with a washcloth. At that time she said, 'Chelle, I think I have AIDS.' She didn't look good, but AIDS wasn't really around yet. And Gia *always* had dark circles under her eyes. And her weight always shifted, too. When she was on methadone it was up, on heroin she ate a lot of sweets. She just looked like she had been on a drug binge. And I thought she was telling me she had AIDS as one of her things to make me feel sorry for her.

"So I got her cleaned up, and I kept saying, 'You can't stay here,' you know, and then finally I said she could spend the night. I still didn't know if she was lying about the AIDS or not. We went to bed. In the morning, she said she was going to get something for breakfast. I asked if she needed money, she said, 'No, stay there.' What I didn't know was that she had already taken all my tip money from my jeans and she went off to buy drugs. So I sat in the living room and waited for her. I was *so pissed*.

"She came back about two in the afternoon, when she thought it was safe and I was at work. She still had her key, she thought she was just going to hang out at the house. And she walked in and I was fighting her to get into her pockets to find the dope. We were just pushing and shoving and all that. We threw each other around. And she was trying to run out the door and I grabbed the shirt off of her, so she wouldn't run out. I pulled it off her, and she ran out the door like that. I called the police on her. I wanted her brought home.

"The next thing I heard she was in the hospital in Philadelphia and she had pneumonia."

They were not thrilled to have Gia Carangi as a patient at Warminster General Hospital, nestled back off the redundantly named Street Road in Philadelphia's northern suburbs. Even at inner-city hospitals, where staff was accustomed to hard-luck cases using emergency room doctors as primary care physicians, the junkies were considered the scum of the earth. At a suburban hospital, the concept of treating a beaten-up IV drug user who looked like Street Road's first street person, and a *woman* yet, was a little difficult to grasp. Especially since the girl was registering as a welfare recipient, but was accompanied by a mother who appeared to be at least middle class—and who was acting nearly as touchy as the staff was feeling about this odd case.

"They did everything they could to avoid admitting her to that hospital," Kathleen recalled. "I had to beg them."

Kathleen explained that her daughter's symptoms included weakness, extreme shortness of breath and fever—and a history of long-term IV drug use. But she told the doctors she believed it was primarily depression that Gia was suffering from. She was having crying spells that wouldn't stop. The doctors ran a series of tests, the results of which suggested that depression was the *least* of Gia's problems. She had bilateral pneumonia, bone marrow depression with anemia from drug-related toxicity and extremely low blood cell counts. The doctors thought they had better rule out AIDS.

The hospital staff was extremely paranoid about the AIDS virus. It was June of 1986. AIDS news was in the papers every day, Perry Ellis had just died very publicly from the disease on May 30, and the Second International Conference on AIDS had just concluded in Paris. But in the trenches, hospital workers were still getting sketchy information on the disease and weren't sure whether to trust what they were getting. In inner-city hospitals, where the first AIDS cases had been concentrated, there was already a routine to the panic, a sense of fear and experience. Warminster General Hospital had treated, at most, a half dozen AIDS patients. Each one caused a certain sector of the staff to don rubber gloves for the simplest of procedures—like taking a temperature—and full body suits for anything more complicated.

When AIDS was suspected, Gia was immediately rushed into an isolation ward. A doctor trying to explain fear as caution might insist that she was isolated to keep her from picking up any additional infections from other patients in her immune-depleted condition. But according to her charts, she was released from isolation only after it was determined that she probably had AIDS-related complex "and not communicable AIDS disease." Even in June of 1986, it was clear to the medical profession that AIDS was not the type of communicable disease that required patients to be isolated in order to prevent an epidemic. But nurses and doctors on duty at hospitals don't always believe what the medical journals insist they should.

"I'm not sure if they didn't trust what the literature was saying or just had never worked with somebody with AIDS," recalled Patrick Kenney, who was psychiatric nurse at Warminster at the time and, as the staff's only openly gay member, had taken on the added responsibility of being the hospital's AIDS expert. "Some of the medical staff wanted nothing to do with Gia. They were petrified of her. There was a staff problem with the moral issues of how she got AIDS. The majority of staff responded well to the teaching I was doing, but a few were irrational. They were going in in space suits just to check on her—gloves and gowns to take her temperature. But it wasn't just her. There was a physician who had AIDS here. They wore gowns to take his temperature, too. I tried to explain to them why this was *not okay,* what is the message you're sending? But then, most patients tend to be accepting of whatever the staff says."

Kathleen was not accepting of what the staff said—echoing outrage that Gia was too weak to voice—and was quickly branded "difficult" by many responsible for Gia's day-to-day care. After observing what they considered to be the unusual relationship between mother and daughter, they began referring to Kathleen as "that bitch."

After eight days in the medical unit—her AIDS having been determined to be the noncommunicable kind, her pneumonia successfully treated with erythromycin—Gia was transferred to the psychiatric unit. She was diagnosed as having a schizoaffective disorder with some psychotic features and significant depression. She had talked about thoughts of buying a gun and committing suicide. She was having hallucinations and feeling paranoid.

When her crying began to abate and she was speaking coherently, she pieced together what had just happened to her. After her fistfight with Rochelle, Gia had run topless out into the street. A construction worker had given her his windbreaker to cover up, and she proceeded to wander aimlessly into one of the neighborhoods where she bought drugs. It started to rain, and she lay down on a mattress next to a Dumpster and fell asleep. Then something violent happened to her. She told one friend she was raped by a man who found her there. She told a nurse in the psych unit that she was turning a trick and the guy had beaten her up. She told her mother that all the bruises were from her fight with Rochelle.

"I still do not believe that Gia was raped then," said Kathleen. "Gia eventually told me *everything,* or gave me enough information to put everything together. Nothing she ever said leads me to believe she was raped. She told me one time in a fit of anger, 'Well, I've been raped twice, but don't even think twice about it because I dealt with it in group.' And I don't know whether to believe that or not.

"But Gia knew I have very strong feelings about rape. I always said I would rather be dead than have to live with that for the rest of my life. I can't imagine anything worse than that. And she knew that. So probably she just said it to me for shock value, to vent her anger." Even after all the years of her daughter's drug addiction—or perhaps because of it—Kathleen still had a strong, motherly capacity for self-deception.

After whatever happened on the sidewalk in Atlantic City—hours later, Gia thought—she got to a phone and contacted her father. He cleaned her up as best he could and put her on the bus back to Philadelphia so her mother could take her to the hospital.

Although the hospital had had several patients on the medical side with AIDS, they had never had an HTLV-III positive psychiatric patient. It was the first test of their ability to counsel a victim of this new terminal illness and get her better medical information than what the doctors had—provided by the local AIDS task force. Patrick Kenney was becoming a national figure in the drive to educate nurses about AIDS. He had served as the American Nurses' Association representative to a conference sponsored by the Surgeon General in 1985 and was writing a book for nurses to use in preparing AIDS plans. Subsequently, there were at least a few nurses on the psych side who were acting appropriately around Gia.

"Her reaction to our reaction was odd," recalled one nurse. "She thought she was going to be treated like she had the plague. She knew she had AIDS-Related Complex (ARC) and would go into AIDS and just expected more people in space suits. I sat down cross-legged on her bed. She said, 'Aren't you afraid of me?' I said, 'Are you going to have sex with me? Are you going to share needles with me?' I think she was kind of shocked and surprised that we were willing to touch her."

Gia was put on lithium to battle her depression. After it began to take effect, she called Rob Fay and asked him to come to the hospital. They had been out of contact for close to a month, which he assumed meant that Gia was using again and couldn't face him. When people disappeared from the rehab and meeting community, the recovering people feared the worst. Rob had just buried one of his best friends from the program, who had committed suicide by jumping in front of a moving car after returning to drugs. He was thrilled to hear that Gia was still alive.

"I knew something was really wrong because she came toward me like she was going to hug me and then she sorta turned sideways," he recalled. "I said, 'What the hell is this kinda cheese hug here?' And we went off into a little side room, where there were a few other nuts and their parents, and a radio was playing kinda quiet. She said she had been diagnosed with ARC, and I made some bad joke because I didn't know what ARC was, y'know. And she told me, 'No, listen to me, *this is it!*' She told me about AIDS-Related Complex and we just sat there and cried.

"And it was funny as shit, we used to have this song in rehab, 'Don't Forget About Me,' or something like that. It came on the radio. We're sitting here with all these people in similar situations, all these people with their parents who are fairly distraught, and she just kicked in. She cranked the radio up real loud and we started dancing and, y'know, it was a real special moment right there. One guy started making an advance toward the radio, and I just looked at him and he knew it was the wrong move."

While the psychiatric staff was heartened by the presence of this outside friend, they were still trying to make sense of the relationship between Gia and her mother—which had been made even more complicated by the diagnosis. "Patient very verbal about frustration, anger, guilt," read her chart for June 22, 1986, "uncertain in ability to make future plans ... feels hurt by mother's reactions and feeling that mother is acting like she has it, too." Then the staff learned the reason for Gia's uncertainty about her future plans. She suspected that she wouldn't be allowed to move in with her mother after her discharge, which was only a few days away.

"At that point, I didn't know much about AIDS," recalled Kathleen, "and I had to accept the fact that my daughter was dying. And, of course, they were treating us like we had the plague. When I walked into that hospital, whereas nurses are usually very compassionate, nobody spoke to me. Just whispers. They stayed away from me, walked on the other side of the hall when I passed. So, I'm trying to deal with all this and get my shit together and try and support her and it's freaking me out. And then Henry says he's worried he's going to lose his job if Gia comes to live with us. 'If she has that, she can't come back here,' he said, 'I'll help you, she can stay in a hotel, but she can't come back here. I might lose my job.' It was hard for me to hear that. I didn't feel that I could really go against him. I knew that, given enough time, I would be able to get him to let her come home. I didn't know what was going to happen if my neighbors found out.

"She forced me to tell her over the phone one day that Henry wouldn't let her come home. They put pressure on her to force me. She trapped me into saying it. Finally, I told her what Henry said and she hung up. I called back and talked to the nurse and they calmed her down."

The hospital support staff was astonished by the unfolding family drama. "I had to unofficially sort of soothe things over," recalled one nurse, "I just finally said to the mother, 'She's your daughter, you can't turn your back to her!' And she had no response, she just kind of had a blank expression. She said *he* wouldn't let her come home, *he* didn't want her home."

The nurse was incredulous. "I don't know, to me, unconditional love is unconditional love: no matter who they kill," she said. "I never had it. I'm an adult child of an alcoholic myself. When your child has a fatal disease and no life of her own how can you turn your back on her? Unconditional love *has to be there*. That's what got me so riled up. I feel I overstepped my bounds, in saying all that. I made a judgment call but I'm supposed to stay neutral. I just had a hard time comprehending the dynamics of that family."

Besides her discharge plans, Gia was also upset about the treatment she had received on the medical side. She asked to be given a copy of her medical records, which the hospital refused. She also asked for an afternoon pass from the psych unit to go to Norristown to look for a place to live, and called Rob Fay to see if he could help. He called Dawn Phillips, who only knew Gia from their conversation after her self-disclosure at Eagleville but had become friendly with Rob during her recovery. She saw him at Norristown meetings, which she attended at least once a day.

Dawn was less wary about AIDS than whether Gia could

stay off drugs. Assured that Gia was clean and would be attending meetings, she offered whatever room there was in her tiny Norristown apartment. There was no bed to offer, because Dawn was sleeping on the floor on a foam mat herself—or sometimes on the couch. She told Gia they would figure out something.

In the meantime, Kathleen had forced Henry to reconsider. "I said, 'I cannot live with this, this is her home, she has got to come back here,' " she recalled. "He told his bosses what the story was, and they were really good about it. They said, 'Look, Henry, your trouble is our trouble. It's okay.' Henry came back and told Gia she could move back in. I called her back—the whole thing had taken less than twenty-four hours. But she had already made arrangements to stay with this other person. She thought it would be better for her to go to the meetings. But I wanted her here."

Gia was discharged June 26, 1986, with a prescription for more lithium, a referral to a local mental health center and the AIDS task force, and a prognosis of "Fair."

Sharon Beverly had moved back to Philadelphia from New York when her mother took ill in 1984. She had remained the only friend from the old days with whom Gia stayed in contact. "We usually talked on the phone," she recalled. "She had always called to tell me she was in one of these drug centers, then she'd call to tell me she was clean and working. It was like that when she was in New York, and it just continued. She called me from Eagleville, then she called and said she took a job at the mall selling jeans, which seemed pretty weird. But she felt that's what she had to do. They told her in therapy that she had to humble herself.

"From that point on, she was never the same. She just lost that glow, that fun side of her. She was losing it little by little, but by this time she was drained. The last time I saw her, she looked really different. They had her on lithium, she just looked like a different person. Her hair was different, it was thin and dull, and she didn't have that glow. She kind of was like a zombie.

"Gia always said she wanted to be a guitarist. I was telling her that I was getting ready to move back to New York, and I was doing some singing at the time and writing. So I asked her, 'Do you know how to play guitar now?' And she said, 'A little bit.' And I said, 'Come on, y'know, we'll do something together, you play guitar and I'll write the songs.' And she said, 'No, it's too late for that.'

"She'd call me and we'd do silly things on the phone like watch *Friday Night Videos* together and talk about life. At that time she had become spiritual. She was reading the Bible. She was reading a lot of things. She was saying, 'I think God has a big plan for me, but I don't think it's in this life.' She said one thing that I couldn't believe. She said, 'I can't believe you're still my friend. You're the only person who's been through all this with me. I can't believe you're still my friend.'

"She still couldn't imagine someone just loving her for herself. She was really mean to me at times, said really mean things to me. She stole from me. I didn't care. I forgive things like that. She wasn't herself when she did those things. I always knew that she had a really good heart. Even when she was ruthless, she had that kind of innocence about her."

When Gia moved back to Norristown, word spread quickly among the Eagleville community that she had been using and was dying of AIDS. "She came back here and everybody heard she had AIDS," recalled Rob Fay, "and they were all . . . one minute, 'Oh we really care about you,' and then she's got AIDS and nobody's around. I was real upset. I would confront people if I saw them on the street. A lot of people were afraid they were going to get the disease. The rumor got out that I was gay with AIDS. I got tested. I hadn't slept with her and I never shot drugs with her, but I didn't know anything about AIDS, really. I was just as naive as all the other people. And we had spent a lot of time together, you know, used the same chopsticks, the same fork and glasses. I didn't know any better, and I just didn't want to be surprised all of a sudden. Then the first test came out positive. It was a false positive, but once it was on the street as a rumor—well, we're all a bunch of junkies.

"Her mom was strange about the whole thing. The day

Gia was moving into Dawn's apartment, we were sitting out front—Kathy, Gia and myself. And Kathy was talking to me, asking me things like 'Are you afraid of Gia now because she has AIDS?' And she was asking like she was talking to a three-year-old, you know? And that was the only time I heard her mention that Gia had AIDS."

"You can't imagine if you haven't lived through it what it's like to have a child diagnosed with AIDS," recalled Kathleen, beginning to cry. "It's just, you just can't imagine the nightmare. Henry couldn't handle her having AIDS. My mother didn't come see her the whole summer. She wouldn't let my nephew come see her. Gia was here and she was *dying*.

"I was afraid to tell anybody what was wrong with her. People didn't know much about AIDS back then—neither did I—and *nobody* ever talked about women getting it. I didn't know if I was more upset because I was losing her or more upset that she had AIDS. I took her one day for a ride in the car. We were in the Corvette. I pulled over into a little park area, and I said, 'Gia, I could just pull away from here and hit the gas pedal and let go of the wheel of the car.' And she just sat there and looked at me. And I realized I couldn't do it to her, as badly as I wanted to do it to myself. But that's the way I was feeling, that my life was over, too."

Dawn Phillips was working full-time and going to numerous AA and NA meetings while she and Gia shared her tiny apartment. But she still had an opportunity to see how Gia was struggling with her illness and her relationship with her family. "I remember coming home one day and Gia's mother was there and I had just seen a movie, it was a lesbian movie, *Desert Hearts*," recalled Dawn, who was also gay. "This woman in this movie [a beautifully tomboyish openly gay woman] reminded me to a *T* of Gia. That woman was like Gia, especially the way she was about being gay. And I said, 'Gia, I saw this movie, you have to see it,' and as soon as I started saying what the movie was about, her mother got out of the conversation completely. She didn't want to talk about *that*.

"Her mother wanted her to move home, and Gia didn't want to go. But what was happening was she was getting sicker and sicker, and I wasn't really able to be there to take care of her. She would go home more often, and finally she just moved back, although we still saw her.

"There weren't a lot of people around for her. Just me and Rob, Cheryl, a couple of the counselors from Eagleville she still called. She had one other friend I took her to see one day, that girl she lived with in New York, Sharon. I remember, on the way to Sharon's she wanted me to take her to a place that has these great steak sandwiches, Dellesandro's. We went for a cheesesteak.

"Rob stuck with her. I think that Rob sincerely liked Gia as a person and a friend but, let's face it, Rob also wanted to go out with Gia. Desperately, he wanted to be with her. She knew that. She was thinking about somebody else. She was still talking about her counselor from Eagleville. Gia told him that. It wasn't a secret between them. I don't know if he totally believed her when she said she wasn't interested in men. He could believe she wasn't interested in him: he just couldn't believe that she was totally gay. Or maybe he just hoped. But, I'll give him credit, even if he could not go out with her, Rob was close by, being her friend.

"Look, I have no doubt Gia was gay. Why would somebody want to live a life that is not easy to live in this society, put up with so much abuse, live in fear? Who in their right mind would do that if they didn't *have to?* I know people that have been sexually abused that are still straight. Their relationships have put a strain on them, they need therapy. But I don't think abuse *makes* somebody gay."

One gay counselor who worked with Gia felt differently about her sexuality. "I think her gayness was almost a reaction and I don't know if it was a true gayness," he said. "There are some people ... well, I have a female friend who I used to be *engaged* to, so you have to be careful of labeling yourself gay. I have lesbian friends who there is no question about — their identity and affection is at that end of the Kinsey scale. Gia would have taken affection from *anybody.* It's hard to see in this setting, but I don't know that she got from *women* what she wanted either. Gia reminded me of a Push-Me-Pull-You. A dance-away lover — when she gets close to somebody she dances away. She had love–hate relationships."

* * *

Gia was able to get some medical information from the local AIDS task force and asked Rob to go to some peer counseling for friends of AIDS victims. She had less luck getting mental health help for herself. A counselor from Eagleville tried to refer Gia to the best female psychiatrist she knew.

"She refused to see Gia because she was HIV-positive," recalled the counselor. "She didn't want to have that slip out and get to her other patients. She told me that the research and stuff about AIDS was being minimized. She was afraid of Gia using her bathroom and shit like that. What could I tell Gia? She was so depressed, she wanted to see somebody. I told her that the psychiatrist's caseload was full and I talked to her when she called me at home."

Gia was able to get some counseling at a mental health center in Norristown. But her counselor there, though sympathetic and dedicated, was untrained in counseling AIDS patients. She did not realize that Gia was terminally ill.

"It was my understanding that she had been diagnosed with ARC," recalled the counselor. "I didn't know that meant she would die. To be honest, I didn't think she *was* going to die. I kept telling her, 'You have ARC, you don't have AIDS.' She said, 'I don't care if you say I have ARC, I'm gonna die.' She wanted to deal with death issues. As a therapist, I was not really listening to what she was telling me. Here I was encouraging Gia to feel better and she was dying. We weren't at odds, but I was hoping for the best and she was doomed in what she knew was going to happen.

"I had spoken to a psychiatrist who specialized in people diagnosed with AIDS or ARC, and spoke to Gia about joining the support group. But she felt it would be all men. She had a great issue with the fact that there wasn't a whole lot for women with AIDS. She felt isolated. She had no comrades, and she felt very awkward and alone and *marked* in terms of having this disease." At that time, fewer than 750 women in the United States had been diagnosed with AIDS, and fewer than 1,900 internationally. Women made up less than seven percent of the world's AIDS patient population.

"She looked like an old lady, she looked terrible," the therapist recalled. "Her skin was wrinkled, she sort of hobbled around. Later she started walking with a cane. She shook, she was just sick. Drugs were still an issue with her. She was committed to not doing them anymore, but she still had her works in her house, and she had some heroin residue. She would spend time looking at the works and looking at the residue. She was really going through a grieving process of saying good-bye to heroin. She went through a ritual of slowly letting go of the heroin addiction and, in a sense, almost had a burial. Eventually she threw everything away, and she was angry at the drug. She told me that she thought she got AIDS through heroin.

"Gia had good insight. She understood a lot of her problems. That's what makes someone so troubled, so interesting. An individual who has more than just *the behavior,* but has some insight and psychological depth to go with it makes for a more in-depth experience—for the therapist, too. But if you don't translate that depth into behavioral changes, it means nothing.

"I met her when her health was failing. Her physical limitations were so great that her psychological understanding was more in line with her behavior. I saw her in a unique position, because she *couldn't* do what she used to do. She thought of herself as wild. A lot of the wildness was driven by how she felt about herself. It drove her to get attention from her mother and she did excessive behavior intentionally to get attention."

By this point, Gia had decided that she and Rochelle had no place in each other's lives. Rochelle disagreed with Gia's decision. At the depths of her own drug craziness, Rochelle was continually calling and writing. Gia felt she was being harassed. She was dying and, frankly, making peace with Rochelle was low on her list of priorities.

"The biggest thing she was trying to put to rest was her relationship with her mother," the therapist said. "She was *desperately* trying to find the good in it."

On August 6, 1986, Way Bandy was booked to do a session at Scavullo's studio. He arrived so exhausted—delirious, really—that the models had to do their own makeup. Scavullo was only partially astonished by the makeup artist's uncharacteristic professional lapse. Helen Murray—who had bounced from Calvin Klein to scouting models for Wilhelmina to agenting, and was currently representing Bandy—had called the studio ahead of time to say that he would be late. She also told Scavullo, "Way is sick"—by then the industry code-words for AIDS. The photographer was horrified and frightened.

"My first instinct was not to let him in my apartment, and then I thought, 'You bastard,' " Scavullo recalled. "So I took him up and massaged him and gave him tea, and gave him love and support . . . And I'm glad I did. My first instinct was to run. Thank God the better half of me came through."

The next day, *Vogue* editor Grace Mirabella arranged for Bandy to speak with her husband, a surgeon at Sloan-Kettering, who convinced the makeup artist—who hadn't seen a medical doctor in years, preferring natural cures—to check into New York Hospital. He was first put into a tiny room, but Bandy's friends conspired to pull strings. It turned out that Maury Hopson had done the head nurse's hair for her wedding nineteen years before. Bandy got a suite overlooking the Fifty-ninth Street Bridge. And on August 13, while listening to Maria Callas sing the third act of *Tosca* on his cassette player, Way Bandy died.

One of his last dying acts was to ask Hopson and Murray to make sure that his cause of death was accurately identified in his obituaries. He had been upset by the way Perry Ellis, and his company, Manhattan Industries, continued to deny the designer's cause of death. Bandy wanted to assure that the end of his career in the ephemeral craft of makeup would have a more lasting impact.

In the spirit of his request, Bandy's obituary was not only accurate, but Murray, Hopson and Scavullo granted interviews with a number of journalists to make even more public the death of this very private man. Bandy had been one of the best-known, openly gay men in the world, but had never spoken out about AIDS or even associated himself publicly with AIDS causes because of fear of how it would affect his career. In death, he became the first gay man to publicly share—with the gay and straight worlds—not just the fact of AIDS-diagnosis, as Rock Hudson had, but the panic of AIDS-paranoia and the horror of AIDS-death.

His posthumous openness also gave the nation a sterling example of just how irrational people who knew better could be about the disease. When obituaries pointed out that Bandy had made up Nancy Reagan for a *Harper's Bazaar* session with Scavullo four months before his death—the pictures were about to appear in the magazine's September "10 Most Beautiful Women" feature—the White House announced that Bandy hadn't really *touched* the First Lady that much. "Maybe he was with her fifteen minutes," Nancy Reagan's press secretary explained to a *Washington Post* reporter. "She uses very little makeup . . . She had seen the obit in the paper and was surprised and sorry. She knows there was nothing more than a handshake. And we've all been told by the medical community that you can't contract the disease that way."

Bandy's friends expressed their outrage over the White House statement—"Unfuckingbelievable," Murray told one reporter. "How dare she say that? It must have taken him forty-five minutes to an hour to put her face on, and overall, Way and Francesco had to have been there for four or five hours." They also used the media window of opportunity caused by Bandy's death to publicly air what life in the previously fast lane had been reduced to.

Bandy's health fanaticism apparently had been pushed into high gear as the AIDS crisis forced the world's gay communities into reevaluating their lifestyles. Hopson told a reporter that both he and Bandy had a "running crazy period" but in 1984, the two, who had never been lovers, both decided to become celibate. "It's a very barren life when you don't have sex," Hopson explained. They also went on strict macrobiotic diets, which were said to build up immune systems. Still, they were fearful, both of the disease—which felled Bandy's ex-lover, novelist Michael Gardine, in 1985—and the growing antigay backlash. Hopson admitted they had been scared away from public association with AIDS-related causes for fear of destroying their considerable careers.

"There was one model," recalled Hopson, "who horrified most people in the industry because she refused to have any male homosexual do her makeup. Then she called up Way for a makeup lesson, and was going to have the company pay him to teach her how to do her own makeup for the jobs. Well, ha, ha, ha. I'd really like to rub her nose in it today. Oh, God, how funny. She calls Way! He refused to give her the makeup lesson, by the way."

Hopson and Murray discussed how Bandy's eccentricities had prevented him from admitting his physical deterioration or asking for help. In his last months, he was portrayed as a man trapped by his own mystique. When his doctor asked why he had avoided treatment, he said he had taken on "a Greta Garbo existence."

"One sad thing is, once the rumors started to fly around about Way," recalled Murray, "part of me knew that his career, for all practical purposes, was probably over. True. People *loved* talking about it. Even if he had come out of the hospital with good, old-fashioned pneumonia, the [AIDS label] would have hung over his head. That's what's so disgusting, the stigma. And the people who were doing most of the talking were people who didn't even know Way ... people on the fringes of the business."

On August 14, Gia wrote a letter to her Aunt Nancy that she never mailed:

Dear Nancy, I hope your fine & every thing's OK. As you know I won't be seeing Dodekins [Rochelle] it isn't any good between us it hasn't been for me since I went into Eagleville. I told her but she didn't hear me. I love her but don't want to be her lover or anyone else's. The Boys are as bad as the girls.

I miss Barbara terribly. She's always on my mind. I always told people how funny she was. I wonder if she knew how much I loved her. My Mom said she did.

My friend Way died today. I upset about him he helped me get jobs went first moved to NYC. I used to have a blast working together. He made me a bracelet I still have it. He was amazing if he wasn't gay I would have try to marry him. Death makes life seem unreal. Unreal in the sence that you can't hold onto it. When I was in the Mental Ward the last time I was lying in my bed and I kept imagining Rod Sterling coming through doorway saying little about another dimension, in another time. I am falling asleep ...

Bandy's death also hurt Gia for other reasons. "She was upset that when Way died, nobody called her," recalled Rob Fay. "All the people who claimed to be her friends. I think that when Way died she realized that she wasn't as important as she had come to think she was. I think that's when she realized that a lot of it was bullshit and people who said they cared didn't care.

"I think when he died she also knew it was comin' for her."

Although Gia had days when her strength seemed almost normal, she had just as many when she was completely debilitated. "I was talking to her on the phone one night," recalled Dawn Phillips, "and she was having trouble talking. After we said good-bye, it took her fifteen minutes to hang up that phone. She was in bed, she wasn't near the receiver, and since I usually wait for the other person to hang up, I waited. I could hear her struggling to hang it up, she was in pain. It was like fifteen minutes—I looked at the clock. At one point I even tried calling out to see if she was okay. She eventually hung it up, but I knew how bad she was at that point."

It was her physical deterioration that caused rumors to circulate among her old friends in the clubs. The rumors were started after she came out of Warminster, when she went into Center City to get her hair cut by Maurice Tannenbaum. The former Mr. Maurice had himself come full circle. He spent four years doing commercial photography in New York, followed by six months in Europe trying to get more artful, more editorial work. Disgusted, he returned to Philadelphia, took a masters in photography and did some hair out of his house. Finally, he opened his own salon in Center City.

"She came in and she had lost about fifty percent of her hair," Maurice recalled. "It was the first time I had seen her in a while. She was obviously sick. In fact, I actually started hearing about two months before she died that she was dead."

Her living situation at home was not altogether peaceful.

Her older brother Joey, who lived in Atlantic City with his wife and their two children (she was pregnant with her third), was out of work and spending time at his mother's house over the summer finishing her basement. At the same time, Joey's first wife had moved back from California with their eleven-year-old daughter, taken up residence in Atlantic City and gotten involved in a lifestyle that had the family in an uproar.

"I started getting all these phone calls from the other grandmother," recalled Kathleen. "It was a lot of partying and bad stuff going on. We were trying to get the organization that handles children and youth in New Jersey to take her out of there. The social worker handling it at that point wanted Henry and I to get her, and take her away from the mother and that situation. She couldn't live with her father. He had no room, he wasn't working at the time. It was a mess."

In the midst of this mess, Joey observed the way Gia was interacting with Kathleen and Henry. "I couldn't understand what was going on there," recalled Joey. "Gia was saying she had to get out of there. They weren't being as nice to her as they were letting on. I heard them arguing about what she was doing with her money, and stuff like that. They wanted her food stamps from her and really cruel, nonsense stuff. I finally had to leave. I couldn't believe what was going on. I would take her out to breakfast sometimes and she would pull out a bunch of money and offer to pay. She'd say, 'Just don't tell them that I got any money cause they'll take my money off me.' I said, 'They don't want your *money.*' I just thought she wasn't feeling well or something. Then I heard them arguing about it, 'We know you've got money, what are you doing with your money,' and stuff like that. I took her to the store one day. She wanted to get some juice, she liked Hawaiian Punch and she got a few cans of that, and some lox, and I heard them upstairs, and they were up there counting down what she got."

"She was treated like a dog in that house," Nancy Adams said. "You know how you see movies about people in institutions, locked up with the key thrown away? That's how it was. We couldn't call there, she couldn't call us. Kathleen had her locked up. Gia would call Rochelle and I at the salon, collect. She said she was sick and lonely, and they were always fighting about money. She thought Kathleen and Henry were afraid they were going to get stuck with all the medical bills. I guess that was a legitimate concern, but Gia's happiness and well-being just didn't seem to be motivating factors here. You see people on television dying of AIDS and you see the family pulling together for one last minute of quality time and she didn't have that. She didn't have anything."

"It was not like that at all," Kathleen said. "We would have given her *anything* if we thought it would help. She had food stamps here. Sometimes she gave them to us, sometimes she wouldn't, and she would get all hyper and bent out of shape.

"Gia has never been the easiest person in the world to live with. You would think another woman in the house would be a help, but she was never a help. If I cooked something one way, she wanted it another way. When she was dying, food was something that you knew she had to eat, and you tried to give her something that you knew she liked. But, because of the nature of the disease, she would smell food cooking and be hungry, the smell would cause her nose to run and her mouth acted up. And any time she tried to eat she was completely miserable. She could taste the cardboard from the box whereas the day before she couldn't. If you washed the dishes in certain detergent she could pick up on it. One night I had a beautiful rib roast and string beans, but by the time she got to the table she was having an allergic reaction to it. Then she started ripping into me. I was very upset.

"I was still working at Spiegel and Gia was home by herself. Joey's daughter came to visit us and, because I was working, Gia and her spent a lot of time together one weekend. Gia took her to play miniature golf, to McDonald's. Gia could start out doing something and be okay, and then she would tire easily. One of the big fights we had was because I didn't want her to drive my car anymore. I was just concerned that something would happen and she wouldn't be up to the situation. She was probably in denial as to how far along she was, and she was upset that I was taking away some of her independence. But I was very concerned that something would happen to her."

18

Beautiful Friend,
The End

In contemplation of her fate, Gia wrote:

> *Life & Death*
> *energy & Peace*
> *if I stoped today*
> *it was fun*
> *Even the terriable pains that have burn me & scarred*
> *my soul it was worth it for having been allowed to*
> *walked where I've walked. Which was to hell on earth*
> *Heaven on earth back again, into, under, far in between,*
> *through it, in it over and above it.*

Gia didn't want her life to pass improperly. "She was really concerned with dying, she wanted to do it right," said Rob Fay. "She didn't want to go to hell. We used to watch Oral Roberts and them guys on TV. We'd laugh at it, but the right questions were there. At least that was a place where they talked about that kinda stuff.

"She knew that somebody would want to do something with her life story. She said, 'I don't want it on no Monday Night Movie, *The Adventures of Carangi*.' She didn't want any bullshit in it. She didn't want her mother to tell her story. If Kathy hears that and she's hurt, well, I'm sorry, but

378

that's what Gia wanted. She didn't want the bullshit. She wanted to make a couple of videos addressing children, especially young girls. To them, a cover girl is like a goddess, y'know.

"What she wanted was for the kids to see what it can do. She wanted to tell the kids, y'know, that you don't have to do this. You don't have to get high, you don't have to run from things because it doesn't get you anywhere. We talked about a video and she would say, 'Look at where it got me.' She didn't care about Jagger and all of them guys. That part of the story meant nothing to her. She just wanted to help keep anyone else from goin' through what she was goin' through. It's one thing if you get hit by a bus and you're dead, y'know. But to have to sit there every morning and say, 'I better live today because I might die today,' was— well, I can't imagine it.

"She wanted to talk to those kids about drugs. It isn't the drug itself. I can't stress this enough—Gia's life didn't go downhill because she discovered heroin. She'd have gone there eventually, it didn't matter what drug she used. Coulda been peanut butter sandwiches. Heroin was just escapism at its best. Somebody's a junkie nodding out, you hit 'em with a bat he doesn't know it. You are *away* when you're high. That's what she wanted to do, to get away, to run. And she couldn't run anymore.

"She didn't want to say, 'Don't ever do drugs.' She used to fuck with Nancy Reagan and the 'Just Say No' thing. Yeah, eight-year-old kid in the ghetto making three grand a week sellin' dope—'Just Say No!' It doesn't *work* that way. And she knew that. She wanted to get down to the issues of why people are gettin' high and why drugs are killin' people. I don't believe anybody gets high for recreation. You get high to escape your day. 'Shit, I had a rough day in the office, give me a couple of martinis, let me light a joint.' It's escape, no matter how you put it. CEO of some, big, GM or something, or some guy who digs ditches. One goes home and has a beer and the other goes home and has his butler bring him Dom or somethin' like that. It's the same thing. It's not being able to face life on life's terms, as it comes. That's what she wanted kids to know: you can handle *anything* that comes your way. You don't have to go gettin' high, you don't have to run from anything.

"And I never went and got a video camera. We just put it off and put it off."

In September, Joey's wife had her baby, which set off another round of family angst. The issue of where his daughter from his first marriage would live continued to worry everyone. And then, the issue of whether Gia should be allowed to visit the new baby—come near the baby, *touch* the baby—became another battleground.

"I didn't know that much about AIDS," recalled Joey Carangi, "and then I started hearing how deadly it was and stuff like that and I started listening up on this stuff. I wasn't worried about myself, but then Gia was supposed to come visit with my mom, and my wife was due to go in the hospital any day to have a baby and I was worried about her coming. I didn't think it was a good idea. Not that I would tell her not to come, but I didn't think my mother should bring her."

Gia came anyway, and none of the imagined problems materialized. At the end of the family get-together, Gia was dropped off at the Atlantic City station to catch a bus back to Philadelphia so Kathleen could stay a few extra days with the new baby. Instead of taking a bus, she walked over to the salon to see Rochelle and Nancy. "The girl looked like walking death," Nancy recalled. "To leave somebody that sick in a bus terminal? I just didn't get it."

"Her mother, who cared about her *so much*, didn't know where she was," Rochelle recalled. "We went out to dinner and she paid for it. Where she got the money I don't know. She told me she was sorry for this and that, and that she loved me. She said she was contemplating moving back to Atlantic City. She was supposed to call me the next week, to make plans to get together for Halloween. Gia *loved* Halloween.

"She was saying that she had ARC. She said you could live for ten to twenty years with it. I didn't think she was gonna die. In 1986, people didn't know too much about it."

But while it may have seemed important to Rochelle, a chance for another new beginning, Gia's visit to her was only a minor aspect of the trip to Atlantic City. Her agenda in challenging the family wisdom on the matter was clear. Her goals very specific. "In the scenario with the Atlantic City trip," recalled one of her counselors, "Gia thought that her *mother* was telling the mother of the newborn not to let her come visit because she had AIDS. When Gia got down there, she found out that it was her brother and his wife, and not the mother. She cared *very deeply* that it wasn't her mother. In fact, she was ecstatic.

"Gia was, by this time, so desperate for signs of her mother's love. It is so sad to think here are two people and all they wanted each other to know was that they loved each other, and they couldn't do that in a way that was normal and straightforward. It's amazing that people can spend their whole lives trying to get another person to say they love you."

On October 18, 1986, Gia went to Hahnemann University Hospital—a teaching hospital in Center City which treated many of the city's first AIDS cases—to see her oncologist, Dr. Wilbur Oaks. The doctor had no plans to admit her. She was in for tests and an office visit, as she had been several times over the summer. Gia's most immediate problem was persistent vaginal bleeding—a permanent period— which left her, among other things, severely dehydrated. She was put on birth control pills to try to stop the bleeding. When that wouldn't work, a hysterectomy was considered. Since Gia was focusing more and more on childlessness as her biggest regret, the hysterectomy would have been an especially symbolic blow. On the 18th, Gia went in for an ultrasound, but was so dehydrated that technicians couldn't get her bladder full enough to see it, no matter how much water they forced her to drink. Oaks decided she would have to be admitted.

"She was indigent, on medical assistance," recalled Dr. Oaks. "The AIDS patients are costly and the end result is so grim, but we don't turn anyone away. She was one of the very first we had, certainly the first woman. I had seen her over the summer a few times, and by the time she was admitted her personality was strange. She was pretty much sociopathic at that point. She looked like she'd been through a hell of a lot. And it's hard to know what you should do when they look like they're in distress. One thing we had to do was discuss the 'code status' with patients and family.''

The code status—whether Gia would be put on life support if her health failed, if she "coded"—was, initially, an easy decision to make. Gia and Kathleen had had many conversations over the summer about final arrangements. Much to the rest of the family's shock, a funeral plot had already been discussed—near her aunt Barbara Adams, but in the open sun because Gia always liked to lay and have the sun fall on her face. And Gia had already expressed her desire *not* to end up on life support. It was agreed that, if the situation arose, there would be no unusual heroics employed.

But code status seemed to be the only thing the family could agree upon. During Gia's hospital stay, Kathleen took complete control of her daughter's life, pitting herself against family and friends. She decided who and what could be told about Gia's condition. Although Gia had been quite open about her diagnosis of ARC several months before, Kathleen was now insisting that she had been hospitalized for "female problems" that had mostly been caused by her long-term drug use. When old friends called, Kathleen could not bring herself to admit to them that Gia was terminally ill. Besides the personal stigma attached to such an admission, she was afraid that the local press might get hold of the story. She was under the impression, probably mistaken, that reporters had been snooping around Hahnemann trying to get information on her famous daughter.

Kathleen also decided who could visit Gia in the hospital. Immediate family were allowed in. Joe Carangi would drive up to Philadelphia from Atlantic City to see his daughter almost every day after work, often accompanied by one or both of Gia's brothers. Kathleen immediately barred Rochelle, claiming that Gia had specifically stated that she didn't want to see her old girlfriend and had even written a note saying that she now hated her. Nancy didn't come because she was sure she wouldn't be allowed in either. She got reports from Gia's old high school friend Vicky, who knew how to get in and out of private hospital rooms unnoticed from years of doing deliveries for her family flower business.

"The whole thing at the hospital was horrible, just horrible," recalled Joey Carangi. "Kathleen wouldn't let any of Gia's friends in. She had everybody flagged from going upstairs to visit. I saw a few of her friends sneak up when Kathleen wasn't there. But as far as Kathleen was concerned, she didn't want nobody up there to see her, nobody, and she was playing like she was the doctor, taking care. Grieving mother. *Right.*"

Rob Fay *was* allowed to visit, although he was "walkin' on eggshells all the time to make sure *I* could get in there," he recalled. "Rochelle wanted to see Gia. I talked to Gia about it, and she wanted to see Rochelle, but she knew the mother wouldn't let her. I tried to hook the two of them up on the phone, but it didn't work out. Kathleen blamed a lot of Gia's life on Rochelle, which was bullshit. I think part of the reason she took the drugs was to show her mom that *she* wasn't in control, as much as she would like to think that she was. But, whatever Gia did, she did to herself. Nobody made her do anything, she knew that. There's nobody to blame in this whole thing but Gia. She shot the dope, let's be real.

"When I first went to see Gia, they made me put on this gown, y'know, nine hundred gloves and all this head shit and everything. I was, like, devastated, I had never seen anything like that. And when I came out, the nurse who helped to undress me with all this stuff, she could see that I was crying. Kathy came up to me and she was like real vague about everything. She was not saying, like, Gia will be all right, but she was real vague about the AIDS. That was the only time they had me put on the gloves and all that. After that I just walked in.

"They still told me not to touch her, y'know, but that was bullshit. And when Gia was awake, we were like old buddies. We used to sit and watch TV all cuddled up together, and there was no problem."

Although some of Gia's relatives and friends would never forgive Kathleen for her behavior during the hospitalization, several of Gia's counselors felt they understood exactly what was going on. "My perception of what happened at the end," said one counselor, "was that Gia wanted this type of nurturing from her mom and she set it up so that she got it before she died. I know some people thought it might not have been a good idea. But you have to understand that this was this woman's *daughter* and they had been fighting for position most of Gia's life. Any woman you talk to who has lost a child—that's the hardest thing, the hardest grief to get over. I think Gia felt that her mother was finally there for her. Everybody prepares to die. That might have been Gia's way.

"I believe that people are basically good. And I believe that every parent really loves their kid. They might just not know how to do it in a way that *helps* their kid. This is what I think Gia came to feel at the end, that her mom did love her but just didn't know quite how to do it in a way that Gia needed it."

Some recognized the same phenomenon, but interpreted it less charitably. "It's ironic, isn't it?" Nancy Adams recalled. "Gia always wanted her mother's attention. And now she finally had it—and she paid for it with her life."

For a week or so, it was unclear how sick Gia was. She was given blood and medication, her brothers convinced her to eat, and on some days she looked healthier than she had in months. She was well enough one day to insist that her mother give her the cash she had left in her wallet. "She really had this trip about money," Kathleen recalled. "I had taken her wallet out of her pocketbook because I didn't think it was safe to leave it there in the hospital room. I had just washed my hands and gone through this whole sterile procedure when she demanded the money. I said, 'What are you going to do with this?' They were hooking her up again to a drug she didn't like. It made her sick. Maybe she thought she'd be able to bribe somebody to get her out of the hospital."

One afternoon, Kathleen left the hospital for dinner and came back in the evening. When she did, Gia was having trouble breathing, and the doctors were debating whether to put her on a respirator. Kathleen went into the room, and thought she noticed a red spot on the bedsheets under Gia's hand. She pulled back the sheets to reveal her daughter lying in a pool of blood, and immediately ran out into the hall screaming for a doctor, a nurse, anyone. Help came, but the gloves everyone was wearing were soon so covered with AIDS-infected blood that "we knew we were in trouble," Kathleen recalled. "I finally told the nurse to go sterilize her hands."

When Gia was out of immediate danger, a new debate began over code status. Kathleen had changed her mind. She now insisted that her daughter *should* be put on life support, and pushed Gia to sign new consent forms.

"They brought the paper and I said, 'Gia, just sign it,'" Kathleen recalled, "and she said, 'Thank you very much for making my decision for me.' She had to make such a big deal out of everything ... reading it, whether she understands it or not. I just said 'Sign it.' I was a nervous wreck." Gia finally signed the forms, and she was moved to another room to be put on oxygen.

"As they were moving her, a doctor came out and said to me, 'What do you think you've saved her for?'" Kathleen recalled. "She said, 'If you were out in California, you wouldn't be putting her through this. You'd sign a paper when you went into the hospital so you wouldn't go through this.' I thought, 'How cruel can you be, to say this to me?' Yet that's what she thought we should have done.

"Every doctor said there was some hope she could come off the respirator. But then everything went wrong that could go wrong. Enlarged liver, enlarged spleen, her kidneys went. They punctured her lung, which had to be drained all the time. I'd leave and everything would be fine, and I'd come back and would be hit with another bombshell. At the end, she was spared absolutely nothing. Every organ in that girl's body failed.

"Then I had to fight because they decided that she wanted to die. She didn't want to die, she just wanted to get the hell off the respirator. She wanted to go to Disneyland; she thought she could still beat it. She would write me notes, 'We can buy oxygen, we can get a tank at home, take me home, take me home!' And I would explain almost every time I walked in there, 'Gia, if I could get you to the elevator, I would take you home. But you'd be dead before we got to the door.'"

The hospital staff even tried to convince Kathleen to have someone else appointed Gia's guardian. "The psychiatric nurse misinterpreted something Gia said," Kathleen recalled, "and I thought I was going to have to go and have somebody appointed her guardian. I said, '*I'm* the next of kin. She can't speak for herself. *I* have to be the one. *I* talk for her.' The doctor agreed with me. They wanted me to sign the paper so that if she had cardiac arrest they would not do the heroics. I wouldn't do it. Because, if I did that, they would cut back on treatment."

Gia was kept on a respirator for nearly a month. Her room was decorated with flowers. Kathleen was surprised the hospital would allow flowers in such a sterile environment, but when she found out she filled the room with Gia's favorite yellow roses. There were also a few toys: a stuffed monkey, with Gia's money pinned to it, and a yellow butterfly toy Rob Fay had hung from the IV holder above her.

Dawn Phillips managed to sneak in to see Gia one more time, and found her restrained in her bed so she wouldn't keep pulling out the tubes in her body. The nurse undid the restraint when a visitor came, and Gia took Dawn by the shoulder and tried to pull her close.

"She was pulling my face towards her and trying to say something," Dawn recalled, "but with the tube in her mouth, she couldn't. No one else was in the room, and I began to get frightened. I didn't know what she wanted, and she couldn't tell me. I didn't want to react to being so close to her ... yet, there was fresh blood and saliva coming from her mouth. This made me nervous. I was pulled almost to her face when a nurse came in. Then I backed up. The whole time I was fighting my tears. When I go to the waiting room, I walked by Gia's mom and Rob, who were there speaking ... I just began to cry. When I went over to talk to them, Kathy was saying we weren't supposed to be there. I said, 'Don't you think Gia needs to know she has friends who care about and love her, too?' Kathy began saying something about Gia's appearance ... I went back in to see Gia. That was the last time I ever saw her."

Rob got to see Gia one more time after that. Before he left, she handed him a note that said "I hope."

A few of the nurses gave Gia lots of extra care. "There was one girl who would take care of her like a young child," Kathleen recalled. "She got to know Gia the way I knew Gia. She would comb Gia's hair, get her all fixed up. I took in ribbons. Gia didn't like ribbons, and she would take the ribbons out. Then they would tie her hair up with a piece of hospital string, and she was satisfied with that." One day Kathleen looked at Gia's legs and decided they didn't look right, so she found a basin and washed her daughter's feet. But at other times, Gia didn't want her mother to look at her atrophying extremities. "Her nightgown would get pulled up and she didn't want me to see her," she recalled. "Gia would force the nightgown down, and it was amazing that someone on a respirator would still have that pride."

The last holiday she and her mother were able to celebrate together was Halloween. "She had pumpkins in the room," Kathleen said, beginning to cry. "I went out at lunchtime and brought her a great big scary hand and some little cat. And I laid the cat on her head and put the scary hand on her. When Dr. Oaks came in, I said, 'You have to show Dr. Oaks your Halloween outfit.' And she reached over with the hand and pretended like she was scary. He couldn't *believe* that we celebrated Halloween."

The last week nobody was allowed to visit but Kathleen. Rob Fay, among others, was livid. But Gia was on life support, rarely conscious. And her physical deterioration had been so extreme that Kathleen was sure she wouldn't want anyone to see her like that.

"She died around ten in the morning," Kathleen recalled. "I saw them wash her and the flesh fell off her back. I had my Bible with me. Usually, when Gia went anyplace she took her Bible with her, but she made me leave hers at home so it wouldn't get messed up or lost or something. I hadn't read it all day. I had just left her father in the waiting room. I was reading her the Twenty-third Psalm, the Lord is my shepherd. I had read it through once and I started again and I got to 'the Valley of the Shadow of Death.' And I saw something out of the corner of my eye. I looked up and the nurse that was on duty was running out of the room and the machines were going haywire.

"I ran to her and sobbed, 'Oh, my baby, my baby,' and she was gone. They took all the hoses out of her. It was over. We went home. Luckily, the first undertaker we went to had no objections to preparing an AIDS patient. He just encouraged us to keep it a little quieter than we wanted to, suggested we not do an obituary in New York. He said we should have a closed casket, because he didn't know how she would look. But I did have to pick out what she would wear anyway.

"Anytime I ever picked out anything for her, I was never sure if she would like it. Because even if I was positive in my mind, it would always turn out that she wouldn't like it. He suggested a dressing gown and nice lounging pajamas, to make sure it was big and roomy. I wanted some member of the family to see the body, but he wouldn't allow it.

"Her father walked in and saw it was a closed casket and had a fit. But Gia and I had a pact that if she wasn't going to look her absolute best, it should be a closed casket. She didn't want people looking at her if she didn't look good."

Epilogue

The memorial service for Way Bandy was held at the Japan House in Manhattan on Thursday, November 13, five days before Gia's death. It was attended by more than two hundred people—all the *fashionistas*, and all the people Bandy had made beautiful. Besides the eulogizing, the event was also used as a fund-raiser for New York Hospital's Laboratory for AIDS Research. An envelope for contributions was slipped into each program.

The service was extensively covered in the media. And the following March, when *Vanity Fair* did a feature on the decimation of talent in fashion and the arts from AIDS, a description of the service was used as the opening scene. As part of the article, photographs of fifty AIDS victims were offered in memoriam. Among them were Bandy, *Interview* editors Robert Hayes and Peter Lester, model Joe Macdonald, *GQ* editor Jack Haber and *New York* magazine writer Henry Post. Only two of those memorialized were women, record producer Lyn Hilton and Esme Hammond, a friend of the New York music scene and the wife of legendary record producer John Hammond.

Gia Carangi's funeral was held on November 23 at a small funeral home in suburban Philadelphia. Kathleen and Henry Sperr did their best to contact the people in Philadelphia and New York who they thought should know. Some of Gia's Philadelphia friends chose not to attend because of their anger at Kathleen—either because she hadn't let them in to see Gia or she hadn't told them when they called that Gia was terminally ill. Nobody from the fashion world attended the funeral or sent flowers, although several weeks later, a Mass card arrived from Francesco Scavullo, who later recalled, "We were hysterical crying in the studio when we heard."

At the time of Gia's death, no obituaries ever appeared in major newspapers, magazines or trade publications. Only a small death notice appeared in *The Philadelphia Inquirer*. She would never be mentioned in any of the myriad articles about AIDS in the fashion industry.

"You know, this will sound awful," recalled one hairstylist, "but I remember when her father called me and said she died, I wondered why he called me. He said, 'I know you were very good friends with my daughter.' It would have been awful for me to deny it, wouldn't it?"

"I remember asking a photographer, 'Where is this Gia, whatever happened with her?'" recalled German *Vogue* fashion editor Suzanne Kolmel. "He said, 'You know that she *died*. And at the end, she sold *pizza.'*"

"About three months after Gia died, I was working with Sandy Linter for *Harper's Bazaar*," recalled one top model. "And, somehow or another, Gia's name came up, which *never* should have happened anyway, but it did. Sandy was doing my makeup, and about halfway through she said, 'Excuse me,' and she left and walked around the block for about twenty-five minutes."

In early April of 1988, the morning show *AM Philadelphia* did a segment on AIDS. After the program aired, co-host Wally Kennedy received a phone call from a viewer who had been touched by it.

"She said, 'I saw your show and I think it just scratched the surface,'" Kennedy recalled. "She said, 'I've had some personal experience with AIDS. My daughter died of it. It really was such a waste. She was a great kid and had a lot going for her.'"

Kennedy asked the woman his standard questions: Who was she, what did she do, was she from Philadelphia? The woman said she was a suburban housewife. "She said, 'My daughter was a pretty successful model in New York,'" Kennedy recalled. "I said, 'Yeah, yeah,' thinking *every* mother's daughter is a pretty successful model in New York.' Then she said, 'Her name was Gia.'

"I immediately took the woman's name and asked around the station. Everybody had the same reaction I did. First, they had no idea Gia was dead. And second, they were shocked that she had died of AIDS. I called the woman back and asked her to come in and speak to one of our producers. After meeting with her, we decided to do a show.

"She wasn't beating me over the head. She wasn't hawking herself. It was a nice kind of mutual thing. I wanted her as much as she wanted me. The only reference she made was that 'Some day somebody's going to write a book about this.' My guess is that a lawyer put a bug in her ear."

Not long before Kathleen's *AM Philadelphia* appearance her husband, Henry Sperr, moved out. He left Kathleen alone in the house in Richboro—except for her granddaughter. Joey Carangi's thirteen-year-old daughter had moved in with the Sperrs the day Gia died, which raised a few eyebrows among family members—especially when she enrolled in an acting class at the John Casablancas Modeling and Career Center in nearby Langhorne.

"Henry claimed the separation was because of Gia," said photographer Joe Petrellis, who had remained friendly with the family and still used Henry as his accountant.

"When Henry left after Gia had died, he had a lot of career problems at that point," Kathleen recalled. "But I think the whole thing, dealing with all we dealt with, and how I was after she died ... even before I got home from the hospital, he wanted to take all the pictures down, all the covers on the wall. I still have her shoes in the closet. I couldn't let go and he wanted me to let go. It bothered him that I was as upset as I was. He came back later."

Gia's father called Rochelle before the show to let her know it would be on. "I had run into him in the casino before that," she recalled. "He just gave me a big hug and a kiss and he started crying. He knew Kathleen. He knew she'd do anything to get on TV. She wanted to be the model, the superstar. So now she was doing it through Gia's death. He used to kind of laugh at her. Like a joke. A *bad* joke."

In August of 1988, Joe Carangi suddenly took ill and was rushed to an Atlantic City hospital for emergency surgery.

He was diagnosed as having an inoperable brain tumor and died several weeks later. His son Michael briefly tried to take over his last remaining luncheonette, Joe's Place. But family squabbles between the children of Joe's three marriages soon made such a smooth generational transition impossible. When Joe's Place finally closed, two framed magazine photos of Gia were still displayed on a shelf above the grill.

In March of 1989, the *Chicago Tribune* reported on the latest good fortune that had accrued to twenty-two-year-old local hero Cindy Crawford, the former Northwestern University student who had become a New York–based supermodel with the Elite agency. Crawford was negotiating a potentially lucrative contract with Revlon to appear in print and broadcast ads, packaging, display and sales materials for all the company's cosmetics, fragrance, haircare, beauty treatment and suntan products. She would have to work for Revlon only twenty days a year for three years—at a base annual fee that would later be reported at $600,000. Her first ads would appear in the fall, just after the July release of the first Cindy Crawford calendar.

The Revlon contract was smaller than the one Paulina Porizkova had recently signed to represent all the various products produced under the Estée Lauder name—reportedly valued at $5 to $6 million. But it increased interest in Crawford, who had already done over 200 magazine covers worldwide in three years and had further seeped into the public consciousness when the pop star Prince included a lusting song about her, "Cindy C," on his never-released and ardently bootlegged *Black Album*.

As her first Revlon ads began to appear in September of 1989—and she started hosting a show called *House of Style* on MTV—Crawford finally crossed the line between supermodel and celebrity. Her romantic link with movie star Richard Gere, who she would later marry, cemented her position in the gossip-column world as a name that readers were already supposed to know.

Crawford had grown up in De Kalb, Illinois, the middle child of an electrician and a housewife, who separated when she was a freshman in high school and later divorced. Her first modeling job, at sixteen, was a 1982 bra ad for the Marshall Field's department store. The next year, the small local agency that represented her became the Chicago office of Elite. When Crawford graduated from high school, she was sent to Europe, where she worked the *alta moda* in Rome—Patrick Demarchelier, shooting for Italian *Vogue*, made her cut her hair and dye it—and did a few sittings in Paris. From there, British *Vogue* sent her to Bermuda. And from Bermuda, she returned directly to Chicago and promptly quit the business before anyone could lop off the prominent mole next to her mouth. An excellent student, she enrolled in college as a chemical engineering major. But she soon came under the tutelage of Victor Skrebneski, who was still Chicago's only nationally important fashion photographer, just as he was when he discovered Wilhelmina Cooper in the 1950s. Crawford dropped out of college after a semester, and for two years she made a six-figure income modeling in Chicago. Her mole was reborn as a beauty mark.

Crawford was brought to New York by Elite's Monique Pillard in 1986. She quickly became the epitome of what modeling had grown into—coldly sexual, calculating, businesslike, any pretensions to art dismissed, any discussions of being a muse rendered amusing. Perhaps modeling had always been this way. But now the *models* knew it, too.

In one of her earliest national magazine interviews, for *GQ* in 1988, Crawford had attributed her success to Paulina's "paving the way for girls with tits." That wasn't really the case at all. But it was always prudent to backslap someone who was still working and visible and higher up than you on the food chain. And it was always safe to assume that the business, like the public it served, had a collective memory that reached back only one or two monthly magazines. That was especially true by the late eighties, when greed and AIDS and the War on Drugs had rendered unfashionable everything that had ever seemed delightfully out of control about the Uncommon Era of the late seventies. Nostalgia was "Out." Amnesia was "In." If no one was going to forgive, it was probably best to forget.

On October 30, 1989, *New York* magazine did a cover story on Crawford, anointing her as "The Face" and describing her as "a model for the nineties." She was described by the magazine as "an intelligent, olive-skinned, brown-eyed brunette with a full-blown figure ... cast as Everywoman precisely because she is so unlike the thin, white-bread blondes who once dominated modeling."

This time, when asked about her early years in the business, Crawford did the politically incorrect thing and told what the *fashionistas* knew was the truth.

For years, she had been sold on her resemblance to another model, whose time had passed too quickly but whose look was still very much in demand. The makeup artists sometimes even did her face to look exactly like her visual prototype.

That's why Crawford had a nickname in the business. They called her Baby Gia.

"But more wholesome," Crawford was quick to point out. "She was wild. Completely opposite me. She'd leave a booking in the clothes to buy cigarettes and not come back for hours."

And then she paused: "She's not living anymore."

It was an epitaph no more revealing than the "Beloved Daughter" etched on Gia's headstone.

Appendix
Names & Fates

As I put together *Thing of Beauty*, I was frequently amazed and too often stunned by the fates of the people whose paths Gia had crossed. Gia's New York datebooks and address books—which were given to me by her mother—served as my Rosetta Stone, but they are also memory books for an erased generation. A disproportionate number of the people mentioned in the books (or their close associates) had died before I even came to this story. Before I started, photographer Bill King, model agent Zoli, designers Giorgio di Sant'-Angelo, Willi Smith and Patrick Kelley and hairstylist Bob Fink had all been memorialized like Perry Ellis, Way Bandy, Chris von Wangenheim and Wilhelmina Cooper before them. A good number of these deaths will someday be attributed to AIDS.

Many more people died during the course of my research. It got to the point where I started reading *The New York Times* death notices every day to see which potential sources were gone: Steve Rubell, Halston, photographer Guy Bourdin, and fashion illustrators Manning and Tony Viramontez are just a few of the people who were alive when I started and whose biographical information I ended up verifying from their obituaries.

On at least five occasions, people who had agreed to speak with me, or were considering my request, died before the interviews could take place. Gia's father, Joe Carangi, had

agreed to an interview for the original article I did about
Gia before his sudden death from a brain tumor. I spoke
with photographer Ara Gallant at the beginning of my book
research, and we agreed to meet the next time I was in LA,
where he had relocated. When I called many months later
to schedule the actual interview, Gallant was not at the
Santa Monica number I had for him. I subsequently learned
that Gallant had committed suicide in Las Vegas. He was
supposedly depressed about returning to drug use: I've still
never seen an obituary for him. I was trying to arrange an
interview with Kesia Keeble when she died, reportedly from
untreated breast cancer. (Since her husband, fashion writer
John Duka, had died of AIDS, there was much initial speculation that she had it as well.)

Keith Gentile, a Philly friend of Gia's who gave me a
great interview and led me to several key sources, died of
AIDS several months after I met him. When we spoke, he
apparently didn't know he was even sick. Another good
friend of Gia's, referred to in the book by the pseudonym
Vicky, died in a car crash on the way to Atlantic City during
the winter of 1989, just as Gia's aunt Barbara had four years
earlier. Rochelle had called Vicky only a few weeks before
the accident to convince her to speak with me.

When I tried to contact Wilhelmina executive Karen Hilton, I found out she was in a coma from a crippling stroke,
from which I understand she is now slowly recovering.

And, finally, as of this writing, Rochelle Rosen* is battling
liver cancer. When I did the interviews for this book, she
was still living and working at the Jersey Shore; she had a
new long-term lover and her biggest health concerns had
been alleviated by consistently negative HIV tests. She has
now moved back in with her parents and is receiving aggressive medical treatment.

About those people mentioned in the book who are still
alive and whose whereabouts are knowable, I can report
the following:

Kathleen and Henry Sperr still live in the Philadelphia
suburbs with Kathleen's teenage granddaughter from her
son Joey's first marriage.

Nancy Adams still lives and works at the Jersey Shore.

Appendix: Names & Fates

Michael Carangi lived and worked at the Jersey Shore until marrying an Australian woman who tracked him down after reading a version of my original *Philadelphia* magazine article on Gia, which was reprinted in the Australian edition of *Cosmopolitan*. They have since relocated to Australia.

Joey Carangi, his wife and three children still live at the Jersey Shore. While I was researching the book, Joey wasn't speaking to his mother, but I understand they're now in communication.

Dan Carangi recently took over a luncheonette in Atlantic City.

Maurice Tannenbaum, after moving to New York and working at Pierre Michel, recently set up his own small Manhattan salon and still comes to Philadelphia weekly to do his clients there.

Sharon Beverly* is a successful makeup artist, specializing in film and TV commercials, based in Los Angeles.

Karen Karuza left Philadelphia, where she owned a business that sold Catholic religious icons as collectibles, and relocated to Oaxaca, Mexico, where she teaches and, at this writing, is pregnant with her first child.

Toni O'Connor* lives and works in the Chicago area.

Joe McDevit (the former "Joey Bowie") is a successful makeup artist, specializing in fashion photography, based in New York.

Ronnie Johnson* is a successful makeup artist shuttling between Philadelphia and New York.

Roseanne Rubino works in corporate sales at Tiffany's in New York.

Rob Fay has remained drug-free and married a woman he met during the last year of Gia's life. The first of their two children, a daughter, was named Jimi Gia Fay.

Cheryl Paczkoski and Dawn Phillips, both of whom have remained drug-free, live and work in the Philadelphia area.

Patty Stewart lives and works in South Jersey.

Lance Staedler is a successful freelance photographer who recently moved his base from New York to Los Angeles.

Michael Tighe, after destroying his photography career in the late seventies, spent four years living as a heroin addict. He eventually entered the tough Day-Top program in North Jersey, where he spent his twenty-seventh birthday and achieved some notoriety when he was interviewed there by Geraldo Rivera for an ABC series on heroin use called *Chasing the Dragon*. He left the drug program early because he felt pressured by its administrators to do more public speaking and began using heroin again. "In the program, you're talking about it, you're thinking about it all the time," he said. "They call it 'shooting dope without shooting dope.' So when you get out of the program, the first thing you want to do is shoot dope." He went on a binge for two weeks and then stopped completely, with the moral support of his family and his best friend, actress Amanda Plummer. He is once again a successful freelance photographer, doing mostly celebrity portraits and movie posters, and based in LA.

David Cohen is now a nationally known hat designer based in New York.

Denis Piel has his own film production company, Jupiter Films. He directs shorts and commercials around the world, and occasionally does still photography.

Harry King stopped doing hair for several years to take pictures, and later to write screenplays. He recently returned to doing some hairstyling.

Sara Foley Anderson was the head of the Wilhelmina agency's W2 division, until recently accepting a position as senior bookings editor at *Harper's Bazaar*.

Helen Murray is an independent *fashionista* agent based in LA. She represents photographer Sante D'Orazio and several others.

Lizzette Kattan married an Italian economist with whom she has two children. They split their time between Milan and a home in Switzerland; Lizzette started a children's clothing company and was also recently named ambassador from Honduras.

Charla Carter is a freelance writer, fashion editor, and stylist based in Paris.

Kay Mitchell left the modeling business after an unhappy experience running her own agency, Legends. She repaired to Ohio, where she spent most of the eighties building a series of regional modeling competitions, and returned to New York in 1990 to put together a national scouting company to service the top agencies.

Robert Hilton, who had been separated from his wife, Karen, for years before her stroke, lives in North Jersey with their two children and does drug rehab work in New York City.

Grace Mirabella was fired as editor-in-chief of *Vogue* and replaced by former British *Vogue* editor-in-chief Anna Wintour. Soon after, Mirabella was hired by Rupert Murdoch to create her own namesake fashion publication. *Vogue* fashion editor Jade Hobson went to *Mirabella* as well. Grace Coddington came to American *Vogue* from the British edition as a fashion editor.

Polly Mellen changed jobs at *Vogue* not long after Anna Wintour took over, accepting a freelance fashion editing contract with the magazine that allowed her, for the first time in more than three decades, to work outside of *Vogue*. A year later, after a flap about her appearing as a model in an ad, she shifted to a similar position with the new Condé Nast beauty magazine *Allure*.

Patrick Demarchelier recently made a high-profile contract shift from *Vogue* to *Harper's Bazaar*.

William Weinberg and Fran Rothschild both left the Wilhelmina agency after it was bought out by German businessman Dieter Esch and his daughter Natasha.

Juli Foster lives in central Florida and still does some modeling.

Christie Brinkley married singer Billy Joel. They have one child, and Brinkley does some modeling work for *Cover Girl* and *Sports Illustrated*.

Esme Marshall lives in North Jersey with her daughter and is trying to get back into modeling.

Jerry Hall married Mick Jagger. They have three children. Hall has appeared in several recent films and on the London stage.

Janice Dickinson went through rehab and married British-born film producer Simon Fields. They have one child and live in Los Angeles. After several years away from the business, she has recently done some European runway modeling and is trying to make a second career in photography.

Patti Hansen did some acting and married Keith Richards. They have two children and live in Connecticut and England. After years away from the business, she appeared on the cover of *Mirabella* to announce a return to modeling.

Lisa Taylor lives in Los Angeles and recently began modeling again when Calvin Klein featured her in a campaign celebrating mature women.

After Taylor's comeback, and a Barney's ad by Steven Meisel featuring Lauren Hutton (and other stars of the generation just before Gia's), many of the top girls from the 70s signed with agent Bryan Bantry, who mostly represents photographers and hair and makeup artists. They are going to try to create a new market for top models in their 40s— instead of just the occcassional nostalgia shots—and convince America that beauty is truth, not youth. Among the models are Janice Dickinson, Patti Hansen, Bitten, Shaun Casey, Lise Ryall, Lois Chiles, and Marisa Berenson.

The following people in the fashion industry are basically in the same lines of work—still freelance or associated with the same companies—as they were during the late seventies and early eighties. They are, however, all much bigger deals now, have more "side projects," command higher fees and, in some cases, have even moved on to *emeritus* status.

Irving Penn, Richard Avedon, Arthur Elgort, Albert Watson, John Stember, Mike Reinhardt, Francesco Scavullo, Alex Chatelain, Victor Skrebneski, Jacques Malignon, Aldo Fallai, Jean Pagliuso, Francois Lamy and Andrea Blanche are all still top names in fashion and commercial photography.

Sandy Linter, John Sahag, Maury Hopson, Ariella and Rick Pipino are still top names in hair and makeup, doing salon and studio work. Sahag now also owns his own successful salon.

Eileen Ford, John Casablancas, Monique Pillard and Jo Zagami are still the top people at Ford and Elite, respectively.

Since the publication of *Thing of Beauty,* I have had many requests about where to find published photos of Gia. This is a completely arbitary list of pictures—most of which are mentioned in the book and should be accessible in libraries and used-magazine shops.

Appendix: Names & Fates

American *Vogue*

Glamour

British *Vogue*

French *Vogue*

401

Italian *Vogue*

3/79:	Lamy shots, pages 410–23, 654–59
1, 2, 3/80:	Back covers are Gia Armani ads by Fallai
4/80:	Gia in Armani groupage
5/80:	Best of Avedon Versace ads
2/81:	Cover by Grignachi

German *Vogue*

10/79:	Piel collections shots, outtakes from American *Vogue*
4/80:	Florida shots by John Stember, pages 96-97, 101–13
12/83:	Fur & leather supplement by Watson

American *Harpers Bazaar*

8/79:	Gia by Scavullo, page 139
9/79:	Gia by King, pages 236, 246
10/79:	Gia by Pullman, page 145
11/79:	Gia by Pullman, pages 190–92

American *Cosmopolitan*

Covers 4/79, 7/79, 1/80, 7/80, 4/82

Italian *Bazaar*

7–8/78:	(double issue) Citicorp Building by Von Wangenheim plus many others
9/78:	Rome and Paris collections by Von Wangenheim and Elgort, plus groupage by Demarchelier and others

Several photos of Gia are also available in books. There are three in the out-of-print book *Fashion: Theory* edited by Carol Di Grappa and published by Lustrum Press. The Helmut Newton shot used in poster form in the opening of *Thing of Beauty* is reprinted in both the Pantheon Photo Library paperback on Newton and the book *Private Property*. The book *Scavullo Women* has two photos of Gia and an interview with her; the *Yves St. Laurent 1958–1988* book has Denis Piel's 1979 collection photo of Gia with the harlequins. In terms of more disposable fashion-related books, photos of Gia are on the covers of *Cheap Chic* and *Hot*

Tips: 1000 Fashion & Beauty Tricks and inside *Disco Beauty*. I am told that Arthur Elgort will soon be releasing a book of his fashion work that will include several unpublished shots of Gia.

For information on actual prints of photographs of Gia, which are likely to be quite expensive, contact the individual photographer's agent. The easiest way to identify an agent is to look up the photographer in one of the photo annuals that you can find in many libraries—like *Black Book, American Showcase,* or *Graphis.*

Acknowledgments
& Afterstuff

Kathleen Sperr was my first source for the *Philadelphia* magazine story that grew into this book. A difficult, but nonetheless, brave woman, Kathleen, for reasons I never completely understood, opened up her life and her relationship with her late daughter to an astonishing level of scrutiny. She believed that the story of Gia's life was worth telling no matter how it reflected upon her. And it was often she, in the early years of this project, who led me to the people with the most damning things to say about her. Kathleen trusted the process of uncompromised journalism. She would have liked to make some money, she wanted to review my work before publication and she made me jump through an awful lot of hoops. In fact, at this writing, I have no idea if we're still speaking. But she neither demanded nor received any compensation or other conditions for her on-and-off cooperation over the last four years—including my last interview with her, for the book, which lasted nearly five hours.

When the techniques of reporting and psychological profiling are used in family situations—a thorny, hybrid process I can only describe as "investigative psychotherapy"— sources like Kathleen Sperr are absolutely crucial and difficult to come by. They also, by their cooperation, open themselves up to charges of media-hounding by those family members and friends who don't believe in the process.

Acknowledgments & Afterstuff

For a journalist to suggest that someone's motivation in granting an interview is somehow more ethically compromised than the interview request itself is the height of cynicism and self-delusion. I was extremely fortunate that hundreds of people allowed me access to their public and personal lives in researching *Thing of Beauty*. And many people also assisted me in the research and writing of the investigative stories on teenage suicide and child sexual abuse in *Philadelphia* magazine that laid the groundwork for this project. They taught me how to interview them and how to be worthy of the extreme levels of trust required of the process. But every such undertaking begins with one person and one open wound. And it was Kathleen's pain and frankness while we sat drinking coffee in her kitchen that started this one.

I met Kathleen because of a phone call from *AM Philadelphia* host Wally Kennedy after her original appearance on his program. Wally knows lots of journalists, and he could have called any one of them. I'm grateful that he chose me.

I had inspirational research assistance on this project from Sean Sperry, David Borgenicht, Laura Loro, Erin Friar and Sally (Luongo) Hyman. Merv Keizer checked the facts. Helen Flaherty transcribed a lot of the interviews; XyWrite software allowed me easy access to the raw material.

Thanks to Cindy Cathcart at the Condé Nast library; Sherry Handlin at the Butterick archives; Anne Walker at the Philadelphia AIDS Library; Don Monroe, keeper of the Warhol archives; the library folk at the Fashion Institute of Technology in New York, Philadelphia College of Textiles and the *Philadelphia Inquirer*. Xanthipi Joannides at *Glamour* arranged several crucial interviews for me; Sallie Dinkel and Greg Christianson, both formerly of *GQ*, did some of my homework; Reenie McDonnell, Michelle Nader, A. D. Amorosi and my old Jewish Y Men's Health Club–mate Bob Bosco helped find unfindable sources and set scenes. New York sleeping accommodations courtesy of casas Rich/Fried and Green/Kaplan.

All my sources worked very hard through sometimes grueling interviews, but I'd like to especially thank Sharon Beverly,* Rob Fay, Karen Karuza, Rochelle Rosen,* Nancy Adams, Monique Pillard, Kay Mitchell, Lizzette Kattan (who also took care of us in Milan), Felicitas Oeltze von Lobenthal (who did the same in Munich), Francesco Scavullo and Sean Byrnes (the first fashion people to speak with me, triggering a chain reaction of cooperation among the *fashionistas*), Polly Mellen (whose cooperation also opened many doors, as did that of Marc Balet and Sara Foley), Michael Tighe, Robert Hilton, Giampiero Paoletti, Claude Brouet, Maurice Tannenbaum, David Uosikkinen, Fran Chalin, Margie Dameshek and Sue Lubin. Special thanks to all the sources I'm not allowed to thank by name.

Most of the quotes in this book are from interviews I conducted or are clearly attributed to the places where they originally appeared. There are a handful of quotes from public figures that I took the liberty of including without direct attribution. It's only fair to acknowledge the appropriations: Maury Hopson would not speak with me, but Dick Polman of *The Philadelphia Inquirer* provided raw interviews with Hopson from his coverage of Way Bandy's death; the out-of-print book *Fashion: Theory* was a wellspring of insight, especially since co-publisher John Flattau allowed me to use the interview he taped with Chris von Wangenheim for the book; Anthony Haden-Guest spent an afternoon walking me through his various *New York* modeling stories, from which I retrieved some of the more verifiable anecdotes, and he graciously loaned me some of his files; Lynn Snowden gave me an unpublished piece about her own modeling career, and I used several quotes from her *Mademoiselle* story on Esme Marshall; John Lombardi helped me out with several sources, and wrote both the Arthur Elgort profile for *American Photographer* and the piece for *High Times* from which I got ideas and factoids about "heroin as mass hip"; Brad Gooch's *Vanity Fair* story on club culture was very helpful, and contained the Anita Sarko quote I used; Judy Klemesrud wrote the *Esquire* cover story on "The Year of the Lusty Woman"; Marie Winn wrote the *Times Magazine* profile of Alexander Liberman; Jennifer Allen wrote the five-part New York *Daily News* series on modeling I mentioned (which Joel Seigel kindly fetched from the about-to-strike *News* library); Peter Wilkinson spoke with me about his interview with Patti Hansen for *New York Woman,* from which I got a quote; some Avedon background and a quote came from a 1978 *Newsweek* cover story on him; a few Ann Simonton quotes came from Susan Faludi's *Mother Jones* piece; Tony Shugaar's *Spy* article on Terry Broome was of help; the *Sports Illustrated* twenty-fifth anniversary swimsuit issue was, of course, a compendium of facts I needed; Mark Stevens's book *Model* noted the D'Arcy phenomenon; and Timothy White's interview in *Musician* was the source of the Bowie quote; the Cindy Crawford interviews were with Bruce Buschel *(GQ)* and Michael Gross *(New York).*

Nora Magid was my writing teacher at the University of Pennsylvania, my mentor and my first professional colleague. She died while I was finishing the final draft of *Thing of Beauty,* and I hope she forgave me for paying more attention to the work she inspired me to do than I did to *her* during the last years of her life.

Nora passed me on to Ed McFall, who was the reporting teacher I never had and has remained a good friend. Ron Javers gave me the job at *Philadelphia* magazine in 1982 and the editing that led to most everything else. Both he and the magazine have given me a lot. Ron and publisher Herb Lipson—and later, Herb's son David—also indulged me several professional courtesies that allowed this book to happen.

The music column I used to do for Art Cooper at *GQ* was my only contact with the printed world while writing *Thing of Beauty.* My editors there, especially Paul Scanlon, helped me piggyback book research onto their assignments. In a wonderful twist of fate, the person to whom I owed the most thanks at *GQ,* Eliot Kaplan—who also helped out with a draft of this book and has been a pal since childhood—is now editor-in-chief of *Philadelphia,* where I owe him other thanks.

I had written only one piece for Wayne Lawson, my editor at *Vanity Fair,* when he took it upon himself to filet this book down into a magazine excerpt and then sold the idea to Graydon Carter. When I tell other writer-friends about Wayne's efforts, they are pleasantly stunned to hear that there are any editors like him left in the magazine business. So am I.

On the art side of things, where I learned a lot of noneditorial stuff needed for this project, thanks to Amy Herling, Alfred Zelcer, Tracy Diehl, Russell O. Jones, Greg Klee, Ken Newbaker, Patricia McElroy, Michael Jones and Heidi Volpe—as well as photographers Mary D'Anella, Jim Graham, Dan Kron and Pepe Botella, and hair-makeup guy Marc Carrasquillo.

This book happened because Loretta Weingel-Fidel, my agent, did a great job selling it and listening to me whine during it, and Jane Rosenman, my editor, worked hard on it through three rigorous editing passes. (Jane, you proved *TNR* wrong.) Bill Grose, the editor-in-chief of Pocket Books, let us do what we wanted and never asked us to shy away from the tough stuff. Photo editor Vincent Virga gave us a burst of perspective and made visual sense of it all. And Lisa Levinson and Donna Ng were two of the many Pocketeers who deserve thanks.

On a more personal note, I'd like to thank my friends Joel and Lisa Perilstein, Loren and Jill Feldman, Geoffrey Little, Diane Douglas, Jeff Rosenschein and Doug Sherman for their unending support. In the area of work pals, thanks to Barbara Fallon, Polly Hurst, Carol Saline, Janet Bukovinsky, Lisa DePaulo, Judy Prouty; Sandy Bloom, Ruth Ann Ryan, and Edith Shapin; Steven Levy and Teresa Carpenter; and Rob Hyman for the tune.

My family has always been amazingly supportive of what I do for a living—even when they were baffled by it or, worse, forced to be the *subject* of it. To my parents, Estelle and Jerry, my brothers, Jeff and Dan, my Nana and Poppop, my in-laws, Joan and Ed, the Schultzes, the Caplans and the rest of the crew, I can only say thanks for loving me and trying to answer my questions.

My wife, Diane Ayres, smoothly answered every query I had about what it was like to be a girl and took a lot of time away from her fiction writing to make sure that *Thing of Beauty* got done. Her first two novels were also teeming with insights I couldn't possibly have written this without: I hope she sees what I got from them as homage rather than appropriation. Diane edited all the drafts of this book and the original Gia article, and sat through endless discussions with me about everything from Keats to Bowie, and back again. She is my miracle.

Index

Index

411

Index

Index

Index

Index

Index

416

Index

417

Index

418

Index

Index

Index

Index